# GABRIEL WARD LASKER

WAYNE STATE UNIVERSITY

# PHYSICAL ANTHROPOLOGY

## SECOND EDITION

EDITION
EDITION
EDITION
EDITION
EDITION
EDITION

HOLT, RINEHART AND WINSTON   New York   Chicago   San Francisco   Atlanta
Dallas   Montreal   Toronto   London   Sydney

Illustrations from *Human Biology* are reproduced by the
kind permission of Wayne State University Press, and
those from the *American Journal of Physical Anthropology* by the kind permission of the Wistar Institute
of Anatomy and Biology.


Portions of this book appeared in a different form in *The
Evolution of Man* by the same author, © 1961 by Holt,
Rinehart and Winston, Inc.


Library of Congress Cataloging in Publication Data

Lasker, Gabriel Ward.
    Physical anthropology.

    Bibliography: p. 381
    Includes indexes.
    1. Physical anthropology.   I. Title.
GN60.L33   1976              573              75-23386

ISBN 0-03-089757-2

Copyright © 1973 by Holt, Rinehart and Winston, Inc.

Copyright © 1976 by Holt, Rinehart and Winston
Printed in the United States of America
7 8 9 0      074      9 8 7 6 5 4 3

# PREFACE TO THE SECOND EDITION

Those familiar with the first edition of this book will perceive three major changes in this revision. First, responses to the earlier edition suggested that if the material could be even more fully explained its usefulness would be enhanced. Such fuller explanation and clarity are the chief purposes of this new version, and every page has been scrutinized to that end. In addition, we have instituted a number of features that should help gain clarity. We have enlarged the type size for the legends to the figures, and these are full explanations often covering for a second time the material in the text. We have introduced a system of boldface type to refer the reader to the glossary (itself expanded) and to the map on the end papers which gives the location of sites of discovery of fossils important in the story of human evolution, and we have introduced many cross-references to the figures and the text.

The other two changes are substantive. First, I have altered the dating of geological epochs. These are traditionally determined by the fossils they contain. Since animal species in different parts of the world differ, an epoch may not occur at exactly the same time everywhere and it may be considered to start later in marine deposits than on dry land. I consider this unsatisfactory and now prefer arbitrarily to consider the beginning of the Lower Pleistocene epoch (the time of the great glaciations) to coincide with the Olduvai Event (a period of normal polarity during an epoch when the South Pole was the North Pole). And I consider the Middle Pleistocene to begin with the present Brunhes Epoch, when the north-pointing compass last began to point north. The polarity of rock is frozen in when the rock solidifies and therefore it is possible to distinguish geological deposits that have normal from those that have reversed polarity. The Olduvai Event lasted from about 1,900,000 to about 1,600,000 years ago and the Brunhes Epoch began about 690,000 years ago. It is not yet customary to date the Pleistocene by magnetic reversals but since these phenomena were worldwide (all other geological occurrences—even the great glaciations—are geographically restricted) magnetic reversals are likely to become the key reference points in time for dating widespread developments such as the emergence of *Homo sapiens* in Africa, Asia, and Europe.

The other substantive change deserves brief mention. When a fossil or other specimen is discovered and deposited for study in a museum, it is given a numerical designation that is never changed thereafter. These designations often give way to a scientific name and/or to a nickname, but these latter kinds of names may be changed as our knowledge of the specimen increases. In the few places where I speak of a particular specimen (rather than of some population of organisms) I have introduced specimen numbers. It may not be practicable for students to memorize such designations, but if any reader wishes to compare what I say about specific fossils with any account in the research literature he will need to have access to the number by which the fossil is known.

Those who reviewed my previous work have made a number of specific suggestions and have called attention to a number of errors (charitably considered minor by them). I acknowledge with pleasure the suggestions of these reviewers: K. A. R. Kennedy of Cornell University; William Pollitzer, the editor of the *American Journal of Physical Anthropology;* F. S. Hulse, himself the author of an excellent general textbook of physical anthropology, *The Human Species;* F. E. Johnston, Professor of Anthropology at the University of Pennsylvania; W. M. Krogman (whom I stopped to visit in 1937 on my way to my first course in anthropology—with Hooton at Harvard—and whose work I have followed with admiration ever since); M. S. Goldstein, whose research on Mexican migrants greatly influenced my own; and S. L. Larnach in Australia. Criticisms of other books of mine (including some in reviews by Dr. E. W. Count, formerly professor of Anthropology at Hamilton College; Professor D. F. Roberts in England; and A. J. Kelso and E. E. Hunt, Jr., professors of anthropology at the University of Colorado and at Pennsylvania State University respectively) have also influenced this work.

In addition, instructors who have used the prior edition as a textbook have provided suggestions. (I acknowledge the helpful suggestions of Drs. Noel Korn of California State University, Northridge; Eugene Giles of the University of Illinois, Urbana; Jack Prost, University of Illinois, Chicago Circle; Milford Wolpoff and Stanley Garn, both of the University of Michigan; David Dietrick,

Long Beach City College; S. L. Washburn, University of California, Berkeley; and many colleagues here at Wayne State University, including David Carlson, Mark Weiss, and Bernice Kaplan.) Mr. Brian Heald and Mr. David Boynton, at Holt, Rinehart and Winston, have been most helpful.

These changes have, I hope, made this second edition of *Physical Anthropology* more effective in fulfilling its original objective: to serve as an introductory textbook for basic courses in physical anthropology. Much of the recent work in physical anthropology is in three directions: human biological ecology, molecular anthropology, and primate behavior. I have therefore attempted not only to cover traditional aspects of physical anthropology, but also to show the significance of these newer trends of biological anthropology. Thus, I have prepared a chapter on human adaptation (previously published in slightly different form in *Science*). Molecular biology is now viewed in anthropology as an extension of the study of human variability and its evolution at a finer level, and I have introduced examples of molecular mutants and of their evolution. The study of behavior of nonhuman animals (ethology) is for the anthropologist a foundation for examining human behavior and its origin and evolution. I have therefore included examples of different aspects of the behavior of nonhuman primates from the multitude of recent studies.

Besides this new material on contemporary man and the nonhuman primates today, a wealth of fossil materials has been discovered that bear on human evolution. Brief descriptions and discussions of their significance are incorporated in the present account.

There are numerous textbooks of physical anthropology available. One of my motives for adding yet another was that those purporting to be introductions almost invariably overinterpret the evidence and dogmatically assert conclusions which cannot be affirmed with confidence on the basis of presently available evidence. Thus, the application of computer analyses to measurements has fostered so-called multivariate methods in which variabilities in numerous respects are considered simultaneously: the arrays of numbers generated in this way often cannot be referred back to the anatomy they are supposed to represent and, to that extent, their functional significance is speculative or even imaginary.

Furthermore, in some of the available textbooks there is an overzealous willingness to ascribe a specific function to every anatomical characteristic. Indeed, form does have functional meaning, but it is not yet always possible to know that meaning. The wide range of comparative studies of different groups of man and of different animals in all sorts of natural and artificial environments has created firmer bases for interpretation. It unfortunately remains true that much casual and premature speculation is published, which can prejudge the issues and discourage the necessary painstaking research. For instance, although many textbooks would have you think otherwise, it is almost pure speculation to deduce the diet of fossil humans from the details of their teeth. Scientific detachment requires the presentation of unsettled questions as such. And I hope any failures to do so adequately in the pages that follow are neither numerous nor grave. In any case, the conclusions I have reached should be treated as tentative and subject to continuous reevaluation. Where several possible interpretations seem more or less equally plausible, I have therefore tried to mention the alternative views, together with an outline of the arguments.

Some topics have been deliberately omitted. Thus, since any attempt to classify the people of the world into races is highly arbitrary and of dubious value, none is attempted. I have therefore subordinated the question of race to a discussion of differences and similarities between members of various subpopulations of the human species. The possible existence of differences between such groups in biological capacities is acknowledged on the basis of ecological differences with different selection pressures, but alleged findings of racial differences in intellectual endowment are rejected since environment greatly influences all kinds of psychological test scores.

Progress in the science of physical anthropology—indeed, in the natural sciences in general—is not so much marked by the appearance of books and monographs as by the publication of specific research in scholarly periodicals. To encourage the reader to look at some of these original publications, I have cited many such articles as well as a number of books and reviews. Since the literature on physical anthropology is extensive, however, the citations are often only examples drawn from a larger documentation of the points. The chief American periodicals carrying research reports concerning physical anthropology are: *American Journal of Physical Anthropology, Human Biology, Science,* and *American Anthropologist.* I have selected many references from these journals because of their ready availability in libraries. Likewise, since science of the past is encompassed in the present, I have not always tried to cite the author who first proposed a specific idea, but have tried instead to cite those who best state a modern view of the matter.

I hope that the reader will participate in the sense of scientific adventure that anthropologists experience when they resolve previously disputed points and add to human knowledge.

Mrs. Alice Hand and Mrs. Denise Lozano have applied to this book skills gained in helping to edit the quarterly journal *Human Biology.*

*Detroit, Michigan*                                                        G. W. L.
*October 1975*

# CONTENTS

CHAPTER **1**

# PHYSICAL ANTHROPOLOGY AS A FIELD OF SCIENCE

Discussion of the questions of physical anthropology, the study of human biology, is not confined to university classrooms. It spills over into physicians' seminars, schoolroom classes in social studies, the public press, TV talk, and even casual conversations. What are the differences between men and women and to what extent are they determined by expectations of other people rather than by inherent biological factors? How do children grow up to be so different? Are there any "inferior races," or are the differences between groups of people merely skin deep and of no functional significance? What have been the sources of human erect posture? of the bare body lacking fur except for a little hair on the head, face, armpits and pubic region? Whence arose the human capacities for abstract thought and communication by means of language? Are the monkeys and apes our close cousins? And are those fossil skulls and bones found in Africa really missing links?

The methods of science do not always answer such questions directly. Human biologists rephrase these questions in such a way that examination of the facts (whether by simple observations or by more elaborate experiments) provides new and more precise questions. The primary purpose in setting forth what is now known of physical anthropology is to provide a frame of reference into which future evidence can be meaningfully fitted. The principle of science

1

upon which this faith in a continued growth of knowledge rests, is that still unknown facts are based on the same natural laws as those already observed and recorded. The explanations under which known facts are subsumed must also apply to everything we will ever discover. True, present explanations may involve errors and in that case they will have to be modified. Science is a system for the accumulation of knowledge, thus we never know all there is to know and the frontiers of science are eternal as past errors are corrected and present understandings are refined. In the past our reconstruction of the origin of man has contained error because of seriously fallacious assumptions about the processes of nature, such as the notion of "mixed blood," whereby an individual was supposed to represent a melding of the races of his parents. We now realize that individuals acquire their hereditary characteristics not as a whole but piecemeal and randomly, through various lines of descent in the family tree.

In at least one case the course of human evolution was misinterpreted because of widespread belief in the authenticity of a fossil "Piltdown Man" that proved to be a hoax. But it is instructive that the fraud was eventually exposed because the supposed evidence did not fit well with other facts. The skull was modern in form but thick; the jaw was apelike but the teeth showed a human type of wear. When other evidence made it probable that a human type of jaw evolved before the large human skull was fully formed, and a careful examination of the specimen by chemical methods revealed that the jawbone, though apelike, was modern, Weiner and his colleagues (1953) had another good look under the microscope and established that the jaw and teeth were those of a modern young female orangutan whose teeth had been cleverly ground down and stained to simulate a fossil ape-man.

Fortunately, science rarely has to deal with deliberate deceit. However, conclusions reached with all good will, but on limited evidence, often have to be reevaluated. At different times the earliest geological strata that contain the characteristic cold-weather mammals of the **Pleistocene Epoch**\* (the Ice Age) were thought to have been formed 200 thousand years ago, then 600 thousand, then a million. Now geologists and physicists estimate that the deposits go back about two million years. **Australopithecus,** a fossil form belonging to the human family that occurs in these deposits, was at first considered by most physical anthropologists to be too apelike to be directly ancestral to us since it was thought to be so recent. Now that we know that these deposits are older and that *Australopithecus* also lived in the preceding **Pliocene Epoch,** almost all physical anthropologists consider *Australopithecus* a lineal ancestor of ours.

Many problems of physical anthropology remain open, however. For example, the molecular evidence, the examination of the detailed nature of the chemicals of which different species are composed, reveals a very close affinity of humans with the anthropoid apes (Goodman et al., 1971). This would imply, according to Sarich and Wilson (1967), that chimpanzees and we still had

---

\*Terms in **boldface** are defined in the Glossary.

common ancestors as recently as 4–5 million years ago. Paleontologists claim, however, that a fossil, **Ramapithecus,** belonging to our line of descent but not to that of the chimpanzee, occurred in the **Miocene,** 10–14 million years ago (Pilbeam, 1972), and by this evidence the common ancestors are pushed 6–10 million years further back than Sarich and Wilson's dates. A possible explanation of the discrepancy is a theory that evolution in the human line had been slowing down (until the technological revolution and population mobility of the last few centuries) and that the molecular similarities between human and chimpanzee have persisted for a long time; although the small number of differences between humans and chimpanzees would seem to imply a more recent common origin, if the rate of divergence has been slow it may go as far back as the Miocene (Goodman et al., 1970). But this theory of evolutionary deceleration is not accepted by all students of the problem. There is a widely held view that molecular changes are random events and occur at a constant rate. The search for still more evidence continues.

We should not expect all the problems to have been solved. Looking to our animal origins for evidence of our innate nature, one writer, for instance, may see the general adjustment to each other of animals in the wild and think of nature as idyllic and peaceful; another sees only predator and prey and he may think of nature as "red in tooth and claw." The physical anthropologist tries to account for both patterns and the relationship between them. He looks at the whole gamut of interactions between animals of the same species— especially among species closely related to us, the nonhuman primates. He also analyzes the differences in behavior among many species, including humans, to see how much they depart from each other and specifically to evaluate the distance we may have come in developing our own idiosyncratic nature.

These and other questions about humans are not confined to physical anthropology, however. Human beings are studied in many ways, from different points of view and by various techniques. Among these special interests in the study of humanity are the evaluation of its accomplishments: the critical analysis of the development of literature, music, the graphic and plastic arts, and even the history of political and economic events. These are the *humanities.* The study of human beings also includes scientific examination of the human body and its functions (the morphological and behavioral sciences: human anatomy, human physiology, psychology, and sociology).

*Anthropology* (the term means the *"study of man"*) encompasses these humanistic, behavioral, and biological aspects. In fact it differs from the other disciplines mentioned above principally in its concern for the interrelationship of these aspects. Its approach is also inclusive in that it subsumes the study of people of all parts of the world and of all time. Its methods are therefore primarily comparative, one individual with another, one epoch with another, and even the comparison of human beings with apes and monkeys.

The study of *prehistory* is one of the branches of anthropology. The word "history" is normally reserved for the study of written accounts of past events. Prehistory therefore covers the events in human affairs before writing was invented. These events are known from examination of the houses, tools, and bones of ancient humans that are dug up and analyzed by archaeologists. *Prehistoric archaeology* thus is a major subfield of anthropology.

*Cultural anthropology* is the study of those aspects of human behavior and its products that we learn from our predecessors. Some cultural anthropologists focus on social relations between people and prefer the name *social anthropology*. They often start with a study of the family and of kinship. Learning one's culture is made possible by culture's most characteristic invention, symbolic language, and *anthropological linguistics* is the branch of study concerned with this general phenomenon.

There are other anthropologists who specialize in specific aspects of culture. Economic anthropology deals with livelihood activities throughout the world. Political anthropology deals with the formation of groups larger than families and with the different ways in which conflicts between factions are resolved. Medical anthropology encompasses the study of attitudes toward disease and of healing practices, including everything from witchcraft to the organization of a hospital emergency room. The anthropology of education considers learning and how the culture is transmitted to the young in various societies. These studies do not have distinct enough bodies of method and theory to be considered separate disciplines and are considered subfields of cultural anthropology.

*Physical anthropology,* although united to cultural anthropology and archaeology by shared attitudes of approach and by the need for some of the same research skills, has its own biological methods.

## Physical Anthropology Defined

Physical anthropology is the study of the physical aspect of humans: the study of human evolution and biological variation. Physical anthropology is concerned with the sources of variation and directions of change among both individuals and groups, past and present. The sources of variation lie in genetic differences and environmental modifications of the genetic potential. The directions of change originated in the past, in differences as they arose over long spans of time through evolution. However, even in today's short spans of time the tendencies to new variations and change of human form continue. Those interested in variation study the growth and development that account for differences in anatomical structures, organs, and tissues. They also compare the physiological responses of different groups of individuals to metabolic tests (such as body temperature or respiration rate after cold exposure or after exercise or under other conditions). Physical anthropologists must also take account of innate differences among individuals of different sizes or shapes and, particularly, among groups from different places in responding to various test conditions and measurements. Scientists working on these problems are often concerned with providing norms for the use of physicians who must evaluate disease. Thus, weight and stature norms for children of each sex of various ages from different places serve as standards for measuring the state of individual growth. Only in this way can the abnormal growth caused by malnutrition or endocrine (glandular) diseases be discovered and evaluated. In fact, this aspect of physical anthropology, sometimes labeled Human Biology, is placed among the basic medical sciences in some universities.

*Physical anthropology,* on the other hand, is a term preferred by those who wish to be closely identified with basic humanistic studies. They ask such questions as: what is a human being and how has the **species** evolved? Physical anthropology thus includes the study of human fossils. Many fossil bones with bearing on our evolution have been found. The earliest ones share many features with monkeys, apes, and other animals. Other are more similar to those of modern humans.

Much of the progress made in discovering these specimens and revealing their meaning is the work of scholars who identify themselves as archaeologists and **paleontologists** as well as physical anthropologists. As a group they are probably best described as human paleontologists. It is human paleontologists who have searched for and, when found, examined and reconstructed skeletons of animals—of types now extinct—that may have been our forerunners. To paleontologists we also owe our knowledge of the fishes, horses, dinosaurs, and other animals and plants of past ages, hence also of natural evolution in general. Paleontologists, together with geologists, have collaborated with physicists to provide reliable dates for a study of the calendar of human evolution.

Physical anthropology also relies heavily on studies of the comparative anatomy of present-day vertebrates (animals with backbones) and especially of the group to which we belong, the **Primates.** It relates the anatomy of these present-day animals to the information gained from studies of fossil primates.

The contributions of *primatology* to anthropology are not limited to studies of the skeleton and soft parts, however. Experiments performed on living monkeys and apes provide examples of biochemical constituents (such as blood serum enzymes), physiological functioning (such as muscular strength), nervous responses (such as responses over nerve pathways after electrical stimulation of nerve cells), and even behavior (such as responses to being deprived of all social contact from birth on). Studies of primates in the wild indicate some of the varieties of individual behavioral patterns (such as the building of nests) and of social interaction (such as the maintenance of permanent groups) that would have been available to human ancestors if they were once similarly adapted. That is, as archaeologists push back the story of human history to earlier and earlier times, the stone tools made by early man are progressively simpler and less varied, and less and less distinguishable from unmodified pebbles that were never used as tools. Likewise the first shelters and clothes must have been relatively inefficient by later standards. But they served well at the time and therefore it is safe to assume that these early ancestors of ours lived only in moderate or warm climates and managed in ways similar to the way present-day nonhuman primates live in the wild in similar zones. There is still room for argument as to whether, at any particular stage, our ancestors lived in the forest or in open grassland or both. Precisely because present-day monkeys and apes live and can be studied in a wide variety of natural environments, from dense tropical forests to treeless plains (savanna), the study of their varying adaptations to these differing conditions can indicate the most plausible modes of life of our early forerunners.

At some times the primary emphasis of physical anthropology is on long-range history; in other circumstances the subject of study is generation-to-generation processes. Each may throw light that is necessary if we are to see a rounded image of the other. If, for example, we wish to understand the biological differences among people, we need to know something about how these differences have arisen. To understand their origin it will help to know whether and, if so, how and to what degree, biological differences between individuals and between groups determine the way people think and behave. While these are questions for physical anthropology, those concerning people's behaviors and attitudes are within the wider framework of social science, involving the contributions of cultural anthropology and other behavioral sciences. Students of animal communication, for instance, use evidence from all these fields. In physical anthropology, as in the other natural and social sciences, some of the greatest advances of recent years have been made in respect to questions for which answers have been sought through several areas of knowledge.

The physical anthropologist studies processes by which physical characteristics of individuals come to vary in frequency in groups and by which the characteristics of populations change from generation to generation. To the extent that the biological characteristics to which this refers are transmitted through sexual reproduction, these processes are called genetic. *Pedigree genetics* deals with the transmission of genetic differences between individuals in the family. A pedigree is a family tree or genealogy. *Population genetics* concerns the statistical effect of all the pedigrees in the population. This is expressed as increases and decreases or maintenance of the frequencies of genetic characteristics within whole populations or samples of them. The physical anthropologist's contribution to population genetics is to apply human demographic and ecological data (of birth rates, death rates, marriage practices, nutritional intake, health conditions, and so on) to the study of human population genetics. In human beings, cultural factors frequently influence the establishment, perpetuation, and occasional disappearance of biological differences. Geneticists call simple genetic variation within populations **polymorphism**— genetic variations that are inherited in a known way and exist in considerable frequency. Two examples of such polymorphisms are the Rh-blood group system and **hemoglobin** variations, which occur in the blood of many individuals, normally with no ill effects (see Chapter 5). When special tests are applied to blood samples from different population groups, the Rh-negative condition is found in about 15 percent of White Americans, but the trait is rare or absent in American Indians. Sickle-cell hemoglobin occurs in over 15 percent of many

African populations but is very rare in Europeans. Both these systems are poly-morphisms because the variants are common in some populations. The variant forms are passed from generation to generation in definite ways.

What probably concerns the anthropologist most about human inheritance are the factors that lead to genetic stability or to change in such polymorph-isms in local groups of people and in the whole human species. For example, physical anthropologists seek to understand the changes in the distribution of blood groups and hemoglobin in historic times (such as the introduction of the Rh-negative trait into some Indian tribes and the frequent occurrence of the sickle-cell condition in American Blacks) through the application of the principles of theoretical and experimental population genetics gained from other organisms, while taking into account the special circumstances of human marriage patterns and exposure to, and treatment of, human diseases. For ex-ample, polymorphic frequencies can be modified by migration, inbreeding, in-fectious diseases caused by unsanitary conditions, and successful treatment of genetic diseases.

Because size and form affect biological function, physical anthropologists are also concerned with **anthropometry**—measurement of dimensions and pro-portions of the head, face, and limbs, or of the skeleton, taken by standardized procedures. The genetics of anthropometric traits is complex, and various dimensions are interrelated and subject to a variety of modifying influences. These very complexities provide the physical anthropologist with a challenge to understand functionally significant characteristics (such as stature) in this way and to add to that understanding by examining past human biology through measurements on fossils.

Other branches of biology, as they develop, are also rapidly applied to physi-cal anthropology. Thus, in recent years biochemistry has created a *molecular biology* (see Chapter 4). The structure, working, and evolutionary transforma-tion of the specific chemical molecules within cells are examined, identified, and traced by new "labeling" and separation techniques, and such tools as the electron microscope may make them visible. Geneticists have examined the hereditary nature of, and the mechanisms responsible for, molecular variation. The findings of molecular genetics—the molecular differences between spe-cies and the relative frequencies of different molecules in the same species—require for their explanation an understanding of how these species live, or have lived in the womb, or how their ancestors lived in the distant past. These are, of course, the very kinds of questions that challenge the historical anthro-pologist.

The physical anthropologist's problems and solutions often involve one more set of conditions than those of the geneticist or biochemist: culture. In studies of human beings the critical questions are only rarely accessible to the precise tools of breeding fruit flies in bottles or testing blood specimens with chemical reagents. Economic and social influences affect diet and activity, for instance, and thus influence some of the most significant aspects of human bodily form. The answers are often statistical statements that describe probabilities, tendencies, and trends. *Human ecology,* the interaction between us and our environment, is reflected in our adaptation to that environment, whether this be the result of an inherited attribute or a product of our life experiences.

## Applied Physical Anthropology

Finally, variations in human physique, whatever their cause, challenge the physical anthropologist for a description and an explanation. Sometimes the answers have practical significance, as, for example, in the relation of a person's physique to the probability of incurring one or another disease. And as we literally hem ourselves in, our clothes, chairs, cars, and capsules provide a challenge for the application of physical anthropology to the design of our surroundings.

Although the application of the findings of physical anthropology to practical problems does not represent a separate subject area, knowledge of quite unexpected kinds sometimes proves useful. Thus, the cause and mode of spread of kuru, a tropical disease prevalent in the Faure of New Guinea, was not adequately explained biologically (it was thought to be inherited) until it was shown that it is an infectious disease transmitted by the former practice of cannibalism. The organism lodges in the brains of its victims and the brain was the part traditionally given to old women to eat. Kuru thus principally occurred in old women. This relationship does not preclude the presence of genetic factors. A hereditary group-specific protein in the blood serum, $Gc^{Ab}$, is more common in individuals and populations with kuru than in those without. The relation of human variation to questions of health and disease often involves knowledge of the distribution of diseases in human populations in relation to the distribution of normal anthropometric and genetic traits.

Besides health, there can be applications of physical anthropology to matters of convenience and safety, such as the fit of clothing, furniture, vehicles, and workspace. Conscious application of our knowledge of human variation has begun to replace trial and error in designing many products of human use such as airplanes and automobiles.

It should be clearly understood that physical anthropology does not stand alone in any of these subject areas. But no other discipline seems suited to the task of the synthesizing of human biology. Specifically, the processes of human evolution and differentiation require for their understanding knowledge gained from the adoption of specialized research methods first developed in other biological and behavioral-science disciplines. Human evolution and differentiation also require for their study further refinement of general principles and concepts.

## Anthropology and Human Biology

Since physical anthropology utilizes methods and concepts from so many other branches of science, one may ask how it is to be distinguished from them.

As an aspect of biology, physical anthropology can be considered as one approach to human biology. It is the approach that attempts to place the problems of human biology in the widest context. This approach is more often to humanity as a whole, or to human populations, than to individuals. Furthermore, the subject of physical anthropology is people, and people are the only culture-bearing animals. Physical anthropology is the science that deals with the interaction of sociocultural and other environmental factors with genetic processes in human biology.

As an aspect of the study of humans, physical anthropology is aligned with the rest of anthropology through its concern both with cultural influences on human biology and with biological preconditions for the development of culture. In anthropology, each scholar tends to specialize in one method of approach, but our evolution can only be understood by making a gestalt—a whole—out of this diversity of approaches. Perhaps a simple set of examples will illustrate this. The study of the history of a language is quite different in character as well as in subject from the study of the history of marriage customs or the history of pottery. These, in turn, differ from the study of the history of our anatomy. Chimpanzees communicate by a variety of sounds and gestures and can command numerous "meanings," but it is only with great difficulty that one was trained to "say" three English words and use them in appropriate context. Language and verbal communication is perhaps the most distinctively human of all behaviors.

Most animals have very well defined seasons of estrus during which females are receptive and males are interested. Women and men, on the other hand, schedule their sexual activities throughout the year according to menstrual cycles and inclination as well as by elaborate rules dictated by the culture (which vary from society to society but always include some tabus). The development of family life no doubt required for its stability this shift to more-or-less continuous possibility of sexual relations and the unique delay in maturation of the human young.

Chimpanzees can select some leaves and use them to sponge up water to drink, but only a human can acquire the image of a complex finished artifact, such as a bowl or jug for the storage or transport of fluids, toward which the clay is shaped and molded.

In the past a great deal of confusion has been caused by failure to consider the separate influences of language, other aspects of culture, and biology. Nevertheless, one must not overlook the fact that factors from these different domains influence each other. Language and culture determine the very existence of differences through their roles in determining the nature of the society and the rules for the selection of mates. Differences in culture influence the differing milieus of the societies within which biological differences evole. However, in the end, all history depends on the kind of animal we are and the way we have come to be. The biological evolution of a being who will talk, stay mated, and cook food in the pots made for that purpose is basic to the history of language, marriage, and pottery.

The differences in cultural characteristics between the Egyptian and the Eskimo, the Samaritan and the Seminole, the Hutterite and the Hottentot, can be studied only by using the methods of analysis of the cultural anthropologist. But the very existence of culture and the occurrence of cultural differences depend on a special kind of organism with suitable brain, tongue, and vocal chords for talk, the altered sexual rhythm and delayed maturity suitable to durable family organization, and suitable hands to make pots. Only we combine these traits with adequate mental capacity to conceive, remember, and transmit these ideas: that is, to develop culture. As our forebears began to rely on the products of culture, they must have adapted biologically to this way of life. The further development of human capacities, and the evolution of an organism possessing them, must have depended mainly on the growth of culture itself. In many of the areas that are now inhabited it is doubtful that people could survive without clothes, shelter, and organized society. Yet they have survived and adapted, evolving in response to both the physical and the cultural aspects of their environment. Our further survival no doubt depends on continuing biological resilience and, especially, on our ability to anticipate the threats to continued existence and to gain support for the plans and social sanctions needed to frustrate the threats.

Physical anthropology continues to forge ahead and attract the attention of a growing number of research workers. Some of the concepts and controversies of a previous generation (racial types, for example) have been demonstrated to be sterile. Some fundamentalists still think that evolution is at variance with special creation and some reactionary politicians have attempted to gain favor with such people by trying to legislate that evolution can only be taught as one of several "theories" of human origin. Nevertheless among thoughtful people debates about the theory of evolution have given way to descriptions of the changes that have taken place in various organisms and an analysis of the principles operating such changes.

## Summary

Physical anthropology is the study of human biological variation and evolution. It is concerned with the processes of evolution and the resultant biological history of the human species and with human biological variation and its causes.

The subject matter of physical anthropology can be divided either on the basis of the methods applied or on the basis of the problems with which research is concerned. In physical anthropology, as in many other fields of knowledge, only some of the methods are special to the field whereas others are borrowed. Furthermore, many of the methods developed in respect to one set of problems are then successfully applied to other types of problems. Since this book is intended as an introduction to the present state of knowledge in physical anthropology and not as a handbook or manual for training practitioners, the organization is based largely on the subject matter and not on the methods. First we shall deal with some principles of biology as they apply to man, with evolution (the processes leading to general stability combined with gradual change in biological organisms), and with the variety of such organisms that are the products of evolution—especially those most similar to ourselves. Then we shall take up the principles involved in the evolutionary changes in organisms and apply these principles to the study of our fossil relatives, beginning with earlier ones and coming down to more recent predecessors. We shall briefly consider some methods such as anthropometry (measurement of the body) and their application to the study of human growth and of racial differences. Finally, we shall consider some of the major problems the world now faces and speculate on the possible helpfulness of physical anthropology to us in forming our point of view in response to them.

# CHAPTER 2

# EVOLUTION

## The Process of Change

There is no longer any doubt among scientists about the fact of evolution as the central process of nature. Organic evolution is a general principle of biology, applying equally to all forms of life. Among biologists who have considered the evidence there is overwhelming acceptance of the thesis that we evolved in the same way that other animals did. In their evolution, species often progressively diverge with time from other related species. In our development, we in this way left behind us some of those traits that are more or less common to other advanced organisms that populate this globe. We have also acquired traits that distinguish us from the rest of the animal world. Some of the evidence is reviewed in this book, and we shall see (Chapters 6, 7, and 8) that the mechanisms which brought about this transformation and continue to operate in us today are similar to the mechanisms of evolution in other organisms.

By **evolution** is meant any change in hereditary endowment continuing through successive generations of time. It is a lawful change in the genetic composition of the members of a **breeding population.** The technical meaning of *breeding population* will be discussed later (pp. 81–83). It will suffice here merely to mention that it is the group of individuals among whom mates are found.

Since there are different degrees of probability that any one individual will mate with any other, the exact boundaries of a population may not be clear. Therefore evolution is often considered to be a property of **species,** groups of organisms (animals or plants) that are homogeneous enough to breed among themselves and have fertile offspring. When organisms are separated by time or space so that there is no direct way to know if they would interbreed, they are considered members of the same species if they are about as similar to each other as are members of species that do. Evolution thus consists of all the ways in which inherited qualities develop and permeate a species while others decline or fail to be preserved. Both processes may go on simultaneously with different traits in the same population, while still other hereditary features may persist and pass unmodified from generation to generation. Ordinarily the term "evolution" is used only for continuous changes that have gone on for many generations, but this process is the accumulation of changes going on from fathers and mothers to sons and daughters. In essence, evolution is the accumulation of genetic changes between successive parents and offspring. The differences one can see between a father and his son provide living evidence of the evolution that has been proceeding throughout many generations. If it were not for such differences between parent and child, however slight they may be, there could be no evolution.

The difference between the random changes that occur between one generation and the next and the seemingly purposeful evolution extending over many generations baffled serious thinkers of the past, of course, and efforts to account for changes in species included incorrect naturalistic explanations as well as appeals to mystery. The fact of evolution seen in generation-to-generation change requires explanation and that will occupy much of this book (see especially Chapters 7, 8, and 9) but these changes are the substance of evolution and that deserves a few examples here at the outset.

A child sometimes resembles one of his grandparents but not his father or his mother. Whatever degree of resemblance is demonstrated to earlier ancestors must have come through the parents, but the extent to which the genetic makeup of an earlier ancestor will be communicated cannot be predicted. No one knows in what member of a large family a noteworthy physical feature of a grandfather will reappear or whether it will reappear at all. Such a hereditary trait may occur in only some of the offspring, express itself to various degrees, or become modified. The process of evolution is continuous change over time. It may vary in rate, however. Indeed, when there are no changes whatever in environment or habits and when members of the population do not mate with those of other populations, one may see merely small chance fluctuations in physical characteristics from generation to generation without continuing evolution in any direction. In nature there are instances of so-called living fossils, such as the opossum and the horseshoe crab, that have remained almost the same over millions of years (see Fig. 13-10). In human beings however, especially in the last several centuries, increased population mobility and far-reaching changes in living conditions must have accelerated the rate of evolution. Human evolution has probably never been faster than now, at least in respect to features that adapt us to modern living conditions.

Sexual reproduction ensures that each successive generation differs from the one before it. (This takes place through a process called **meiosis** that will be described on pp. 24–30.) The relatives of a newborn infant sometimes say, "He is the image of his father." At most, however, the child merely resembles one of his parents. One never sees a child who is identical in every feature to either parent. Photographs show that individuals look quite different from the way either of their parents appeared at the same age. Variation is present among members of a family and among families and groups. Such variation can be thought of as a result of evolution. If there were no change, how could descendants differ? On the other hand, further evolution, especially large changes over long spans of time, largely depends on variation at the same time that it is responsible for ever-diverging types and increasing ranges of variation. Evolution is both the cause and the effect of variation.

We are not always aware of the extent of variation. When one looks at people, the differences within a foreign family or group, the basic kind of variation, may be difficult to see. To some observers, "All Chinese look alike." This is because the features in which the Chinese differ from our own group of people are so strikingly evident that one may fail to notice the differences which exist among individual Chinese—variations that they find perfectly adequate for identifying their acquaintances. For example, the skinfold of the eyelid that gives the almond-eyed appearance to the Chinese has innumerable variations (Fig. 2-1). We have plenty of visible proof for the fact that evolution is at work among us to produce cumulative effects of group differentiation. Such evidences consist of observations of what happens within the family and the population and what has happened between species over long spans of time. Future evolution will depend on future conditions, and uncertainty about future conditions makes prediction of the future course of evolution difficult. Unlike some other scientific principles in which the number of factors entering into predictions is small most evolutionary events depend on the very large number of possible changes in living conditions. It is therefore difficult to predict what future organisms will be like. But for the past, the salient conditions are known or can be inferred, and evolution provides the explanation.

## Evolution Through Unequal Increase in Numbers

One example of evolution as a fact that still operates among us is the continuous change in the proportion of different groups in the population of the United States. Some groups—the American Indians, for example—have decreased in numbers. In 1600 there were 900,000 to 1 million in the continental United States. Although there are now again over 800,000 Indians in the United States, the number had shrunk to about 350,000 in 1920 (LaFarge, 1960). On the

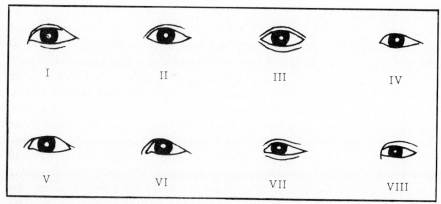

FIG. 2-1    Some of the types of eyelid skin folds seen among Oriental peoples. Many human features exist in a variety of forms, and the combination of features makes it possible to distinguish all individuals—even twins. From A. Gibaut and G. Olivier: *Anthropologie des Tibetains orientaux.* Publications hors serie de L'École Français d'Extreme-Orient, 1965. Reproduced by permission.

other hand, some of the immigrant groups from Europe have multiplied steadily as well as rapidly.

Changes in the proportions of the groups that make up the world population likewise go on generation after generation, as would be expected from the different reproductive rates of various countries. National populations differ genetically; hence the changes in the relative sizes of these populations demonstrate human evolution because of the resulting shift in the genetic composition of the world population. One used to hear talk of a "Yellow peril"—the supposed result of large population increases in eastern Asia. This concept not only rested on racist values, it also was based on an error of fact: namely, that the populations of eastern Asia had a greater rate of increase than those of the rest of the world. If the relatively high reproductive rates of one race can be considered a threat to other races, then the peoples of Asia and Africa might have been justified in speaking of a "White peril." In 300 years the population of Europe has increased sixfold, and this growth rate should be doubled again to take account of increases in European populations living outside Europe (Sax, 1956). In the same period the population of Asia increased only fivefold and those of other parts of the world even less. This means that the average person of the physical types present in Europe some 300 years ago has today several times as many living descendants as has a typical non-European individual of that day. Europeans have colonized North America, Australia, New Zealand, and to lesser extents South and Central America, Asia, and Oceania. The result has been a significant evolutionary change in humanity as a whole. Such change is not a problem in itself. There is no Yellow peril, White peril, or Black peril, although today there is a peril of excessive numbers of all types of people in relation to available natural resources.

## Facts and Theories

But what about the long stretch of past evolution? What facts have we to demonstrate that it really took place? What biological changes occurred during ancient geological epochs and the glacial and postglacial periods that resulted in the human species of today? There is now much fossil evidence for all sorts of intermediate forms that show the nature of our relationship to other animals, and new finds are being added continuously. Some of these are of apelike humans, some of humanlike apes, monkeylike apes, monkeylike lemurs, mammallike reptiles, reptilelike amphibians, amphibianlike fishes, and other intermediate links between animal forms. Our problem is not in finding missing links as such. It is in establishing the genetic interrelations of fossil forms, the order in which these forms have occurred, and their ways of life. To solve this range of problems it is important that the search go on for more complete skeletons and for variant types from different places and geologic times. The general picture, however, is already clear.

Evolution is a fact rather than a theory. However, theories are needed to explain facts and relate them to each other. Such theories have the additional advantage that they can help to anticipate the course of events that have not yet occurred. There is adequate scope for the elaboration of theories about evolution.

These theories deal with highly complex interrelationships among the molecular components of cells and the cells that form animals, and between the animals and their environments. Evolutionary theory, like historical theory in general, is not so much a system of precise prediction of the future of humanity as it is a help in the reconstruction of the past and a guide to the general nature of our biological future. Evolutionary theory has been developing and changing, especially with the application of new genetic principles to natural populations. It has been modified, first by Mendelian genetics, then by population genetics, and lastly by molecular genetics. That these theories continue to be debated and modified does not cast in doubt the fact of evolution itself; further refinement of evolutionary theory makes the fact more understandable rather than more probable.

The general fact of evolution had been noted before Charles Darwin. A self-consistent but falsely based theory had been previously proposed. The idea, usually incorrectly ascribed to Lamarck, is that the environment modifies the genetic constitution and that changes in the environment produce inheritable changes in organisms. We now know that the genetic constitution is impervious to such direct influences.

Of great importance in the development of the theory of human evolution was the publication in 1859 of Charles Darwin's *Origin of Species*. In his book Darwin presented the idea of evolution through **natural selection.** This natural process, he said, causes "survival of the fittest" or continued life for those types of animals and plants best adjusted to the conditions in which they live, and death for those that are not so well adjusted to these conditions. The nature of the environment thus limits (selects) the kinds of organisms that will flourish. Especially during periods of progressive changes in the environment, the corresponding progressive changes in groups of organisms tend to be limited to those features that can adapt them to their changing surroundings. Such a way of life with its environmental possibilities and limitations on the evolving organism is called an **ecological niche.** Natural selection is explained in Chapter 7 and **adaptation** is discussed in detail in Chapter 9.

Darwin was not the first to present such a theory, but surprisingly the theory was first applied to explain why species do not change. In the 1830s Edward Blyth published several articles showing that species of organisms are buffered from change by the premature death of the unfit. That is, deviants are adversely affected. This process, now called **normalizing selection,** in fact slows and stabilizes evolution by eliminating offspring that differ greatly and maladaptively from their parents. It was the establishment of *progressive evolution,* however, and its firm foundation in the numerous facts assembled by Darwin and his followers, that produced a revolution in biological thought. Progressive evolution is the selection of changed offspring that are better adapted than their parents.

Darwin's studies of animals throw light on the origin of humanity. Thus, characteristics that help us to survive had become established and spread in our forebears because they were passed on from one generation to the next. Every chance variation that worked better tended to be preserved. Darwin and Alfred Russel Wallace, a naturalist who presented the idea of natural selection simultaneously with Darwin, at first said nothing about human beings. Nevertheless, both critics and defenders of natural selection immediately saw that the theory of selective survival would apply to us. In fact it was the implication that our forebears had been nonhuman rather than the idea of evolutionary change in general which sparked the bitter controversy.

Darwin turned to the question of human evolution in a later work, *The Descent of Man,* published first in 1871. His argument for the relationship of humans to other animals was based on the similarity in anatomy to which T. H. Huxley had already drawn attention. The anatomical resemblances between humans and other primates that persuaded Darwin are in the general plan of the skeleton, muscles, nerves, viscera, and, especially, the brain. At that time there were virtually no fossils available to help support their contention, and Darwin and Wallace themselves at times had misgivings as to how "survival of the fittest" could work in humans. Once the question of our kinship to the apes had been raised, however, and the anatomical similarities had been demonstrated, the search for evidence of "missing links" and the development of explanatory theory began.

Another striking event in the history of evolutionary theory was the discovery of the mechanism of inheritance, since this explains how variation (the very substance of evolutionary change, as we have seen) is achieved and maintained. It had previously been thought that the mixing of parental fluids caused the similarity between parents and offspring. The misleading term "mixed blood" reflects this old misconception. Now we know that there is no direct mixing of parental bloods or other fluids in the offspring. The genetic mode of transmission using coded nucleic acid causes offspring to acquire parts of the hereditary endowment of both parents. On the basis of experiments in cross-breeding peas, Gregor Mendel showed that his results could be explained only if there are discrete particles **(genes)** transmitted from parents to offspring.

This theory of *particulate inheritance* was published in 1865 but was not understood by others in Mendel's lifetime. Although biologists had developed the cell theory and added to knowledge of cell division and reproduction, it was not until the present century that the climate of scientific thought was ready for an adequate theory of genetics.

By the early 1900s, however, the theory of evolution had been refined and human fossils had been found and examined. The applicability of evolutionary theory to humans was widely accepted and was soon to be supported by additional finds and by an understanding of the relevance of the principles of human genetics. The beginnings can be traced a little earlier, but the scientific study of evolution in genetic context is purely a phenomenon of the twentieth century.

## Summary

Evolution is continuous change in hereditary endowment. Human evolution is a fact manifest in genetic differences between parents and offspring, in differences between groups, and in the fossil record. Evolution is also a set of theories that explain the facts. Darwin's theory of natural selection and Mendel's theory of the gene, both propounded over a century ago, are the basis for the twentieth-century development of satisfactory explanations of the increasing number of established facts about human evolution.

# CHAPTER 3

# THE BIOLOGICAL
# BASIS OF LIFE

## The Origin of Life

About 2,300 years ago, the Greek philosopher, Aristotle, described the border-line between the inanimate and the living as doubtful and perhaps nonexistent. The gradual transition in nature which he suggested has since been demonstrated and we have begun to understand the course of the evolution of life.

It is possible that life originated either on the earth or elsewhere, to be transported here later. Radio telescopes aimed at the Milky Way have discovered sources emitting microwave signals of just those wavelengths associated with certain molecules. In this way astronomy has revealed many chemical compounds and radicals (parts of compounds) in interstellar dust clouds. These include the hydroxyl radical (OH), water ($H_2O$), formaldehyde ($H_2CO$), methanol ($CH_3OH$), ammonia ($NH_3$), carbon monoxide (CO), a highly reactive molecule with a carbon-carbon double bond ($H_2C:CHCN$), and also HCN, $CN_2$, $H_2$, and $HC_3N$. In all, at least 22 molecules (half of them organic—that is, carbon-containing—molecules) have been found, all but 4 of them since 1968. Two of these (the OH radical and CO) have also been identified outside our galaxy.

If living organisms or even complex organic molecules were transported to a lifeless earth from elsewhere in the galaxy, however, they must have been embedded in a meteor or they would have been destroyed en route (Urey, 1962). Since this hypothesis requires that one postulate two heavenly bodies able to support life and a vehicle between them which also could do so, the suggestion that life as we know it originated on earth is more plausible. Furthermore, some biologically necessary molecules have not been observed in space and those that do occur are in clouds of gas and dust where they are shielded from ultraviolet light that might otherwise destroy them. Such "clouds" condense to form stars and similar protective conditions do not exist then. Stars developed to the stage of our sun would not shield the molecules adequately.

Living things are distinguished by their capacity to grow, reproduce, and interact with their environment. They require a source of energy (food) that they metabolize, and they excrete waste products. Especially in animals, considerable energy is utilized in the breakdown of food for use by the body in maintaining life processes, and there is a marked capacity to respond to stimuli and to move. But plants as well as animals share these functions.

The chemical reactions that synthesize organic substances take place in the living cell and utilize materials and energy from food. Knowledge of the cell has grown with the perfection of molecular techniques. Among these techniques, are those of histochemistry, the localization of specific chemical products within cells, and electron microscopy, by which fine structure can be made visible. The branch of science that deals with intracellular processes in these ways is called cell biology. Knowledge of cell biology provides a foundation for embryology (the science of development), genetics (the science of transmission), and ecology (the study of interaction with the environment). Biology, the science of life, is therefore largely dependent on knowledge of the structure and function of cells. Life itself depends on the way cells function. The activities of cells involve the interplay between the molecular chemical constituents and the organized cellular subunits called **organelles.**

The various parts of the cell have different functions. The cell nucleus contains the **chromosomes** that guide the cell's reproductive function (see Chapter 4). The material outside the nucleus, called **cytoplasm,** serves as the "chemical factory" for the functions of growth and the production of energy. Membranes fulfill many functions in cells. They serve as barriers: physical barriers selectively transmitting only certain substances. Membranes serve as insulation, as a base for chemical reactions, and, of course, they give shape and substance to cells.

Certain cell types in multicelled animals lack the capacity to reproduce and have no cell nucleus. Instead of reproducing themselves they are formed from other types of cells. However, development of multicelled animals required the prior existence of cells with all three functions: reproduction, growth, and production of energy. An adequate description of the origin of life must therefore explain cells with nuclei, cytoplasm, and membranes (Fig. 3-1).

All chemical compounds that contain carbon atoms are called "organic."

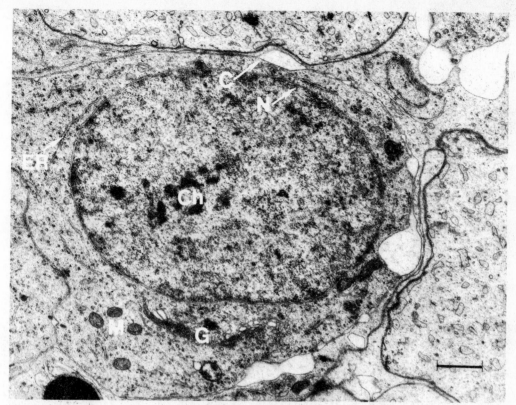

FIG. 3-1    Mammalian cell: *C*, cell membrane; *N*, nuclear membrane; *Ch*, chromatin (chromosomal material); *M*, mitochondria (metabolic energy center); *ER*, endoplasmic reticulum (the dark grains are ribosomes); *G*, Golgi apparatus (the packaging station for synthesized protein). The line = 1 micron. Electron micrograph of rabbit testis courtesy of Dr. Maurice Bernstein, Wayne State University, Detroit, Michigan.

Some, such as carbon dioxide ($CO_2$), are simple, contain few atoms, and can readily be synthesized. Others, such as starches and proteins, are complex, may contain hundreds of atoms, and are very difficult to synthesize. The cell nucleus, cytoplasm, and membrane consist of complex organic compounds. How could the materials present in the world before life existed synthesize such compounds? So far as we know, the naturally occurring complex organic compounds of today are all the results of life processes: life seems always to be dependent on prior life. Rot, decay, and fermentation, which reduce organic compounds to simpler compounds and chemical elements, also occur only as a result of life processes. It takes live yeasts, molds, or bacteria to decompose animal and plant tissues to water and simple gases.

Imagine, then, a time before there was life. Even if organic compounds were not being synthesized in cells, at least there would be no microorganisms to degrade such organic compounds as existed.

Since there was nothing to cause compounds to decay, the natural process of change, "chemical evolution," would have led to increasingly more complex, not simpler, compounds. Eventually, some complex compound achieved the ability to make more material like itself. This was the first step in the origin of life. This reproduction must have been confined within a structure that can be called a primitive cell, and such a cell would then have acquired the ability to reproduce copies of itself. What we call life began in this way, with the development of the capacity to break down the surrounding substances to utilize their constituents for the creation of descendants.

Studies of radiations from stars and galaxies, as well as theories concerning the origin of the earth, point to an original atmosphere that contained methane, nitrogen, and water instead of the present atmosphere of nitrogen, oxygen, carbon dioxide, a little hydrogen, and traces of other gases. In 1953 S. L. Miller began the first successful experiments to produce **amino acids,** the chemical building blocks of the *proteins* (Fig. 3-2) found in all forms of life. His purpose was to show how this could be done **abiogenetically** (derived without life or products of living things). He used combinations of gases forming atmospheres of the type believed to have been prevalent on earth at one time. When he subjected these atmospheres to electric spark discharges, they yielded a wide variety of organic compounds, including not only formic acid but also even amino acids and a vitamin. Besides the sparks (which simulated natural lightning) other energy sources such as heat, light, and radiations of various types produce similar results (Friedman and Miller, 1969). Ultraviolet light (which simulates sunlight) under some circumstances can break down mole-

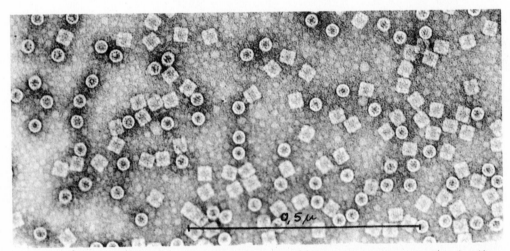

FIG. 3-2   Protein molecules as seen in the electron microscope. Note the size ($1\mu=$ about 0.00004 inches) on the scale and compare the size with that of a virus and bacterium (Fig. 4-3). This particular type of molecule ($\beta$-hemocyanin) is the shape of a cork, and some were end-up and appear circular whereas others were on their side and appear square. Specimen: Dr. Van Bruggen, University of Gronigen, Netherlands. Photographed through Zeiss Electron Microscope EM 9.

cules, but under others, presumably including primitive earth conditions, it can produce a variety of amino acids (Sagan and Khare, 1971). Even in the absence of water, a mixture of three gases that are known to exist in interstellar space (ammonia, methanol, and formic acid) forms amino acids when exposed to ultraviolet light (Wollin and Ericson, 1971). Ultraviolet light can also stimulate the production of nucleotides from such gases. Nucleotides are the essential units of the nucleic acids that are necessary for reproduction (Stephen-Sherwood et al., 1971).

Some students of the subject believe that the metabolic functions of cells came first and that only after a long period of evolution would natural selection shape the reproductive process (Hanson, 1966). In any case, constituents of the proteins and nucleic acids of living cells have been synthesized in the laboratory under primitive earth conditions. No one has yet come close to creating a living cell from primitive "air," however, but the chemical steps have been shown to be plausible. To create a cell one would need high concentrations of the chemicals in well-formed confined spaces, and a good deal of time. Perhaps the tiny amounts of essential substances were concentrated in spray or evaporating pools, or were "shaped" and modified by compression among inorganic crystals such as in the interstices in clay.

Synthesis of proteins and nucleic acids must entail chains of successive stages. Until life began, the nonliving environment could have held quite complex substances. However, once any complex of carbon-containing molecules was able to metabolize parts of its environment, and accurately reproduce itself, to be alive, its descendants would begin to use up all the natural chemical food on which they grew. If some descendant were modified in the direction of being able to grow on some simpler substance, this form would have an advantage and would multiply in a world in which the original "food for life" had become scarce (Horowitz, 1945).

Each time this happened the descendants added a new capacity to synthesize and, at the same time, the world lost some complex organic substance achieved by nonlife processes. The gap between the most complex nonorganic substances and the simplest forms of life increased. The gap could hardly have been jumped by a single event; many steps were probably involved, so that what were originally purely abiogenetic chemical syntheses began to take place within the organism. They became biological processes. The increasingly long chains of life processes progressively eliminated the complex chemically synthesized substrates on which the first rudimentary forms of life had depended. Thus, with the disappearance of the complex freely-occurring compounds, and the replacement of rudimentary forms of life by more complex ones, the gap constantly increased between the kinds of chemical substances found within living things and those found independently of living things (Fig. 3-3).

The first plausible theory of the origin of life emphasized the step at which particles were formed in the "primeval soup" containing the substrate. A. I. Oparin, a Soviet scientist, developed this theory in 1924 (see Oparin, 1957;

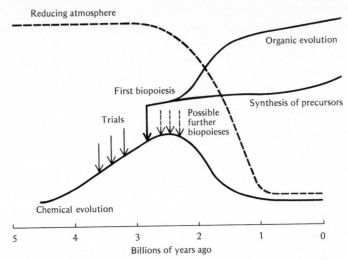

FIG. 3-3   Probable origin of life (biopoiesis). Several unsuccessful starts (first three solid arrows) and several successful trials (dashed arrows) are postulated. Once successful organisms had evolved, chemical evolution regressed as organisms broke down the more complex precursors. Furthermore, the reducing condition of the atmosphere was superseded by an atmosphere with free oxygen. From *Heredity, Evolution, and Society* by I. Michael Lerner, W. H. Freeman and Company. Copyright © 1968.

and Keosian, 1964). Colloidal suspensions form tiny droplets within which chemicals can become concentrated and reactions take place. In attempting the abiogenetic synthesis of proteins, S. W. Fox (1960) was able to produce substances from amino acids that are in some ways like proteins. They are capable of assuming the shape of little uniform spheres that can be seen under the microscope. In some cases the electron microscope reveals differentiation and such cell-like characteristics as double-walled membranes in the droplets.

Simple cells such as the one-celled animals (protozoa) are already complex structures possessing not only the capacity to grow, reproduce, and evolve, but also the chief biochemical themes of all living things. Despite the difficulty of simulating these structures in the laboratory, the approach to the abiogenetic production of the essential units, especially of high-molecular-weight nucleotides that might reproduce and evolve, has allowed us to view the origin of life not so much as a possibly unique event of some distant past, but more as a reproducible process that occurs under specific, albeit rare, circumstances.

## Mitosis and Meiosis

There are two ways in which organisms can reproduce: by simple multiplication and by bisexual reproduction. Simple multiplication of cells is called **mitosis.** Mitosis is a nuclear phenomenon—a mechanical process that ensures equitable distribution of genetic materials. **Meiosis** is a process in bisexual reproduction. It involves the reduction of the amount of genetic material in a sex cell **(gamete)** to half the usual in such a way that when a male gamete (sperm) fertilizes a female gamete (ovum), the full complement of genetic material for the individual is reestablished. In the process not only is the genetic material halved, but each essential part of it must be halved so that the reconstituted fertilized ovum has all the properties necessary for its development.

Many unicellular organisms reproduce by mitosis. Mitosis is the process by which a cell transmits the identical genetic material of its **chromosomes** (Fig. 3-4) to two daughter cells. Ordinary (nonsex) cells in multicellular organisms also multiply by mitosis. This process can be seen in preparations fixed and suitably stained for microscopic study (see Figs. 3-5 and 3-6). In mitosis the chromosomes (literally "stained bodies") in the nucleus of a cell which is about to divide gather on a plane near the middle of the cell. The nucleus disappears as such and each chromosome is seen to be made up of two strands called **chromatids.** These paired strands separate and are drawn in opposite directions towards the sides of the cell. There they reform cell nuclei and the cell itself pinches in two to form two cells.

In the case of sexually reproducing plants and animals the sex cells undergo a special pair of divisions, called meiosis, which reduces the number of chromosomes to half. This reduction is obviously necessary if a sperm is going to fertilize an ovum and start a chain of cell divisions in which the number of chromsomes is the same as that of either parent. If two sex cells join together to produce a complete genetic blueprint, each single sex cell—male or female—can contain only half a blueprint. During the first of two divisions the chromosomes come together into homologous pairs of similar size. This pairing is unlike any process during mitosis. The chromosomes are seen to consist of a **centromere,** a central structure from which radiate the chromatids, the strands that form the arms.

The chromatids of each homologous pair—but not the centromeres—double to form pairs of sister chromotids, each pair attached to a single centromere. These chromatids then tend to intertwine with their opposite numbers belonging to the homologous chromosome and to exchange corresponding regions. The exchanges are called *crossing over* **(chiasmata)** and permit, as will be seen later, the recombination of genetic information. The reformed units then untwine.

The *first division* of meiosis results in one of each homologous pair of (doubled) chromosomes going to each daughter cell. Then the two daughter cells themselves split in the *second division*. During this the centromeres of each chromosome split, with the previously doubled chromotids going one to each cell. We are left with four cells, two containing a set of centromere-chromatids chosen haphazardly from one complete set of homologous pairs of chromosomes, and the other two containing the opposite numbers of these homologous pairs.

When a sperm fertilizes an egg, the single chromosome sets from the two cells are joined together into a new paired set in the fused nucleus of the

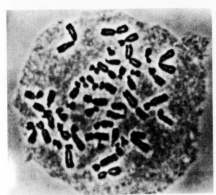

FIG. 3-4 *Left:* Untreated human bone-marrow cell undergoing mitosis. The 46 chromosomes of this human female cell are clearly visible. *Below:* The karyotype. The microphotograph shown in Fig 3-4 *(left)* was cut apart and remounted to show the 22 autosomal (nonsex) pairs and the pair of X chromosomes of the normal human female cell, matched for form and size and classified into groups. In the normal male karyotype there would be one X and one Y chromosome instead of two X chromosomes. Photographs courtesy of Dr. E. R. Powsner, Wayne State University, Detroit, Michigan.

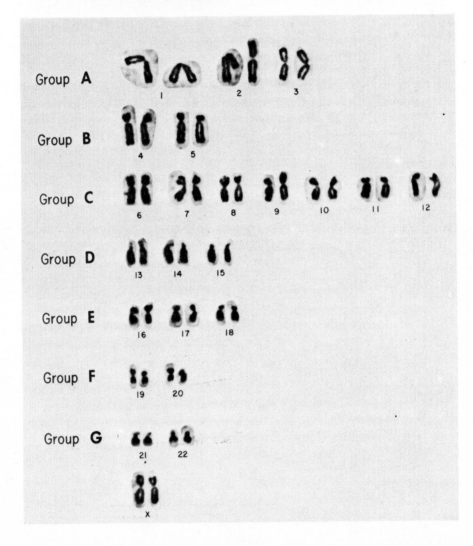

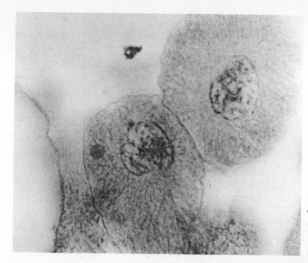

FIG. 3-5 The mitotic process. *1. Interphase:* Chromosomes are a mass of tenuous threads. Their light staining may result from hydration and diffuseness of nucleic acids.

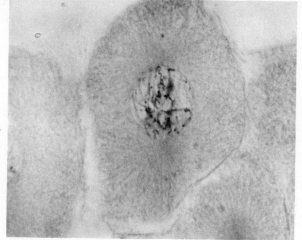

*2. Prophase:* In preparation for division, chromosomes shorten and thicken; individual chromosomes separate from the mass of threads and move out toward the nuclear membrane. The spindle is beginning to form and the nuclear membrane is beginning to disintegrate.

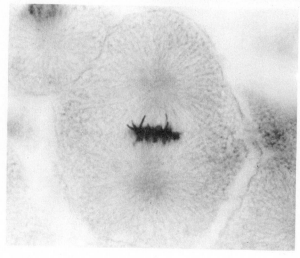

*3. Metaphase:* Metaphase is the period of equilibrium between convergence of chromosomes at the equator and their divergence toward the poles. Spindle fibers seem to be discrete and not "lines of force" as was once thought, as they can be seen by the electron microscope, and the entire mitotic apparatus, including spindle fibers, can be isolated from the rest of the cell by treatment with detergents.

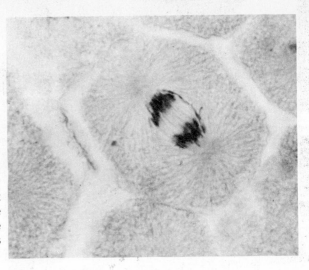

4. *Anaphase:* Anaphase occurs suddenly when the equilibrium is broken by division of the centromeres that had held the chromatid pairs together. The chromatids, now daughter chromosomes, move apart toward opposite poles, with the divided centromeres leading. The spindle and cell are lengthening in this photograph.

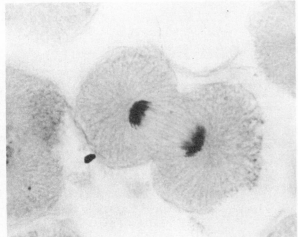

5. *Anaphase:* This photograph shows the cell pinching in two.

6. *Telophase: (bottom)* Cell membranes have almost completely reformed, and daughter cells are connected only by the intermediate body of Flemming. In later telophase the spindle vanishes, the nucleolus and nuclear membrane reappear, and the cell reasumes the appearance of interphase. Photographs courtesy of the Upjohn Company, Kalamazoo, Michigan.

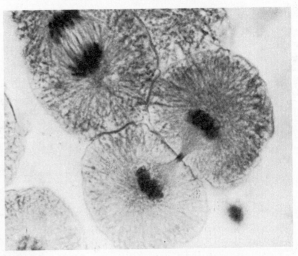

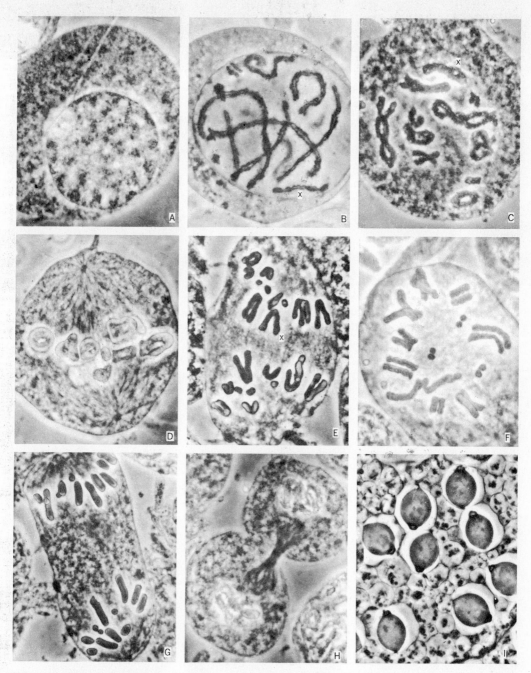

FIG. 3-6   Meiosis. Formation of grasshopper sperm. Compare with mitosis shown in
Fig. 3-5. A. Spermatocyte. These cells have a full complement of chromosomes but
give rise to gametes by meiosis. B. Early prophase. The chromosomes are slender and
paired. C. Later prophase. The chromosomes are double and paired and crossovers can
be seen. D. Metaphase. The chromosomes are shortened and converge at the equator.
E. Anaphase. F. Prophase of second division of meiosis. G. Anaphase of second
division. In this division the chromosomes are single and rodlike. H. Telophase,
Spermatids, the products of meiosis, will soon become sperms. Reproduced by permission from A. M. Winchester   1969   *Biology and Its Relation to Mankind* (ed. 4).
New York: Van Nostrand Reinhold, p. 578.

fertilized egg. The process of fertilization leads to an essentially equal amount of chromosomal material coming from each parent. Because of the reduction division, however, any given chromosome or part of a chromosome may come from either one or the other of the parent's parents. Because of the crossing over at chiasmata, part of a chromosome can come from one grandparent, part from the other. Fertilization is thus responsible for the uniting of two diverse but similar stores of genetic information into new combinations, and since it is the combination that determines function of the organism, the offspring may have a more or less favorable functional capacity than either parent. Fertilization also initiates the series of mitotic divisions and cell specializations that account for the growth and differentiation of the embryo.

## Summary

Life consists of the ability to grow, reproduce, and interact with the environment. These traits themselves evolved in an atmosphere different from the present atmosphere of the earth. Some organic chemical radicals have been detected in interstellar space, but the development of complex molecules from these simple ones probably occurred here on earth, although under very different conditions than occur today. Evolution of living things required cells with membranes to confine the chemical reactions and concentrate the molecular products, and with chromosomes to control growth and reproduction. In mitosis cells divide and multiply. Meiosis and fertilization are processes in sexual reproduction by which special sex-cells with half the usual complement of chromosomes are formed and come together to reconstitute cells with the normal complement. In so doing the coded information of the chromosomes of the two parents is recombined in the offspring.

# CHAPTER 4

# THE PRINCIPLES OF GENETICS

## Molecular Genetics

The chemical examination of the structural elements of cells (histochemistry or cytochemistry) has permitted, among other things, the analysis of the materials responsible for essential life processes: the materials that cause the continuity from generation to generation and determine the development of the individual. These substances are nucleic acids. There are two kinds of nucleic acids in cells: deoxyribonucleic acid (called **DNA,** for short) and ribonucleic acid **(RNA).** The DNA of a cell is found primarily in the **nucleus**—specifically in the **chromosomes.** The RNA, however, occurs primarily in the **cytoplasm.**

Two lines of evidence led to the identification of DNA as the effective genetic material. One involved the demonstration that bacteria of one kind and appearance could be transformed into those of another kind and appearance by DNA from dead specimens of the latter. First it was shown as long ago as 1928 that mice would die if simultaneously injected with heat-treated bacteria of a virulent strain (that contained the virulent molecules of DNA but had been killed so they could not reproduce) and with harmless forms of living bacteria. Then, in 1944, Avery and his colleagues showed that an extract containing the

DNA of the virulent bacteria would transform the benign strain to the lethal one (as shown both in the appearance of the bacterial colonies of the strain and in the capacity to kill mice (Fig. 4-1).

The other line of evidence comes from an experiment which shows that only the inside (DNA) and not the outside coat (protein) of a virus can infect bacteria (Fig. 4-2). Hershey and Chase (1952) did this experiment with a virus **(phage)** that infects bacteria. These simple parasitic organisms consist of DNA and a protein coat (Fig. 4-3). Phage was grown in cultures that transferred a marker to

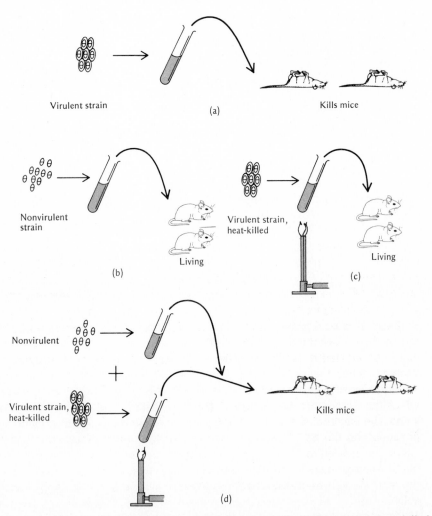

Virulent strain
(a)
Kills mice

Nonvirulent strain
(b)
Living

Virulent strain, heat-killed
(c)
Living

Nonvirulent

+

Virulent strain, heat-killed
(d)
Kills mice

FIG. 4-1 Bacteria transformed from nonvirulent to virulent. DNA from a heat-killed virulent form was added to living nonvirulent culture and transformed it so that it killed mice. Redrawn from *Cell Heredity* by Ruth Sager and Francis Ryan. New York: John Wiley & Sons, Inc., 1961. Reproduced by permission.

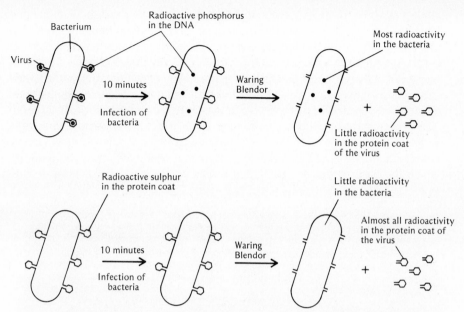

FIG. 4-2   An experiment which shows that, in virus infection of bacteria, DNA alone enters the bacteria and effects reproduction of the virus. Redrawn from *Cell Heredity*, by Ruth Sager and Francis Ryan. New York: John Wiley & Sons, Inc., 1961. Reproduced by permission.

the DNA of phage. This marker was radioactive phosphorus, which took the place of ordinary phosphorus in the DNA. It served as a marker because one could later measure the amount of phage DNA by the strength of radioactivity given off. Other experiments labeled the protein coat of phage with radioactive sulfur. After infecting bacteria with one or the other of these strains, the remains of the virus were knocked off the bacteria by shaking them. Location of the tracers then showed that in those experiments in which it was the protein that had been labeled the sulfur was always in the part knocked off outside the bacteria. Since the sulfur marked the protein, the protein could not effect reproduction of the virus *within* the bacteria. However, in those experiments in which the DNA had been labeled the phosphorus which labeled it was always within the bacteria, showing that DNA alone effected the reproduction of the phage within the host bacteria. Even though this neat experimental method cannot be applied to all types of cells, other kinds of experiments and reasoning by analogy have led to the conclusion that the nucleic acid (usually DNA but in some viruses RNA instead) controls the genetic identity of all types of cells.

The chemical structure of DNA (Fig. 4-4) provides the clue to the way it works in reproduction. This structure was inferred in the classical work of Watson and Crick (1953 a and b). DNA consists of sugar, phosphate, and a nitrogen-containing base. The diffraction (bending) of X-rays by the molecule made it possible to "see" how the molecule is put together and showed that the DNA molecule is in the form of two intertwining spirals of alternating sugar and phosphate. These spirals are held together by chemical bonds between pairs of bases, like rungs of a spiral ladder, which in turn attach to the sugar. The only way a stable three-dimensional structure could be achieved, Watson and Crick argued, was if the four bases known to occur in DNA—adenine (A), guanine (G), thymine (T), and cytosine (C)—pair in only two ways: C with G, and T with A. This exactly fits another fact: although DNA from different kinds of animals varies in the proportions of the four bases, the amount of C is always approximately equal to that of G, as is T to A. It follows that if we know the order in which the bases occur on one strand of DNA we can state the order on the

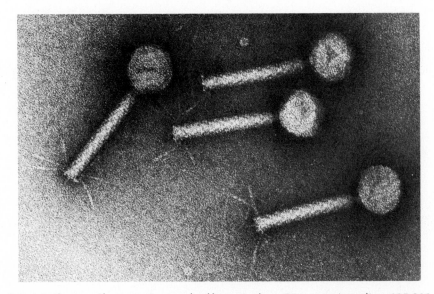

FIG. 4-3 *Above:* Electron micrograph of bacteriophage P2, approximately × 185,000. The head contains tightly packed DNA, which is injected into a host bacterium via the tail. (From R. C. Williams and H. W. Fisher: *An Electron Micrographic Atlas of Viruses,* 1974. Courtesy of Charles C Thomas, Publisher, Springfield, Illinois) *Opposite, above:* Bacteriophage infection and reproduction. Redrawn from M. W. Strickberger: *Genetics.* New York: Macmillan, copyright 1968. Reproduced by permission. *Opposite, below:* A bacterium (*Escherichia coli,* the common intestinal bacterium). Compare the size (1 $\mu$ = about 0.00004 inch) with that of the viruses and protein molecules (Fig. 3-1). This bacterium is being infected by a virus (phage T2), and one phage is attached to its surface above the lower end. The ability of viruses to inject their nucleic acid into bacteria and other cells and to have the nucleic acid "command" the cell to produce more virus is the basis of transmission of virus diseases. It is also similar to the way higher organisms use DNA to reproduce. Specimen: Prof. Kellenberger, Univ. ·Geneve. Photographed through the Zeiss Electron Microscope EM 9.

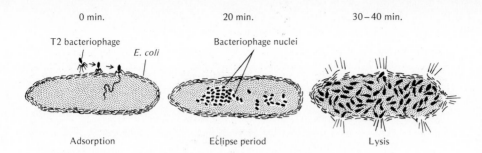

| 0 min. | 20 min. | 30–40 min. |

T2 bacteriophage · *E. coli* · Bacteriophage nuclei

Adsorption · Eclipse period · Lysis

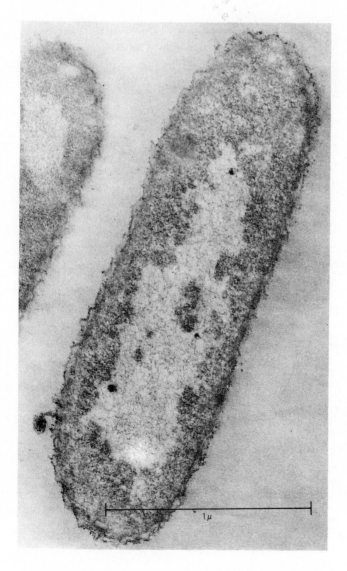

$1\mu$

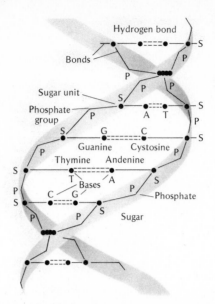

FIG. 4-4   DNA's double helix, with two intertwined spirals, held together by pairs of nucleotides arranged stepwise along the inner aspect. Note that hydrogen bonds link each A to T and each C to G. Redrawn from C. J. Witkop, Jr.: "Advances in dental genetics." *Journal of Dental Research 42*, 1263, 1963. Reproduced by permission.

other strand. The two sets are complementary. Opposite each C there must be a G and opposite each T an A. Watson and Crick argued that the process of duplication of chromosomes must involve a splitting apart of the two strands of DNA in such a way that each half separately would pick up its complementary bases and thus would reform a complete double spiral. Since the two spirals

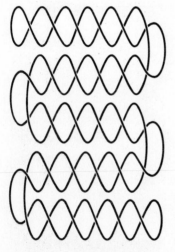

FIG. 4-5A   The double spiral of DNA is actually a thin, continuous, circular molecule doubled on itself repeatedly in the relatively short, wide state of the chromosome at metaphase.

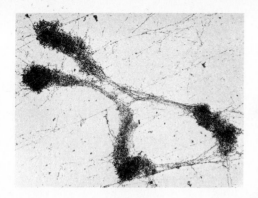

FIG. 4-5*B*   Chromosome fibers. A chromosome from a human white blood cell treated with trypsin to dissolve much of its protein and reveal the DNA strands. Note the redoubling on themselves and the existence of numerous interarm fibers, especially at the centromere and at the ends of the arms. D. E. Moore and J. G. Abuelo, *Nature 234,* 467, 1971. Reproduced by Permission.

are interlocked, the unwinding must start at one point and proceed down the spiral while newly doubled DNA—two spirals with exactly the same base sequence as the original one—are being constructed behind.

Actually DNA is apparently a thin circular molecule doubled on itself by ropelike windings and incorporated with protein to produce the essential structure of the relatively thick metaphase chromosome (Fig 4-5A, B).

The role of the DNA molecule in chromosomes undergoing division was demonstrated in an experiment (Taylor, 1958) in which cells were grown so as to incorporate radioactive hydrogen (tritium) in the DNA. This is a marker that shows itself in developed photographic emulsion. After one mitotic division the tritium marked all the chromosomes equally, indicating that each daughter chromosome had received one-half old and one-half new material. At the next division, however, the tritium marked only one of each pair of chromatid strands (with occasional exchanges resulting in partial labeling of both sisters). At the next division some pairs of chromosomes were entirely free of tritium, indicating that all the DNA of these cells had been newly synthesized (Fig. 4-6).

How can DNA control the whole structure and function of the organism? How can it make corn look like corn or sponges look like sponges? Cellular structure is dependent on proteins. The catalysts (called enzymes) that control the chemistry of life are themselves such proteins. Proteins are organic compounds that consist of one or more **polypeptide** chains. These chains are strands of **amino acids** strung together in some fixed sequence. Proteins themselves are synthesized on the surface of tiny structures (one kind of cell **organelle,** called **ribosomes**) that are seen in electron microscope photographs in the cytoplasm of cells (see Fig. 3-1).

RNA is a nucleic acid with bases arranged in a linear fashion, like DNA. Unlike DNA, however, these bases form a single rather than double strand. Furthermore, one of the bases of DNA, thymine (T), is replaced by uracil (U) in RNA. But otherwise the structures are so similar that RNA can be coded with a base sequence complementary to one of the pair of strands in a specific DNA. The coded RNA is formed in the nucleus of the cell, with the DNA there

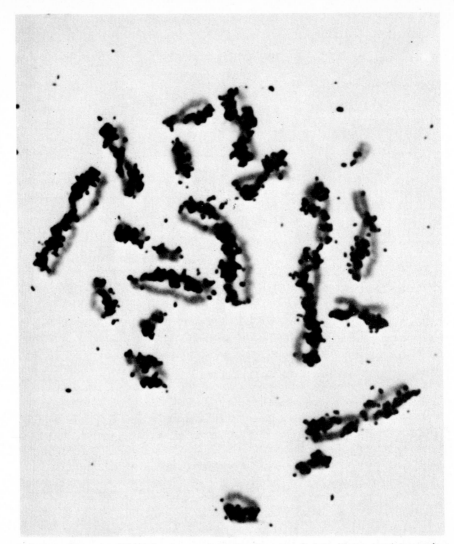

FIG. 4-6   The role of DNA in chromosomes undergoing division. In an experiment first conducted by Taylor (1958) cells were grown so as to incorporate radioactive hydrogen (tritium) in the DNA. The cells were then allowed to go through several mitotic divisions. After one division the tritium marked all the chromosomes; after a second division, shown here, it marked only one chromatid strand. The parts of chromosomes without tritium contained newly synthesized DNA. Half the DNA was newly synthesized at each mitotic division. The figure, photographed through the microscope, superimposes an ordinary photograph and an autoradiograph in which the radioactivity in the chromosomes exposed the film placed next to them to create a pattern of black dots. Note the few instances where both sister chromatids are labeled because of interchange (crossover) between chromatids. Courtesy of D. M. Prescott, University of Colorado.

forming a template (Fig. 4-7). This RNA, called messenger RNA (mRNA), passes out of the nucleus to the ribosomes in the cytoplasm with the coded message. The complex of ribosomes plus attached mRNA is called a **polysome.** The segment of DNA that codes the polysome constitutes the **gene,** the genetic unit that determines the exact nature of the protein to be synthesized by the polysome (Fig. 4-8). However, the concept of the gene goes back to Mendel (1865) (see p. 42)—long before the roles of DNA and RNA were known—and

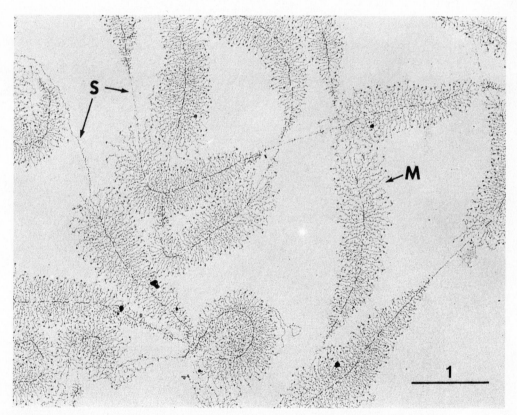

FIG. 4-7   DNA with genes (matrix units, M) in the process of coding for RNA. The structural arrangement shows many thin fibrils of RNA coming off each of the several matrix units like feathery portions off the stem of a quill. The matrix units are separated by nonmatrix (S) units of the same DNA strand. The feathery part would be equally wide throughout if the RNA had all developed to the same stage. The narrow parts of the "feathers" have therefore been photographed at an earlier stage of RNA production than the wide ends. This is consistent with the concept that RNA molecules are sequentially initiated (from the thick end to the thin end of each gene). The scale at the lower right equals 1/1000 of a millimeter. From O. L. Miller, Jr., and B. R. Beatty: "Visualization of nuclear genes." *Science 164,* 955, 1969. Copyright 1969 by the American Association for the Advancement of Science.

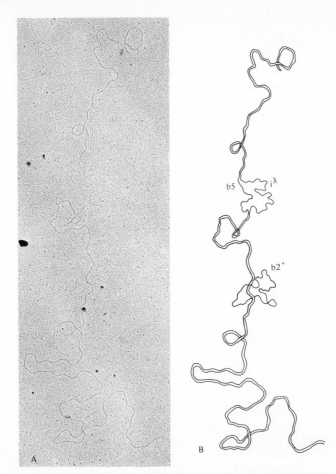

FIG. 4-8 Electron micrograph (A) and tracing (B) of double-stranded DNA (produced by annealing together two slightly different kinds of DNA) showing single-stranded loops on which specific genes are located. The loops of single-stranded DNA represent the differences between the two strands, hence apparently carry the genes in respect to which the two kinds of DNA differ. From B. C. Westmoreland, Waclaw Szybalski, and Hans Ris: "Mapping of deletions and substitutions in heteroduplex DNA molecules of bacteriophage lambda by electron microscopy." *Science 163*, 1343, 1969. Copyright 1969 by the American Association for the Advancement of Science.

most genes (including all human ones) still cannot be "seen." So in this and other books one will find the term "gene" used as a name not for a bit of DNA but for the concept of how such a bit of DNA works.

A second kind of RNA—also coded—is present in the cytoplasm. Its molecules are much smaller. It is soluble and is therefore designated sRNA. Depending on its base sequence it is capable of attaching itself to one or another of the amino acids that are to enter into the protein. It is also able to attach itself to mRNA: C bases to G ones, U bases to A. This *complementarity* lines up the sRNA, carrying amino acids, at the appropriate places on mRNA. The sRNA molecules then give up their attached amino acid to a developing chain of amino acids. The chain is called a polypeptide, a building block of protein, and the process is known as *sequential synthesis*.

Ribosomes are themselves composed of a third kind of RNA, the exact function of which is still not known, but the ribosomes travel along the coded mRNA (which is attached by one end to a special membrane) reading the message, collecting the sRNA with amino acids, and discharging completed polypeptides through the membrane. The messenger RNA is then ready to begin another identical molecule and the sRNA is free to pick up more amino acid and to repeat the cycle, while the polypeptide chain bends and adheres to itself or to other chains. The structure of the protein molecule is exactly the same each time the coded message is read from messenger RNA complementary to the same segment of DNA. Since the DNA of different cells is all derived from the same fertilized egg, a multicelled organism can produce quantities of protein of a uniform kind. The amount of DNA in a human cell, for instance, can code for the production of a very great number of proteins.

In the process of **mitosis** (see p. 24) the chromosomes of daughter cells are identical to those of the cell from which they were formed. However, the daughter cells themselves may differ in form and function. Thus, nerve cells, muscle cells, connective tissue cells, and all other cells derive by a long series of mitoses from a single fertilized ovum. The process by which these tissues develop is called **differentiation.** Most of the key steps in human differentiation occur in the embryo. They do not all occur simultaneously, however, but in stages. The stages are marked by the initiation and subsequent shutting off of the synthesis of each polypeptide, in concert with that of all the others so that there is an orderly development of one structural detail after another. The controls of the process of differentiation are themselves coded in sequential pairs of bases in the DNA. The segments of DNA that initiate a process of protein synthesis are known to be near the DNA that codes mRNA with the sequence for that particular synthesis. Shutoff mechanisms are also coded in DNA, and one theory concerning sequential production of different proteins is that the genes for them are closely linked and that expression of one of them precludes expression of the others (Kabat, 1972).

All cells of the body derive from the same fertilized ovum and have identical DNA, but cells of different tissues have different functions. Therefore, the functional differentiation must depend on the position of cells relative to each other. That is, each step of differentiation depends on the state of the anatomy already achieved. Holliday and Pugh (1975) speculate that a modification of DNA occurs through a process called "methylation" which deactivates the DNA, and that the process could begin at one point on the DNA ladder and progress along the ladder a specific distance during each of a specific number of cell divisions, so that, after a particular number of divisions, a tissue would be composed of cells each differentiated to the identical extent.

Since there are only four kinds of bases in mRNA (U, C, A, and G) one base can code only 4 possible messages, and two bases can write only 16 messages (that is 4 × 4: these are UU, UC, UA, UG, CU, CC, CA, CG, AU, AC, AA, AG, GU, GC, GA, GG).

In turn each of these pairs can be followed by any of the four kinds of bases. There are thus 64 (16 × 4) possible messages of three sequential bases on one of the two strands of the DNA spiral. Such a sequence of three bases is called a **triplet** or **codon.** There are only 20 different essential amino acids in proteins, however, and some different triplets have the same meaning. As I have said, most RNA has all four kinds of bases. Some have only one or two kinds, however. Starting with RNA of only one kind of base it is possible to synthesize polypeptides with only one kind of amino acid. From there N. W. Nirenberg and others (1963) have worked out, one at a time, the codes for each of the amino acids. These are all triplet (three-letter) codons in which the "letters" (A, C, U, and G) are the RNA bases. Since RNA triplets bind a specific amino acid the code was "broken" by adding first one amino acid and then another to a given triplet to determine which one was held by it. The decoding has been directly confirmed. The complete base sequence that codes for the protein of the coat of bacteriophage MS2 has been worked out and compared with the sequence of the 129 amino acids of the same protein. As can be seen in Fig. 4-9, most of the amino acids can be coded by any of several different base sequences. The code is therefore called "degenerate." But any triplet can determine the laying down of only one amino acid in the peptide. What is sometimes called the "one to one to one principle" implies this exact correspondence between chromosome DNA, messenger RNA, and a peptide of a protein. The addition or deletion of three consecutive bases in a sequence leads to the addition or deletion of one amino acid in the peptide, but an addition or deletion of one or two bases anywhere along the chain alters all the subsequent triplets as they count themselves off in threes. Studies of "errors" of these kinds have helped reveal the nature of the code.

A process called reverse transcription involves coding DNA from RNA. An **enzyme,** reverse transcriptase, causes this reaction. Research on reverse transcription is of great interest because it has, at least in theory, the potential for changing the inherited instructions of DNA and might therefore provide a way to correct human hereditary diseases or to improve the strains of domestic plants and animals. However, since it is at least conceivable that harmless bacteria or viruses could be changed into harmful ones for which there would be no known cure, some of the researchers in this field have ceased certain types of potentially dangerous experiments and have called on all others to do so also until safe methods can be developed.

## Mendel's Principles

Long before the nature and role of nucleic acids were suspected, in fact even before the nature of cell reproduction had been interpreted from what could be seen in the microscope, the basis of genetic theory had been established through the analysis of breeding experiments. In 1856 Gregor Johann Mendel

| | | | |
|---|---|---|---|
| U U U = phenylalanine | C U U = leucine | A U U = isoleucine | G U U = valine |
| U U C = phenylalanine | C U C = leucine | A U C = isoleucine | G U C = valine |
| U U A = leucine | C U A = leucine | A U A = isoleucine | G U A = valine |
| U U G = leucine | C U G = leucine | A U G = methionine-F starts polypeptide chain in bacteria | G U G = valine |
| U C U = serine | C C U = proline | A C U = threonine | G C U = alanine |
| U C C = serine | C C C = proline | A C C = threonine | G C C = alanine |
| U C A = serine | C C A = proline | A C A = threonine | G C A = alanine |
| U C G = serine | C C G = proline | A C G = threonine | G C G = alanine |
| U A U = tyrosine | C A U = histidine | A A U = asparagine | G A U = aspartic acid |
| U A C = tyrosine | C A C = histidine | A A C = asparagine | G A C = aspartic acid |
| U A A = terminator | C A A = glutamine | A A A = lysine | G A A = glutamic acid |
| U A G = terminator | C A G = glutamine | A A G = lysine | G A G = glutamic acid |
| U G U = cysteine | C G U = arginine | A G U = serine | G G U = glycine |
| U G C = cysteine | C G C = arginine | A G C = serine | G G C = glycine |
| U G A = terminator | C G A = arginine | A G A = arginine | G G A = glycine |
| U G G = tryptophan | C G G = arginine | A G G = arginine | G G G = glycine |

FIG. 4-9 The genetic code of RNA. Each of the 64 three-letter codons (called "triplets") has one and only one meaning, but the code is "degenerate" in that most of the amino acids can be laid down in the polypeptide chain by more than one such codon. Some of the codons are punctuation, and can initiate (AUG, GUG) or terminate (UAA, UAG, and UGA) a polypeptide chain.

began experimenting with the breeding of peas in the garden of an Augustinian monastery of which he later became the abbot. His results were published in 1865 in the proceedings of the natural science society of Brno, in what is now Czechoslovakia. Mendel selected for study pure strains of peas with pairs of sharply contrasting characteristics. He then crossed peas in respect to each of seven contrasting features. The hybrids resulting from the crosses were regularly of one or the other parental type, rather than intermediate between the two. Thus, all crosses of round-seeded peas with wrinkled-seeded ones resulted in round peas. Inheritance was clearly not a matter of blending. Peas can be self-pollinated (that is, fertilized with their own pollen) to produce genetically pure strains. Mendel noted that when his hybrid peas were self-pollinated approximately three-fourths of the third generation showed the characteristic of the second-generation parent plant, whereas the remaining one fourth showed the characteristic not present in the parent but only in one of the grandparents. Self-pollination of round-seeded hybrid peas yielded 5,474 round-seeded ones and 1,850 wrinkled ones, almost a 3 to 1 ratio (actually 2.96 to 1).

To explain this ratio, Mendel assumed that the characteristics of the peas were the result of formative elements (subsequently called *genes*) inherited from the parent plants. He argued that in pure strains the genes exist in pairs of the same kind and breed true but that in crosses between strains there are different kinds of genes which make up the pairs. Since these hybrids are indistinguishable from one parent but possess a gene it lacks, Mendel argued that one allele is dominant over the other. In the next generation, self-pollination of plants which had one of each kind of gene would yield plants with three kinds of genetic constitution. In the example cited, rounded is **dominant** and wrinkled is **recessive,** hence all hybrids (called the $F_1$ generation) yield rounded peas, but when these $F_1$ peas are self-pollinated the resulting $F_2$ peas of the next generation have the two alleles in a series of chance recombinations and give about one in four pairings with two recessive alleles, one in four with two dominant alleles, and the remaining half of the cases with one of each type but indistinguishable from the pure dominant. The visible characteristics are referred to as the **phenotype,** while the term **genotype** designates the genetic constitution. In the subsequent elaboration of Mendel's views, each gene was conceived as occupying a fixed position **(locus)** in the genetic material. The alternative genes at a locus **(alleles)** determine variations in a trait: for instance the genes for round and wrinkled seeds in peas. A plant or animal with like alleles is called **homozyotic** (like-egged) as distinct from a hybrid genotype with different alleles **(heterozygotic).** Thus, two genes for wrinkled is a homozygotic recessive genotype, two for rounded is a homozygotics dominant genotype and one of each is the heterozygotic dominant genotype. Homozygotic round-seeded peas and heterozygotic round-seeded peas are indistinguishable, however, because the round-seeded trait is dominant (Fig. 4-10).

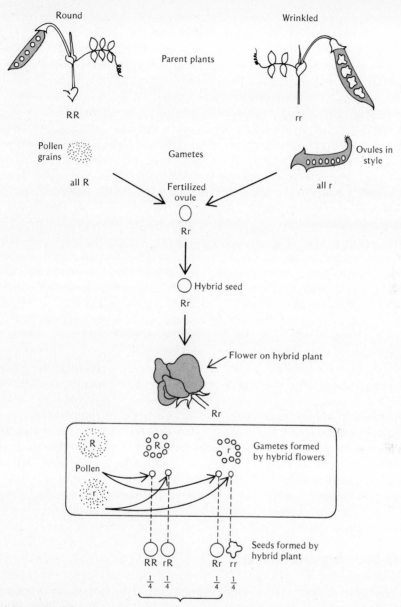

FIG. 4-10   Mendel's experiment explained. R is the gene for round seeds, r is the gene for wrinkled seeds. Redrawn from C. Auerbach, *The Science of Genetics*. New York: Harper & Row, Publishers, 1961. Reproduced by permission.

In some cases Mendel crossed plants in respect to two different sets of characteristics, such as yellow and rounded by green and wrinkled. In these cases he noted that in the $F_2$ generation the genotype for one character was independent of that for the other. Since there are three possible genotypes for each pair of alleles, and any of the three of the first can go with any of the three of the second, $3 \times 3$ or 9 possible genotypes exist for two pairs of alleles. But since there are only two phenotypes for each, there are only $2 \times 2$ or 4 phenotypes in all. In Mendel's experiments the pairs of characters seemed independent. Each phenotype occurred approximately in the frequency predicted by the theory that all $F_1$ plants were heterozygous for both traits and that the genes segregate independently in the $F_2$ generation. We now know that there are cases of linkage, however, and they will be discussed below.

Mendel's contribution was stated in the form of three laws. Briefly stated in modern terms these are:

1. *The law of unit inheritance.* The characteristics of parents are passed on to descendents unchanged (as units). There is no blending of parental characters. Even recessive traits, such as wrinkled and green in peas, although they do not manifest themselves in the $F_1$ crosses from pure-bred lines, may show up unchanged in later generations.

2. *The law of segregation.* The pair of genes of a parent separate; only one from each parent passes to the offspring. Thus, heterozygotic $F_1$ plants with round peas can yield $F_2$ plants of all genotypes.

3. *The law of independent assortment.* Different pairs of alleles are passed to offspring independently so that new combinations of genes present in neither parent are possible. $F_1$ pea plants from a cross of round and yellow (both dominant) by wrinkled and green (both recessive) will be round and yellow, but the $F_2$ generation will also contain some round and green, wrinkled and yellow, and wrinkled and green plants because the genes for the traits assort independently. The genes for round are just as likely to be associated with those for green as with those for yellow.

Genetic linkage (see below) of genes on the same chromosome was later shown to be an exception to this law and the combinations do not always occur in the predicted ratios.

## Linkage and Crossing Over

When the relationship of Mendel's experiments to developing knowledge from the microscopic examination of cells was pursued, it was appreciated in principle that independent assortment would not apply to two genes in the same chromosome. And as the number of genetic experiments increased, results of some were at variance with the statistical expectations of Mendel's third law. In 1911 T. H. Morgan explained it. When segregation is not at random, he said: "instead of random segregation in Mendel's sense we find 'association of factors' that are located near together in the chromosomes." In these cases the genes are said to be **"linked."** Mendel had concluded that the characteristics studied by him assorted independently. Later experiments with the same seven characteristics of peas studied by Mendel have shown, however, that two of them are linked; in fact, linkage to still other characteristics which had not been studied by Mendel shows that his seven characteristics are located on four of the seven chromosomes of peas (Lamprecht, 1961). Two genes far apart on the same chromosome may have so high a likelihood of crossing over between them that no linkage is detectable even though both show linkage to genes lying between them.

In the species of fruit flies that have long been one of the favorite subjects of breeding experiments, there are only four pairs of chromosomes. Two genes carried in the same chromosome do not assort independently. A recessive anomaly of the eye *(scarlet)* and a recessive defect of the wings *(curved)* are both in the same (the third) chromosome. If one crosses fruit flies having one defect with those having the other, the $F_1$ generation will be heterozygotic in respect to both traits and show the dominant normal conditions. $F_2$ descendants or backcrosses (mating of $F_1$ individuals back to the parental line) will tend to show only one of the two defects, because most of the chromosomes have the gene for one defect or the other, as in the grandparental generation. Thus, there will tend to be a lack of chromosomes with both or neither of the defective genes. However, some instances of the third chromosome in fruit flies do in fact have both or neither of the linked genes. The explanation is **crossing over** (see p. 25). During **meiosis** chromosomes are not transmitted as wholes. When they come together and then separate, similarly situated parts of a pair are interchangeable and chromosomes often exchange segments. The segments are said to cross over. This can be seen in the microscope as **chiasmata** (the points where chromatids cross) (see Fig. 4-6). The genes that these segments contain are not visible under the microscope. However, in fruit flies the effect on the $F_2$ generation of the crossovers can be counted in breeding experiments, and the frequency of *scarlet* and *curved* in that generation should equal the frequency of chiasmata between the loci for *scarlet* and *curved* on the third chromosome. Six percent of the chromosomes of *scarlet* and *curved* cross over per generation. this is close linkage. In general, crossing over is so frequent that two genes far apart on the same chromosome may assort independently. In that case it will not be evident that they are on the same chromosome unless both are shown to be linked to a third gene located between them. If two genes are closely linked (if they are near each other on the chromosome) the crossover rate is low. Nevertheless, the possibility of crossing over is repeated every generation so that in the long run combinations occur in the same proportions as would be the case with random assortment. Within one family the defect of the wing and the eye will go together, in another the gene for the defect of the wing will go with the gene for normal eyes. A study of the whole population would show no association of the linked conditions; the traits are only associated within particular pedigrees. The numerous genetic conditions known in the most commonly studied species of fruit fly all fall into four linkage groups which correspond with the four pairs of chromosomes.

## Sex Linkage

If one examines the chromosomes of ordinary human cells one finds that those of men and of women differ. Women have 23 pairs of chromosomes (see Fig. 3-4, bottom), but men have 22 pairs and two unmatched chromosomes. One of the two unmatched chromosomes is small and is called "Y," the other is large and is called "X." One of the 23 female pairs is identical in size and form to the male "X" and is known to be two Xs. Since males have both kinds in ordinary cells, male gametes have only one, either an X or a Y. Female gametes have one or the other of the pair of Xs. Ova fertilized by an X-bearing sperm have two Xs and develop into females. Ova fertilized by Y-bearing sperm have an X and a Y and develop into males. This is the way sex is determined in people and in many other organisms.

Although the Y-chromosome determines maleness, virtually nothing else is known about it. The X-chromosome, however, is large and is known to carry many genes. In females these genes behave like genes on any other chromosomes, but since there is only one X-chromosome in males, the effect of X-chromosome genes in males is different. In males there can be no heterozygosity for genes on the X-chromosome. A gene on the X-chromosome which is recessive in females will be functionally indistinguishable from a dominant in males. This circumstance permits one to identify X-linked genes. For instance there is a very rare gene for the bleeding disease, hemophilia. It is recessive and therefore the disease occurs in females only in the extremely rare circumstance where they inherit it from both parents. Males, however, have only one X-chromosome, which they inherit from their mothers, and sons of heterozygotic mothers may have the disease. Hemophilia turned up in both the Russian and Spanish royal families and from the genealogies it seems evident that Queen Victoria was the carrier and transmitted it to some of her male descendants. Other sex-linked genes are those for **color-blindness** (see p. 106) and **G6PD deficiency** (see p. 76). Since men have only one X-chromosome the frequency of the gene for these conditions is the frequency of the condition in males. Since men transmit their Y-chromosome but not their X to sons, boys never inherit X-linked genes from their fathers. In descent through females these sex-linked conditions do not segregate independently—they are all on the same chromosome. Sex linkage is the special property of allelic genes on the X-chromosome and should not be confused with those differences between the sexes which are determined by having two X chromosomes or one X and one Y.

## The Rediscovery of Mendel's Laws

Mendel's studies were lost from notice for 35 years. He had established his point by statistical demonstrations and in his day scientists were unaccustomed to such methods. But by 1901 the presence and functioning of the chromosomes were known, and these paired structures could now provide a physical basis for the Mendelian laws of genetics. Three botanists working separately each rediscovered the principles of Mendelian genetics and each also belatedly learned that Mendel had already demonstrated the principles long before. They confirmed Mendel's findings on peas and beans and showed that the principles also apply to many other kinds of hybrid plants. Within two years a physician, Sir Archibald Garrod (1902), published similar statistical findings in pedigrees of human families with hereditary diseases. The study of genetics has gained momentum ever since.

Not all genetic characteristics show the dominance that Mendel observed in the seven traits he studied. For example, crosses between white and red evening primroses lead to pink hybrids. This is a case of *nondominance*. As knowledge of genetics has advanced, nondominance has been seen to be frequent. The gene coded in DNA determines a particular peptide. Therefore both alleles of a pair determine the proteins of the organism. It may happen, however, that one gene in the heterozygotic state can lead to the synthesis of adequate amounts of a particular peptide, with the result that the homozygotic condition cannot be distinguished from it. Such a gene is dominant. As new and finer criteria and biochemical tests are applied, instances formerly considered to show just dominant and recessive phenotypes can be differentiated into the three classes. For a pair of allelic genes $A$ and $a$, there are heterozygotes ($Aa$) and the two kinds of homozygotes ($AA$ and $aa$).

Phenylketonuria (PKU) is a rare congenital metabolic disorder usually associated with mental defect. It is inherited as a recessive. When the heterozygotic parents of patients with PKU or some other recessive disease can be distinguished from homozygotic normal individuals, the help these parents can get from genetic counseling is obviously great, as they can find out in advance whether they are liable to have children with the disease. Thus, with sensitive biochemical tests individuals can be shown to be *carriers*. Both members of a couple may be carriers and have low but adequate levels of some essential enzyme. If this low level indicates that they are both heterozygotic carriers they would be in danger of having children with none of the needed enzyme. They may wish to forego reproducing rather than run the risk of having children with such a defect. Furthermore, any children they do have can be examined while very young so that those with the disease can be treated in infancy, the only known way to avert serious brain damage. On the other hand, of course, screening other members of the families of patients for carriers spares noncarrying couples the concern caused by the presence of such genetic disease in their relatives.

## Quantitative Inheritance

Before Mendelian genetics was developed it was already well known that the extent of expression of some characteristics in children is partially (but only partially) related to the extent of these characteristics in the parents. Francis Galton, a younger cousin of Charles Darwin, studied the inheritance in man of traits such as stature and **dermatoglyphics** (literally "skin writing"—the general term for fingerprints and similar patterns on the palms of the hands, toes, and soles of the feet). These complex characteristics sometimes take forms in children intermediate between those of their parents. This is because they depend on several genes, not on a single major pair. Furthermore, environmental and hereditary factors interact (see Chapter 9).

In the face of these complexities it is not surprising that Galton failed to discover Mendelian laws. Instead he established a dichotomy between influences of "nature and nurture" and he introduced the use of human twins as a method of assessing the degree of heritability. Identical twins are formed from the division of one fertilized egg. They are therefore called **monozygotic** (one egg) twins. They have identical heredity and any differences between them are the result of environmental influences. Sometimes one twin receives more nourishment than the other within the womb; differences in stature between the members of monozygotic twin pairs may represent such environmental influences. Sometimes, especially in cases of separate adoption, one twin experiences a way of life different from that of the other during growth and development; identical twins reared apart tend to show greater differences in psychological attributes than in physical characteristics because of this kind of environmental influence. Although there are phenotypic differences in stature and other measurements even when the genotype is identical, in general monozygotic twins are more similar to each other than **dizygotic** (two-egg) twins formed from separate ova separately fertilized. Genetically, dizygotic twins are only as similar to each other as are other brothers and sisters, and it is only among dizygotic pairs that twins can be of unlike sex.

The extent of **hereditability** of some specific quantitative characteristic is generally measured by comparison of the degree of divergence in respect to that characteristic which is shown by pairs of monozygotic twins compared to that shown by dizygotic twins. Since the difference between the two members of monozygotic pairs can be ascribed to "environment," and since the environmental influence will be much greater in some situations than in others (such as being brought up in separate foster homes rather than by the same parents) such hereditability indexes, in addition to presenting other theoretical problems, vary from population to population.

Another way to compare pairs of twins is through **correlation,** a measurement of the extent to which the sets of data relate to each other. Such methods can also be used on brothers and sisters, parents and children, and so on, for the same purpose. Correlation coefficients and related statistics can be used to see how any two sets of data go together, such as thighbone length and body height (used in estimating stature from the skeleton), or stature at some age or stage in childhood and stature in adulthood (used in making a formula to predict the adult stature of a growing child).

## Summary

Nucleic acids (DNA and RNA) are spiral molecules of linearly arranged bases. They are so formed that they can exactly determine the configuration of other linearly arranged molecules on a one-to-one principle.

The order of sequences of bases in DNA determines the order in RNA. A triplet "word," a codon of three sequential bases, determines which amino acid is integrated into a specific sequential position in the formation of a peptide, the structural unit of protein. The DNA is in paired chromosomes, information from only one of each pair being transmitted to each offspring. This mechanism determines Mendel's laws of inheritance: (1) *unit inheritance* (characteristics are passed unchanged; there is no "mixing of blood"); (2) *segregation* (the pair of genes of each parent separate and only one of each pair is transmitted to each offspring); (3) *independent assortment* (in general, which of one pair of alleles is transmitted does not determine which of another pair will be). Two genes linked on the same chromosome do not assort independently, however. Females have two X-chromosomes whereas males have an X and a Y, and the sex of offspring is determined by whether they get an X (and are female) or a Y (and are male) from their fathers. Genes on the X-chromosome (sex-linked genes) are never passed from father to son. Some quantitative characteristics are genetically too complex for Mendelian analysis but the significance that genetic factors have upon them is revealed through studies of twins and other relatives.

# CHAPTER 5

# BLOOD GROUPS, HEMOGLOBINS, AND SERUM PROTEINS

In the preceding chapter I discussed how the genetic process operates in individual organisms and in transmission of inherited characteristics to their offspring. As I have already pointed out, the significance of this process in terms of evolution lies in the way it affects genetic transmission within the breeding population. The most significant population from this point of view is the **species,** the largest group within which all the individuals are potential co-ancestors of each other's descendants. Thus, all dogs belong to a single species because although it may not be possible to successfully mate the largest breed with the smallest, both can be mated with dogs of intermediate size and all breeds are therefore at least indirectly interfertile. The application of the species concept to specific cases may not be easy, however, because it may be impossible to know about interbreeding in the wild, and behavior in captivity is not a valid test. For this and other reasons the definition of species has to be modified and qualified to make it universally applicable, but a genetic definition—a group whose members are capable of interbreeding and producing fertile offspring— serves best in respect to humans and the study of human evolution.

Every species shows considerable variability among its members. This variability is the basis of natural selection, a selection dependent on the advantage of one type of individual over another (see Chapter 7). Such "Darwinian **fitness,**" as it is called, is measured by the relative number of progeny reaching adulthood. Survival of the fittest can have permanent significance for the species only when the variability has a genetic basis and the more fit transmit different characteristics than do the less fit. In wide-ranging species there are both differences between individuals in the same place and differences between average individuals of different regions. Such species (among which is the human species) are called **polytypic species.** All sorts of characteristics that vary between peoples from place to place have been studied in the past. Many of these differences are in purely cultural characteristics, such as traits of language and nationality, and these do not mark humans as polytypic in the biological sense. Other characteristics, including most physiological measurements, are biological but are subject to considerable modification according to circumstance. A few, such as fingerprints, are fixed but we do not know exactly how they are transmitted. The different sorts of characteristics are all involved in human evolution. To better understand the process of evolution, however, it is best to begin with the generation-to-generation tracing of known genetic entities.

The application of human genetics to the study of human evolution could not proceed far if it were based merely on a knowledge of rare hereditary anomalies and diseases. The need is for a group of conditions that are inherited in a large proportion of normal individuals and whose relative frequency can be studied in different human populations. This need is being met by the growing list of inherited substances that can be identified in human blood (Giblett, 1969; Livingstone, 1967; Mourant, 1954; and Race and Sanger, 1954).

We know by the traditional methods of physical anthropology (and even from casual observation) that many characteristics, such as skin color, nose size, and hair form, differ among human groups. But in structures such as skin, nose, and hair, genetic potential is expressed to a varying extent, and differently at different times throughout the course of development. The relationship between a particular base sequence in the DNA of a chromosome and the end result can rarely be identified in the genetics of quantitative characteristics. On the other hand, by examining components of blood specimens, it is possible to identify very small differences. Blood is a complex substance. If it is collected in a syringe and allowed to stand it separates into two parts: one, a reddish mass composed of red blood cells and of the fibrinogen that causes them to clot; and two, a clear fluid, blood serum, containing the serum proteins. Both fractions of blood contain many varying substances. The serum contains a variety of proteins. The red cells have blood group substances on the surface and contain **hemoglobins** and red cell **enzymes.** Minor differences in the amino acid sequence of a protein in the blood serum and in enzymes, for instance, are caused by corresponding differences in the nucleic acids that code for these molecules. Many of the variants are inherited in such a simple way that one can assume that they are the result of single variations in the DNA code. Some polymorphic variants reach high frequency in some human populations. One kind of **polymorphism** (see p. 112) involves balanced selection (see Chapter 7), but it is best to define polymorphism without reference to the mode by which it is maintained. Using the criterion of gene frequency above 10 percent in some human populations, there are about 20 polymorphic variations in 13 or 14 different human red cell blood group systems, a number of additional polymorphisms among the 23 or so distinguishable serum proteins, and at least 4 common ones among the several score known human hemoglobin variants. There are also normally occurring variations in the nature of some enzymes, but most of the numerous hereditary conditions in which a particular enzyme is deficient or lacking are too infrequent to be classed as polymorphisms. Besides polymorphisms in respect to the genes that determine proteins in the constituents of blood, there are a few that affect substances in other body fluids, such as one **amino acid** (designated BAIB) in urine and the secretor factor (see p. 64) and other components of saliva (Azen, 1972).

Analysis of the pedigrees of polymorphisms shows many to be due to allelic or closely linked genes. Those that are allelic or linked are called a system. There are 13 or 14 different human red cell blood group systems, and most of the other polymorphisms constitute separate systems. There is no evidence of linkage between systems and most of them are known to be inherited independently of each other. They are also independent in evolution. Gene frequencies of one system can change while those of another do not. There are enough mutually independent systems of blood group **antigens** (see p. 55) and changes in the relative frequency of allelic genes is generally slow enough to permit anthropologists to classify present-day populations into historically meaningful patterns that reflect historic relationships over many centuries. When national or tribal groups are classed according to the frequencies with which they possess the genes for the different antigens, fewer and smaller differences are usually found to exist between neighboring groups and those with common origins than between groups with more distant origins. Thus, for instance, on the basis of their blood groups, Hottentots and Bushmen of southern Africa are variant African populations and are not similar to any of the more distant peoples (such as certain Asiatics) to whom it has been claimed they are related (Singer and Weiner, 1962). In other words, the blood group antigens provide an index of the genetic similarity of populations such as the Hottentots to Bushmen and African Negroes. If one uses blood group gene frequencies to measure genetic similarities and differences, the grouping of populations are usually very similar to those based on external characteristics (da Roche et al., 1974) but this need not be true for any single genetic trait.

Variations in hereditary molecular traits are not confined to differences within a species. Interspecific differences are also of interest. In general, the exact form of a given protein differs among different species. Species closely related to each other in anatomical traits are usually also similar in molecular characteristics. In fact, in closely related species some molecules are indistinguishable and seem to be identical. This is true of cytochrome C, for instance, a molecule that occurs with only small variations in a very wide range of species. Human and chimpanzee cytochrome C are indistinguishable and macaque monkey cytochrome C differs from that of humans and chimpanzees in only one amino acid. Presumably all closely related species with a particular molecule in identical form inherit it through DNA with the identical code sequence for amino acids. They may, however, spell the code with slightly modified base sequences. Likewise, small modifications in a protein imply small differences in the DNA sequence. Interestingly enough, related species sometimes show similar variants. It is possible that in these instances the intraspecific variations go back to the common ancestors of these related species. For instance, reagents prepared from human blood for blood grouping tests in people reveal corresponding differences among apes; likewise reagents specially prepared for testing monkeys also reveal differences within each species tested (Wiener and Moor-Jankowski, 1963; and numerous other publications of these authors reviewed by them in 1971). Molecular anthropology is thus involved both in comparisons within species and in comparisons between species. Differences in both are interpreted as caused by variations in the base sequences of DNA. In some cases the number or proportion of amino acid substitutions can be counted; in others the distance is measured by the strength of a reaction. In either case different interspecific differences may be expressed in terms of a common unit of measurement by which one could state how many times greater is the difference between two species (for instance, chimpanzee and human) than between members of one species (such as among people). Figure 5-1 shows that in various tests humans and chimpanzees are much more similar to each other than are humans and rhesus monkeys.

## Antibodies and Antigens

When a blood group substance is introduced into the blood stream of another person by blood transfusion, a number of substances, called **antigens,** on the surfaces of the erythrocytes (red blood cells) of the transfusion may react with substances (called **antibodies**) in the host's blood serum. This reaction is similar to that of blood serum with bacteria, which stimulate the production of antibodies capable of combining with the bacterial substance and hence serving as antibacterial agents. Although there are several kinds of interaction, all help protect against repeated attacks of the disease caused by a specific kind of bacteria. The study of such interactions between substances and serum antibodies is called *immunology* because, in the case of bacteria and viruses, the interaction of the antibodies with bacteria and viruses destroys these organisms and thus affords immunity to disease.

The study of such reactions in humans has permitted the classification of human red cell antigens. The hereditary antigens are present from birth, and the individual keeps the same kind throughout life. Possession of a particular antigen is inherited according to Mendel's principles. Possession of antibodies

|  | Human/Chimpanzee | Human/Monkey | Source |
|---|---|---|---|
| DNA (nonreassociation) | 2.5% | 10.1% | Kohne, 1970 |
| Hemoglobin (mutations) | 1/579 | 15/287 | Goodman et al., 1972 |
| Fibrinopeptides (mutations) | 0/30 | 7/25 | Doolittle and Mross, 1970 |
| Carbonic anhydrase (immunological) | 4 ID | 50 ID | Wilson and Sarich, 1969 |
| Carbonic anhydrase (mutations) | 1/115 | 6/115 | Tashian et al., 1972 |
| Albumin (immunological) | 0.0% | 3.7% | Goodman, 1968 |
| Albumin (immunological) | 7 ID | 35 ID | Wilson and Sarich, 1969 |
| Transferrin (immunological) | 0.0% | 3.7% | Goodman, 1968 |
| Transferrin (immunological) | 3 ID | 30 ID | Wilson and Sarich, 1969 |
| Gamma globulin (immunological) | 0.19% | 3.4% | Goodman, 1968 |

FIG. 5-1   The evolutionary distance between humans and chimpanzees and humans and rhesus monkeys. Although the units of measurement of evolutionary distance differ in the different studies, the distance between humans and chimpanzees is in all cases less than a quarter of the difference between humans and rhesus monkeys. (Some of the data are cited by S. L. Washburn, personal communication.) (*Mutations* = minimum number of point mutations per number of shared codons; *ID* = immunological difference.)

in the serum, however, is not usually inherited. Antibodies are formed (or selected) in the **gamma globulin** molecules of serum exposed to the antigen.

## The ABO Blood Groups

The interest in blood groups sprang from the practice of transfusion of blood from one person to another. Such experiments began at least as early as the seventeenth century. They were usually uneventful, but in a few instances the recipient of the blood died following the transfusion. In 1900 Karl Landsteiner, who later received the Nobel prize for this work, discovered why. He noticed that when the red cells from the blood of one individual are mixed with the serum of another, the cells may clump—a reaction called **agglutination.** Landsteiner (see 1945) and his students found that they could group human beings into four types on the basis of these reactions. The four types can be explained by the presence or absence of either or both of two substances (the A and B antigens) on the cells. The property of agglutination was soon associated with the transfusion accidents; for instance, transfusing A-type blood into a B-group patient could produce a severe reaction. Blood typing for purposes of blood transfusion began. Only compatible blood is now used.

Serum known to contain antibodies to a specific antigen is called an *antiserum* to it. The A and B antigens can be identified by tests using two types of antisera, containing antibodies called anti-A and anti-B respectively (Fig. 5-2). When a drop of anti-A serum is added to a drop of blood, the red cells may remain in normal suspension or they may clump together. This reaction can be seen under a microscope or with the naked eye. If the blood reacts to anti-A by clumping of its red cells it must contain the A antigen. If the blood reacts to anti-A but not to anti-B, it is therefore called type A; if, conversely, it reacts to anti-B but not to anti-A, it is type B; if it reacts to both anti-A and anti-B, it is called type AB; and if it reacts to neither, it is called type O. Some false reactions (called pseudo-agglutinations) occur but they can be distinguished by their microscopic appearance and by other tests.

Although it was believed from the start that the blood groups were inherited, it took many years before enough evidence had accumulated to permit a German mathematician, Felix Bernstein (1924), to describe the mechanism. He showed that the inheritance of the blood groups could be explained as due to three alleles (alternate forms of the gene occupying a specific lucus on a chromosome). The allele for antigen A (designated $I^A$) and for antigen B (designated $I^B$) are equally dominant, but that for O (designated $i$) is recessive; thus, as each individual could have only two of the genes (one on each chromosome), all human beings would be $I^A$, $I^Ai$, $I^BI^B$, $I^Bi$, $I^AI^B$, or $ii$. But $I^AI^A$ would be indistinguishable from $I^Ai$, and $I^BI^B$ from $I^Bi$. In all authenticated cases of parents and children tested, the variant types found would be explained by this system. Thus, for example, two type AB ($I^AI^B$) parents can never have a type O ($ii$) child, since there is no source for either $i$ gene. Likewise, two type O ($ii$) parents can have only type O offspring since there is no source for $I^A$ or $I^B$ genes. (See Figure 5-3.)

This principle can be used to demonstrate that a particular man is not the father of a child putatively his; that is, in a particular case one can test the blood of a child and that of its mother and say that the blood of the father must have been of one of several types and could not have been of any other type. Such evidence is used in court cases of disputed fatherhood. The evidence is negative, not positive: one can point to certain individuals who could not have been a parent of the child; one cannot say who, among the others, was the parent. In addition, in some instances identification of the blood type of the red cells of a blood stain has permitted police officers to say that the blood is not that of some particular suspect or victim. Furthermore, antigens similar to those of the human blood groups react with blood of different species and permit experts to determine whether a certain bloodstain is human at all and, if not, what it is.

The reason why transfusions of blood of the wrong type (or from any other species of animal) produce serious and sometimes fatal results, is that human blood contains antibodies, as we have noted, as well as antigens. The red cells

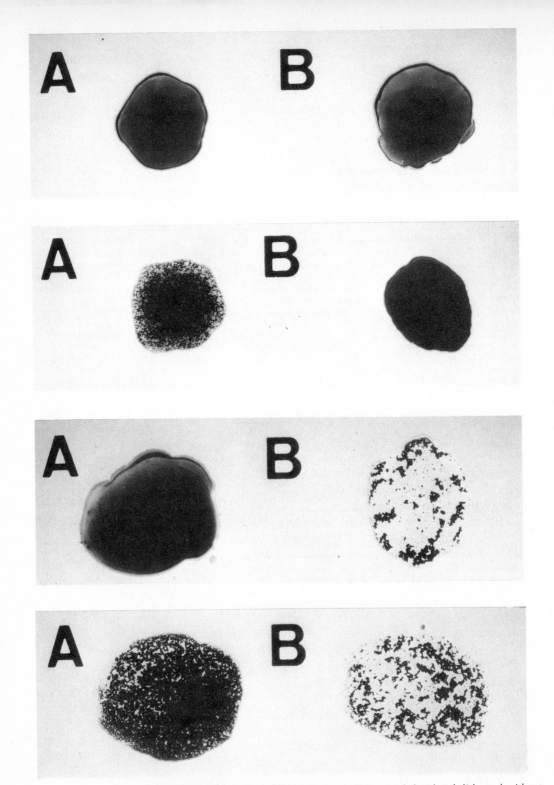

FIG. 5-2 *Top:* Human red cells mixed with anti-A serum on left side of slide and with anti-B serum on right side. The reaction of both is negative. The cells (and hence the individual from whom they came) are therefore classified as Group O. *Second:* The same testing procedure was followed. The reaction with anti-A is positive. The cells and individual are therefore Group A. *Third:* The same testing procedure. Group B. *Fourth:* The same testing procedure. The reaction of both is positive. Group AB.

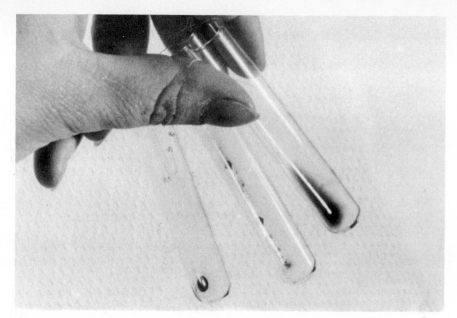

FIG. 5-2 *(continued)* An alternative test for blood groups. Left to right, 4+, 3+, negative.

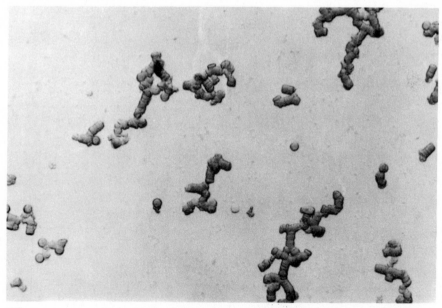

FIG. 5-2 *(continued)* A false positive reaction (pseudoagglutination) is caused by the stacking of red cells, flat surface to flat surface. It can be distinguished by microscopic appearance, as here, or by other tests. Photographs courtesy of Colonel Frank R. Camp, Jr., Director, the Blood Bank Center, Fort Knox, Kentucky.

| Blood group | Genotype | Red blood cells have antigen | Serum has antibodies |
|---|---|---|---|
| O | *ii* | none (universal donor) | anti-A and anti-B |
| A | $I^A I^A$ or $I^A i$ | A | anti-B |
| B | $I^B I^B$ or $I^B i$ | B | anti-A |
| AB | $I^A I^B$ | A and B | none |

FIG. 5-3   Relationship between ABO blood groups, genotypes, antigens, and antibodies. There are four ABO blood groups. Blood of Group O has neither antigen A nor B on the red blood cells, and is therefore a universal donor, since these cells will not agglutinate in the presence of either A or B antibodies. The genotype of a type O individual is *ii* (homozygous for the gene *i*). Individuals of type O have both anti-A and anti-B antibodies in their serum, however. It would therefore agglutinate red cells from type A, B, or AB donors, and type O individuals can receive blood transfusions only from type O donors. Similarly, type A individuals have at least one $I^A$ gene, have A antigen on their red cells and anti-B antibody in their serum, and so on.

of the donor are agglutinated if the recipient has antibodies to their antigens. Fortunately, blood donors of type O have red cells that are not normally clumped and destroyed by anyone else's serum, and so group O persons are called universal donors: in an emergency, their blood can be given to persons of other types.

The world distribution of the ABO blood groups is better known than that of any other human polymorphism. They are also the most commonly used marker in studies of paternity, so-called race mixture, and for distinguishing monozygotic twin pairs (in whom all blood groups are identical) from dizygotic twins who can differ. The world distribution of ABO blood group gene frequencies (Fig. 5-4) is now well worked out (Mourant et al., 1958).

Selection for ABO groups will be discussed in Chapter 8.

## MNS, P, and Rh

Karl Landsteiner, the discoverer of the blood groups, continued his experiments, and in 1927 he and one of his associates discovered that when rabbits were injected with human blood, a few of the animals produced an antiserum capable of reacting with some, but not all, human blood specimens (Landsteiner and Levine, 1927). The antigen in the human blood thus identified was designated M. It differs from the A and B substances in that the antibody was not found in human blood; to test for the human antigen the antibody was prepared in rabbits. A second substance, N, which occurs in some individuals who have M and in all non-M individuals, was soon found by Landsteiner and Levine (Fig. 5-5). There are two alleles, M and N, which correspond to the two substances. The individual with an M gene on each of a pair of chromosomes is of type M; likewise the individual homozygous for N is of type N; but the blood of heterozygous individuals reacts with both kinds of antisera, and they

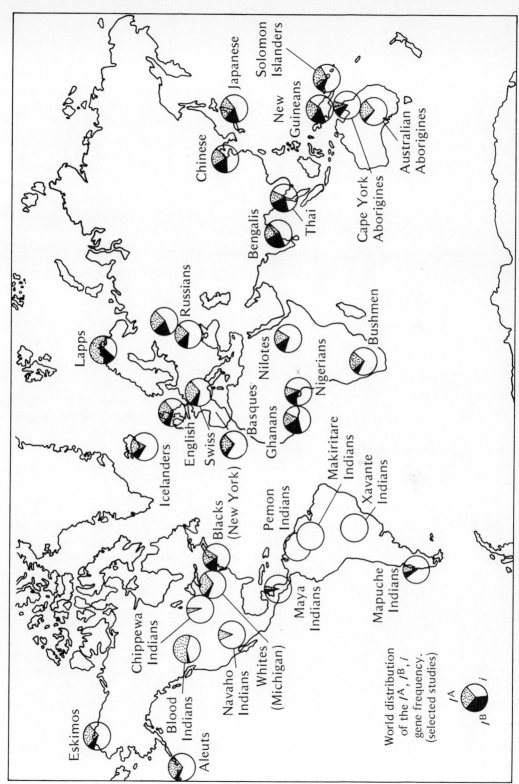

FIG. 5-4  ABO blood-group gene frequencies of selected populations. Redrawn from a map prepared by R. M. McDonald.

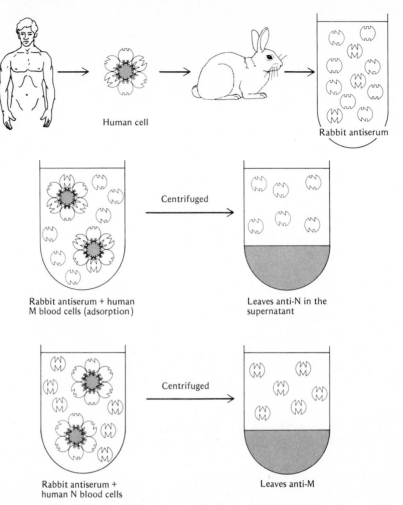

Human cell

Rabbit antiserum

Rabbit antiserum + human
M blood cells (adsorption)

Centrifuged

Leaves anti-N in the
supernatant

Rabbit antiserum +
human N blood cells

Centrifuged

Leaves anti-M

FIG. 5-5 Preparation of anti-N and anti-M serum by injecting blood from an MN individual into a rabbit. Redrawn from Andrian M. Srb, Ray D. Owen, and Robert S. Edgar: *General Genetics* (ed. 2). San Francisco: W. H. Freeman and Company. Copyright © 1965.

are of type MN. There is thus no Mendelian dominance: *M* and *N* are expressed equally and are codominant.

More recently two additional antisera, anti-S and anti-s, have been prepared. One or the other or both of these reacts with all blood specimens. S and s are closely related to M and N because the frequency of S is not the same in individuals of type M, MN, and N. The system may therefore be referred to as the MNSs or simply the MNS system.

Landsteiner and Levine also prepared a third type of antiserum in rabbits, one which identified a human antigen they called P. This is independent of the

ABO and MNS systems. In the past, the test sera for P were often unreliable, and anthropological use of this reaction must be made cautiously and with this difficulty in mind.

Beginning in 1939, Landsteiner and his associates—especially Philip Levine and A. S. Wiener—made another series of discoveries. In that year Levine and R. E. Stetson noted an unusual case of a woman patient of blood group O whose serum agglutinated blood of her group O husband during a transfusion. Her blood serum was also found to agglutinate the blood of some other group O persons. The following year Landsteiner and Wiener (1940) injected rabbits with the blood of rhesus monkeys and found that the resulting anti-rhesus antibodies in the rabbit blood serum agglutinated not only the blood of other monkeys but also that of some humans. It was then shown that the same people react to both kinds of antiserum, rabbit and human. The antigen they show is called Rh because it occurs in the blood of rhesus monkeys.

In the years since the original discovery, a series of subtypes of the Rh antigen have been established. According to one view these are caused by the presence of various combinations of dominant genes (C, D, and E) or their recessive alleles (c, d, and e) on a small segment of the chromosome responsible for the Rh type. If this theory of linked genes is correct, the linkage must be very close, because authentic cases of crossing over have not been found. The alternative view is that enough different kinds of allelic genes appear at the one locus to account for the variety of Rh types. This sharp difference of opinion may in part represent nothing more than a difference in views concerning the nature of the gene. The gene is, after all, an abstract concept describing the genetic behavior of a segment of chromosome containing a particular sequence of base bars of DNA. Whether a variation is considered to occur within one gene (allelic difference) or within several closely linked genes along the chromosome will depend on the somewhat arbitrary boundaries assigned to the gene.

Selection in the Rh system will be discussed in Chapter 7.

## Additional Blood Types and the Secretor Factor

Not only are there subgroups of Rh, but there is at least one important subgroup of A, (A$_2$), and there are also several subtypes of M and N. In addition, there are a large number of other antigens that are independent of the previously mentioned systems or related in still unknown ways (Table 5-1). These are usually named for the individual in whom the antigen was first found and bear such names as Lutheran, Lewis, Kell, Duffy, Kidd, and Diego. New types continue to turn up from time to time. They often are discovered when an individual receives repeated transfusions for some disease and then develops serum antibodies for an antigen of a type he or she lacks but which was in one or more of the transfusions.

One additional factor related to the blood groups is of value in anthropology. In some individuals evidence of their ABO status is found in saliva and in other

Table 5-1   **The blood group systems in man**

| | Year of discovery | Number of known antigens[1] |
|---|---|---|
| ABO | 1900 | 5 or more |
| MNSs | 1927 | 29 |
| P | 1927 | 3 |
| Rhesus | 1940 | 28 or 30 |
| Lutheran | 1945 | 2 or 3 |
| Kell-Cellano | 1946 | 9 |
| Lewis | 1946 | 3 |
| Duffy | 1950 | 2 |
| Kidd | 1951 | 2 |
| Diego | 1955 | 1 |
| Auberger | 1961 | 1[2] |
| $X_g$ | 1962 | 1 |
| Sciana | 1962 | 2 |
| Dombrock | 1965 | 1 |

[1]There is some dispute about the distinctiveness of some of these, and new ones are occasionally being discovered. In most systems there are also "silent" forms in which no antigen is present. In the ABO system there is a gene h for suppression of a substance H. Since A and B are formed from H, homozygous hh individuals have the silent "Bombay" phenotype and fail to react in tests of their ABO antigens. There are also about 24 very rare "private" antigens and about 9 almost universal "public" antigens.
[2]The Auberger system is possibly with the Lutheran system.

body fluids. These individuals are called secretors. In other persons of the same groups the substances are not dissolvable in water and do not occur in the saliva. Besides anti-A and anti-B sera that can be used to test the saliva of A, B, and AB individuals, there are anti-H antibodies that react with saliva of some group O individuals and can be produced from various plants. Most secretors also have the Lewis antigen, but it is doubtful that these are two results of a single gene.

Persons lacking A or B antigens have the corresponding antibodies (anti-A or anti-B respectively). In the other blood group systems antibodies are not normally found in individuals who lack the antigen. These other systems therefore have less immediate significance for blood transfusion. Nevertheless, from the point of view of genetic research, these factors are equally interesting. Taken in aggregate, the blood groups permit geneticists to plot the frequency distribution of a considerable number of human genes (see, for example, Fig. 5-6). At least one anthropologist, William C. Boyd (1950, 1964), one of the first and strongest advocates of the application of genetic methods to anthropology, has used the distribution of the blood group genes to divide the human species into **races.** Most anthropologists would now prefer to study the various blood group systems, variations, distributions, and changes with reference to ecological settings, disease, and migrations, without invoking any concept of race that applies to overall appearance. Race is a vague term and reasons for not using it are discussed in Chapter 21. Analyses of geographic distributions of blood groups are a substitute for, not an adjunct to, racial classification and its interpretation.

# Hemoglobin

Hemoglobin is a protein that has varying forms in humans and animals. These variants are identified by giving them letters of the alphabet. Hemoglobin is found in the red blood cells. In the lung a large surface area is exposed to the air on one side and to the pulmonary blood vessels on the other. Hemoglobin in the red cells in the blood of those vessels is capable of picking up oxygen from inhaled air and transporting it through the blood stream to all parts of the body, where it gives the oxygen to the tissues. This oxygen transportation is one of the functions of circulating blood. The oxygen-depleted hemoglobin (reduced hemoglobin) is returned via veins to the heart and then via the pulmonary arteries from the heart to the lungs, where the cycle begins again.

The amounts of hemoglobin in the blood vary. A hemoglobin deficiency is called anemia and may be a serious disease. One kind of anemia is the result of insufficient iron in the diet. Iron is one of the necessary constituents of hemoglobin. Iron-deficiency anemia may be treated by adding iron-containing foods or medicines to the diet. Other anemias are the result of defects in the hemoglobin itself.

Two methods, chromatography and electrophoresis, are often used to study proteins. Both have been used to study hemoglobins. Furthermore, a combination of both in studies of the separated fractions of hemoglobins, a method called **fingerprinting,** has proved particularly helpful (Fig. 5-9A). First the

FIG. 5-6   World distribution of the Duffy gene $Fy^a$ (the amount of black in the circles indicates the gene percentage in that sample). The map does not include all published values. There is a general cline (or slope) ranging from high values of the gene in North America, East Asia, New Guinea, and Australia to low values in Africa. The clines are not necessarily smooth, however, and some local populations are atypical of the region—"ripples in the gene pool." Data from N. A. Barnicott, 1964.

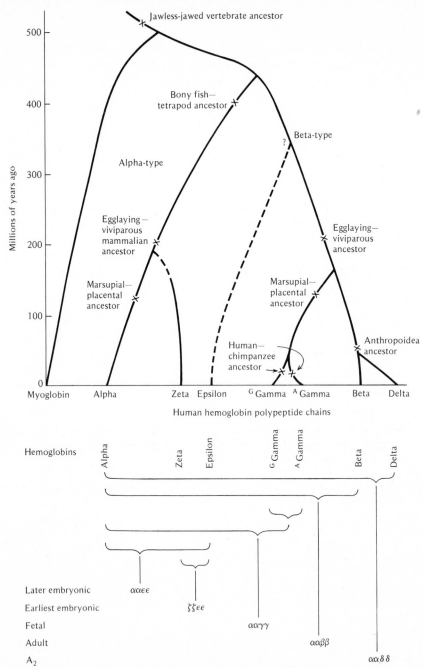

FIG. 5-7 *Above:* Lines of divergence in the evolution of human myoglobin and hemo-globin chains. These polypeptide chains—myoglobin, alpha ($\alpha$), beta ($\beta$), gamma ($\gamma$), delta ($\delta$), epsilon ($\epsilon$), and zeta ($\zeta$)—contain parts of their amino acids in common. The extent of these common sequences implies that all of these globins evolved from

hemoglobin is broken into pieces by the digestive **enzyme,** trypsin. There are thirty of these pieces, called peptides, in normal adult hemoglobin. The peptides are then "fingerprinted" by being separated both by electrophoresis and by chromatography. In electrophoresis an electric current is run across wet paper on which the mixture of pieces has been placed at one spot, and the molecular fragments are drawn at different rates depending on their electrical charges, sizes, and shapes. Then, in chromatography, the fragments are permitted to diffuse in a different direction. Under given conditions a given fragment will always diffuse the same distance on the paper. In this way the absence of one of the usual peptides or the presence of a new one can be detected.

A still further precision in identification of proteins is obtained by a detailed plotting of the sequence of **amino acids** in the peptides. Although a complicated process, automation of the tests has permitted the complete sequencing of hemoglobins and other protein molecules from an increasing number of species and the partial analysis of molecules from many other species.

The hemoglobin molecule consists of four polypeptide chains. It is these long chains that are broken into peptides by digestion with trypsin. There are several kinds of polypeptide chains in hemoglobin (Fig. 5-7). The principal kind of normal adult hemoglobin, hemoglobin A, has two each of the two kinds of polypeptide chains called by the Greek letters alpha ($\alpha$) and beta ($\beta$) respectively. The minor component of hemoglobin, $A_2$ (not to be confused with the blood group $A_2$, with which it has no connection) contains two alpha ($\alpha$) chains and two chains of a third type, delta ($\delta$). In the new born (and sometimes in others) there is a fourth type of hemoglobin polypeptide chain, gamma ($\gamma$), and it forms so-called fetal hemoglobin. A fifth kind of chain, epsilon ($\epsilon$), and a sixth, zeta ($\zeta$), are involved in the formation of hemoglobins in embryos. These six types of hemoglobin polypeptide chains differ considerably from each

---

the same primitive form. Myoglobin is less similar to the hemoglobin chains than they are to each other, and primitive hemoglobin must have diverged from primitive myoglobin before the hemoglobin chains diverged. By similar logic, the most ancient divergence among the hemoglobin chains was between the alpa and zeta types, on the one hand, and the beta, delta, gamma and epsilon, on the other. Since some simple jawless fish have a hemoglobin chain less similar to the myoglobin and hemoglobin chains of jawed vertebrates than their myoglobin and hemoglobin chains are to each other, it is believed that the evolutionary distinction between hemoglobin and myoglobin in the jawed animals occurred after their separation from the jawless fish about 500 million years ago. But since the carp has both alpha and beta type chains, by similar logic we believe that the separate evolution of alpha and beta chains took place before the evolutionary separation of land animals and fish about 400 million years ago since land animals and jawed fish both have alpha and beta type chains. Furthermore, by this line of reasoning, Goodman et al. (1975) have inferred the approximate dates of separation of all the types of hemoglobin chains found in man except epsilon, which has not yet been sequenced. Professor Goodman kindly provided unpublished as well as published information for this figure.

*Below:*    The different kinds of hemoglobin polypeptide chains combine in groups of four (two of each of two kinds) to form hemoglobins.

other and from that of myoglobin, a similar protein found in muscle. They also differ in amino acid sequence from the corresponding chains of other species. Nevertheless all chains share some of the same amino acids in the same sequence in the same part of the chain. By comparing the sequences in these chains, it has been shown that human $\beta$ and $\delta$ chains have more of their sequences in common than either has to the human $\alpha$ chains. The different hemoglobin chains apparently evolved from the same precursor and those chains that are more similar, such as $\delta$ and $\beta$ chains, apparently differentiated in evolution more recently. The $\delta$ and $\beta$ chains were apparently differentiated in evolution by gene duplication, after which event the sequences began to become less similar. Boyer et al. (1974) note that all these hemoglobin chains have some triplet codons which are invariable, and that such variations as do occur are not at random in different parts of the chains. They therefore conclude that all the hemoglobins are "visible" to natural selection and that natural selection allows almost no variation in the functionally essential parts. That is, if the differences were due to pure chance one would expect them to occur with similar frequency in all parts of the molecule.

Among closely related species, there are only a few differences in the amino acid sequence of a particular peptide chain. There is, for example, one difference in the $\alpha$ chain and one in the $\beta$ chain between gorilla and human. Also a score or more of distinct variants are known for both the $\alpha$ and $\beta$ chains among humans; in all but one of these only a single amino acid substitution occurs. Some of these variants are associated with anemias, and, since the amino acid substitutions in the chain are determined by modified base pair sequences in DNA, these are hereditary diseases.

One of these hereditary diseases is sickle-cell anemia. If a drop of blood from a person with this disease is kept away from oxygen of the air (either by keeping it in a closed container or by treating it with a reducing agent) the red blood cells assume bizarre sicklelike shapes when viewed under a microscope (Fig. 5-8). Some other individuals who do not have anemia have red blood cells with the same property but usually less marked in character. J. V. Neel (1951) and others were able to show that these nonanemic individuals are heterozygous sicklers (carriers of the anemia), and that the anemia occurs if the gene for the sickling condition is inherited in the homozygous state. Chromatographic, electrophoretic (Fig. 5-9B), and combined (fingerprinting) methods demonstrate that sickling is due to a variant hemoglobin (hemoglobin S). These studies show that in sickle-cell anemia hemoglobin S is the only hemoglobin present, but that in the heterozygous state there are both hemoglobins S and A.

Some cases of sickle-cell anemia were found in children, one of whose parents had the sickle-cell trait whereas the other parent did not. This presented a puzzle at first, since the anemia is supposed to occur only in the homozygous state and these children were heterozygous. When their hemoglobins were studied by chromatographic and electrophoretic methods (Fig. 5-9A and B), however, they were seen to have not one but two abnormal hemoglobins, one of them S and the other with one of two distinct rates of migration in the filter

FIG. 5-8  Human red blood cells (erythrocytes) that have been coated with gold-paladium metal vapor and shown by scanning electron microscopy. *Left:* normal cells. *Right:* cells from a sickle-cell anemia patient that have been deprived of oxygen by treatment with sodium metabisulfite. Cells from such patients have a normal appearance in the presence of oxygen but when deprived of oxygen the surface is modified and they assume bizarre forms some of which are elongated or sickle shaped. Magnification 3000 times natural size. Photograph courtesy of Dr. Marion I. Barnhart, Wayne State University, Detroit, Michigan.

paper or starch. These patients had hemoglobins S and C or S and D. Hemoglobin C differs from A (and also from S) in one specific substitution of an amino acid in the molecule, hemoglobin D, another. However, as can be seen in Figure 5-9C, many pairs of amino acids, such as histidine (his) and lysine (lys) have the same electrical charge, and substitution of one of these for the other has no effect on electrophoretic migration. There are thus many hemoglobins that cannot readily be distinguished from normal (A), others that cannot be distinguished from S, and still others that cannot be distinguished from C. Hemoglobin D turns out, on detailed analysis of the sequence of amino acids in the molecule, to be several different hemoglobins, which all have the same electrophoretic mobility.

Sickle-cell hemoglobin shows a change in a single peptide of the $\beta$ chain (see Fig. 5-9A). When the specific changed spot in the fingerprint was further studied by sequence analysis it was shown to result from a single amino acid

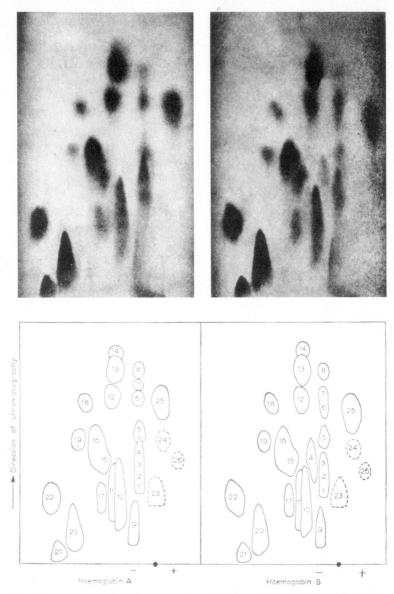

FIG. 5-9A  Peptide fingerprints of hemoglobins A and S. After treatment with trypsin, an enzyme that breaks up proteins, the hemoglobin protein is broken in a uniform way into subunits called peptides. The diagram shows that hemoglobin S (sickle-cell) differs from hemoglobin A (adult) in the position of peptide 4. This shift in position is known by sequence analysis of the amino acids to be caused by the substitution of one of them (valine) for another (glutamic acid) at one position (number 6) in the beta chain of the hemoglobin (see Fig. 5-9C). From V. M. Ingram: "Abnormal human haemoglobins." *Biochimica et Biophysica Acta 28,* 539, 1958. Reproduced by permission.

| Phenotype | Genotype | Fitness | Hemoglobin Electrophoretic Pattern | Hemoglobin Types Present |
|---|---|---|---|---|
| Normal | Hbᴬ H H Hbᴬ | 0.98 | | A |
| Sickle-cell trait | Hbᴬ H H Hbˢ | 1.24 | | S and A |
| Sickle-cell disease | Hbˢ H H Hbˢ | 0.19 | | S |

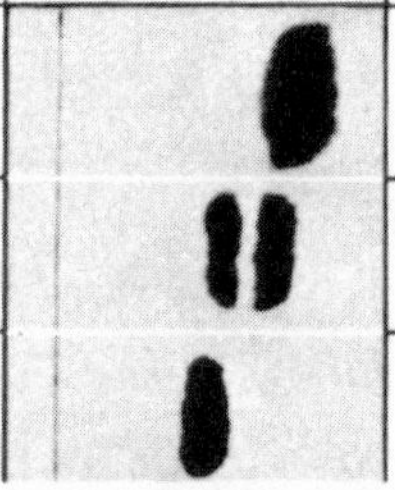

Fig. 5-9*B* This schematic diagram portrays the electrophoretic patterns of hemoglobins A and S. Hemoglobin A is normal; hemoglobin S is the sickle-cell hemoglobin. Fitnesses, as measured in this figure, are the probabilities of survival and reproduction for each type as a percent of the average fitness of all members of the African populations living in a region where the risk of malaria is high (see Chapter 7). These fitness values would not hold for the same people living in the United States. Where there is no malaria, individuals with "normal" hemoglobin are as fit as those with sickle-cell trait. The measure of fitness is relative to the environment. From I. Michael Lerner: *Heredity, Evolution, and Society.* San Francisco: W. H. Freeman and Company. Copyright © 1968. After Anthony C. Allison.

substitution of valine for glutamic acid in the sixth position of the $\beta$ chain (Fig. 5-9C). Hemoglobin C has lysine at that same locus. Now that the genetic code for messenger RNA is known, it can be shown that each of these changes can be accounted for by a single point mutation: GAA to GUA and GAA to AAA, respectively (see Fig. 4-9).

Hemoglobins S and C are found most frequently in Africans and in descendants of Africans elsewhere in the world. In general all the abnormal hemoglobins are more frequent in populations of the tropics. The anthropological significance of this in relationship to the distribution of malaria will be dis-

| | 1 | 2 | 3 | 4 | 5 | 6 | 7 | 8 |
|---|---|---|---|---|---|---|---|---|
| | | + | | | | − | − | + |
| Hemoglobin A | val | his | leu | thr | pro | glu | glu | lys |
| | | + | | | | | − | + |
| Hemoglobin S | val | his | leu | thr | pro | val | glu | lys |

FIG. 5-9C The first eight of the amino acids in the beta chain of hemoglobins A and S. They differ only in the sixth position where valine (val) is substituted for glutamic acid (glu). Since glutamic acid has a negative charge and valine is neutral, in electrophoresis the peptide that contains this sixth position migrates at different rates in the two kinds of hemoglobin. A positive charge at the left terminal end and a negative charge at the right end have been omitted from the diagram.

cussed in Chapter 7. Since the structure of hemoglobin is known in great detail, its variants are also a useful tool for assessing the degree of molecular similarity among primates and other animals.

## Serum Proteins

When blood stands it coagulates and the red cells clot. The clear yellow fluid that remains is blood serum. Similarly, if whole blood is centrifuged the red cells segregate at the bottom of the tube. Other cellular constituents form a whitish layer above them. On top is a clear yellowish fluid called blood plasma. Unlike serum, plasma contains fibrinogen (which causes clotting in whole blood). Both serum and plasma contain soluble serum proteins that can be separated from each other and studied by electrophoresis (Fig. 5-10).

In one-dimensional electrophoresis about six major factors are separated. The ones that move most rapidly toward the positive electrode are called prealbumins. They are followed by the most abundant serum protein, **albumin,** and the alpha 1, alpha 2, beta, and **gamma globulins.** The alpha globulins are usually separated into those that move rapidly toward the positive pole (alpha 1) and those that move more slowly (alpha 2). Gamma globulins, the blood proteins that form antibodies, actually migrate in part toward the negative pole. Two-dimensional starch-gel electrophoresis reveals many additional distinct proteins and variants (Fig. 5-11).

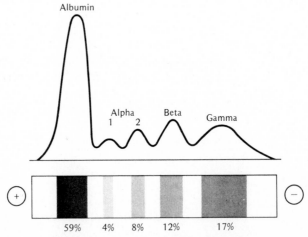

FIG. 5-10   The serum proteins separated by electrophoresis. When introduced at the right they migrate at different rates toward the positive electrode. The majority of the protein consists of albumin. The proteins that migrate next most rapidly toward the positive electrode are called alpha 1, alpha 2, and beta globulins, respectively. The slowest migrating proteins consist of gamma globulins. The wavy curve at the top is a trace of the optical density across the stained proteins which have been separated by electrophoresis diagrammed at the bottom.

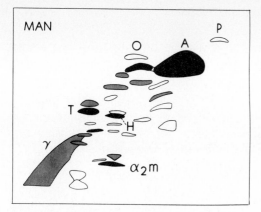
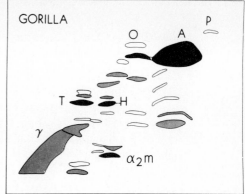
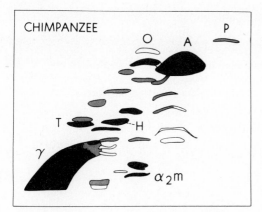
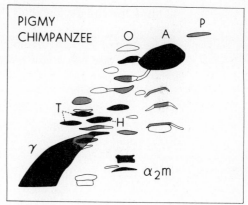
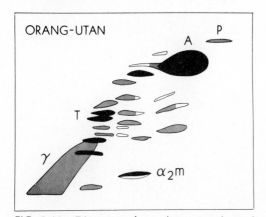
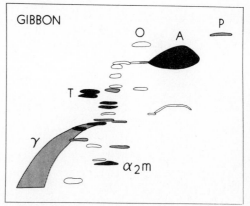

FIG. 5-11  Diagrams of two-dimensional starch-gel electrophoresis patterns of hominoid blood sera comparing some of the specific proteins. *P*, prealbumin; *A*, albumin; *O*, orosomucoid; *T*, transferrin; *H*, Haptoglobin; $\alpha_2 m$, alpha$_2$ macroglobulin; and $\gamma$, gamma globulin. Shading and size indicate relative amounts of the different proteins. When a population shows common variants in one of these proteins it is an example of polymorphism. Transferrin in chimpanzees provides examples of such polymorphism (see Fig. 5-13). From Morris Goodman: "Serological analysis of the systematics of recent hominoids." *Human Biology 35*, No. 3, 1963. Reproduced by permission.

## Albumin

The most abundant serum protein, albumin, shows several polymorphic variants. One was found in relatively high frequency in Mexican Indians; another (called albumin Naskapi) occurs in up to 25 percent of individuals in several Canadian and United States Indian tribes. Francis Johnston and his colleagues (1969) have shown that both of these variants occur in Indian tribes, such as the Navaho and Apache, of the region in between, the southwestern states.

## Haptoglobin

One of the alpha 2 globulins, **haptoglobin** (Hp), combines with hemoglobin. When it is separated from other serum proteins by electrophoresis, haptoglobin can be stained with hemoglobin and thereby identified. Three different types, Hp1-1, 1-2, and 2-2, are of common occurrence. The haptoglobins are inherited in a simple way. One of the types (1-2) is due to heterozygosity for $Hp^1$ and $Hp^2$ genes, whereas the other types (1-1 and 2-2) are homozygous; Figure 5-12 shows the geographic distribution of the gene frequencies. In addition to variant forms of haptoglobin, quantitative modifications have been found to occur quite frequently in Blacks in the U.S., Brazil, and Africa (Azevedo et al.,

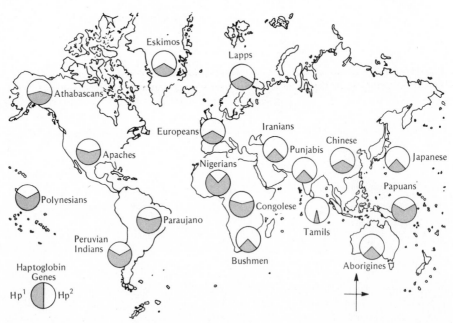

FIG. 5-12 World distribution of the $HP^1$ and $HP^2$ haptoglobin genes. Selected populations. $Hp^1$ varies from a frequency of 0.1 in Tamils to 0.7 in Nigerians. Data from R. L. Kirk, 1970.

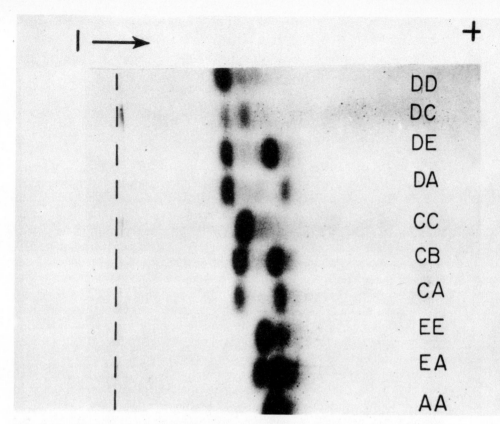

FIG. 5-13 Photograph of electrophoretic separation of different chimpanzee serum transferrins. The samples were inserted at the dashes on the left and moved different distances toward the right, the + pole of the electric field. The polymorphism in chimpanzees, as in humans, leads to many different molecular forms (A, B, C, D, E) and frequent occurence of heterozygotes with two different spots with different mobilities (DC, DE, DA, CB, CA, EA). Photograph courtesy of Professor Morris Goodman, Wayne State University, Detroit, Michigan.

1969). One of these variants is the absence of observable haptoglobin (ahapto-globinemia, HpO) and another involves reduced synthesis (Hp2-m).

## Transferrin

Certain beta globulins are **transferrins**—that is, they have the chemical property of binding iron. The serum proteins are separated by starch-gel electrophoresis and the gel is then treated with a radioactive isotope of iron ($^{59}$Fe) and placed in the dark on photographic film; the radioactive emissions from the iron expose that part of the film at the transferrin spots. In this way many variations in mobility of transferrin have been identified in the serum of human beings, apes, monkeys, and other animals (Fig. 5-13). Genetically homozygotic transferrin is represented by a single spot. Heterozygosity yields two spots, however, because the heterozygotic individual has two kinds of alleles and each allelic gene produces a distinct molecular form of this (and other) proteins. Interestingly enough, compared with humans, chimpanzees and macaque monkeys have an equal or even greater variability in their transferrins (Buettner-Janusch, 1961; Goodman et al., 1965, 1967).

## Other Serum Proteins

The gamma globulins are complex and are formed of units of unequal molecular size (as shown by layering in the ultracentrifuge). The molecules of immunoglobulin (as they are also called) consist of pairs of "light" (short) and "heavy" (long) polypeptide chains. The dominant type of adult serum antibody, the IgG class, consists of two pairs of light and two pairs of heavy chains so bound together that they give two sites with which antigen can combine. It is this double-ended structure that causes antigens and antibodies to form masses that precipitate: red cells to clump together when treated with antisera to antigens on their surface, and viruses to be inactivated in the blood stream. Besides a series of hereditary diseases affecting the synthesis of these immunoglobulins there are also a number of normally occurring factors (Gm and Inv types) that are tested for by immunological methods involving inhibition of the agglutination of red cells.

The Gm factors associate man closely with the chimpanzee and other higher primates. In Fact, Ruffié (1971) considers humans more closely related to chimpanzees than to any other primate largely because these two species alone possess Gm(6) and Isf(1). As with other serum protein variants, the Gm, Isf, and Inv types are inherited and vary in frequency in different populations. For instance, the Gm types distinguish the eastern Asiatics from the people of India, but show the connection of so-called Mongoloid peoples of Northeast India to the neighboring eastern Asiatic populations (Vos et al., 1963) (Fig. 5-14). Similarly these Gm types distinguish different linguistic groups in New Guinea and show one of them to be similar to southeastern Asians (Giles et al., 1965).

There are many other serum proteins, some of which vary among individuals. One set of alpha 2 globulins is called the Group-specific (Gc) component. Another varying system is that of prealbumin.

## Red Cell Enzymes and Enzyme Deficiency

Some drugs (especially an antimalarial, primaquine) produce a temporary hemolytic anemia (one in which red cells are destroyed). This occurs more frequently in Black males than in others and has been shown to be due to a deficiency of the enzyme glucose-6-phosphate dehydrogenase **(G6PD),** which normally metabolizes glucose in the red cells. Tests have been developed that allow surveys and family studies of the trait. The deficiency is inherited and is **sex-linked** on the X chromosome. Since males have only one X chromosome,

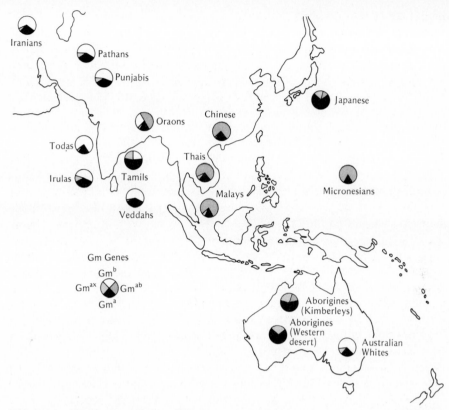

FIG. 5-14   Distribution of *Gm* alleles in various populations in South and Southeast Asia and Australia. Note that the Oraons (who show so-called Mongoloid characteristics in other respects also) resemble East Asians in having the *Gm*<sup>ab</sup> allele but resemble other West and South Asians in having *Gm*<sup>b</sup>. Data from Vos, Kirk, and Steinberg, 1963.

which either has or lacks the gene for the deficiency, there are no heterozygotes in males and counting the gene is relatively straightforward in them. However, females heterozygous for the gene show various degrees of deficiency or none at all.

When G6PD deficiency occurs in Europeans, as it does quite commonly in some populations bordering the Mediterranean Sea, the disease is severe and occurs in response to a great variety of drugs. When enzyme-deficient Europeans eat broad beans ("fava" beans in Italian), or even if they breathe the pollen, they also get the anemia, and the disease is called **favism.** Blacks with the enzyme deficiency do not show this response to fava beans. The G6PD deficiency in them and the gene responsible is, therefore, different from that in Europeans. Nevertheless, the condition is sex-linked in all populations. G6PD itself varies. Starch-gel electrophoresis separates two main types of G6PD, presumably because of amino-acid substitutions similar to those of hemoglobins. One type, A, occurs only in persons with African ancestry. Also like sickle-cell hemoglobin (see Chapter 7), the G6PD deficiency is found in people whose ancestors have lived in areas of the world with a high incidence of malaria, a parasitic disease carried by certain types of mosquitoes (Motulsky, 1960). Thus the incidence of the deficiency is high in many parts of South and southeast Asia, in parts of New Guinea and Melanesia (but not among Australian aborigines), in Arabia and western Asia (notably among Israelis from Turkey, Iraq, Yemen, North Africa, and Persia, but not among North and East European Jews) (Fig. 5-15). Africans from the torrid zone and their descendents in the Western Hemisphere show high incidences, as do some populations of Greece and Italy.

Individuals who inherit the deficiency are better equipped to resist malarial infections. A study in Nigeria (Luzatto et al., 1969) shows that in children infected with falciparum malaria (the kind involving the most virulent organism) the malaria parasites are more frequently found in normal than in enzyme-deficient red cells. Females who are heterozygous for G6PD deficiency have both types of red cell, normal and deficient, and the parasite infestation was 2 to 80 times lower in the deficient cells.

Many other enzyme variations and deficiencies occur. Most of them are known to be inherited. Skin, even that of Whites, has melanin pigment which is dependent for its production on enzymes. **Albinos** (see Fig. 9-5) lack one of the enzymes. Universal or generalized albinism (in which melanin pigment is completely or almost completely lacking in the hair, skin, and eyes) is a recessive. It is of anthropological interest because of the wide range of inci-

FIG. 5-15   Distribution of high frequency of glucose-6-phosphate dehydrogenase (G6PD) deficiency. This enzyme deficiency is apparently caused by any of several different genes, all sex-linked. It seems to be another case of balanced polymorphism involving selection for resistance to malaria (compare with Figs. 7-2, 3, 5). Data from A. Motulsky, 1960.

dence, from rare in Europeans (about 1 in 20,000) to frequent (about 1 in 200) in such American Indian populations as the San Blas Cuna of Panama and the Hopi, Zuni, and Jemez Pueblos of New Mexico (Jones, 1964; Woolf and Dukepoo, 1964). Albinism also occurs in many other vertebrate species.

Other enzymes are also of anthropological interest because of variations among individuals, populations, or species. One other polymorphic system deserves mention, although it has so far been little applied to anthropological studies. A complex series of antigens (the HL-A system) occurs on the white blood cells (leukocytes). The HL-A types are determined by genes in two closely linked loci on the sixth chromosome and their diversity is responsible for the difficulty of performing surgical organ transplants (such as kidney transplants and heart transplants) from a dead human being to a live one without risk of rejection. The techniques for testing the HL-A antigens are too time-consuming for routine population surveys but the significance of compatible matching in organ transplantation and other medical applications is so critical for patients that an increasing body of data is being collected. A long list of polymorphisms in White, Black, and Japanese populations indicates that enough is now known concerning genetic individuality so that theoretically, at least, it makes possible the identification of the true father in cases of disputed paternity (Chakraborty et al., 1974).

# Summary

Polymorphic genes are variant alleles occurring in appreciable frequency in some populations. In anthropology, the geographic distribution of polymorphic genes is studied and analyzed. Blood group antigens are molecular configurations on the surface of red blood cells determined by polymorphic genes. ABO, MNS, P, Rh, secretor, and other such traits are identified immunologically. Various hemoglobins, including sickle-cell hemoglobin, are identified by a whole series of methods that permit exact location of the altered amino-acid sequence in the hemoglobin molecule. Serum proteins, including albumin, haptoglobin, transferrin, and others, also occur in polymorphic frequencies. Many enzymes also vary, and hereditary deficiency of one (G6PD) occurs chiefly in populations where malaria is endemic, that is, regularly present throughout the population.

CHAPTER **6**

# STABILITY AND CHANGE IN GENE FREQUENCIES

Darwin's main contribution to the understanding of evolution is the theory of natural selection. This theory states that of two somewhat different plants or animals, the one whose inherited characteristics better adapt it to life under a given set of prevailing circumstances has the better chance of leaving offspring. This is true whether or not the competing organisms belong to the same group, so long as they are living the same kind of life in the same place, that is, so long as they occupy the same ecological niche. Natural selection not only means "the survival of the survivors," it also implies that on the average a new generation composed of the offspring of such survivors will be more fit than the last generation. Because the new generation is, on the average, descended from the fitter members of the previous generation, evolution progressively favors the genetically fit. Charles Darwin and Alfred Wallace independently arrived at this principle by 1858. Since then no data have been uncovered to contradict it, and much confirmatory evidence has been advanced.

In 1867, however, an engineer called Fleming Jenkin criticized Darwin by arguing that if a fitter variant arises in some population, the offspring will have to mate with one of the less fit kind and thus dilute the new characteristic. After several generations the advantage would have so difused as to be of little benefit and all members of the population would share the trait, so further selection would be impossible. Darwin never solved this dilemma, and it remained for the rediscovery of Mendel's laws to show that a beneficial characteristic would not be diluted. We now know that many characteristics do not strictly follow Mendel's laws, but fitness in respect to these characteristics does not become "diluted" because they are the results of combinations of genetic traits that do follow Mendel's laws. In fact, natural selection leads to the combination of genes into systems of genes that work well together.

The gene theory led naturally to the definition of evolution in terms of changes in gene frequencies. After the rediscovery of Mendel's laws, W. E. Castle showed the effect of selection on gene frequencies and demonstrated that as soon as selection is arrested the frequency remains stable at the level then attained (Li, 1967). The application of genetics to evolution is called the synthetic theory of evolution. R. A. Fisher (1930), Sewall Wright (1931, 1932), J. B. S. Haldane (for example, 1932), Th. Dobzhansky (1937), Julian Huxley (1943), and others developed the theories of population genetics that classify changes of gene frequency according to four possible causes. These are usually listed as: (1) **mutation** (the process by which an established gene is transformed into an **allele** not present in earlier generations), (2) **natural selection** (the differential survival of organisms that carry specific alleles that better equip their possessors to leave progeny), (3) *random* **genetic drift** (the chance production of progeny with more of one or another specific allele), and (4) **migration** (the introduction of individuals with different alleles or different ratios of alleles from another breeding population). These four causes of change in gene frequency will be discussed in this chapter and the following two.

It has been shown that complex interactions of genes with each other influence evolution and that a theory based on single genes may not suffice in many instances. Nevertheless, any circumstance that causes a breeding population progressively to change the frequency of alleles in its **gene pool,** as the sum total of its genes is called, is a significant evolutionary factor. In fact, simultaneous change in many gene frequencies, generation after generation, is certainly the usual situation in evolution, but the case of a change in the frequency of a single gene, such as that which determines **achondroplastic dwarfism** (the dwarfism involving short limbs—a simple dominant genetic condition) is easier to elucidate than, for instance, multiple genetic factors influencing stature. In any case, the more complex situation involves many of the same principles as the simpler one.

## The Breeding Population

What is a population to a geneticist? Some describe the **Mendelian population** as "a reproductive community of sexual organisms that share in a common gene pool." This begs the question, however, since the gene pool is "the corporate genetic endowment of a whole population " or, in a more restricted sense, "all the alleles of a particular locus on a particular chromosome in a population."

The circularity of reasoning in this definition of population is the inclusion of a genetic criterion, the gene pool, in the definition. To escape the dilemma the population must be defined in other terms: the population consists of those among whom mates are found. Thus the human **breeding population** is the *endogamous group* (those who breed with each other) of the social anthropologist. The breeding population can be thought of retrospectively (the community of ancestors of those alive in a population today) or, perhaps better, prospectively (those who will have descendants in common). In any case *population* in this sense is held together by social behavior—specifically the social behavior of selection of mates—and among human beings selection of mates is determined in turn by both geographic and cultural factors. This is not to say that biological features, such as skin color, are not involved, but (since there are no known bars to fertile interracial unions) "race" enters the definition only insofar as social perception of it influences breeding behavior.

The *genetic breeding population*—the mated and fertile adults of a population—may be easier to define than to delimit. In bisexual species, including humans, any adult member of one sex is capable of fertile mating with any such member of the other sex, but the probability of actual mating is by no means uniform. The population can therefore be conceived at several levels: a small local community among whom most mates are found, a wider compass among whom some mates are found, or the whole species among which all groups are potential ancestors of descendants in common. The comparative study of human populations must, of necessity, deal with the subpopulations. F. P. Thieme pointed out in 1952 that religious, caste, racial, economic, educational, class, and other cultural factors affect the selection of mates. Human breeding populations are therefore geographic-social subgroups partially separated by these criteria. When these subgroups are predominantly endogamous and rather tightly bounded by social restrictions against marriage with outsiders (as sometimes happens with religious sects) they are called **isolates**. Language differences also tend to isolate populations from each other. Furthermore, isolates are formed in any species by natural geographic barriers to migration. In humans there may be effective barriers in the cultural ecology also, since people may be slow to move to areas where their traditional way of life is not practicable and disinclined to mix with others who practice a different life style. Economic self-sufficiency also contributes to effective isolation, of course.

Even when there are no discrete boundaries and no distinct isolates there may be effective isolation by distance. Thus, if transportation is primitive, people may choose their mates near at hand and hence from a relatively small number of individuals of the opposite sex. Geoffrey Harrison and his colleagues (see Boyce et al., 1967; Kücheman et al., 1967) have shown that in a rural area near Oxford marriages entered in the parish records reflect the fact that, until about a hundred years ago, almost all men there married girls who lived within half a day's walk. The breeding population in this situation can be conceptualized as the people within a circle that encompassed some fraction of the mates. For rural European villages, circles that include half the mates are small but marriages with individuals far outside the circles (often at great distances) prevent the formation of effective isolates even under these conditions. Similarly, D. Roberts (1956) found that among the Dinka of the Southern Sudan in Africa many marriages were within the local group of villages, most were within the tribe, and virtually all were within the same major subdivision of the Dinka people. Nevertheless the number of exceptions to endogamy at each level prevented the isolation from being effective.

The population geneticists thus conceptualize the local population either as a series of "island" isolates or as a circle drawn from the center of a more or less homogeneously populated surface. The island model is more or less satisfactory for some small and widely scattered groups of hunters, gatherers, and primitive agriculturalists. Progressive isolation by distance, however, seems to provide a more general model at various levels of social and economic development. In either case, among humans, sociocultural as well as geographic factors are important in delimiting the genetic breeding population.

Although populations are defined in social terms, it remains the task of the population geneticist to measure the genetic differences between populations and to explain them not only in specific instances but also in terms of the general principles that account for the maintenance or change of the genetic characteristics of the group.

## Random Mating

The reason for so much concern with the definition of the "genetic population" is that although the individuals within the population differ, it is convenient to describe a population which shares a common gene pool. To share the gene pool equally, mating must be at random. **Random mating** in a sexually reproducing species means that an individual has a chance of mating with another of a particular genotype in proportion to the frequency of that genotype in the opposite sex. Thus, since blood groups do not enter into visible features, the likelihood that a woman will mate with a man of blood group O under conditions of random mating is 45 percent if 45 percent of the males are blood group O. The assumption of random mating of this kind is consistent with observed genetic findings in many studies and has permitted the development of a body of theory that accounts for much population genetics. When, however, the genotype frequencies of mates are nonrandom, for instance, if women of O type marry men of O type more frequently than do women of other blood group types, the theory alerts one to look for explanations of the exceptions. In any case, since random mating is measured in terms of genotypes, the existence of **assortative** (nonrandom) **mating** (matches in which particular characteristics of one mate are associated with the same or some other characteristic in the other mate) in respect to one characteristic may leave the mating pattern in respect to another characteristic essentially random. Thus, taller men may marry taller women and the converse for short men, but since stature is in no way related to blood groups (within populations, at least), the mating will still be random insofar as the blood groups are concerned.

## The Hardy-Weinberg Law

If we assume random mating, we can come to certain conclusions about the distribution of genotypes. Consider, for example, a gene pool of two alleles, $A$ and $a$, whose frequencies are $p$ and $q$, respectively (and where $p + q = 1$, because there are no other alleles). The genotypic frequencies can then be obtained by expansion of the square of the binomial $(p + q)^2 = p^2 - 2pq + q$. The same formula would apply to any number of alleles—with three, for example, the square of the trinomial $(p + q + r)$ would be

$$p^2 + 2pq + 2pr + q^2 + 2qr + r^2$$

This formulation implies that once the proportions of the genotypes reach equilibrium they do not change from generation to generation. The principle was known to Castle (Li, 1967), but its formulation with its implications was apparently independently developed by a British mathematician named Hardy and a German physician named Weinberg. It is therefore traditionally called the **Hardy-Weinberg Law** or the Hardy-Weinberg Equilibrium. It is an equilibrium because, in the absence of other forces, the process of random mating will tend to establish and maintain these values.

Let us consider a gene pool in which the frequencies are $p_A = 0.9$ (90%) and $q_a = 0.1$ (10%). Assuming no selective advantages or mutations, we can obtain the genotype frequencies from the following square,

|  | Maternal | |
|---|---|---|
|  | $p_A = 0.9$ | $q_a = 0.1$ |
| $p_A = 0.9$ | AA .81 | Aa .09 |
| **Paternal** |  |  |
| $q_a = 0.1$ | Aa .09 | aa .01 |

which, of course, is equivalent to $.9^2 + 2(.9 \times .1) + .1^2$, and gives us a genotype composition of 81 percent $AA$, 18 percent $Aa$, and 1 percent $aa$.

The $F_2$ generation of this population will have six types of matings, and a similar box can be constructed

Maternal

|  | $p_{AA} =$ .81 | $q_{Aa} =$ .18 | $r_{aa} =$ .01 |
|---|---|---|---|
| $p_{AA} =$ .81 | .6561 | .1458 | .0081 |
| $q_{Aa} =$ .18 | .1458 | .0324 | .0018 |
| $r_{aa} =$ 0.1 | .0081 | .0018 | .0001 |

(Paternal — row labels on the left)

which is the same as the trinomial expansion above,

$$p^2 + 2pq + 2pr + q^2 + 2qr + r^2,$$

or

$$.6561 + 2(.1458) + 2(.0081) + .0324 + 2(.0018) + .0001.$$

The genotype composition may then be expressed in tabular form as follows:

| Mating | Frequency | Offspring | | |
|---|---|---|---|---|
| | | AA | Aa | aa |
| AA $\times$ AA | .81 $\times$ .81 | .6561 | | |
| AA $\times$ Aa | 2(.1458) | .1458 | .1458 | |
| AA $\times$ aa | 2(.0081) | | .0162 | |
| Aa $\times$ Aa | .18 $\times$ .18 | .0081 | .0162 | .0081 |
| Aa $\times$ aa | 2(.0018) | | .0018 | .0018 |
| aa $\times$ aa | .01 $\times$ .01 | | | .0001 |
| | | .81 | .18 | .01 |

or 81 percent AA, 18 percent Aa, and 1 percent aa, the same genotype composition as the $F_1$ generation. A graphic summary of the values of AA, Aa, and aa for all values of p and q is given in Figure 6-1.

The significance of this law in human population genetics is that if the genotypes are not in substantial agreement with equilibrium values one must look for an explanation in some exception to the assumptions of the law. Sometimes the matings are far from random, or certain genotypes tend to die young. Then the ratio of phenotypes may not fit the ratio of $p^2:2pq:q^2$. Misclassifications of genotypes may also be revealed through departures from equilibrium values.

In the case of dominance, the Hardy-Weinberg Law may be used to estimate gene frequencies. Roughly speaking the recessive gene (say a) will occur in homozygous state (aa) in $q^2$ frequency if the population is in Hardy-Weinberg equilibrium. The frequency of the recessive gene therefore is the square root of the frequency of the homozygous recessive genotype.

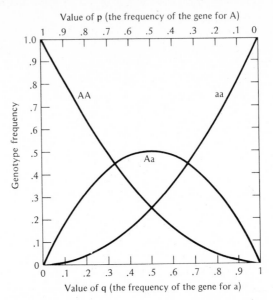

FIG. 6-1    If there are two allelic genes, *A* and *a*, occurring at frequencies *p* and *q* respectively, the Hardy-Weinberg Law predicts that by random mating the genotypes *AA*, *Aa*, and *aa* will be in the ration of $p^2$: $2pq$: $q^2$ respectively. These values have been plotted for every value of *p* and *q*. Note that in a two-allele system *q* = 1 − *p*.

For example, total albinism is a recessively inherited condition in which the individual has ivory white hair and pink skin and eyes. Albinism occurs in somewhat different frequencies in various populations. In Norway about 1 in 10,000 individuals are albinos, for instance. Since albinos in Norway live about as long as other individuals, we may assume that roughly one birth in 10,000 is that of an albino. Thus we may estimate the gene frequency, *q*, as $\sqrt{1/10{,}000}$ =.01 (1 in 100) in Norway. Since each individual has two chromosomes that can carry this gene, 1 person in about 50 carries the gene and can have albino descendants.

## Inbreeding

Full first cousins are the offspring of a pair of brothers, a pair of sisters or a brother and sister. If first cousins marry and have a child, the child (see Fig. 6-2, left) has six great grandparents rather than eight.

If the child (#7) has the gene for albinism on one chromosome there is 1 chance in 2 he got it from his father (#5), another 1 chance in 2 (making it 1 in 4 overall) that his father got it from his mother (#3), another 1 chance in 2 that she in turn got it from her father (#1)—making the total chance 1 in 8. There is another chance in 2 that that great grandfather (#1) transmitted the gene to his son (#4) (making it 1 in 16), a further half chance that the man (#4) transmitted it to the child's mother (#6) (making it 1 chance in 32) and a still further half chance that she passed it on to her child (#7) on his other chromosome (overall, 1 chance in 64).

However, since the child has two chromosomes for which this sequence could be true, the chance of his having the gene at the albinism locus identical for both of them by reason of his having descended two ways from that great grandfather (#1) is twice 1 in 64, which equals 1 in 32. This only accounts for the one great grandparent, however. The chance of having received a gene in common from the great grandmother (#2) is also 1 in 32, so the overall chance in this instance $= 2 \times \frac{1}{32} = \frac{1}{16}$. We say that the inbreeding coefficient (F) of full first cousins is $\frac{1}{16}$ or in the decimal system $F = .0625$. The general rule for calculating it is to trace the path from the individual to any common ancestor through the individual's father and back through his mother and to raise the fraction $\frac{1}{2}$ to the power of the number of traced steps less one. This is repeated for every common ancestor and the inbreeding coefficient is the sum calculated from all such loops. In Figure 6-2, right (a diagram of the same case) the dotted line has six links so we reduce this number by one and raise $\frac{1}{2}$ to the fifth power. We do the same for the solid line. The total inbreeding coefficient is calculated in this example as

$$F = (\tfrac{1}{2})^5 + (\tfrac{1}{2})^5 = \tfrac{1}{32} + \tfrac{1}{32} = \tfrac{1}{16} = .0625$$

Let us apply the calculations of Fig. 6-2 to the question of albinism. If the gene frequency in a randomly breeding population is 1 in 100 (.01) then in first

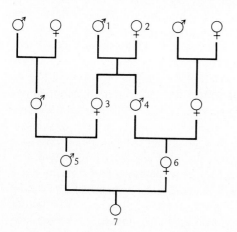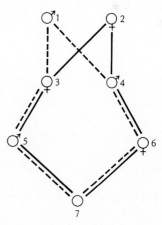

FIG. 6-2 *Left:*   A pedigree showing the offspring (#7) of a first-cousin marriage between #5 and #6. *Right:* The same pedigree showing method of calculating the inbreeding coefficient of #7 from the great grandmother, #2 (solid lines), and from the great grandfather, #1 (broken line). ♂ = male, ♀ = female, ○ = child.

cousins the rate of the condition will be raised approximately $.01 \times .0625 = .000625$ above the rate in the general population $(.01 \times .01 = .0001)$. The rate in offspring of first cousins (some 7 in 10,000) is much higher than the incidence in the general population (1 in 10,000) but the risk is still rather small. Nevertheless, if one counts the number of cousin marriages in the parents of cases of albinism and other relatively rare recessive conditions, one finds a higher incidence than in the population at large. This is true whether or not the group mates at random. It merely reflects the fact that rare genes occur in few family lines and are concentrated in those few families.

The high frequency of cousin marriages in the parents of albinos and progeny with other inborn errors of metabolism was observed by Sir Archibald Garrod (1902, 1923), and his description of this constitutes the first application of Mendelian genetic principles to human beings.

In considering the desirability of marriages between cousins or other relatives, it is well to bear in mind that there is a somewhat greater chance of the offspring having recessive diseases. The rarer the disease the greater the risk in relatives compared with nonrelatives. That is because the incidence of a recessive disease occurs with the square of the gene frequency whereas the inbreeding effect is a constant fraction of the gene frequency ($F \times$ gene frequency). Thus, as one deals with genes with the frequencies .01, .001, and .0001 the frequency in the diseases would be approximately .0001, .0000001 and .00000001 respectively while the inbreeding effect in first cousins would be approximately .0006, .00006 and .000006. Looked at in another way, a gene so rare that it was unique could be homozygous only in the inbred descendants of the unique case.

When looked at overall, however, the differences are not large. Schull and Neel (1965) found that, among one group of Japanese children, mortality was about 90 per thousand in the offspring of unrelated parents and about 105 per thousand in the offspring of first cousins (Table 6-1). Major congenital defects occured in 85 per thousand and 117 per thousand respectively. Although there are many difficulties with studies of this kind, these tendencies are paralleled in data on Europeans and Americans. Furthermore, a high proportion of the few offspring of brother-sister and father-daughter unions followed from pregnancy have congenital defects (Adams and Neel, 1967) (Table 6-1). On the other hand, inbreeding has no effect on the frequency of dominantly inherited diseases; most offspring even of related individuals are healthy; and, from the point of view of society, the increase in deleterious homozygotes does not represent an increase in the frequency of genes with deleterious effects. In fact, because of the increased mortality one would predict an eventual *decrease* in the frequency of deleterious genes in the population. In any case, as implied by the Hardy-Weinberg Law, a single generation of outbreeding would offset all previous inbreeding, no matter for how long it had occurred. This is because the inbreeding loops (Fig. 6-2, right) must come back to the same individual (#7) or they cannot affect his chance of inheriting the same gene through both his mother's and his father's lines from some more remote common ancestor of theirs.

**TABLE 6-1    Effects of inbreeding**

| Schull and Neel (1965) | Noninbred control | Offspring of first cousins | Difference (%) |
|---|---|---|---|
| Child mortality (%) | 9.0 | 10.5 | 17.2 |
| One or 2 major defects (%) | 8.5 | 11.7 | 37.5 |
| Minor defects (%) | 7.9 | 9.8 | 24.1 |
| Average birthweight (grams) (corrected to age 10 years) | | | |
| Hiroshima | 2659 | 2631 | 0.9 |
| Nagasaki | 2598 | 2573 | 0.9 |
| Adams and Neel (1967) | Controls | Offspring of father-daughter or brother-sister | |
| Died in infancy or had major defect | one of 18 | six of 18 | 500 |

Schull and Neel, after an analysis of their own studies in Japan and other data from elsewhere, conclude that the slightly higher incidence of some defects in some studies of offspring of first cousins may be caused by other than purely genetic factors. Adams and his coworkers concluded that the rate of death and defects in children of close relatives is higher than would be expected on the basis of the findings with cousins.

## Mutation

New possibilities arise because of combinations of alleles. If the alleles are rare, any given combination will be very rare. If different genes are polymorphic, various combinations occur repeatedly and new characters may become established.

The only way in which totally new possibilities arise, however, is through change in the gentic material itself—a change that can be transmitted. Several varieties of such changes have been observed, ranging from a change in the code for a single amino-acid substitution (a **point mutation**) to transposition of pieces of chromosome, duplication or deletion of whole chromosomes or segments of them, or even to duplication of the whole set.

It has been argued that mutations could have little to do with evolution because those actually observed in the laboratory or in man are nearly always detrimental (or at least neutral). This argument has little weight, for mutation does not act alone to produce evolution. It does so chiefly in the presence of other factors, such as natural selection, and serves merely to account for the presence of variation. In a more or less well adapted animal or plant, most changes would be for the worse, assuming environmental conditions to remain unchanged. But in a period of changing environment and new opportunities, a greater range of mutational changes would be advantageous and likely to "take hold." So far no one has been able to predict which genes will mutate or the direction mutations will take, although mutations can be greatly increased in frequency by some chemicals, such as mustard gas, and especially by X-ray and other types of radiation.

Mutations are generally disadvantageous from the standpoint of survival, for the simple reason that the form or organ that changes is already the outcome of a chain of natural selection for fitness that reaches far into the past. The established genes, therefore, are advantageous. Nevertheless, the capacity to mutate (but at a low rate) is itself selectively advantageous. With a changing environment the advantage of some mutations will outweigh the disadvantages of having tolerated disadvantageous ones. The possibility of change and its occurrence in one individual or a few individuals prevents the whole evolutionary line from facing extinction. Thus, among insects, mutations resulting in resistance to DDT were probably disadvantageous to the survival of the insects until man discovered and applied this insecticide. The spread of DDT-resistant strains of many different insect species implies that there are often such mutations (even when there is no use for them) and manifests the value of mutation for survival. This may explain why mutation is an attribute of all living things. The rates of mutations of specific genes in humans and other animals are normally between about 5 and 50 per million births. Some such rate may be the optimum, naturally established through natural selection. Lower rates may not provide the species with enough resiliency in changed circumstances; higher rates may upset the equilibrium of well-adapted species. Although any given mutation is rare, some mutation in the individual's chromosomes is a common occurrence, since there are millions of base pairs in the chromosomal DNA. Some mutation rates for specific defects are given in Table 6-2, and mutation rates for humans and bacteria are compared in Figure 6-3.

Rates of mutation have recently climbed above spontaneous rates because **mutagenic** chemicals and radioactive materials have been widely introduced into the environment. If this increase is minor, natural selection (through death and sterility of *mutants,* the carriers of mutations) can probably maintain our species. There is, however, some disagreement among experts as to what can safely be considered "minor." Actually, there is no set limit. There is no way accurately to predict the genetic effect on mankind of caffeine, drugs such as LSD, material for chemical warfare, hydrogen bomb experiments, discharge of waste from atomic energy installations, the widespread medical and dental use of diagnostic X-rays, and so on. So far we have probably raised human mutation rates relatively little, but we have no reliable way of counting "moderate" increases in undesirable recessive mutations or of appraising their possible long-run effects. The effects of radiation are better understood than those of ingested and inhaled chemicals. Any penetrating radiation that reaches the ovaries or testes is capable of producing mutations in germ cells. The number of such mutations is greater the longer and more intense the exposure to radition. There is, however, still no way of predicting in which individual mutations will occur or what mutations will ensue.

H. J. Muller (1950), who won the Nobel Prize for discovering that radiation increases mutation rates, believed that not only is the rate of deleterious

TABLE 6-2   Mutation rates for various diseases

|  | Rate in gametes per 100,000 (= rate in individuals per 50,000) |
|---|---|
| **Dominant** | |
| Achondroplastic dwarfism (short stature with very short limbs) Copenhagen | 4 |
| Retinoblastoma (an eye tumor) Michigan | 2.3 |
| Huntington's chorea (a disease involving involuntary contraction of muscles) Michigan | less than 0.1 |
| **Sexlinked** | |
| Muscular dystrophy, Duchene type (atrophy of muscles) Ireland, Utah | 4–9 |
| Hemophilia (bleeding disease) Denmark, Switzerland | 2–3 |

The conditions are in some cases, such as hemophilia, known to be compounded of several different diseases, each of which is inherited. The reported rates are therefore the sum of the rates for all loci which can produce the disease (data from Stern, 1960).

mutation increasing, but also that the elimination of harmful mutants is decreasing because of the increase in effectiveness of medical treatment. Some hereditary enzyme defects, such as diabetes mellitus, can be treated by dietary control or by providing the missing enzyme or a substitute as a drug (insulin in the case of diabetes). Since affected individuals live to reproduce, this relaxation of selection (see p. 106) further increases the **load of mutations.** thus, the numbers of individuals dependent on the medical treatments continue to grow. This is not necessarily a problem unless the treatments themselves are burdensome or become unavailable. It is, for example, possible that mutations toward hairless bodies accumulated in the human species as his use of clothing developed and the lethal implications of hairlessness vanished. We do not consider it necessary to rue the fact and to conjure up the vision of possible exposure nude in the snow, however. "Load of mutations" is a relative term useful only in respect to specified conditions.

## Summary

Evolution can be explained in terms of mutations and of changes in the frequencies of alleles, provided that allowance is made for the fact that the action of a number of genes is not merely the sum of their individual effects. Gene frequencies can be sampled in a breeding population. Genetic theory is generally based on the assumption of random mating within the breeding population. One test of random mating in respect to particular genes is whether

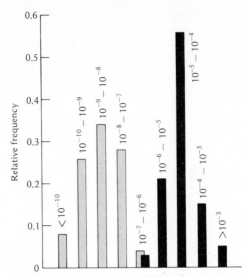

FIG. 6-3    Most rates of mutation in humans (black bars) are between $10^{-4}$ and $10^{-5}$ (1 per 10,000 and 1 per 100,000). In bacteria (gray bars) the most frequent range is between $10^{-8}$ and $10^{-9}$ (1 per 100 million and 1 per billion). The difference is at least partly caused by the fact that human genes determining the conditions studied consist of considerable lengths of DNA, and any of many types of change along this length can produce the mutation. In bacteria the methods of testing generally involve the rate of reversion of a mutation to the "normal" condition, and hence only the specific type of change in the specific codon which is the exact reverse of some prior mutation is involved; any other mutation only compounds the one being tested and will go unobserved. Redrawn from K. C. Atwood: "Problems of measurement of mutation rates," in W. Schull (Ed.): *Mutations*. Ann Arbor: University of Michigan Press, 1962. Reproduced by permission.

the genotype frequencies are in Hardy-Weinberg equilibrium. Inbreeding is not random in respect to genotypes and hence leads to frequencies of homozygotes higher than the equilibrium values calculated by the Hardy-Weinberg formula. Repeated mutation also alters gene frequencies. Radiation and some chemicals increase the mutation pressure.

# CHAPTER 7

# NATURAL SELECTION

One of the synthesizers of the "synthetic theory of evolution," the expression of evolution in genetic terms, is Theodosius Dobzhansky. He paraphrases Darwin's argument in a few sentences.

> Any organism needs food and other resources in order to live; the resources are always limited; the number of individuals of any species is therefore also limited. Any species is capable of increasing in number in a geometric progression; sooner or later the state will be reached when only part of the progeny will be able to survive. The statistical probability of survival or elimination, despite accidents, will depend on the degree of adaptedness of individuals and groups to the environment in which they live. This degree of adaptedness is in part conditioned by the genetic endowment. Therefore, carriers of some genotypes will survive, or will be eliminated more or less frequently than will the carriers of other genotypes, and the succeeding generations will not be descended equally from all the genotypes in the preceding generations, but relatively more from the better adapted ones. Therefore, the incidence of better adapted forms will tend to increase and the incidence of less well adapted ones to decrease. (Dobzhansky, 1962, pp. 128–129)

Natural selection is clearly reflected in the structures of animals. Ability to run, swim, or fly, and specific ways of acquiring food, such as sharp teeth or the anteater's long tongue, would all be adaptive in certain environments, and in those environments would be naturally selected. The term "natural" refers only to the contrast with "artificial" selection by us of seed in agriculture or of sires in animal husbandry. It need not be limited to the wild. Furthermore, cooperative behavior can be just as natural as stark aggression. "Selection" also has a special meaning—that there are biological variants favorable in terms of the circumstances under which their selection occurs. Do not confuse "natural selection" with some supposed internal (orthogenetic) selection toward specific ends. Fitness is defined by the test of survival, not by "fitness" in some evaluative human sense such as the "physical fitness" achieved through exercise. Semantic shifts in the meaning of "natural" and of "fitness" have repeatedly plagued the development of evolutionary science. Thus, Teilhard de Chardin (1959) extends evolutionary concepts beyond the naturalistic realm in which they can be scientifically tested.

Even Darwin, since he was unaware of Mendel's work, did not know how variation could be produced and maintained. He was therefore unable to resolve Jenkin's dilemma (see p. 80) and fell back to some extent on the earlier notion of Lamarck that development of structures through use would somehow lead to their becoming genetically transmissable. That is, Darwin partially abandoned the idea that favorable changes resulted solely from selection. The notion that an acquired characteristic can ever be genetically transmitted has no shred of scientific evidence to support it, however. Some older experiments, and others in Russia during Lysenko's suppression of genetics in the USSR, were supposed to demonstrate direct influences of the environment on the hereditary "stuff." Some of these, such as cold adaptation of plants in Siberia, were not carefully conducted and show nothing. Others, such as short-tailed rats born to those whose tails had been amputated, were outright frauds—the tails of the offspring had also been cut off.

The hypothesis of the inheritance of acquired characters has been generally discredited. There is, however, the possibility of some heredity besides the principal chromosomal mechanism, and there are instances where life in the uterus, mother's milk, or parental care conditions the offspring and may hence lead to similarities across generations other than those determined by the chromosomes.

In any case, Darwin saw, and collected from other observers all over the world, numerous examples of evolution through natural selection. Examples of natural selection are usually most clearcut in those larger groups in the taxonomic hierarchy (for the classification of organisms, see Chapter 10) where some major adaptive function has spread to a whole group. Thus, the carrying of young in the womb during early development and subsequent suckling with milk at the breast evolved in all the placental mammals and must have been selected because of the protection and sure nutrition thus afforded the young. There would be selection against progressively earlier parturition and weaning. (Similarly, delayed parturition and weaning would be selected against by the increased chances that the mothers would succumb to these burdens.)

Differences of lower **taxonomic** significance, such as between two **species** of the same **genus**, are of less dramatic selective significance. Often species are distinguished solely on the basis of differences in size or color. These differences also may be naturally selected, of course. Thus, white fur is obviously selected for its value as concealment among animals that live in snowcovered places. Many such species also have thick fur for warmth, and large body size and relatively short limbs are also naturally selected for the preservation of body heat (see Chapter 9).

Subspecific differences, on the other hand, may be small and not important enough for survival to permit their ascription to a specific mode of natural selection. In humans, serious doubt exists as to which of the various "racial" differences may have been naturally selected by what environmental circumstances in what times and places. There is, for instance, considerable controversy concerning what advantages to survival in given circumstances there may be in blond or straight human hair. We are still not certain whether a very high frequency of a **phenotype** (such as hair form or color) has become so because it was advantageous. One of the best recorded instances of evolution within a subspecies, however, is the change of color of several species of English moths. In recent years, with the increasing prevalence of smog, the moths have darkened appreciably. Color in these moths is an inherited characteristic, and the dark moths apparently have been selected for survival in the darker environment. Under modern industrial conditions they are less conspicuous to birds that would have preyed on them had these species retained their former light color. Experiments with the placing of light- and dark-colored specimens on soot-coated trees of the industrial zone showed that the light ones were more visible and were more often eaten by birds than the dark varieties which have evolved there in recent decades (Fig. 7-1). On the other hand, in experiments in unpolluted woods of other districts, birds captured proportionately more of the dark than of the light moths. (These and other observations of camoflage in natural selection are described by Hardy, 1965.)

In humans the predictive application of the concept of natural selection to differences among populations is difficult. For example, many very different areas of the world have received large numbers of European colonists, African slaves, and Chinese coolies, and members of each of these human populations have succeeded in establishing themselves in a wide variety of environments. Although there is some evidence that populations long resident in extreme environments may be genetically somewhat better adapted as well as conditioned by their life experience, there is little to suggest that immigrants are biologically significantly less well adapted than the local population in most situations (see Chapter 9). The differences in environment between two parts of the world such as Asia and America probably make less difference in respect to human biological requirements than the changes over time in one place (such as the United States from our parents' childhood to our own). This is because human **adaptation** is mediated by human culture, which shields us from many direct effects of geographic differences, but cultural aspects of the environment

FIG. 7-1  *Left: Biston betularia,* the peppered moth, and its black form, *carbonaria,* at rest on a soot-covered oak trunk near Birmingham, England. *Right:* The same two varieties at rest on a lichened tree trunk in unpolluted countryside. From the experiments of Dr. H. B. D. Kettlewell, University of Oxford.

are themselves changing rapidly. Biological diversity within the population itself is therefore adaptive. All groups of man studied show considerable biological variability. Human populations have both larger and smaller, stronger and weaker, more aggressive and more complacent members. This variability probably is a reflection, in part, of genetic diversity. Since whole groups are sometimes selected for survival or extermination and variability favors survival, the advantage for the group of genetic diversity among its members probably accounts for the preservation of considerable variability in respect to numerous characteristics in man.

## Balanced Polymorphism

There is one special case, *balanced polymorphism,* in which evolution can be seen at work not in changing gene frequencies but in maintaining them. In balanced polymorphism an equilibrium exists in which several different alternative alleles are maintained in a population. If the heterozygous individuals *Xx* (of a gene *X* and its allele *x*) are more viable and are to some extent favored for survival both over individuals who are homozygous *XX* and those who are homozygous *xx*, the population is likely to achieve a balanced polymorphism. Both *X* and *x* genes will tend to be maintained in the population by the selection for survival of the *Xx* individuals. Since matings between two *Xx* individuals will produce roughly one *XX* and one *xx* individual for every two *Xx* individuals, selection will continue in every generation. Furthermore, depending on the relative pressure of selection against *XX* and *xx* individuals, there will be some ratio of *X* to *x* in the general population that will be in equilibrium. That is, in balanced polymorphism there is some ratio of *X* to *x* at which any increase in the relative frequency of either allele will tend also to increase force of natural selection against that allele and thus tend to return the ratio to its former balance. If *xx* individuals are more severely selected against than *XX* individuals, at equilibrium the frequency of the *x* allele will be less than that of *X*.

### Sickle-Cell Anemia

We have already described sickle-cell hemoglobin and the serious disease, sickle-cell anemia (Chapter 5). The gene for the hemoglobin (and hence for the disease) is frequent in some peoples of tropical Africa and India, and in their descendants in other parts of the world (Fig. 7-2). The question arises as to why the severe natural selection against the gene for such a condition would not have kept the frequency of the gene at a very low level. A. C. Allison (1954) noted that places with a high incidence of sickling in Africa often are the very places infested with the most serious and virulent forms of malaria parasites (Fig. 7-3). Since malaria is virtually universal in these regions he experimented with innoculating sicklers and nonsicklers with malaria and then treating with modern drugs those in whom it "took." He found that the heterozygous sicklers are relatively resistant to the malarial infection compared with those with no sickle-cell gene—the so-called "normals" (Table 7-1).

A double natural selection is at work here: a selection against homozygous sicklers, many of whom die of anemia and hence fail to reproduce, and, in the tropics, a selection against homozygous "normals," many of whome die of malaria. This is an example of balanced polymorphism. The biological price of maintaining many heterozygous individuals in the population, however, is the birth of numerous homozygotes of both types. These types are not equal in numbers: the selective pressure against sickle-cell anemia is more extreme than that against susceptibility to malaria. But there is some point, an equili-

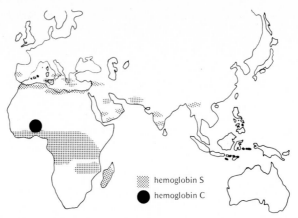

FIG. 7-2   Distribution of hemoglobins S and C. Sickle-cell (S) hemoglobin is a hereditary variant in humans. It occurs frequently in individuals in areas where falciparum
malaria is endemic (compare with Figure 7-3). The homozygous condition—sickle-cell
anemia—is a very serious disease. The heterozygous condition affords resistance to falciparum malaria and apparently reduces the malaria mortality, especially in young
children.

Another variant hemoglobin, C, is frequent in heterozygous form in some populations in or from West Africa. Hemoglobin C also produces a severe anemia if homozygous (hemoglobin C disease) or if heterozygous with the gene for sickle-cell anemia
(hemoglobin S-C disease). Redrawn from Arno G. Motulsky: "Metabolic polymorphisms and the role of infectious diseases in human evolution." *Human Biology 32,* 45,
1960. Reproduced by permission.

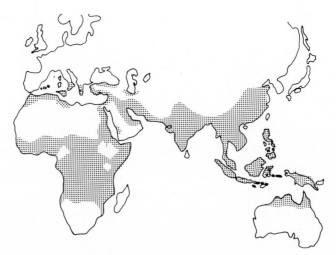

FIG. 7-3   Distribution of falciparum malaria. Redrawn from Arno G. Motulsky: "Metabolic polymorphisms and the role of infectious diseases in human evolution." *Human
Biology 32,* 43, 1960. Reproduced by permission.

TABLE 7-1    Mechanisms involved in sickle-cell anemia polymorphism

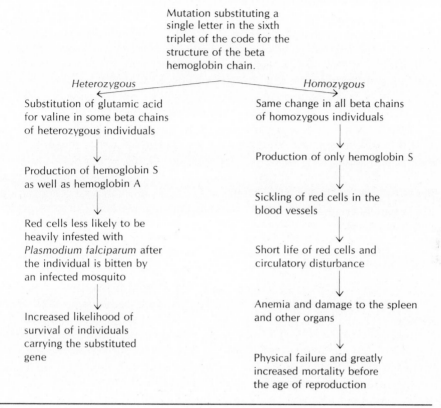

Mutation substituting a single letter in the sixth triplet of the code for the structure of the beta hemoglobin chain.

*Heterozygous*

Substitution of glutamic acid for valine in some beta chains of heterozygous individuals

↓

Production of hemoglobin S as well as hemoglobin A

↓

Red cells less likely to be heavily infested with *Plasmodium falciparum* after the individual is bitten by an infected mosquito

↓

Increased likelihood of survival of individuals carrying the substituted gene

*Homozygous*

Same change in all beta chains of homozygous individuals

↓

Production of only hemoglobin S

↓

Sickling of red cells in the blood vessels

↓

Short life of red cells and circulatory disturbance

↓

Anemia and damage to the spleen and other organs

↓

Physical failure and greatly increased mortality before the age of reproduction

brium, where the pressures will be in balance. This point will be different in different places, depending on the prevalence of malaria; and hence even at equilibrium the frequency of the sickle-cell gene will vary from place to place. This may account in large part for the great geographic differences in the frequency of the sickling characteristic: as much as 40 percent or more in some parts of Africa, nearly 10 percent in American Blacks, but virtually none in large parts of Europe and Asia (it does occur in some parts of India, Turkey, Italy, and Greece). F. B. Livingstone (1967, 1969a) has plotted these distributions and made the calculations that show the extent of the differential selection among the three genotypes *SS, Ss,* and *ss.*

Although the observations of Allison have not been confirmed by further direct experiments, there is indirect evidence for the malarial theory of the sickle-cell polymorphism. In many studies of children in places with endemic falciparum malaria, it is found that the proportion of sicklers is smaller in infants and young children than in older children and adults. Since the sickling trait is congenital and does not change with age, this observation must mean that more nonsicklers than sicklers die in infancy and young childhood, presumably from the ravages of the first onslaught of malaria before acquired immunity is developed. Another observation concerning the sickle-cell trait (Workman et al., 1963) is that among Blacks in the United States the frequency of the sickle-cell gene (usually about 7–9 percent) would imply more European than African ancestors, whereas a number of other traits indicate, as is generally thought to be the case, that American Blacks have on the average about 80 percent African progenitors. This seems to imply that (although the evidence is still inconclusive), in the absence of selection pressure from malaria favoring the heterozygotes, the few centuries since the slaves were brought to the New World have been enough to begin to shift the gene frequency toward a new equilibrium value, in which a very low rate of sickling would be maintained only by new mutations and new immigration from malarial regions. In fact, if the worldwide campaign against malaria succeeds, one can predict a lowering of the frequency of the sickling trait and, eventually, the eradication of sickle-cell anemia also.

## Thalassemia

Two other diseases, also anemias, seem to have a relationship to malaria similar to that of sickle-cell anemia. They are **thalassemia** and **G6PD deficiency.**

Thalassemia (from the Greek *thalassa*, the Mediterranian Sea and *haima*, blood), is also sometimes called Mediterranean anemia. It received both its names because it occurs frequently in Greece, Italy, and some other countries of the Mediterranean Basin (Fig. 7-4). It is found especially in places where there is (or, until recently, has been) severe endemic malaria, such as the Po valley and Sardinia. The disease is found in two clinical states, *thalassemia major*, a severe disease, the expression of a homozygous condition that blocks synthesis of hemoglobin, and *thalassemia minor*, a minor form, presumably the heterozygous expression.

Genetically the thalassemias are diverse. Some thalassemia (both major and minor) is the result of an interference with the synthesis of the alpha chain of hemoglobin. Most thalassemia, however, consists of a block in the formation of beta chains. The body attempts to compensate; because of the lack of beta chains, individuals with beta-thalassemia major often form more of the hemoglobin types that they can from those composed of alpha and gamma chains (the fetal hemoglobin normal in infants), or of alpha and delta chains $A_2$ hemoglobin, normally a small component of adult hemoglobins). (See pp. 65–68 for a discussion of the different kinds of hemoglobin chains.) Thalassemia is thus a defect in control of synthesis rather than the result of a change in the peptides of hemoglobin itself. However, individuals simultaneously heterozygotic for thalassemia and for an abnormal hemoglobin such as sickle-cell hemoglobin also have severe disease. The varieties of thalassemias point to the existence of several genes for the condition. In any one population, however,

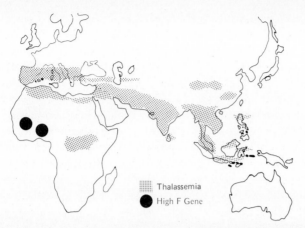

FIG. 7-4   The thalassemia trait is a red-cell abnormality common throughout the Mediterranean area, the Near East, Arabia, India, Southeast Asia, China, the Phillipines, and Africa. The diagnostic term, thalassemia, includes several different genetic entities, all inherited, all producing a similar hematologic phenotype. A fairly well defined thalassemia-like condition is characterized by the presence of large amounts of fetal (F) hemoglobin in heterozygotes. Thalassemia interferes with effective hemoglobin synthesis so that trait cells are deficient in hemoglobin. The homozygous condition, thalassemia major, is a very serious disease, but the heterozygous thalassemia trait apparently offers some degree of protection against malaria. This selection apparently maintains the genes as balanced polymorphisms in malarial environments (compare with Fig. 7-3). Data from Motulsky, 1960.

one variety (hence one gene) is usually predominant and in most cases this is of the beta type. Since one gene predominates it is possible to estimate a frequency for this gene. If a few cases of other types are inadvertantly included such estimates may be slightly too high, but they are not very far off.

Thalassemia is frequent in some malarial zones, and various Italian researchers, among them Carcassi et al. (1957), have attempted to demonstrate the role of heterozygosity for thalassemia in protection against malaria. Direct evidence is lacking, but Carcassi and his colleagues were able to demonstrate that a test for the heterozygotes of thalassemia showed positive in 19 percent and 21 percent of individuals in two Sardinian villages in a low valley, but in only 4 percent and 5 percent in two other nearby villages in the hills. This difference could hardly be due to genetically distinct origins of the populations because there is no history to suggest it and the frequencies of the Rh and MNS blood groups were similar in all four towns; those of the ABO blood groups were as different between the two mountain towns and between the two valley towns as they were between the two zones of altitude. Malaria is the one thing that differentiates the towns of the hill from those of the valley: the hill towns have always been relatively free of malaria, but it was formerly common in the valley towns. This points to the possible effect of malaria as a selective agent in thalassemia.

Other studies (cited by Livingstone, 1967) extend the evidence to other places. Some low-lying malarial areas of Sardinia had less thalassemia than one would expect, but subsidiary explanations (such as recent immigration) seem to explain the lack of the expected "balance" of the polymorphism in these instances.

G6PD deficiency and its relationship to malaria have been described on pages 76–78. Unlike the sickle-cell and thalassemia conditions, the gene for the G6PD deficiency is sex linked and is carried on the X chromosome. Since males have only one X chromosome they either have the condition or not. In females, however, there is a third (**heterozygotic**) genotype and these individuals, like heterozygotic sicklers and heterozygotic thallassemia carriers, appear to be relatively resistant to malaria. In Sardinia, and to some extent in other places where similar studies have been undertaken, there is a strong correlation between the frequency of G6PD deficiency and thalassemia in the local populations. That is, the very villages with a high incidence of the G6PD deficiency also have a high incidence of thalassemia (Fig 7-5). Since both polymorphisms apparently provide resistance to endemic malaria, the influence of either alone is reduced. In the case of thalassemia, the homozygotes have thalassemia major disease and little chance to survive childhood. There is therefore a plausible advantage in having several polymorphisms that provide similar protection, but with each variant gene relatively rare.

Balanced polymorphisms, such as these seem to be, involve continuous natural selection, but little if any change in gene frequencies. The selection goes on continuously just to maintain the equilibrium. Evolution must run just to stand still.

## Rh Incompatibility

Just as there are cases of selection against homozygotes, there can be selection against heterozygotes. An example of this is found in the disease **erythroblastosis fetalis,** a condition apparent at birth. It is characterized by an excessive destruction of red blood cells and a compensatory overdevelopment of those tissues in which red blood cells are formed. The skin may have a yellowish color, and the liver and spleen are enlarged.

The disease is usually due to a difference in Rh blood type between the mother and her infant. The various subtypes of the Rh factor are all inherited as dominants over the Rh-negative condition. Ordinarily the Rh substances produce no untoward reactions during blood transfusions or in any other way. However, an Rh-negative woman can be sensitized against the Rh substances by receiving Rh-positive blood transfusions such as occurred in the case of a woman and her husband reported by Levine and Stetson (1939) and discussed in Chapter 4. This works something like immunity to infectious disease: presence of Rh substance produces, in the serum, antibodies which react with the Rh substance itself. The capacity to produce antibodies to foreign proteins is a healthy attribute in terms of disease; in the case of Rh antibodies, however, the mother can bear Rh-positive children, yet their red blood cells can be

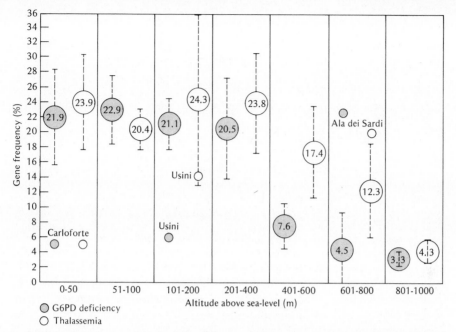

FIG. 7-5   Incidence of glucose-6-phosphate dehydrogenase (G6PD) deficiency and the thalassemia trait in 52 Sardinian villages at different altitudes above sea level. The incidence of these traits is, in general, higher at lower altitudes. This is explained by the higher mortality rates from malaria in the coastal areas. The large circles represent several villages: the average percentage is indicated by the number within, and the range of values by the dotted line. The small circles give data for three exceptional villages considered separately. Carloforte and Usini are low-lying villages in the malarial zone, but their inhabitants migrated to Sardinia from nonmalarious regions. Ala dei Sardi, although high, is reported to have had a high death rate from malaria. (After Siniscalco et al., 1966.)

destroyed by their mother's antibodies. Erythroblastosis fetalis occurs, therefore, in Rh-positive children of Rh-negative women. Cases can occur only when the father is Rh-positive since the positive condition is dominant and can be transmitted by the father to the children even though the mother is negative.

In addition to sensitization by transfusion, an Rh-negative woman may become sensitized from an Rh-positive fetus in her womb (Fig. 7-6). Fetal blood does not cross the placenta freely to flow in the mother's veins, but some antigen does cross, because Rh substances in the fetal red blood cells are able to produce antibodies in the mother's blood serum. The antibodies thus built up in the mother may then be carried in her serum to a subsequent Rh-positive fetus where they react with the red cells to the detriment of the fetus. A peculiar feature of this mother-child incompatibility is that erythroblastosis fetalis apparently occurs less often when mother and father are of different ABO blood groups. It has been shown that fetal red cells can find their way into the maternal circulation. When such fetal cells are of a different ABO group than

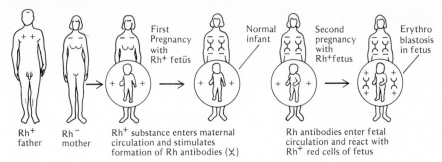

First
Pregnancy
with
Rh⁺ fetūs

Normal
infant

Second
pregnancy
with
Rh⁺fetus

Erythro
blastosis
in fetus

Rh⁺
father

Rh⁻
mother

Rh⁺ substance enters maternal
circulation and stimulates
formation of Rh antibodies (✗)

Rh antibodies enter fetal
circulation and react with
Rh⁺ red cells of fetus

FIG. 7-6   The sequence of events in Rh incompatibility. Since an Rh-negative woman is not born with anti-Rh+ antibodies, it is only after a Rh+ pregnancy or after Rh+ blood transfusions that her Rh+ fetuses run the risk of erythroblastosis fetalis. Redrawn from Adrian M. Srb, Ray D. Owen, and Robert S. Edgar: *General Genetics* (ed. 2). San Francisco: W. H. Freeman and Company. Copyright 1965. Reproduced by permission.

those of the mother (which can happen only when the father is also different), they would be rapidly inactivated, according to Levine (1958), and the fetal cells would have less time to stimulate the production of Rh antibodies in the mother's blood serum. Incompatibility in the ABO system seems to reduce the likelihood of erythroblastosis caused by the development of Rh antibodies in the mother.

Erythroblastosis fetalis can be prevented by treating the Rh-negative mother after her first Rh-positive child. Right after delivery she is given **gamma globulin** (see p. 72) with anti-Rh antibodies. This prevents her developing them in her own serum and thus protects any future Rh-positive child. Furthermore, erythroblastosis can also be treated by blood transfusions to the infant. In former times there were many deaths, however. Every such death removed an equal number of Rh-negative and Rh-positive genes from the population, since the child must have inherited an Rh-negative gene from its mother (since she would be homozygous for the Rh-negative factor), yet must have had the Rh-positive allele to manifest the disease. Polymorphism in such a case would not be balanced; it would be unstable, and one or the other homozygotic type would tend to become universal in the population. If a population at any time had more of one allele than the other, subtraction of an equal number of both through natural selection against hetorozygotes would eventually eliminate the less common allele. Polymorphisms of the Rh type must therefore have to be established by still unknown mechanisms—just as the high frequency of sickle-cell disease in some populations was an enigma until the role of resistance of the heterozygote to malaria was suggested.

## The Evolution of Polymorphisms

In theory, genetic polymorphisms of blood proteins must always pose the threat of maternal-fetal incompatibility since they permit a mother to have fetuses with an antigen to which the mother can form antibodies. Erythroblastosis on the basis of the ABO, MN, and other blood group systems sometimes occurs. Morris Goodman (1963b) has proposed the general theory that as placentas with more efficient transfer of blood to the embryo have evolved, there must have been an increase in the ease of transfer to the mother of fetal antigens; because of this proteins in the blood have tended to be of two kinds: slowly evolving ones with little polymorphism and quickly evolving ones with much more variability. He argues that those blood proteins which appear early in embryonic life are likely to have genetic mutant forms eliminated by maternal-fetal incompatibility and are hence slowly evolving; serum albumin is an example. It might seem that such placentas would not have evolved under the circumstances, but, in the primates, the advantages of an efficient placenta for long gestation seem to have outweighed this consideration.

A random survey of proteins in humans indicates that about 30 percent of them are polymorphic. In fruit flies and mice (and therefore, presumably, in animals in general) approximately 30 percent of proteins are polymorphic. With common variant genes at 30 percent of loci the probability of heterozygosis is very high. In fact, an average human being is heterozygotic for about 12 percent of his genes (Dobzhansky, 1969). Since we have about 100,000 gene loci, we are heterozygotic at about 12,000. Most of these must be incapable of producing antibodies in mothers. This would apply to tissue proteins, which are not accessible to the maternal blood. It would also be true of substances that are not present until after birth, such as gamma globulin. Some other polymorphic proteins are subject to maternal-fetal incompatibilities, however, and in these the adverse selection against some individuals must be balanced by compensating favorable selection of others. In fact, the variation must be a potent evolutionary resource or it would be difficult to understand how the polymorphisms could persist in the face of such maternal-fetal incompatibilities.

The genetic code is degenerate (different messages signal use of the same amino acid in protein synthesis; see pp. 42–43). Mutations of one DNA base to another that produces the same amino acid are neutral and are called "silent mutations." Furthermore, some parts in a protein determine its biochemical processes whereas others have no apparent functional significance. Mutations involving nonfunctional parts are also neutral. Such differences of a neutral nature can substitute one for another without natural selection, and the change is called " non-Darwinian evolution" (King and Jukes, 1969). Natural selection is viewed as an editor who can merely delete messages that are written in functioning parts of the organism. It cannot be the author of the genetic message in the DNA. Natural selection affects the message by correcting the "proof". This "editor" is unable to eradicate neutral changes in the copy since it cannot perceive them. Since establishment of changes in this silent information cannot be by natural selection, it must be by mutation pressure (see Chapter 6) or random genetic drift (see Chapter 8). Some students of molecular genetics believe that non-Darwinian evolution of this kind is an important aspect of evolutionary change.

However, the failure until now to find functional differences does not mean that subtle differences do not exist. Small differences in the availability of a particular substrate or the energy required to utilize it would provide selective advantages even when these do not occur under test-tube conditions (Richmond, 1970). Furthermore, the rates of allegedly nonfunctional changes in different proteins vary both between different peptides and even between different parts of the same peptides—a variation that cannot be explained by a random process such as mutation. In fact, in some instances the functionally most important parts of the peptide chain are known to be the most slowly evolving part (Goodman et al., 1975). Richmond points out that the genetic code itself must have evolved by selection into a mechanism that carries considerable variability of almost but not quite neutral extent. This is the very substance of natural selection. It behooves us to respect variability between individuals that has accumulated by trial and error and that maintains the heterozygosity of individuals as a potent biological resource of the species.

## Relaxed Selection

If a structure was purely neutral, neither advantageous nor disadvantageous, one would expect its frequency to remain relatively constant. In fact, however, any structure without specific function would seem to be somewhat disadvantageous and hence to have a tendency to disappear. Even those that remain recognizable (such as the bony pelvis in the whale or the wings of the ostrich) are greatly reduced in size. It is true, of course, that some such structures, including the human vermiform appendix, seem to be vestigial. It would take only a slight advantage of some unknown kind, however, to balance the small disadvantages of the supposed vestigial structures. Even the risk of appendicitis is relatively small. The reason why nonfunctional structures are generally disadvantageous is probably that they require energy in the form of food calories for their growth and for maintainance of the additional deadweight.

To the extent that apparently selectively neutral structures are, in fact, disadvantageous, there must be a tendency through evolution to lose any capacity if its benefit to the organism disappears. Such a relaxation of favorable natural selection would occur when society develops cultural methods of compensating for a deficiency. For instance, to the extent that diabetes can be effectively treated with insulin one would anticipate that the need of the human body to produce insulin in the pancreas would decrease and the incidence of diabetes (the result of a hereditary tendency toward it) would increase. According to Post (1962) incidence of red-green color blindness in males (hence the gene frequency, since it is sex linked and males have only one X-chromosome) ranges from 5 to 10 percent in Europeans and Chinese, but averages only 2 percent in hunters and food gatherers. Post believes that since the higher frequencies occur in peoples who have had pastoral and agricultural histories for at least three thousand years, color blindness is no handicap to the farmer and herder but is to the hunter and gatherer. This kind of relaxed selection among people in highly protective cultures has been reported in respect to other traits (deviated nasal septum, for instance). The higher incidence of such defects in civilized societies is used as one argument for a return to nature.

However, if "return to nature" means condemning those with minor deficiencies in such capacities as color vision to extermination, it is unlikely any one would abandon the benefits of agriculture for a primitive life in the wild.

## Summary

Natural selection is the process by which some individuals or groups are, by reason of hereditary endowment, better adapted to the environment and therefore are able to leave more offspring than others less well endowed. Natural selection thus involves differences in mortality or fertility. There are instances, balanced polymorphisms, in which natural selection operates against homozygotes and there need be no change in gene frequencies. Sickle-cell hemoglobin and probably thalassemia are maintained in this way. How selection for the Rh polymorphism works is not known; polymorphisms must involve enough favorable selection to offset the disadvantage of the risk of maternal-fetal incompatibility. When changes in the way of life relax the selection for specific features most such features seem to be selected against.

CHAPTER **8**

# RANDOM GENETIC DRIFT

**Random genetic drift** is the third of the four main ways by which changes in gene frequency are effected. It is chance fluctuations in gene frequencies in a population of finite size. In part, human evolution may be explained by chance. This explanation seems a contradiction in terms: saying that changes are due to chance seems to be saying that they are not explained. What is implied in this case, however, is merely that some factors not directly related to biology increase or decrease gene frequency. Thus, if an old man on crossing a street corner, and being rather slow about it, is knocked over by an errand boy on a bicycle who observed the traffic light but not the traffic, the incident is "accidental" as far as the law is concerned. The policeman who hurries to the scene is not concerned with the reason why either the man or the boy should be passing just that particular spot just at that time. To take a more direct example: if the Spanish Armada had conquered the British and occupied England, genes for blue eyes might well be rarer in the United States today. But as far as the fate of the Armada was concerned, eye color either was not relevant or was one of many factors the relevance of which cannot now be determined. Such factors are ascribed to chance and handled statistically in the same way as the factors that determine the roll of an honest pair of dice. Thus we say it is "by chance" that one couple with brown eyes has children while their neighbors with blue eyes are childless. In this way factors of no pertinence to genetics may modify gene frequencies, although this does not preclude a historical explanation if it were possible and worthwhile to ascertain all the unknown or doubtful factors. The cumulative effect of haphazard variation is called *random genetic drift*.

Genetic expectations are frequently expressed as fractions. Thus, in discussing the **Hardy-Weinburg Law** (p. 84) we stated that from a population with two **alleles** of equal frequency ($p = 0.5$, $q = 0.5$) the **genotypes** AA, Aa, and aa would be distributed in the ratio $p^2:2pq:q^2$ respectively, that is ¼AA, ½Aa, and ¼aa. These fractions are only probabilities: in real life the actual numbers are likely to vary. In Mendel's experiment, described earlier, the observed ratio was 2.96 to 1 rather than 3 to 1. Such variations involve changes in the gene frequencies due to chance. Furthermore, chance changes in gene frequencies in the formation of each new generation may or may not lead to cumulative changes. As far as chance is concerned, the likelihood is equal that further shifts in gene frequency will be in the same direction or in the opposite direction (Fig. 8-1). Sometimes the direction of change will be the same for several generations. Sooner or later there might be a whole generation of homozygous AA and no Aa nor aa individuals; at that point the gene for a will

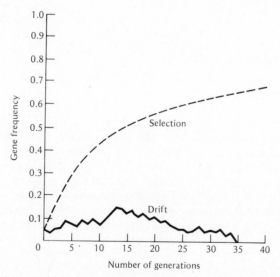

FIG. 8-1  Graphic portrayal of the changes in gene frequency in an allele subject to selection and in one subject to genetic drift for 40 generations (from left to right). An allele subject to selection will increase at a steadily decelerating rate toward some optimal value. An allele subject to drift varies from generation to generation in either direction, and if it ever reaches 0 (in this example in the thirty-fifth generation) it remains there unless reintroduced by mutation or immigration.

have been totally removed from the population (Fig. 8-2). Random drift will have *fixed* one of the genes (*A* or *a*). Therefore all subsequent generations can only inherit the one type of gene—unless the other is reintroduced by mutation or by an immigrant.

One way of explaining random genetic drift is to call it the effect of each generation's sampling of the previous generation's gene pool. It should be apparent that the smaller the population, the more likely are large chance fluctuations and fixations of genes by this process. Sewall Wright (1938) has shown that not only is the total size of the breeding population important, but also the variability in the size of families. Obviously, if a large number of couples had few or no offspring, while others were the parents of many, random genetic drift would have a greater effect than if the distribution of offspring were more even. Increase in variability in family size thus has the same effect as decrease in size of the group. Thus, the greater the variability, the greater the effect of random drift. Since it is also true that the smaller the population, the greater the effect of random drift, the extent of variability can be translated into terms of population size. Geneticists have calculated the amount of random genetic drift that would take place per generation in a theoretical "effective **breeding population**" whose members all had two off-spring per couple. Then for real populations the geneticists estimate the size of the corresponding theoretical effective breeding population that would yield the same amount of random genetic drift. In this way they try to allow for

FIG. 8-2   This graph shows what would happen by random genetic drift to many allelic genes all of which started at a frequency of 0.5 (50 percent) in the population. T = the time in generations and N = the effective size of the breeding population. Since changes in gene frequencies occur only through births and deaths, in evolutionary studies time is measured in generations. The greater the number of generations the more opportunities for chance changes, of course. But the larger the population the less the effect on gene frequency of a given amount of random variation. In fact the influence of generations and numbers are inverse. In the chart (a) For example, assume that at T = 0 all the gene frequencies are 0.5. (b) The alleles would then begin to have different frequencies. (c) By the time that T = N/5 (one fifth as many generations as there are members of the breeding population) various genes would have reached almost every frequency. (d) By the time T = N/2 some of the alleles would have reached a frequency of 1 or 0. Additional generations could produce no further change in these *fixed* genes. (The heights of the bars representing 0 and 1 are not on the same scale. The number of genes fixed always increases with time and decreases with the size of the breeding population.) (e) When the time in generations equals the size of the population (T = N), the frequencies of nonfixed alleles are widely and almost evenly distributed. (f) By the time twice as many generations have passed as there are members of the population (T = 2N) those genes which have not been fixed are equally distributed at all frequencies. (g) From then on the proportion of fixed genes constantly increases and all other frequencies become increasingly rare. Eventually all genes are fixed.

variations in family size. The size of the "effective breeding population" is always less than the number of "real" adults of reproductive age. In several studies of rural communities it averaged about 30 percent of the census of population.

One feature of random variation is its virtual absence in large breeding populations; in them, numerous "chance" events tend to counterbalance each other (Fig. 8-2). Since all organisms are reasonably well adapted to their environment, chance variation—that is, random genetic drift—is likely to encourage unfavorable evolution. For this reason some competent research workers minimize its significance. Others have pointed out, however, that if a species is incompletely divided into partially isolated subpopulations, random variation among these subpopulations would provide distinct "pools" of genes, including some for characteristics unfavorable under those particular

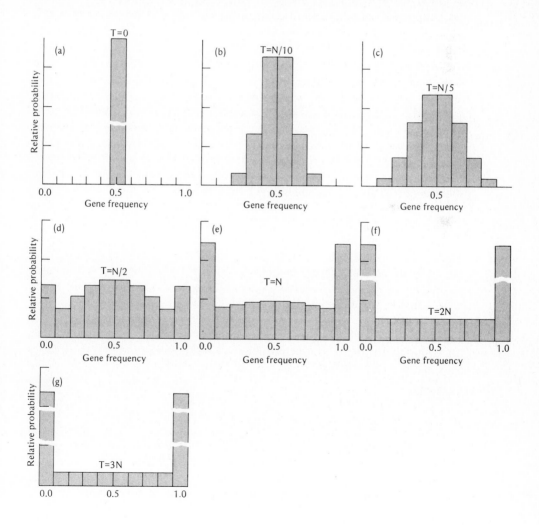

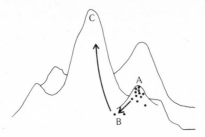

FIG. 8-3   Scheme showing more effective (stable) adaptive niches as peaks and less effective (unstable) adaptations as valleys. A species adapted to the ecological niche represented by peak A could, by natural selection, achieve peak C if incompletely divided into relatively small subgroups that vary (by random genetic drift), so that some individuals would be relatively maladapted in valley B.

circumstances, but which would enhance the possibility for natural selection when the circumstances change. Thus, a small group maladapted to a cold climate could serve as a genetic pool of favorable traits for the whole species in a subsequent warm epoch. Wright (1932) visualized the ways of life as a map with peaks (good ways of life) and valleys (Fig. 8-3). If a species divided into small breeding populations were distributed on such a map, natural selection would attract the populations to the peaks; that is, the groups would adapt to the possible ways of life, sometimes called **ecological niches** by biologists. Random genetic drift would cause the paths to zigzag, however, and sometimes to descend. Although, to that extent, the organisms would be less well adapted, their descent would permit the groups to enter declivities from which the ascent of higher peaks might begin. In other words, a slightly maladapted species with a variety of subpopulations may be more able than a wholly successful one to exploit the environment in some strikingly new way by a radical evolutionary step. The human characteristic of upright gait, for example, could not have started with the fastest ground-adapted quadruped. Finally, the occasional interbreeding between subgroups leads to a sharing of any favorable modifications established in one of the subgroups. Such shared traits might eventually be established in the whole species if they are highly advantageous for survival.

Many important capacities seem to result from combinations of genetic traits. Just as in balanced **polymorphism** of allelic genes (see p. 97), such as sickling, the **heterozygote** is more fit than either **homozygote,** so also there may be favorable combinations of nonallelic genes at different loci on the chromosome or on different chromosomes. One can see the advantage of more or less separate populations for the development and stabilization of such combinations. In partially isolated subgroups scattered over the "map," each experimentally ascends its own peak, but then (by interbreeding) advantageous modifications achieve other peaks. Favorable combinations of genes and genetic systems can thus be altered with considerably less risk of extermination of the species and loss of previous evolutionary gains. Many species, including

our own, are divided into partially isolated subpopulations which differ genetically to some extent; that is, they are **polytypic.** The advantage rests in the fact
that such subpopulations, unlike species, may subsequently fuse and reform in
new adaptive combinations.

Some human breeding groups are small enough for random factors to be
quite pronounced, especially at the outset. The population of the Bass Strait
Islands, Australia, started with 21 adults. The 270 or so inhabitants of the little
island of Tristan da Cunha in the South Atlantic were descended from 8 men
and 7 women who settled there following the Napoleonic wars, and from a few
subsequent immigrants. Pitcairn Island in the Pacific was peopled by the
descendants of 6 of the mutineers of the British ship *Bounty* and 8 or 9
Polynesian women. In 1659 30 white men were sent to colonize the island
of Saint-Barthelemy in the Caribbean, and in 1664 they and their families
amounted to about 100 persons. The population has formed two endogamous
isolates in which genetic drift for blood groups seems to have occurred (Benoist,
1964). Random genetic drift has occurred in the blood group genes in a similar-
sized group in this country—one of the little religious sects, an Old German
Baptist Bretheren community in Pennsylvania (Glass et al., 1952). In 1711,
28 of these German Baptists migrated from Schwartzenau and vicinity to Ger-
mantown, Pennsylvania. They were later joined by several hundred others, but
the sect split into three groups in 1881. In the Bretheren the frequencies of $I^A$ and
$I^B$ are .378 and .025 compared with .258 and .041 respectively in White Americans and .286 and .074 respectively in Germans from the area in Germany
whence the Bretheren emigrated. Another religious community of the United
States and Canada, the Hutterites, migrated to South Dakota between 1874
and 1877. The sect has several separate colonies in which gene frequencies
for the blood groups have drifted apart. Even in small isolates of this kind,
however, there may be some outsiders who come, join the group, and have
children. In the case of the Brethern this immigration has been at the rate of
between 10 and 22 percent per generation, but even this rate has not prevented
significant random differentiation from the surrounding population from which
the immigrants have come. In general, the smaller the effective population
size and the smaller the immigration rate, the greater will be the random variation in gene frequencies. The effective population size multiplied by the immigration rate may be used as a measure of the degree of isolation.

## Drift versus Selection

The distribution of blood groups may exemplify both balanced polymorphism
and random genetic drift. Alice Brues (1954, 1963) has shown that the world
distribution of the blood groups is consistent with the thesis that natural
selection is important in maintaining the balanced polymorphisms, but that
chance factors are important in producing the present differences between
human subgroups. The ABO blood groups are so distributed that the frequency
of the $I^A$ gene varies from 0 to 55 percent, the $I^B$ gene 0 to 35 percent, and the $i$

gene rarely below 50 percent. The majority of possible combinations of relative frequencies of $I^A$, $I^B$, and $i$ is not found in any of the various populations (Fig. 8-4). Brues argues that this suggests natural selection. Otherwise why are not all possible combinations approximated somewhere among the thousands of groups which have been studied? Brues believes natural selection tends to pull all groups toward an equilibrium at gene frequencies of about 25 percent $I^A$, 15 percent $I^B$, and 60 percent $i$. The natural selection of blood groups must have been at work for a very long period of time because blood groups essentially like the human ones are also found in the anthropoid apes. Brues thinks that it is therefore probable that the departures from this equilibrium are due to the action of random genetic drift and historical accident. Indeed, some of the most extreme blood group frequencies are found in relatively isolated peoples—for example, the Basques and the Lapps (see Fig. 5-4).

In addition, however, the selective forces may not be the same in all situations and this, too, can account for local differences. The blood group polymorphisms are known to be related to disease susceptibilities (Table 8-1).

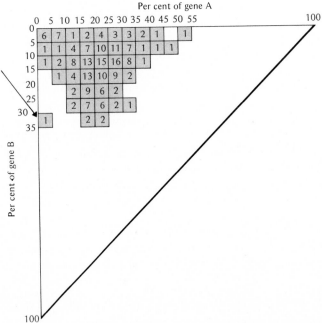

FIG. 8-4   Distribution of 219 representative human populations in respect to frequencies of the ABO blood group genes. Only about 12 percent of possible combinations (the area of the triangle) occur. The isolated case with high B (arrow) represents a report based on faulty method. Brues (personal communication) considers the discovery of a flaw in the aberrant case nice confirmation of her hypothesis. Redrawn from Alice M. Brues: "Selection and polymorphism in the ABO blood groups." *American Journal of Physical Anthropology* 12, 560, 1954. Reproduced by permission.

**TABLE 8-1**    Excess (+) or deficiency (−) of certain diseases in specific ABO bloodgroups and in secretors

| | Number of patients | Blood group | | Secretor |
| --- | --- | --- | --- | --- |
| | | A | O | |
| Duodenal ulcer | 8,272 | +10.0% | +16.8% | +50.0% |
| Gastric carcenoma | 6,795 | +10.0% | | |
| Pernicious anemia | 1,498 | +13.5% | | |
| Leukemia | 1,387 | | −11.8% | |

Results of the kind shown above have been found in many studies, but further research is still needed to explain the findings. Perhaps further chemical analyses of blood group antigens and experiments with them will help explain their function in health and disease.

   An increased frequency of duodenal ulcer in persons of blood group O and in secretors seems to be well established. An increased incidence of gastric carcenoma (cancer of the stomach) and pernicious anemia in persons with blood group A is also reported in many different studies. The dearth of cases of leukemia in blood group O does not hold within homogeneous populations, however. This blood group is rare in Jews but leukemia is very common; heterogeneous populations that contain Jews and non-Jews therefore show less leukemia associated with blood group O. When MacMahon and Fousiak (1958) matched each of 1232 leukemia patients with blood bank donors of the same surname (hence usually of similar ethnic origins) 507 patients and exactly 507 controls (41.2% in both cases) were blood group O.

Thus, persons with blood group O are more likely to have peptic ulcers, and those with blood group A, gastric carcinoma or pernicious anemia. Blood group O is also significantly less common in leukemia patients than in the general population. This is caused by the fact that many leukemia patients are Jewish but blood group O is relatively rare in Jews (MacMahon and Folusiak, 1958). A similar type of explanation, unrepresentativeness of the sample in respect to ethnic origin, or some such could be a factor in respect to other blood group associations. At least, Clarke (1959) found a random association of duodenal ulcer with ABO blood groups and secretor status among close relatives within the same family. Even if diseases such as peptic ulcers and stomach cancer are meaningfully related to blood groups, however, they usually occur late in life and are not likely to affect the number of offspring left behind by persons of the various genotypes. It is hard to see how they would influence natural selection. On the other hand, as Livingstone (1960) pointed out in a review of the subject, infectious diseases that until recently accounted for numerous deaths of infants and youths are likely to have influenced changes in blood group gene frequencies if there is any differences between blood groups in response to these infections.

   Livingstone believes that selection in respect to plague, cholera, smallpox, pneumonia, diptheria, or other diseases may thus account for variation of blood group frequencies. Livingstone (1969a) made calculations of the distribution of frequencies of the ABO blood system, similar to those of Brues (Fig. 8-4) and reached somewhat similar conclusions. However, instead of assuming a single optimal figure, he concluded that the optimum varies and that the geographic distribution of values is not the result of a single optimum (plus random genetic drift) but rather the result of different optima in different places plus considerable migration of people between these places. He was able to assume rates of selection intensity and migration rates that are consistent with the actual distribution of ABO blood group frequencies.

In any case, in some situations the role of random factors is well documented. In the Wellesley Islands off the coast of Australia the aborigines of one island have the highest frequency of the genes for blood group B and for one of the Rh alleles of any population on the subcontinent, but no group A; those of another island in the group have blood group B, no A, and a high frequency of a different Rh allele (Simmons et al., 1962). It is hard to believe that anything but random factors could account for these differences. Similar marked local differences also occur in New Guinea, where people of neighboring villages and of the same linguistic group sometimes differ markedly in blood group frequencies (Giles et al., 1966, 1970).

On the basis of blood group and haptoglobin studies in seven villages in each of two South American tribes, Neel (1970) reports that the differences in gene frequencies between villages are almost as great (85.7 and 92.5 percent as large) as those between twelve different Indian tribes scattered throughout Central and South America. Neel ascribes the intervillage variability to random genetic drift and to the **founder effect** (chance variation in the small original population). He points especially to *fission-fusion,* by which new villages are split from old (fission) by a group of related individuals (fusion).

## Increase in Population Size

Granted that small groups do come to have different gene frequencies—to evolve in various directions—how, one might ask, could this evolution result in major geographic groups with large numbers of people? Obviously, this development would require a substantial expansion in the group through natural increase without the group losing its genetic isolation. Some anthropologists and geneticists consider such population explosion an unlikely event, and hence minimize the significance of random genetic drift. Although admitting the possibility of chance variations, they would deny its importance. In some cases, however, unknown but specific historical influences probably led to just such rapid increases in population. If so, deviant gene frequencies that had resulted from genetic drift could have become fixed in the population of continents or other large areas of the world. For example, on a smaller scale, the people of the Bass Strait Islands, Tristan da Cunha, and Pitcairn have each multiplied more than tenfold; they crowd their little islands, despite the fact that many members of each group have emigrated (Birdsell, 1957; Roberts, 1968).

Similarly, the members of one German-speaking religious sect who settled in the United States and Canada increased from 443 to 8,542 within 70 years (Eaton and Mayer, 1953) and now number about 15,000 people who have descended from only 91 founders (Martin, 1970). The conditions that led to their increase—high incidence of early marriage and group rather than individual responsibility for the children—are present in many peoples. The religious isolates in the United States have available excellent medical attention (with consequent low infant death rates) and yet, until recently, firmly rejected offsetting attitudes common in the American way of life such as late marriage and birth control. Since these isolates differ genetically on the average from other people about them, their way of life with its high rate of natural increase of population has been an historical evolutionary force. Similarly, only a few thousand French ever left France to settle Canada, yet there are now over six million French Canadians, and the French-Canadian gene pool (presumably little changed from that of the immigrants) has largely replaced that of the American Indian in vast areas of Quebec and other provinces.

The enormous relative increase in the world frequency of blondness, light skin color, and blood group $A_2$, which presumably occurred during the centuries of European expansion, can be understood more easily in terms of the development of machines and weapons by Europeans than in terms of the biology of pigmentation and blood. The reversal of the trend to increases in those traits that are most frequent in Europeans and the tendency of other characteristics to increase must also be understood in terms of the introduction of modern medicine in formerly backward areas. Relative to the large effects of modern medicine, sanitation, and birth control, any hereditary differences in fecundity and in natural resistance to fatal diseases probably play a small part, if any, in determining the growth in size of one population rather than another. Whereas differential fertility and mortality within a population may be largely determined by biological differences and social selection, those between populations largely involve the relative effectiveness of their respective technologies (Hulse 1957b, 1968).

Finally, in order to explain the major geographic groups, it is not necessary to postulate a large number of instances in which populations grew inordinately. The number of major racial groups recognized is modest, albeit somewhat indeterminate (Garn and Coon, 1955). On the other hand, the number of human population isolates has been relatively large ever since early **paleolithic** times, and expansion of only a small fraction of them would account for the subsequent racial distributions. The remaining isolates under these circumstances would have become extinct or, more probably, would have merged at a time when their numbers were relatively small, so that their incorporation into wider populations would have had little effect. Small remnant populations submerged in large widespread populations have little effect on the gene frequences of the new mixed group. The further a ripple in a gene pool spreads the lower the height of the ripple.

The examples I have cited of random genetic drift established in a small original population that later expanded are examples of the founder effect. Populations are subject to similar influences at any time their numbers drop. These episodes are called *population bottlenecks*. As the effective population size decreases, the effect of random genetic drift increases disproportionately: episodes of reduction therefore have a disproportionately great significance.

## Migration

The fourth factor influencing change in gene frequencies in the genetic pool is usually listed as *migration*. Migration in this sense is the introduction of genes from outside the **breeding population.** It can function, of course, only when the breeding population is not a completely closed unit. Migration is therefore a factor in all populations, but is not a direct factor in gene frequency changes within the gene pool of the whole human species. Indirectly, as explained previously, migration between the isolates of a partially subdivided species may spread and combine adaptations achieved by random genetic drift and selection in its isolates to produce major adaptive evolutionary changes in the whole species. In monkeys hybrids between different species are frequent in captivity (Chiarelli, 1973; Bernstein, 1974) and sometimes occur even in the wild (Aldrich-Blake, 1968; Bernstein, 1968; Dunbar and Dunbar, 1974); gene flow between species undistrubed by outside cataclysmic changes (such as decimation at our hands) must be rare, however. Interspecific gene flow is rarely considered in discussions of evolution and is unlikely to be an ordinary influence on gene frequencies. It is, however, a possible mechanism of genetic modification among incipient or closely related species.

In the island model of population structure the gene pools are of isolates and the migration is measured as *admixture* per generation. In the model of isolation by distance, however, migration can be viewed as a **gene flow,** a constant gradual diffusion between regions with different gene frequencies.

Since migration can be a significant factor only if there are subpopulations or isolates with distinctive gene pools, it may be simpler to discuss the obverse of migration, that is, degree of isolation. As noted above, both geographic and sociocultural factors lead individuals usually to mate within a group (the breeding population) that shares a common gene pool. From the point of view of the wider general population, mates within the isolated subpopulation are more likely to share genetic characteristics than mates drawn at random from the larger group. Isolation thus tends to further homogamous (positive) **assortative mating**—a match in which a particular characteristic of one mate tends to be associated with the same characteristic in the other mate. When factors in mate selection override propinquity, they are usually based on strong sociocultural bonds and thus also often constitute homogamous assortative mating. Thus, the barrier of physical distance was surmounted in favor of social vicinity after repeal of the Chinese Exclusion Law and passage of the so-called "Bride's Act" of 1947. Some 6,000 young Chinese-Americans rushed to China to marry before the right to bring Chinese-born wives to the United States expired in December 1949. Most of the men went to the very districts where their ancestors had lived, and sought introductions through the usual family channels; they married the very girls they might have married had their fathers never left home. Similarly the Samaritans, never more than a few hundred people, were divided into two tiny groups, one in Israel, one in Jordan, by the division of Palestine, but marriage between these groups has no doubt resumed. Since the blood group frequencies are somewhat different for Samaritans and other Near Eastern peoples, the likelihood of having the same blood groups in mates is higher in these Samaritan couples than it would be in random mixed marriages with other Israelis or Jordanians (Bonné, 1963).

Assortative mating may also be a deliberate choice of mates with similar physical characteristics. Despite the common supposition to the contrary, it is rarely opposites who attract. Assortative mating has two effects: (1) it narrows the number of potential mates and thus limits the size of the effective breeding population; (2) if the similarities are in genetic characteristics, the marriages between persons who are alike disrupts the overall Hardy-Weinberg equilibrium. Preferential mating between like genotypes increases the ratio of homozygotes to heterozygotes. Some populations are divided into separate endogamous castes (groups within the large society who are expected to marry among themselves). When the castes have different gene frequencies the overall increase in the proportion of homozygotes is called the **Wahlund effect** after a Swedish geneticist of that name. If one conducted a large survey of blood groups in the United States one might well find that although the blood group genotype frequencies of Blacks and Whites considered separately were each in Hardy-Weinberg equilibrium, the whole population would show a deficiency of heterozygotes. The Wahlund effect is exactly analogous to the inbreeding effect and can be thought of as a special kind of inbreeding.

## Summary

Random genetic drift is a change in gene frequency caused by the sampling of each generation's gene pool to establish that of the next. In small populations with little migration it may even lead to fixation of a gene by elimination of alleles. In conjunction with natural selection and fluctuation in population size, random genetic drift may have considerable evolutionary influence. Inbreeding, division of the population, and homogamous assortative mating (mating between like individuals) also increase the proportion of homozygotes to heterozygotes.

# CHAPTER 9

# HUMAN ADAPTATION

**Adaptation** is the name given to the series of changes by which organisms surmount the challenges to life. In the broadest sense, biological adaptation encompasses every essential biological process: biochemical, physiological, and genetic. Adaptation can therefore be involved in (1) major evolutionary events, (2) the growth of the individual, and (3) behavioral and physiological changes lasting only hours or minutes. Biological adaptation covers both functional processes and the structures on which they depend. It differs from human biology as a whole chiefly by being limited in its concern to the ways in which the organism relates to the circumstances it must meet to live.

Adaptation implies its antithesis: if one way of functioning is adaptative, another is less adaptive or maladaptive under comparable circumstances. The ability to speed up the heart and respiration rates when one runs is adaptive since it increases the available energy and therefore permits many lifesaving activities such as escape from danger or catching prey. Inability to perform such activities would be relatively maladaptive since it would greatly limit one's mode of life. Adaptive selection is the central theme of the Darwinian theory of evolution—the natural selection of better-adapted organisms and the extinction of the less well adapted through earlier death or reduced fertility. In this sense adaptation is a modification in structure or function that enables an organism to survive and reproduce. The term can apply to a particular organ or the whole individual and to entire populations or the whole species.

Adaptive selection has already been mentioned in connection with changes in, and maintenance of, gene frequencies. It will be further considered in respect to the evolution of different kinds of animals. The more different from each other two individuals or species are, the more able we are to identify the relation of the anatomical differences to different behavior and different adaptation to the environment. Conversely, the peoples of the world today are so similar that it is often very difficult to relate specific structural differences to the specific environmental differences humans encounter throughout the world. The people of both Northwest and Southwest Europe have relatively narrow **(dolichocephalic)** heads, whereas those of the East and Alpine regions have relatively broad **(brachycephalic)** heads, yet among all the proposed explanations no adaptive advantage for either in its own zone has been demonstrated. Nevertheless, questions of differential adaptation remain among the most pressing and the most practical facing human biology today. Are different populations differentially adapted to the differing environments in which they live? Human ecology is concerned with our relation to plant and animal resources and human adaptation to these and to altitude, cold, heat, and the concomitants of migration.

## Altitude Adaptation

Human adaptation to high altitudes involves a relatively small fraction of the world's population. Only about 25 million people (that is less than 1 in 100 of the world's people) live at high elevations. The "thin air" (low atmospheric oxygen pressure) at high altitudes (Fig. 9-1) presents an environmental problem that could not be modified by human inventions until the present century, when bottled oxygen and other such therapies became available for treating mountain sickness. Nevertheless, the way humans live in the mountains is interrelated with their biological response to conditions there (Clegg et al., 1970). People living in the mountains, like those elsewhere, use drugs such as alcohol and coca (the plant that yields the narcotic, cocaine) to lessen their psychological burden. This may alter the nature of their response to the altitude stress and hence affect the impact of the conditions. However, the extent to which these drugs ameliorate the physiological as well as the psychological burden of the altitude seems to be slight (Hanna, 1970, 1971; Little, 1970), although consumption of alcohol can raise the foot temperature of the highland Indians and increase their comfort during the cold of night, and coca also has a mild stimulating effect.

When individuals climb from sea level to an elevation of four thousand meters or more there are large differences in the extent of the response, and some individuals may even die of pulmonary edema. However, a usual response is an increased rate of breathing, an increased pulse rate under

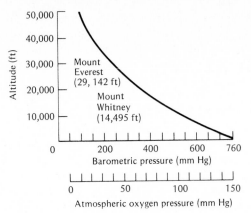

FIG. 9-1   Life at high altitudes involves adaptation to a reduced amount of oxygen. The availability of oxygen is measured by its pressure, calculated as the height in millimeters of a column of mercury (mm Hg) it would support. The oxygen pressure is always proportional to the barometric pressure (about 20 percent of the barometric pressure is atmospheric pressure of oxygen). Barometric pressure falls off with altitude, more rapidly at altitudes above 10,000 feet (about two miles). Changes in respiration, in circulation, in the blood, and even in behavior tend to compensate and occur in human adaptation to high altitudes. Redrawn from A. Vander, J. H. Sherman, and D. Luciano: *Human physiology: The mechanisms of body function.* New York: McGraw-Hill, copyright 1970. Reproduced by permission.

comparable work loads, physical and mental fatigue, interrupted sleep, headaches, and sometimes digestive disturbances and weight loss. After a few days at that altitude there is some short-run "adaptation," including increase in hemoglobin concentrations, but there still are difficulties in working. Families who continue to live there incur increased risks of miscarriages, birth defects, and infant deaths. Individuals reared at these elevations achieve more adequate adaptation and the risks are lower. Those born into populations genetically adapted to the altitude apparently do still better. M. T. Newman and C. Collazos (1957), P. T. Baker (1969), and C. Hoff (1974) report that in the Peruvian Andes growth and skeletal maturation is retarded; the consequent relative stunting is possibly an advantage. Chest measurements do not follow this trend toward small dimensions, however, and A. R. Frisancho (1969, 1975; Frisancho and Baker, 1970) and Hoff (1974) have shown that high-altitude Indian boys in Peru, while developing more slowly than coastal dwellers in other respects, develop a larger thorax and greater lung capacity. Differences in pulmonary function are not found in all studies, however, and apparently do not occur in adults. The right ventricle of the heart, the part that pumps oxygenated blood throughout the body, is also relatively larger in high-altitude populations.

Mountain dwellers thus show the three chief modalities of adaptation: (1) short-run physiological changes; (2) modifications during growth and development; and (3) modification of the gene pool of the population. It is probable that the well-adapted mountain dweller suffers some relative shortcomings when at sea level, but since the Indians who migrate from the Andes to the cities on the coast suffer some of the same kind of social disabilities that Appalachian Mountain folk do in the cities of the United States, analysis of purely biological status is complicated by the concomitants of social status, and the results of studies of such people are difficult to interpret.

One example of the fact that good genetic adaption at one elevation may be bad at another is the case of **sickle-cell** and **thalassemia** traits (see Chapter 7). As noted earlier, heterozygosis confers a degree of immunity to endemic malaria, which is usually worse in some low-lying areas, but at very high elevations even the heterozygotes may have hemolytic crises; that is, they may show the same sort of symptoms as patients with sickle-cell anemia and thalassemia.

# Cold Adaptation

Arctic dwellers provide another example of adaptations. In the Arctic, however, people build houses, wear clothes, and light fires. These cultural traits constitute the predominant adaptations, and they are available for anyone to borrow. For example, the Eskimos have designed fine arctic clothing, and European and American explorers have copied their parkas and mukluks. Furthermore, Eskimos have developed behavioral patterns to meet crises. W. S. Laughlin (1968) and others are contributing much to our knowledge of Eskimo adaptations. Behavioral adaptation is exemplified by an Eskimo who fell into the water. His companion immediately shared half his dry clothing—enough to get both men home, cold but alive.

Despite cultural adaptations, there are times when biological differences count. P. T. Baker (1960) gives an example of the Yahgan at the cold southern tip of South America: it is not that poorly adapted natives die of exposure in snow storms while their better-adapted companions survive, he says; rather, the maladapted group might die of starvation huddled at their campfire while members of the well-adapted counterpart comfortably collect shellfish in the frigid water. Thus, cultural modes (including in this case fire, but little clothing) modify the conditions under which what is probably a genetic adaptation operates. To study cold adaptation in humans one must take account of indoor as well as outdoor temperatures and also activities, clothing, and shelter, and the culturally dictated modes of behavior. For example, other groups than the Yahgan find that with stored food they do not need to stand in cold water. Until recently the Caribou Eskimo killed enough animals in a few days during the caribou migration to last all year unspoiled in the natural arctic deep freeze.

In any case, some degree of cold adaptation is needed in high latitudes. For life, humans must maintain a core temperature close to 37°C (Figs. 9-2, 9-3). In the cold we do this by reducing circulation to the extremities (which therefore drop to lower temperatures than the trunk) (Fig. 9-4). But the vessels of the

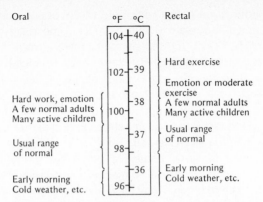

Oral       °F   °C    Rectal

FIG. 9-2 Estimated range of body temperature in normal human beings. Both Farenheit (F) and Celsius (C) scales are shown. Note that the usual range of normal is a little lower in the mouth (more similar to skin temperature) than in the rectum (core temperature). As is always the case in physical anthropology, any measurement such as body temperature varies with conditions, with the individuals, and sometimes between groups. Many studies in human biology involve the establishment of averages, ranges, and other statistics, and of the conditions that determine or modify them. As in the case of body temperature, such standards are of direct importance in the practice of medicine. Redrawn from E. F. DuBois, *Fever and the regulation of body temperature.* Springfield, Illinois: Charles C Thomas, 1948. Reproduced by permission.

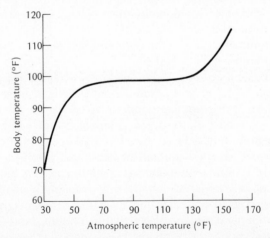

FIG. 9-3 At very low temperatures the core temperature of the body falls and death from cold exposure may follow. At very high temperatures the body temperature goes up and the subject may die in a fever. Over wide ranges of environmental temperatures—from about 60 to 130 degrees Fahrenheit—inside the clothing, the body successfully adapts and the temperature remains steady at about 98.6°F in most individuals. Redrawn from A. C. Guyton, *Textbook of medical physiology.* Philadelphia: Saunders, 1971. Reproduced by permission.

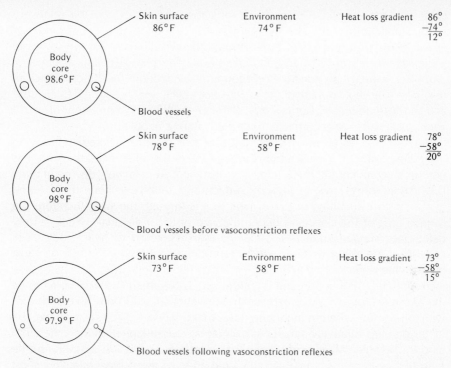

FIG. 9-4   In humans the body core temperature remains almost constant at approximately 98.6 °F. As an example of the way a person adapts to cold, a nude person in a warm room has a skin temperature (86°), between that of the air around him (74°) and his body core (98.6°). The difference between his skin temperature and the air (the heat loss gradient) is moderate (12°) and the heat loss is made up by burning food (metabolism).

As the temperature in the room drops to 58°F (middle) the core temperature drops little (98°), and the skin temperature drops more, but the heat loss gradient increases (20°) and has to be made up by metabolism.

As the room stays cold (bottom) the blood vessels become small (vasoconstriction) and the skin becomes a better insulator. The core temperature remains almost the same (97.9°) but the skin temperature drops (to 73°) so the heat loss gradient is reduced (to 15°) and the amount of heat to be made up by metabolism is reduced.

In freezing cold the blood vessels occasionally open up and close again. This is called cycling and reduces the likelihood of frost bite.

extremities periodically dilate; this cold-induced "cycling" is a widespread phenomenon among mammals and must be adaptive in some way (perhaps through decreased chance of frostbite) although it costs loss of stored heat. Body heat is generated by metabolizing food, burning it up as fuel. Shivering is an involuntary activity that increases the production of heat. All peoples of all places respond to cold in much the same ways. However, some people from cold climates (notably the Central Australian aborigines) have been reported to meet cold sleeping conditions by having the extremities cool off relatively more than the trunk, and also by having lower core temperatures (Schonlander et al., 1958). The subjects of these studies chewed tobacco and the leaves of *Duboisia,* which contain an alkaloid poison. The pharmacological effect of *Duboisia,* rather than genetic constitution, may account for the difference in response. The short-run adaptations differ somewhat in those inured to the cold and in those new to it, but it is not definitely known to what extent (if at all) genetic capacity for acclimatization differs among peoples.

In other species of animals arctic forms tend to differ in predictable ways from those found in more southerly areas. One of the differences, thick fur, has no human counterpart. The Eskimos, for instance, are relatively devoid of body hair. Arctic forms have small body surface area relative to body mass. Some heat is lost in breathing but most heat loss is through the skin; therefore the surface area of the skin (and hence the size of the individual, which largely determines surface area) is a factor in the dissipation of heat. Body mass consists of metabolizing tissues (which produce heat) and fat (much of it just beneath the skin where it may help insulate); hence, increases of weight cause increased heat production and retention. M. T. Newman (1961) applied to us the two rules (or laws) that express these relationships of body size and form with temperature. **Bergmann's rule** states that in bodies of the same shape, the larger one has relatively smaller surface area; cold-adapted animals therefore tend to be large. **Allen's rule** states that short extremities further increase the ratio of mass to surface area and that cold-adapted forms have relatively short limbs. General human body size, as measured by weight or stature, is, on the average, correlated with climate—especially with the temperature in the coldest month.

In continuous populations of large land areas of the Northern Hemisphere, including China, Europe, and the contiguous states of the United States, there is a gradient from larger average size in the north to smaller in the south (Coon, 1939; Lasker, 1941; Newman and Munro, 1955). Nevertheless, these dimensions vary considerably in any one place, and there are numerous exceptions to Bergmann's rule. For instance, Eskimos are squat and have relatively short limbs but are generally small. Some people of East Africa provide an instructive example; they are very tall but slim and their limbs are exceptionally long (Hiernaux, 1968; Roberts and Bainbridge, 1963). In any case, Roberts (1953) showed that the relationship of weight to climate applies on a world scale; Schreider (1951, 1953) extended this to the ratio of surface area to weight; and Newman (1961) concluded that temperature accounts for almost 80 percent of the variance in average body mass of different populations throughout the world, when an appropriate allowance for stature is included.

In humans in general, tall stature is achieved primarily by growth of the limbs (trunk length being much less variable). The real test of the applicability of the rules of Bergmann and Allen to us should, therefore, come in genetically determined tendencies to depart from this nutritionally determined pattern, and to find large size with short limbs in the Arctic and short stature with long limbs in the tropics.

Other details of morphology may also relate to heat balance. Nose form seems to be adapted to the degree of need to moisten the air one inhales. Noses are narrower in colder zones. Nasal dimensions correlate with degree of prognathism (protrusion of the jaws) and with shape of the dental arch. Although this complicates interpretation somewhat, the average ratio of the width to the length of the nose (nasal index) of populations throughout the world is highly correlated with climate—especially with vapor pressure, the amount of moisture in a given amount of air—and there is little doubt that different shapes of nose must be selectively advantageous in different climates (Glanville, 1969; Weiner, 1954; Wolpoff, 1968a). Of the various Mongoloid peoples, Eskimos have the narrowest noses. It is unwise to assume that every morphological feature found in Eskimos is directly a protection against cold, however. For instance, the large, broad Mongoloid face of the Eskimo is more exposed to cold than the smaller face of the European, but frostbite of the face is rarely serious in either people (Steegmann, 1967, 1970).

High altitudes are also cold, and altitude studies must deal with the influence of both altitude and temperature. Some individuals adapted to altitude and cold maintain warmer hands and feet than nonadapted controls (Little et al., 1971). This may serve to maintain more oxygen in these tissues as well as meet the challenge of low temperature in a different way than at sea level (Baker, 1969).

## Heat Adaptation

The regulation of human responses to excessive heat involves at least two distinct types of environment—dry heat and humid heat. When a person works hard in a hot place where either the temperature is extreme, the humidity is high, or the sunlight is excessive, the temperature-regulation system of the body is put under strain. However, after about a week of acclimatization to repeated heat stress the subject acquires more tolerance for these conditions through increased sweating; the degree of cardiovascular strain then decreases (Weiner, 1964).

Most species of primates live in tropical forest environments. In the view of many, our ancestors at one stage also lived in a hot, humid zone with little movement of air but also little direct sunlight. Under those circumstances the heat is well tolerated during rest but hard work produces heat stress.

Essentially nothing is known concerning when our progenitors began to have such bald bodies or whether this antedated the invention of clothing. In dry open country near the Equator, where it is possible that our progenitors evolved their upright posture and a hunting–gathering economy, sweat evaporates more readily than in the humid tropics but sunlight on us and on the objects about us adds a severe radiant heat load to the problems of heat adaptation. Russell Newman (1970) has speculated on the body-temperature mechanism we evolved under these circumstances. Sweating remains important. Wool protects against direct sunlight, but hair encourages sweat dripping, which carries away less heat than does evaporation. The upright posture reduces the surface area exposed to direct sunlight compared to that of a quadruped. Whether hair, at least long straight hair, could be an added protection against heat is problematical. In any case nakedness would have prevented us from adapting to life under desertlike conditions until we achieved ready access to water through use of vessels or had learned to wear loose clothing of some sort. Humans cannot drink very much water at one time but can sweat more per hour than any other mammal so far tested. Before we learned how to carry water with us, human occupation of open plains and savanna therefore required behavior that would make it easy to reach drinking water frequently. Archaeological studies show that early humans often camped near water and relied on their weapons to defend themselves from the predators that frequent water holes. Today, people in dry regions remember for years where water had been found during a drought and know of plant roots and other sources to use in emergencies.

We are unique in our heat-adaptive mechanisms. There is little innate difference between human groups in their ability to respond to heat stress, and short-term acclimatization aside, there is little evidence of population differences. Since heat absorption and dissipation are surface phenomena, the search for possible population differences is logically concentrated on the area of the skin and the nature of its structures: pigment granules, hair, and sweat glands. Groups inhabiting the tropics are, as already noted, generally of small individuals. This increases the surface area relative to mass so that heat produced by activity can be more readily dissipated. Although even moderate activity in a hot environment normally results in some heat storage, excess heat must be dissipated sooner or later, and this is more significant than the somewhat greater capacity for heat storage of larger individuals. Desert-dwellers are generally lean, another way of increasing the relative surface area and therefore, perhaps, of facilitating heat dissipation through sweating.

Pigment is not a simple question. Inhabitants of equatorial zones are dark. This is true of Melanesia, Australia, South India, and Africa, although in other respects the peoples of these areas are very different. Common adaptive modification rather than closely related origins therefore accounts for the similarity in skin color. Numerous theories have been advanced to explain why dark skin color is adaptive in hot climates, and there is still no general agreement. Although light skin reflects more radiant heat, dark skin must protect the body better. Among other things, dark skin inhibits sunburn and sunburn interferes with the sweating response. Dark skin is also less susceptible to skin cancer (which can be a result of overexposure to the sun), is perhaps less attractive to vectors of diseases, and may prevent the synthesis of too much vitamin D, which can be harmful (Daniels et al., 1972; Loomis, 1967). Pigment prevents the ultraviolet rays of sunshine from penetrating the skin to the level where vitamin D is synthesized by their action. In zones with much sun in the summer and little in the winter, the ability to tan in summer would therefore be an advantage. Marjorie Lee and I (1959) exposed individuals of various groups to an ultraviolet lamp and measured tanning by changes in the amount of light reflected from the skin. We found that the capacity to tan varies considerably among individuals—even among those with similar initial pigmentation. Light skin, on the other hand, may be less susceptible to cold injury: Post et al. (1971) have shown that spotted guinea pigs get less frostbite on their white skin areas than on their dark areas. Furthermore, data from two world wars and the Korean War suggest that darker pigmented persons may be more susceptible to frostbite than lightly pigmented persons and this may have exerted selective pressure favoring light pigmentation in regions with frigid climates.

The chief pigment of the skin is melanin (Fig. 9-5). Livingstone (1969b) showed by computer simulation that, on the assumption that control of its

FIG. 9-5   Hopi albino girl with two other Hopi girls, photographed during the period 1897–1900. Albinism is the inability to synthesize pigment (melanin) in the hair, skin, and eyes. It occurs occasionally in all human populations and is inherited as a recessive. The gene for albinism is not equally frequent in all populations, however, and is not so rare in some American Indian tribes as it is in other peoples. Courtesy of the Field Museum of Natural History, Chicago, Illinois.

production is polygenic but based on few alleles at few loci, one can explain the skin color distributions one encounters in going from north to south in Europe, the Near East, and Africa, if there is a small differential advantage of presence of dark color in tropical Africa and vice versa in Europe. His calculations also include the assumptions of some migrations between populations. Such computer "models," as they are called, do not prove that selection under the stated conditions is the basis of the skin color distribution, but they do show that adaptive natural selection for skin color reasonably accounts for it. Low rates of selection and recent migration are consistent with the fact that after some hundreds of years, Europeans in the tropics are still light and Blacks in the United States are still dark. After several thousand years, however, American Indians in the tropics are slightly darker than those of North America, to about the extent Livingstone's calculations would predict. Furthermore, the selective advantages postulated in the model are of a relatively low order, so it is hardly surprising that we still lack direct evidence of the nature and amount of selection that takes place.

The role of human differences in hair in respect to heat tolerance is hard to calculate. Sheep with thick wool can thereby stand very heavy exposure to direct sunlight. Perhaps the retention of head hair in human beings is related to the crown of the head being the most exposed part in the noonday sun, but the influence of hair of different color and form remains to be established experimentally.

It was once believed that Blacks have more efficient or more numerous sweat glands than Whites. Careful counts of areas of skin show no such thing. The only known difference is that obese individuals—Black or White—have fewer sweat glands per given area of skin than thin individuals do. Persons of different body build seem to have approximately the same total number of sweat glands, however (Knip, 1969). After all, ability to maintain body temperature at a constant level is as important to an Eskimo trotting beside his sled dogs as it is to a Bedouin astride his camel.

## Nutritional Adaptation

Nutritional adaptation not only depends on the resources available but also on the mode and degree of utilization. The utilization of food resources is a culturally determined matter. Hunters, fishermen, and food collectors select only a portion of the available foodstuffs. In any one place the limited knowledge and culturally determined technology of the group also restrict farmers and herders to the use of a very small number of edible species. We still know relatively little about differences between populations in nutritional requirements. There do seem to be some inherent differences of this kind. Size itself is the most significant variable. Furthermore, basal metabolic rate seems to be inherently high in populations that have always had a diet of good quality, and low in some poorly nourished populations. Thus, in one region in southern China where a meager diet has been reported, 90 percent of which is from grain (mostly polished rice), basal metabolic rates are low. Neither the immediate diet nor that usual in the population explains all the variability in metabolic rates, however (Roberts, 1952). M. T. Newman (1961), in considering human bodily adjustments to nutrition, reports several instances where the ingestion of necessary nutrients is a very small fraction of the supposed minimal requirements. He concludes that tolerances must vary over the world and that some human populations have adapted to levels of intake that would be fatal to others. On the other hand, ability to get by on less food may be more general. Throughout history most populations of the world have been subjected to repeated famines, and the species must therefore have adaptive mechanisms to meet food shortages.

In addition, time apparently has been adequate for some special adaptations in subpopulations. For example, difficulty in digesting milk sugar (lactose) has been reported as occurring more frequently in some populations than others, and the Chinese, whose cultural practices do not include use of milk from domestic animals, have a high rate of lactose intolerance (Davis and Bolin, 1967; Huang and Bayless, 1968; McCracken, 1971); symptoms from ingesting monosodium glutamate ("Accent"), on the other hand, have not been reported in those who have used this cooking powder for many generations, but have been in Americans, who call it "the Chinese restaurant syndrome" (Schaumburg et al., 1969). One takes it for granted, on theoretical grounds at least, that where specific nutrients are scarce, populations with lower natural requirements for them would thrive, but this must be a minor advantage compared to the possession of adaptive cultural practices for acquiring such nutrients.

A meager supply of food (hypocaloric diet) often occurs in the very environments, the tropics, where soils are leached of minerals and foods of animal origin are scarce. Furthermore, the food ingested must often feed parasites as well as the person. Thus, the increase in weight from tropics to frigid zones, noted earlier under consideration of Bergmann's rule, may be a response to nutritional stress as well as to cold and heat stresses.

As I have noted, nutritional stress also occurs at high altitudes. R. B. Thomas (1971, in press), in a recent study still not fully published, has studied the energy flow (caloric consumption) in the Andean human ecology, and finds that it is always low and frequently disrupted. Thomas finds that in these circumstances slow growth might operate to maintain small size of individuals. It is well to bear in mind, however, that the same energy flow can be maintained with larger individuals if there are fewer of them and the land is less densely populated.

## Plasticity

The adaptations so far discussed are mostly of two kinds; those genetically entrenched in the population by repeated natural selection and those dependent on a capacity to acclimatize in the short run (whether the capacity is equally shared by all subpopulations of the species or not). There is also a third, intermediate, type of adaptation: modification of an individual during his period of growth and development. It may be thought of as a special case of acclimatization, but, since the process is essentially irreversible after adulthood, it deserves separate consideration and it may be separately designated as **plasticity.**

Early in the present century some anthropologists first asked whether the traits that were being used to characterize races could be influenced directly by environmental factors. They did not refer to the theory of inheritance of acquired characteristics, which had already been discredited; nor did they mean Darwin's description of the selective power of the natural environment. The question was: Would people grow up to be physically different if they lived differently? In 1905, Walcher, a German obstetrician, showed that when babies are regularly placed on the backs of their heads, they become broader-headed than do babies who are customarily placed on their sides. In the same year, M. Fishberg compared measurements of the cephalic index (the ratio of head breadth to head length) and stature of Jews in various parts of Europe and in the United States and found that the two groups differed in these respects from each other. If cephalic index and stature could change in immigrants of at least one European group, how could these measurements be used as major criteria of race?

At this time many Americans were concerned with the assimilation of immigrants. Franz Boas (1910) exploited this concern in getting support from the United States Immigration Commission for a survey of the physical measurements of immigrants. Whatever may have been the expectations of the Commission, Boas characteristically set himself a concrete problem and defined it operationally. Are the American-born children of European immigrants significantly different from their parents in such characteristics as cephalic index and stature? If so, do they also differ in the same respects from their immigrant brothers and sisters? Of the various groups Boas studied, his largest samples were of Central European Jews and of Italians from Sicily. In both groups the American-born offspring tended to be taller than their parents; but in the Jews the cephalic index decreased, and in the Sicilians it increased. The measurements of the immigrant brothers and sisters, correlation with the length of the time the parents had been in the United States, and smaller studies of other nationalities led to the conclusion that the changes were the result of some aspect of the American environment that tends to bring about an American type with tall stature and medium cephalic index.

Some anthropologists attempted to explain Boas' findings on the basis of some selection, perhaps a self-selection of immigrants. To examine the possibility of such selection of immigrants, as well as the possibility of changes in the offspring of immigrants, H. L. Shapiro (1931, 1939), in collaboration with F. S. Hulse and W. A. Lessa, both graduate students at the time, undertook studies of two national groups in Hawaii, the Chinese and Japanese. In addition to these groups—both immigrants and those born in Hawaii—the studies included individuals who never left their place of birth in China and Japan, for whom Shapiro coined the word "sedentes." Of the Chinese study only a brief preliminary report ever appeared; the Japanese study, however, has been fully published. The Japanese born in Hawaii were taller and broader-headed, and they differed significantly from Japanese immigrants in this and numerous other respects. However, the immigrants were also different from the sedentes in many dimensions—including many in which those born in Hawaii differed from the immigrants. Shapiro explained the difference between sedentes and migrants on the basis of selection, and that between migrants and Hawaiian-born persons on the basis of factors in the environment during the growth period. The general findings of both Boas and Shapiro have been confirmed by a number of studies (Ito, 1942; Lasker, 1946; Thieme, 1957).

Nevertheless, a number of problems remain. In the various studies, the immigrants measured were older than the subjects born in America, and to some extent this fact might explain the differences. There is a tendency for individuals to decrease somewhat in height after the age of thirty or so, and, in addition, people have been getting taller from generation to generation all over the world; for example, both in Japan and the United States, adult sons are taller than their fathers (and also taller than their fathers were at the same age). Such increases have been going on for 100 years and possibly for 200 or more years. Bowles (1932) has shown that Harvard sons of Harvard fathers were taller than their fathers were at the same age. The sons are larger in most other bodily measurements also; markedly so in the length of their thighs and forearms. Damon (1968) followed some of these same families for four generations and found no further increase in stature in the last generations, however, and he suggested that it is a straw in the wind that the increase in height of each succeeding generation has ended for economically favored American men. Similarly, Froehlich (1970) finds the tendency for increased size to have ended for Japanese men in Hawaii after one American-born generation, but among women in Hawaii size increases were more gradual and extended one more generation.

To take account of secular trends as well as the effects of migration, M. S. Goldstein (1943), a student of Boas, undertook a study in Mexico of Mexican parents and their adult children and a parallel study of Mexican immigrants to the United States and their adult American-born children. He found that the immigrants were larger in the usual respects than the sedentes, that the younger adults in Mexico were larger than their like-sexed parents, and that those born in the United States were larger than their parents. The last difference was the most pronounced, however, and seemed to indicate a growth factor that is especially strong in the United States.

Subsequent studies of Mexicans have confirmed that Mexicans who grow up in the United States are taller and larger in other ways than those brought up in Mexico and that this is not the result of initial differences between those who migrate and those who do not (Lasker, 1952, 1954; Lasker and Evans, 1961).

On the other hand, studies of Italian Swiss in Italy and California by Hulse (1957a, 1968) demonstrate: (1) plasticity in response to environmental conditions that are different in two locations, and (2) a tendency for those whose mother and father were born in different communities (exogamous mating) to be larger than those whose parents were both born in the same community (endogamous mating). This finding is confirmed in some but not in all other studies of the effect of endogamy on the eventual size of the offspring.

What is there in the environment of the United States that accounts for the greater growth here? The pattern of plastic changes is constant in all the studies of migrants, but such studies do not isolate specific causes (Kaplan, 1954). Nevertheless, there is little evidence of significant influences of variation in temperature, altitude, or hygiene. The biggest single factor is diet, and the most significant aspect of food is not the quality nor the vitamin content, but simply the quantity. In the United States, despite much propaganda from the food and drug industries to the contrary, hypercaloric (overabundant) diets are apparently more of a problem for the health of more people than any shortage or dietary deficiency. Overeating is an increasing problem, because Americans expend less and less of the food energy they consume. Coronary heart disease and other circulatory disorders are one of the chief causes of death, and the life insurance companies have found that, on the average, persons of normal weight for height live longer than the overweight and that underweight individuals live still longer.

Large body size would seem to be an advantage in the face of hypercaloric diets; the extra size achieved during growth would provide a larger frame and more metabolizing tissue to consume high-caloric diets in adulthood without creating an excess that can only turn to fat. This may be as important as a small size achieved through the growth period is to an adult who must survive on a diet of very few calories per day. But there are other factors in the equation. Individuals adjust their food intake and even in times of scarcity individuals of different size may have different abilities to acquire food. Cultural factors are important through the enforcement of various modes of food distribution and norms of rationing during shortages.

## Growth

The adaptation of organisms is not only to adult form—important as viability of adults is to the survival of the population. Each developmental stage must also be viable, of course. In humans, growth itself requires considerable nutrients and is therefore a critical part of the nutrient-energy economy. J. M. Tanner (1966) has surveyed the influence of the environment on the growth process itself. During a period of starvation, childhood growth is slower, thereby conserving food energy. But there is also a tendency for maturation to be delayed, thereby preserving the possibility of making up most of the loss if the period of deprivation is not too long and adequate food again becomes available. These temporary interruptions in growth in size with age may have little effect on body form. In virtually every country studied, growth of children was retarded as a result of the wartime food shortages of 1944–1945, but the characteristic population norms in body proportions and eventual adult size were much less, if at all, affected. For instance, Stein et al. (1975), in a large study of the hunger winter (1944–1945) in Holland, find that among young adults the only remaining untoward effect of prenatal exposure to famine (that is, famine while the mother was pregnant) was an increase in the prevalence of certain anomalies of the central nervous system; there was no detectable effect of exposure to famine on the stature, health, or mental performance; however, they also report greatly reduced fertility, retarded fetal growth, and increased risk of early death. The effects of acute famine in postnatal life also seem to be reversible, but one cannot generalize these findings to chronic starvation, which is a more complex problem.

Adverse conditions tend to retard growth, but not equally in all respects. Weight is, of course, immediately affected and height somewhat more slowly. As already noted, there is a general stunting and retardation of bony development in children in the Andes but early and marked chest development occurs. W. W. Greulich (1957) found that in Japan, children of all ages tend to be smaller than American White children in standing height, sitting height, and weight. The Japanese children are also slower in the ossification and maturation of specific bones. In these respects, however, North American-born and also Brazilian-born Japanese children approach American standards (Eveleth and de Souza Freitas, 1969).

Different criteria of maturation show different degrees of influence by nutrition and disease. Eruption of the teeth (Fig. 9-6) seems more resistant to modification than skeletal development (usually assessed by X-rays of the wrist). Sexual development, especially menarche (the age at which girls have their first menstruation), is retarded about two years in populations of lower social status or who for other reasons have poor nutrition; menarche occurs earlier as conditions ameliorate (Burrell et al., 1961; Sabharwal et al., 1966). There is always a positive correlation between different signs of growth and development, however. Growth is thus channelized by genetic factors—no doubt slightly different in different populations—and adaptation is achieved by retardation within the channel in the face of acute stresses on the growth process. When the stress is chronic there may also be some change in the channels.

Some individuals, viewing the way racial differences have been used in the past as an excuse to exploit, enslave, or even to annihilate whole populations, try to deny the existence of any adaptive differences in man. But differences exist both between individuals within the population and, on the average, between populations. Adaptive variability is a great asset to the species, and hence, at least potentially, to future generations of every population. Throughout evolutionary history, however, adaptive traits that were inherent in certain genotypes and differently distributed in various subpopulations have probably given way to species-wide plasticity—an adaptive capacity available to any member of the species if he is subjected to certain conditions during development. Plasticity in turn must tend to be supplanted by the capacity of ever-more-rapid adaptation and acclimatization. The ready reversibility of acclima-

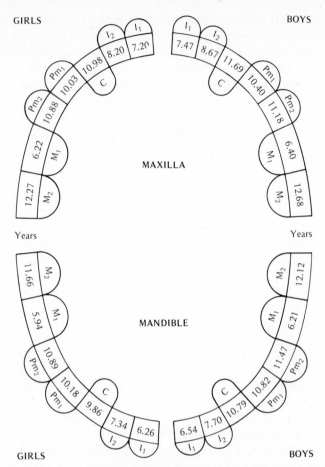

FIG. 9-6 Mean ages of emergence of the permanent teeth. The age of eruption can vary by about two years from these averages but, unlike development of bone, is not subject to as much retardation as occurs in the bones of ill or poorly nourished children. The general order of eruption varies somewhat. However, a child whose first incisors and first molars erupt earlier than the ages indicated in this chart is likely to have the rest of his permanent teeth also erupt relatively early. Redrawn from V. O. Hurme, "Standards of variation in the eruption of the first six permanent teeth." *Child Development* 19, 213–232, 1948. Reproduced by permission.

tization in the individual and of plastic traits in the subpopulation permits adaptation of genetically similar individuals in diverse environments. Thus, red cells and hemoglobin increase when one climbs up a high mountain, but decrease when one comes down; heart rate and blood pressure increase with activity or stress, but decrease with rest, and so forth. Many of these processes are especially well developed in humans, who must have found them necessary as they became one of the most widely distributed species and as they changed environments with ever-increasing rapidity.

The three modes of adaptation (selection, plasticity, and acclimatization) overlap and intergrade in populations and in individuals. The increasing importance of ready response does not eliminate selective pressures. All three modes are still operating and, in this day of rapidly changing conditions, provide a safeguard for the species. At a time when human genetic engineering is discussed and may be implemented, it is well to understand the significance of human variability and human adaptability. Social and political policies that provide opportunities for all will best accommodate varying individuals according to their biological capacities and needs.

## Summary

Adaptation is an aspect of virtually all questions of human biology. Besides their interest in evolution through adaptive selection of the Primates, including humans, physical anthropologists are concerned with biological adaptability as a human attribute. Human beings are one of the most widely distributed species. Human groups have had to adapt to altitude, cold, dry heat, humid heat, and various kinds of diet. Adaptation manifests three overlapping levels: (1) adaptive differences in the extent of inherent capacities in subpopulations long exposed to different conditions, such as differences in the inherited determinants of body form and skin pigment in peoples in different climatic zones; (2) adaptations acquired during the growth period of the individual, such as residual stunting and reduced caloric needs in individuals receiving low-caloric diets throughout childhood; and (3) reversible acclimatization to the immediate conditions, such as the changes that make it easier to work at high altitudes after the first few days there. Greater resilience to change is achieved if adaptations are reversible with each generation or within a lifetime. This implies an evolutionary tendency to shift human adaptability from genetic selection of a fixed response, to plasticity, to reversible adaptability.

CHAPTER 10

# THE CLASSIFICATION
# OF LIVING THINGS

Until the acceptance of Darwin's evolutionary idea, Nature was thought of as a Great Chain of Being ranging in perfection of form from inanimate structures through organisms of increasing complexity to man and ultimately to God. The classification of living things by Linnaeus (1758) and those who followed was therefore on the basis of similarities in complexity. Since Darwin, however, biological classification **(taxonomy)** has been largely based on evidence of common origin. Among organisms, evolutionary relationships are now generally listed under one of two headings: **cladogenesis** (branching origins) and **anagenesis** (originating up or back, that is, descendants and their linear ancestors) (See Fig. 13-1 and the example on p. 194.) Cladogenesis refers to differentiation of one line into several descending ones. Anagenesis refers to change over time within a single line.

When taxonomists classify organisms, they first use a cladistic scheme to place together forms presumed to have branched from common progenitors. But as knowledge increases and finer distinctions can be made, they will also need to separate descendants from linear predecessors; the exact point at which the division is made will arbitrarily separate offspring from their own parents. Although arbitrary, it may be just as useful as a legal definition arbitrarily distinguishing between motor bicycles and motorcycles, for instance. Differences in classification between that used here and that used by others are not matters of being correct or incorrect. Even when there is little or no difference of opinion about which forms are most closely related to each other, there may be a difference of opinion as to how to group the forms. The choice may be arbitrary but it should be compatible with what is known of the evolutionary history of the forms. There should also be no room for ambiguity as to how particular species are being classified; reuse of old terms with new meanings is, therefore, especially to be avoided by those who revise the taxonomy. In fact, it is best to follow the well-known traditional classification system except for correction of outright errors.

To define our place in nature we can start with our widest memberships and then consider our more intimate relations.

R. H. Whittaker (1969) reviewed the evolutionary relations of all organisms. He noted that bacteria and other one-celled organisms are variously classified. Today, rather than try to divide all living things into two kingdoms (plant and animal) it is more common to class the bacteria and similar organisms into a kingdom of their own—the Monera—and to add another kingdom—the Protista—for other one-celled forms. This does not imply that multicellular forms did not evolve from one-celled organisms, but it does allow one to define the animal kingdom more precisely as multicellular organisms that ingest their food. Most animals move in pursuit of food and they have evolved a sensory-neuro-motor complex that makes possible perception of food and movement to acquire it, and digestive, circulatory, and excretory complexes. Regulation of these complexes has required rapid conduction of information along nerves and self-regulating chemical feedback through internal secretions. Whittaker added that the logic of this "has led to levels of structural and functional complexity among animals which are without parallel among other organisms, and ultimately toward complexity of inherited behavior or toward intelligence." The degree of differentiation exceeds that of all other organisms. Man is thus obviously an animal: he moves and feels.

A feature of the animal kingdom—which all animals use in some generations and some (including man) use in all generations—is bisexual reproduction. That is, reproduction is not simply the production of an image of one parent but the recombination of elements inherited from two parents. Bisexual reproduction provides for the possibility of great variability. Only half of the chromosomal material of each parent is involved, and it is a chance matter which of each parent's paired genes are involved in the recombination in the offspring. In bisexual reproduction, therefore, offspring will differ from each other and from each parent. (See also Chapter 4.)

As I have said, single-celled organisms have given rise to multicelled ones with differentiated tissues. Whittaker divides these by the three ways they gain food energy into: (1) *the producers* (plants with their photosynthesis), (2) *the reducers* (fungi), and (3) *the consumers* (animals) (Fig. 10-1). Each of these functions is possible in any setting and so, in turn, there has been a tremendous

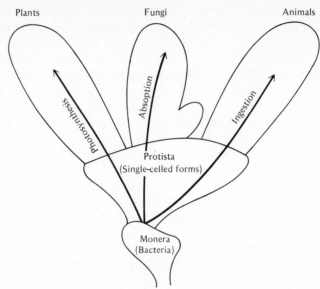

Plants       Fungi       Animals

Photosynthesis

Absoption

Ingestion

Protista
(Single-celled forms)

Monera
(Bacteria)

FIG. 10-1   Five-kingdom system of classifying organisms. Modified after Whittaker, 1969.

differentiation through evolution of variants. The evolution can be depicted as branches of a tree: cladogenic evolution. First among the evolving kingdoms, then in their divisions, and so on down, as each major adaptation has been obtained, the organisms that possess it have not only increased in numbers but also in kinds.

This subsequent diversification of a major type into species adapted to different **ecological niches** (various subsidiary aspects of the environment) is called radiation. The radiations have been compounded with each new major adaptation and the consequent cladogenic, branching, evolution can be pictured as a tree with the oldest and most fundamental modifications at the trunk while later and comparatively minor modifications characterize the twigs. It is the formation of **species** that is the critical step, however, because this is the point at which the different varieties cease to be able to breed with each other. Up to that point they may become more similar rather than more diverse with time. After two species have become reproductively isolated from each other, however, the great majority of further evolutionary changes must make them increasingly dissimilar. That is because for similar forms there are very few kinds of changes that would make them yet more similar, but there are myriads of possible changes that will add to the differences. Once the species level is passed there are no fixed measures, like the inability to breed together, for the extent of differences, but taxonomists use a hierarchical system to name the groups. Each level has a special type of name, beginning with kingdoms for the most fundamental differences achieved by the most ancient branching, and going to subspecies (or varieties or races) for the most minor distinctions. This description of formal taxonomy can be applied only after the fact. At its inception even a radically new adaptation would be classifed as "minor" in these formal terms. Many scholars think that in the case of our own species, *Homo sapiens,* a major new adaptation, the capacity for culture (see p. 186), was established relatively recently (as geological time is measured), and this is one of the reasons why our taxonomic status is still under debate.

## Chordates

The major divisions of kingdoms are called **phyla** (singular, *phylum,* meaning clan or tribe). Among the animals, the human species belongs to the phylum of the *chordates.* These animals are bilaterally symmetrical—that is, the left and right sides of the animal are, for the most part, mirror images of one another. They are distinguished by having, at some time during their life, a flexible cord, the notochord (from the Greek word *noton,* the back, where the notochord is located). Most of them also have a spinal cord; but it is the notochord, not the spinal cord, that distinguishes the phylum Chordata.

Of the chordates, the most numerous group shares still other features with us. This subphylum is the *vertebrates* and includes the fishes, amphibians, reptiles, birds, and mammals. These forms have a spinal cord with a brain at the head end. The cord and the brain form the central nervous system, which coordinates movements and sensations. In addition, vertebrates have a well-developed vertebral column (the spine) to surround and protect the spinal cord. They also have an internal skeleton of bone or cartilage that surrounds and

**Table 10-1 Classification of Homo sapiens in the animal kingdom**

| | |
|---|---|
| Kingdom | Animalia. Including multicelled, ingesting, motile, sensate organisms, among them the chordata. |
| Phylum | Chordata, most of which are vertebrata. Animals with notochords and gill slits. |
| Subphylum | Vertebrata. Fishes, amphibians, reptiles, birds, and mammals. |
| Class | Mammalia. Marsupials, egg-laying mammals, and placental mammals (Eutheria). |
| Subclass | Eutheria. Including rodents, carnivores, and primates. |
| Order | Primates. Including tarsiers, lemurs, and the anthropoidea. |
| Suborder | Anthropoidea. The Old and New World monkeys, and the Hominoidea. |
| Superfamily | Hominoidea. Including the great apes, gibbons, and the Hominidae. |
| Family | Hominidae. Including *Australopithecus* and *Homo.* |
| Genus | *Homo.* Including *Homo erectus* and *Homo sapiens.* |
| Species | *Homo sapiens.* All postglacial and some earlier populations of man. |
| Subspecies | *Homo sapiens sapiens.* Modern human beings. There is no generally accepted system of dividing *Homo sapiens into subspecies but most anthropologists think that we belong to a different subspecies than Neanderthal.* |

protects such organs as the brain and sense organs, and enables the limbs to support and move the body. The vertebrates regularly have locomotor appendages. Except for certain fish, these always consist of two pairs of limbs or, as in snakes and whales, some evidence of descent from animals that had them.

## Mammals

Subdivisions of phyla are called *classes* by biologists. One is the mammals (having *mammae,* breasts). Animals of this distinct class of vertebrates have breasts and nourish their young with milk. Because mammals nourish their young after birth, they establish social relations between female and offspring. Social relations are characteristic, to various degrees, throughout the class and are present in some other kinds of animal. Sustained social relationships are especially useful to human mammals, for the generation-to-generation transmission of culture through learning.

Mammals are warm-blooded **(endothermic)** animals. This means that the body temperature is internally controlled. Mammals can, therefore, remain active in cold weather (Fig. 10-2). The body temperature of some mammals changes somewhat, but even the bear during hibernation does not undergo a slowing of body processes to the extent characteristic of fishes or reptiles similarly exposed to the cold. Reptiles are **ectothermic**—that is, they have body temperatures which vary with the outside temperature. Such animals become sluggish in cold weather. Therefore, in cold environments mammals manage better than reptiles; no crocodiles and few varieties of lizards and snakes are found outside the tropics. The large carnivorous dinosaurs, which were reptiles, may well have been endothermic, however. Bakker (1972) calculates that an ectothermic animal weighing ten tons, by analogy with today's reptiles, could not generate energy for speeds greater than about 3½ miles per hour. Since fossil footprints suggest that the carnivorous dinosaurs ran much faster, he presumes that the mammalian adaptation of body temperature regulation was anticipated in these early reptiles and that their descendants, the birds, inherited their endothermy and their feathers from these warm-blooded dinosaur ancestors. Since large animals have small surface area relative to their weight, the maintenance of a body temperature above that of their environment need not have involved very active metabolism in the body tissues of the large dinosaurs.

The mammals share another main feature with the birds: besides the fact that both are warm blooded, in both the young remain dependent on the adults. In addition, birds and mammals share some secondary features such as efficient body insulation and some systems of communication.

One feature of the mammals is that they learn by trial and error. This gives them a very wide behavioral repertoire, including, of course, human behavior. Other animals sometimes have less-developed potentiality for learning. Thus, some birds inherit their characteristic songs whereas other species of bird learn the details of their song from trial-and-error repetition of what they hear.

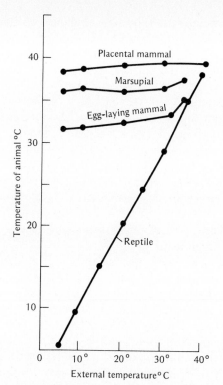

FIG. 10-2   Evolution of "warm-blooded" animals. Reptiles respond almost completely
to the outside temperature and burrow deeply or remain in water to survive freezing
temperatures. There are few reptiles in very cold climates. Even so-called primitive
mammals, such as the egg-laying duck-billed platypus and the marsupial opposum,
change temperature less than their surroundings when the external environment gets
hotter or colder. The placental mammals, such as the cat, maintain almost constant
body temperature whatever the change in the climate within the limits compatible with
life. Mammals, including us, have well developed systems for warming the body
through metabolizing (burning food). Shivering and reduced circulation to the hands
help retain the core temperature of the body. They also have well developed cooling
systems: sweating and increased blood flow to the extremities.

The reproductive mechanism in mammals is marked by economy. That is,
higher proportions of the young survive to maturity than in other classes. This
reaches its maximum in humans, where a high percentage of offspring conceived is born and a majority of those born survive to adulthood. By contrast, most insects and other invertebrates lay thousands upon thousands of
eggs that fail to survive to become reproductive adults.

The class of mammals is divided into three so-called subclasses. These differ
from each other in respect to mode of reproduction. The first of these subclasses is that of the **monotremes.** These mammals, in common with reptiles
and birds, lay eggs as their mode of reproduction. The duckbilled platypus and

the spiny anteater, both of Australia and the latter also of New Guinea, are the only two extant mammals belonging to this subclass. The existence of this subclass suggests that the mammals acquired the capacity to nurse before any of them substituted live birth for egg laying.

The **marsupials** constitute a second subclass of mammals. This group is somewhat more widespread than the egg-laying mammals, and, besides numerous types in Australia, including the kangaroo and the teddy-bear koala, also includes the American opossum. Marsupials are *viviparous;* that is, they give birth to their young rather than laying eggs. The newborn are very immature, however, and must find their way to a pouch on the mother's abdomen, where they can attach themselves to her nipples and remain within the pouch until they are adequately developed to re-emerge.

## Placental Mammals

We belong to the third subclass, the **eutherians,** placental mammals. They develop by a special process in which the egg is shed from the mother's ovary, is fertilized, and then implants itself within the walls of the mother's womb. The **embryo**—the early stage of development of the organism—produces a disc of tissue **(placenta)** on the wall of the womb. The placenta permits interchange of fluids between mother and offspring. While the bird's or reptile's egg must contain yolk enough to nourish the embryo until hatched, as well as a device for storing innocuously the waste products of the developing embryo, the placental mammal utilizes the physiological mechanisms of the adult mother for these functions and for supplying oxygen to the tissues of the embryo. In this way the offspring can be protected until it has grown larger than is usually the size of egg-laying animals at the time they hatch. Other animals, including some snakes and fishes, are viviparous and have the capacity to harbor the eggs within the mother's body until ready to hatch, but only in the eutherian mammals is there a placenta capable of permitting a long intrauterine development and the birth of large infants. The Primates, including us, have well-developed placentas.

## Summary

Taxonomy classes organisms on the basis of common progenitors. Nevertheless, classifications are somewhat arbitrary and may take other factors into account. Thus, multicellular organisms can be divided into producers (plants), reducers (fungi), and consumers (animals). The mammals are animals which nurse their young. They have a system of control of internal temperature that permits them to be active in cold weather. There are three subclasses of mammals, the egg-laying mammals, the marsupials, and the placental mammals. The Primates are placental mammals, hence members of the vertebrate subphylum and the chordate phylum of the animal kingdom.

CHAPTER

# THE PRIMATES

The study of mammals, and especially the study of one order of the eutherian mammals, the primates, is especially pertinent to the study of physical anthropology, because the nonhuman primates provide the closest analogies to us among other animals. Thus, whether one's purpose is to examine human evolution or to learn about human physiology or disease, one needs to be able to recognize general processes that apply in a similar manner to other organisms. One motive for undertaking experiments on primates and other mammals is that the procedures may be impermissible on human subjects. Even when no danger is involved and the studies can be carried out on human volunteers, one may wish to compare the results on people with those on closely related animals not subject to cultural influences. Experiments on nonhuman primates may permit one rigidly to control some of the conditions of the tests in a way not possible with human subjects. Comparative primate studies thus include those of infectious diseases (such as infectious hepatitis), psychological reactions (such as response to rearing in isolation), and neurological mechanisms (such as specific pathways for the conduction of nerve impulses). More specifically, anthropological experiments and observations have focused on individual behavior (such as the studies of locomotion by Napier, 1963, 1964; Prost,

FIG. 11-1   Nonhuman primates are used extensively in psychological and medical research. Increased attention has recently been directed toward the study of social behavior in nonhuman primates. This knowledge provides insights into the development of human social behavior. Here a young macaque monkey seeks close contact with a pseudo-mother (a doll with a terrycloth body). The experiments of H. F. Harlow of the University of Wisconsin concerning affection showed that contact with a suitable surrogate mother was more significant in allaying fear than nursing and that one important function of free arms and grasping hands is the possibility of contact comfort it affords to the infant. Among the hypotheses developed on the basis of psychological experiments on nonhuman primates is the idea that mother–infant contact for long periods of time permits the development of excellent learning, including imitative learning, of the kind necessary for the development of human culture. Photograph courtesy of Dr. Harlow.

1965, 1967; Tuttle, 1967; and others) and social behavior (such as the recording of aggressive **agonistic displays** or adult-infant interactions of animals in the wild—see Chapter 12). In order to select a species of animal for studies of this kind one should, of course, know something about its place relative to other species and specifically its anatomical and **phylogenetic status** relative to us. Let us therefore review the formal taxonomy of the primates and list some of the chief features of the members of the major subdivisions of the order.

It is difficult to define the primates. When any group of organisms first branches off from some other group, it must share most of its characteristics with that other group. These shared characteristics are thought of as **general-**

**ized.** In the case of the primates some members of the order retain generalized features. In fact, there is really no characteristic that is common to all the primates and is not shared with some animals of other orders. For example, prehensile (grasping) hands with freely movable thumbs, a pendulous penis (males), breasts on the chest (females), collarbones, and rings of bone about the eye are characteristic of primates but also occur in other orders and are more or less generalized. Some details of the teeth, such as the shape of the molars, are similar in most primates. They are present even in primitive species of the order and are probably the most characteristic primate traits. In that sense they are **specialized** for primates but ubiquitous, hence generalized, within the order. (See pp. 201–202 for a discussion of generalized and specialized structures.) The way the middle ear is formed from specific bones is also distinctive in primates.

The primates are an ancient group; of the living mammals, only the marsupials and the **insectivores** have left **fossils** of greater antiquity. Furthermore, although we may think of our kind as highly developed, the primates are primitive in that they retain many generalized mammalian features, in respect to which they have evolved less than other orders. This very primitiveness is one of the reasons why the primates have few distinctive features unique to the order. Instead, primates are best distinguished by certain tendencies that are marked in only some members of the order whereas other members retain more primitive conditions in these respects. In this sense the primates display a tendency to keen vision; grasping hands and, sometimes, feet; reduction of litter size to one or two young at a time, and a corresponding reduction of mammary glands to a single pair; and, although the point has been disputed by some students, marked development of the part of the brain, the cortex, that involves highly coordinated sensory and motor functions.

## Classification of the Primates

It may help to delimit the primates and set the stage for a study of our place in nature if we show the taxonomy of the present members of the order (Fig. 11-2). Various authorities group these in different ways. Those interested in experimental or field work with living animals often make rather fine distinctions (see, for instance, Napier and Napier, 1967). Furthermore, paleontologists who have discovered interesting fossils are often tempted to create distinct new categories (taxa) for them. Such taxonomists are colloquially referred to as "splitters," because they tend to split groups into as many recognizably distinct categories as possible. On the other hand, those who are concerned with theoretical or general problems (for instance, Buettner-Janusch, 1973) often need fewer distinctions and they are colloquially called "lumpers," because their taxonomy often ignores minor distinctions. No one system is correct. Grouping can legitimately be done in several ways. Convenience would require arbitrary agreement, but the last widely used system (Simpson, 1945) is now seen even by its author to be in need of revision. Since our purpose is

| Suborder | Infraorder | Superfamily | Family | Subfamily | Genus | English name |
|---|---|---|---|---|---|---|
| Prosimii | Tupaiiformes | | Tupaidae | Tupainae | Tupaia | } tree shrew |
| | | | | Ptilocercinae | Ptilocercus | |
| | Lemuriformes | Lemuroidea | Lemuridae | Lemurinae | *Lemur* | common lemur |
| | | | | | *Hapalemur* | gentle lemur |
| | | | | | *Lepilemur* | sportive lemur |
| | | | | Cheirogaleinae | *Cheirogalus* | mouse lemur |
| | | | | | *Microcebus* | dwarf lemur |
| | | | | | *Phaner* | fork-marked lemur |
| | | | Indriidae | | *Indris* | indris |
| | | | | | *Lichanotus* | avahi |
| | | | | | *Propithecus* | sifaka |
| | | Daubentonioidea | | | *Daubentonia* | aye-aye |
| | Lorisiformes | Lorisoidea | Lorisidae | Lorisinae | *Loris* | slender loris |
| | | | | | *Nycticebus* | slow loris |
| | | | | | *Perodicticus* | potto |
| | | | | | *Arctocebus* | angwantibo |
| | | | | Galaginae | *Galago* | bush baby |
| | Tarsiiformes | Tarsioidea | Tarsidae | | *Tarsius* | tarsier |
| Anthropoidea | Platyrrhini | Ceboidea | Callithricidae | | *Callithrix* | } true marmosets |
| | | | | | *Cebuella* | |
| | | | | | *Leontideus* | } tamarin and marmoset |
| | | | | | *Saguinus* | |
| | | | | | *Tamarinus* | |

| | | Family | Subfamily | Genus | Common name |
|---|---|---|---|---|---|
| | | Cebidae | Aotinae | *Aotus* | night monkey |
| | | | | *Callicebus* | titi |
| | | | Callimiconinae | *Callimico* | callimico |
| | | | Pithecinae | *Pithecia* | saki |
| | | | | *Cacajao* | uakari |
| | | | | *Chiropotes* | saki |
| | | | Alouattinae | *Alouatta* | howler monkey |
| | | | Atelinae | *Ateles* | spider monkey |
| | | | | *Brachyteles* | woolly spider monkey |
| | | | | *Lagothrix* | woolly monkey |
| | | | Cebinae | *Cebus* | capuchin monkey |
| | | | | *Saimiri* | squirrel monkey |
| Catarrhini | Cercopithecoidea | Cercopithecidae | Cercopithecinae | *Cercopithecus* | green monkey and guenon |
| | | | | *Cercocebus* | mangabey |
| | | | | *Cynopithecus* | black ape |
| | | | | *Macaca* | macaque |
| | | | | *Papio* | baboon |
| | | | | *Erythrocebus* | patas monkey |
| | | | | *Theropithecus* | gelada |
| | | | Colobinae | *Colobus* | guereza |
| | | | | *Presbytis* | langur |
| | | | | *Pygathrix* | langur |
| | | | | *Nasalis* | proboscis monkey |
| | | | | *Rhinopithecus* | snub-nosed langur |
| | Hominoidea | Hylobatidae | Hylobatinae | *Hylobates* | gibbon |
| | | | | *Symphalangus* | siamang |
| | | Pongidae | Ponginae | *Pongo* | orangutan |
| | | | | *Gorilla* | gorilla |
| | | | | *Pan* | chimpanzee |
| | | Hominidae | | *Homo* | human |

FIG. 11-2  A classification of the living primates. In formal taxonomy, names are in Latin. Those of families end in "idae," and those of subfamilies in "inae." Names of superfamilies end in "oidea," those of genera are italicized. (Names of species are too numerous to list. They are written with those of their genera and are also italicized.)

general description rather than detailed analysis we shall follow a generally lumping and widely accepted taxonomy (similar to that used by Buettner-Janusch, 1973), which is satisfactory for our present purpose. This is reasonably close to, and readily understandable in terms of, other systems of taxonomy now in use.

Any system of classification must be based on degrees of similarity. Those who study the fossils are particularly concerned with similarities in respect to traits that best show common origins, and they take extinct as well as living forms into account in their schemes. Nevertheless, it is not always certain which traits do so best, and the fossils are often very fragmentary. We shall therefore begin with a classification of the extant (still living) forms.

## Prosimii

The Primates are divided into two suborders. The suborder **Prosimii,** or "pre-monkeys," are represented today by a rather wide variety of generally small, mostly quadrupedal, Old World animals. *Arctocebus* is a representative of this suborder (Fig. 11-3).

One infraorder, the Lemuriformes, is represented by a number of different types that have survived on the island of Madagascar, where no other primates except us, and few other predators, have crossed the straits from the African mainland. Madagascar thus provided a safe refuge for the evolution of diverse species of Lemuriformes. They include the true lemurs, which are quadrupedal and live largely in the trees, on fruit and some leaves and flowers. There are also the nocturnal dwarf and mouse lemurs, which include insects as well as fruits in their diet. These small animals experience seasons of torpidity, during which they deplete stored fat at the base of the tail, much as camels nourish themselves on the fat in their humps. The Indriidae are large, short-tailed animals usually found clinging upright to the large trunks of trees; they make astonishing leaps from tree to tree in this vertical position. They feed on leaves and other vegetable matter, for the digestion of which they possess a long and labyrinthine bowel. Another type of Lemuriforme is the aye-aye *(Daubentonia)*, a peculiar animal with chisellike front teeth that grow throughout life, like those of the rodents, and which it uses to gnaw open limbs of trees in search of grubs. It also has a spindly claw-tipped middle finger (much longer and thinner than its index finger) which it pokes into cavities in trees in search of its food.

The tree shrews, Tupaidae, are small squirrellike animals of Southeast Asia that show some anatomical resemblance in their bones and muscles to the Lemuriformes. In other ways they resemble some nonprimate mammals, such as elephant shrews, which are classed as Insectivora. Unlike all other primates the hands of tree shrews are not adapted for grasping and they retain claws on the fingers and toes. The brain is distinctive. The molecular evidence supports the view that the tree shrews branched off from other primates at an early stage (Goodman, 1966). The reproductive behavior is unlike that of the primates.

FIG. 11-3  *Arctocebus,* an African lorisiform prosimian. These animals can travel along a branch upside down or right side up with equal ease. Photographs courtesy of Dr. W. Montagna.

The male builds a nest in which the young are born. The female then makes occasional brief visits to the nest to suckle the young. There seems no good reason to class the tree shrews among either the Insectivora or the Lemuriformes, and they fit best into their own infraorder, the Tupaiiformes.

The Lorisiformes are lemurlike, generally nocturnal, insectivorous animals of Africa and tropical Asia. Like the true lemurs of Madagascar the lower front teeth of some forms protrude like a comb and are used to groom their fur. The African bush-baby *(Galago)* has long hind limbs and leaping gait.

The tarsier is a small insectivorous animal found on many islands of the East Indies including the Philippines (Fig. 11-4). Although equipped with elongated feet to give it spring for its leaping locomotion, and enormous eyes relative to its small body, a number of details of its anatomy are in some ways humanlike and indeed one anatomist has expressed the opinion that we evolved separately from the other primates from a tarsier-like animal. The common features of humans and tarsiers seem to be the result in both cases of the relative importance of large forward-looking eyes (with a corresponding reduction in the organs of smell) and an erect position of the trunk (with a relatively globular head perched on top). Without implying any linearity of descent by it, the Napiers (1967) consider the grade of development of the tarsier to be a step lower than that of the lemur. There is, of course, no necessary contradiction between a simple level of organization and being closely related to us, but the evidence for both a low grade of development in the tarsier and a close relationship to us lacks real merit. The similarities probably rest on independent causes. That is, the similarities between humans and tarsiers, very small and specialized animals, can best be explained by **parallel** or **convergent evolution.** (See pp. 194–199 for a discussion of parallelism and convergence.) However, the molecular evidence suggests that the tarsier is closer to the Anthropoidea than are lorises, lemurs, or tree shrews (Goodman et al., 1969).

## Monkeys of Central and South America

The rest of the primates, the suborder **Anthropoidea,** sometimes called the "higher primates," consists of the monkeys, apes, and humans. Although members of this suborder have much in common with one another, the monkeys of Central and South America—the New World monkeys **(Ceboidea)**—are clearly distinct from the Old World monkeys **(Cercopithecoidea)** of Asia and Africa, and they in turn are distinct from the apes and us **(Hominoidea).** The most characteristic difference is that all New World monkeys have one more **premolar** (bicuspid) tooth on each side of both upper and lower jaws than do the Old World monkeys, apes, and the human species.

Although the New World monkeys vary among themselves in structure and habits they are classed together as a single infraorder, the **Platyrrhini,** which has only one superfamily, the Ceboidea. All the forms are found in tropical forest environments (equatorial and broken sudan or savanna) from about the Tropic of Cancer to 30° South (well south of the Tropic of Capricorn). Within

FIG. 11-4   Portrait of an adult male tarsier, a small, insectivorous prosimian. It has elongated bones of the foot for leaping, and large eyes adapted to nighttime vision. Photograph courtesy of Dr. W. Montagna.

these limits there are a variety of adaptations, some of which parallel those of Old World monkeys. It is because of these analogies that this independent and isolated radiation (like that of the lemurs of Madagascar) is of interest to anthropologists. The Ceboidea have no direct connection with human evolution.

One family (Callithricidae) consists of the true marmosets (Fig. 11-5) and the tamarins. These little animals retain the prosimians' tendency to have litters, usually giving birth to twins, whereas the rest of the Anthropoidea usually have their young one at a time. Marmosets are omnivorous: their diet includes

FIG. 11-5    The tufted or common marmoset. The marmosets are the smallest monkeys. Small animals generally need food of high nutritious value (such as honey or insects), and marmosets are more insectivorous than other species of monkeys. Photograph courtesy of Robert C. Hermes.

live insects, grubs, and spiders. The marmosets lack third **molar teeth,** a trait they share among primates only with those human beings who congenitally lack their wisdom teeth.

The other family of New World monkeys, the Cebidae, includes the following: The night monkey *(Aotus)* has enlarged eyes for nocturnal vision. The somewhat similar genus, the titi *(Callicebus),* is active in the day or evening; pairs form strong bonds and have been seen to entwine their tails while sleeping. *Cebus* (the "organ grinder's monkey") lives on a varied vegetarian diet in the high trees, much as do the *Cercopithecus* monkeys of Africa, and, despite some marked differences (such as the ability to hold a tin cup with its tail and beg for the organ grinder), it resembles the arboreal Old World monkeys in general body form. The squirrel monkey *(Saimiri),* of about the size the name suggests, can also sit up on its haunches like a squirrel; it eats insects as well as fruit. The gangling spider monkey *(Ateles),* the huge-throated, big-jawed, and loud-calling howler monkey *(Alouatta,* Fig. 11-6), the woolly monkey *(Lagothrix)* and the little known but somewhat similar woolly spider monkey *(Brachyteles)* have vegetarian diets (some live chiefly on leaves, others eat more fruits) and like the *Cebus* they can grasp with their tails. The pre-

FIG. 11-6   The red howler monkey *(Alouatta seniculus)* from northern South America and Trinidad, living up to its name. Photograph by A. W. Ambler from National Audubon Society.

hensile tail actually has skin-ridge patterns on the tip, like our fingerprints, to improve grasp. Patterns in the skin of the fingers and toes, palms and soles, are found throughout the Anthropoidea. The *Cebus* can hang by the tail and arms or legs while feeding among the small terminal twigs of the trees. One subfamily (Pitheciinae) consists of monkeys which have the functional axis of the hand between the index and middle fingers (digits two and three in technical terms) rather than between the thumb and forefinger (digits one and two); among all the primates this is the only form that has this, but even they share the general primate adaptation of a prehensile hand. Lastly, there is one genus of small New World monkeys *(Callimico)* that has the size and form of a marmoset but the dental pattern of the larger Cebidae.

## Old World Monkeys

Old World primates form an infraorder, the **Catarrhini,** which shares a number of characteristics including their dental formula: two **incisors,** a **canine,** two **premolars,** and three **molars** in each half of each jaw: written 2.1.2.3/ 2.1.2.3.

Within this infraorder the Old World monkeys are grouped together as a superfamily (Cercopithecoidea) that consists of a single family (Cercopithecidae) divided into two subfamilies. The chief difference between the two subfamilies is in their digestive systems. One of the subfamilies, the Colobinae, consists of the various leaf-eating monkeys, the colobus monkeys of Africa and the langurs of Asia (Fig. 11-7). These large, colorful varieties have large stomachs that enable them to digest bulky low-calorie leaf foods. On the average, the teeth are high but small and the jaws are less jutting than in monkeys with a more varied diet, but in bones and, presumably, muscles of the limbs, tail, and back, the leaf monkeys do not differ much from the other Old World monkeys, the Cercopithecinae.

The leaf monkeys are classed by the Napiers as quadrupedal semibrachiators, and they have hands specialized for this form of locomotion. The Asiatic Colobinae, however, include forms that spend much time on the ground (but probably only where they can retreat to trees). One unusual group with odd-shaped noses includes the proboscis monkeys *(Nasalis)* of Borneo and the snub-nosed langurs, also called snow monkeys *(Rhinopithecus),* of cold mountainous areas in China.

The other subfamily, the Cercopithecinae, consists of the *Cercopithecus* monkeys, forest dwellers of Africa; the black and white mangabeys *(Cercocebus)* of Africa; the dog-faced baboons *(Papio),* the largest of the monkeys, of Africa and the Arabian peninsula; the macaques *(Macaca),* the usual laboratory monkey, of Asia and North Africa; the patas monkey *(Erythrocebus),* the fastest runner; and the baboonlike gelada *(Theropithecus).* Buettner-Janusch (1973) divides the Cerocopithecinae into three groups, the terrestial baboons and macagues, the largely arboreal mangabeys, and the arboreal guenons, *Cercopithecus.* However, all of these animals spend time on, or frequently descend to, the ground and almost all are at home in, or frequently retreat into,

FIG. 11-7   An infant langur reaches hesitatingly away from his mother, and keeps one hand tightly grasping her fur. The langurs are arboreal leaf-eating monkeys. Photograph courtesy of Dr. Phyllis Dolhinow.

trees. In fact, those most adapted to ground living include not only the hamadryas baboon and gelada but also the patas monkey, which is capable of a very rapid bounding run (like a cheetah), and also has a bipedal stance and a tripod seated position on its hind limbs propped up by its tail. Despite these characteristics the patas monkey is closely related to the tree-living cercopithecus monkeys.

The chief differences among the Cercopithecinae are therefore more a matter of degree than of kind. Baboons grow as big as wolves, some species of guenon monkeys are as small as squirrels; the baboon has a long snout and short tail, the green monkey a short snout and long tail; and different species of macaques vary in size, snout, and tail. The short-tailed forms evolved in response to a more terrestrial life in relatively temperate climates where different sitting postures are more important for the animals than balance is in the trees (Wilson, 1972). Some genera of Cercopithecinae are known to be closely related to each other because, when housed together in zoos, they mate with one another and have healthy offspring (Zuckerman, 1933; Chiarelli, 1973).

Within this subfamily we find a wide range of diets and ways of life. Most live primarily on vegetarian diets of fruits, but the baboons forage on the ground for roots, shoots, and occasionally insects or even small animals. The limbs of baboons are adapted for quadrupedal (four-footed) gait, and therefore resemble those of other ground-living quadrupeds.

Although they are similar in general appearance, there is only a very ancient connection between Old World and New World monkeys. Wild-living African green monkeys are found on the island of St. Kitts in the West Indies, but these are known to have been brought to St. Kitts since the European colonization of the Caribbean islands. Two English anatomists, E. H. Ashton and S. Zuckerman (1951), took advantage of this fact to find out whether there had been any evolutionary divergence of the St. Kitts green monkeys and those of Africa during the 300 years or so of separation. They found that the St. Kitts monkeys are, on the average, slightly different from the African ones. Studies of molecular polymorphisms in the St. Kitts and African green monkeys would be most useful in providing an analogy with short-run evolution (or stability) in respect to human polymorphisms.

## Anthropoid Apes

We are in many ways more similar to the anthropoid apes than to the monkeys; therefore humans and apes are classed in a separate superfamily, the Hominoidea. There are four types of extant apes: gibbon (together with the closely related siamang), orangutan, gorilla, and chimpanzee. The differences of the apes from the monkeys lie in both molecular and gross anatomical details. The anatomical modifications are largely related to locomotion. The arms of apes are long and more freely movable than in the quadrupedal monkeys, but the tail is absent, the lower back and thorax shorter and less supple, and the thorax wide rather than deep.

### Gibbon

The smallest of the four anthropoid apes, the gibbons (Fig. 11-8) *(Hylobates)* and siamangs *(Symphalangus)*, are placed in a family of their own, the Hylobatidae. Their native habitat is in Southeast Asia. They show the anthropoid locomotor adaptation in an extreme form and are the most agile trapeze

FIG. 11-8   The gibbon, the smallest and most agile of the apes. Photograph by A. W. Ambler from National Audubon Society.

artists of all the primates, although to some extent this skill is shared with the spider monkeys, the great apes, and even schoolboys. Their graceful arm-over-arm locomotion is called **brachiation.** A caged gibbon has been seen to swing from one arm and pluck a bird out of the air in midflight. Gibbons are generally vegetarian, however, although occasionally they indulge a fancy for insects, a bird's egg, or even a bird.

The gibbon is also able to walk on its hind legs and apparently always does so on the ground. This rather awkward gait has been described as running but J. H. Prost (1967) found that despite the bounce, both feet were never simultaneously off the ground. When on the ground, the gibbon walks bipedally and holds its long arms up and out for balance, and on a tree limb it can use them as a tightrope walker uses his pole or parasol. In any case the gibbon's bipedal gait is quite different from ours since the gibbon's knee is always bent and it is unable to extend its legs or to get a good push off for a stride. Only human beings are able fully to extend the leg and goose step.

The other apes, the orangutan, the gorilla, and the chimpanzee, are classed together as the Pongidae or great apes. They share the same general body form

**159**

with large head, wide chest, and relatively long arms; many details of anatomy, such as tooth patterns and the presence of laryngeal air sacs; and also some of the same behavioral characteristics, notably the making of nests in which to spend the night.

## Orangutan

The reddish-haired orangutan *(Pongo)* (Fig. 11-9) is now found only in Sumatra and Borneo. The orangutan is a treetop dweller. Young animals may brachiate (Fig. 11-10) but older ones tend to progress cautiously holding on with the rather hooklike hands or prehensile feet as they progress out to the

FIG. 11-9   The orangutan, *Pongo pygmaeus,* of Borneo, now nearly extinct. Photograph by A. W. Ambler from National Audubon Society.

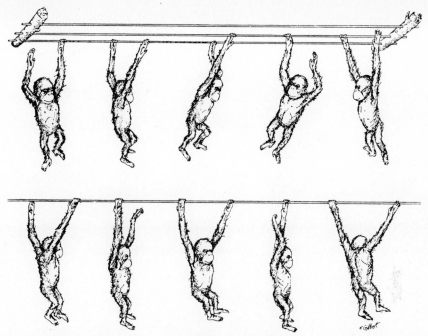

FIG. 11-10    *Top:* (left to right), orangutan brachiating between supports: *bottom:* (left to right), orangutan brachiating along a single support. This type of arm swinging is a natural mode of progression for gibbons, orangutans, chimpanzees, and, to a lesser extent, gorillas. It is associated with a form of the skeleton of the upper limb (especially the shoulder blade) that occurs to some extent also in humans and makes it plausible that our ancestral line passed through a brachiating or semibrachiating arboreal stage. From V. Avis, Brachiation: The crucial issue for man's ancestry. *Southwestern Journal of Anthropology 18,* 119–148, 1962. Reproduced by permission.

small branches in the treetops where they feed. On the thin branches they secure themselves by one or both feet and one hand while using the other hand to eat with. Their legs are short even by comparison with the other great apes. The orangutan's diet is completely vegetarian and includes the wild fruits in which the region is rich (such as the durian, which has a foul smell like that of overripe cheese). The orangutan is now an endangered species in risk of becoming extinct.

Early observers confused the orangutan with the chimpanzee. Although more similar to the chimpanzee than to the gibbon, the orangutan is distinct. Studies of the blood serum of the orangutan indicate that it is quite different in this respect from the African great apes; probably its line of descent has long been separate.

## Gorilla

There are two African great apes, the gorilla and the chimpanzee. Anatomically they are more similar to each other than either is to the orangutan.

The gorilla (Fig. 11-11), by far the largest primate—some weigh 600

FIG. 11-11   A fully grown male gorilla. The knuckle-walking stance is shown clearly. Note that the leg is fully extended on the thigh and that the forearm is also locked in the extended position. Photograph by Ron Garrison, by permisison of the San Diego Zoo.

pounds—is relatively scarce. Some live in the lowlands of West-Central Africa, the remainder in the mountains at the headwaters of the Congo. The differences between the lowland and the mountain gorilla are not great, and were it not for hundreds of intervening miles they would probably interbreed. There are few sizable trees in the mountains of eastern Congo; the gorillas there spend 80 to 90 percent of their time on the ground, although females and young more readily take to the trees. Less is known of the habits of the lowland gorilla since the rain forest is dense.

Gorillas and also chimpanzees are **knuckle walkers** (Fig. 11-11 and 11-12). As shown by R. H. Tuttle (1967), the outer edge of the foot is on the ground but the hand is doubled to support the weight on the middle joint of the fingers. Tuttle thinks this evolved from fist and palm walking as seen in the more arboreal orangutan when he has to get about on the ground. The long forelimbs

FIG. 11-12  Fist walking in a young orangutan (left) compared with knuckle walking in a young chimpanzee. The chimpanzee and the gorilla develop special calluses on the backs of the fingers in this unique way of using the forelimb. From R. H. Tuttle, Knuckle walking and the problem of human origins. *Science 171,* 959, 1967. Copyright by the American Association for the Advancement of Science.

make the gorilla slightly erect even when walking quadrupedally. Like bears, gorillas can easily rear on their hind limbs. In 1861 Du Chaillu wrote that gorillas will rear on their legs and loudly thump their chests. This report seemed so fantastic that his contemporaries were convinced Du Chaillu had never seen a live gorilla and they scoffed at the possibility, since adequately confirmed, that gorillas will charge at a man, stop short, rear up, and beat their chests.

As far as we know, the diet of the wild gorilla is purely vegetarian, that of the mountain gorilla being chiefly bamboo shoots, wild lobelia, and succulent plants that grow at those altitudes. Perhaps partly because of their great size and consequent ground living, the gorillas are in many ways the most humanlike of the great apes. This need not mean, however, that we are phylogenetically more closely allied to the gorilla than to the chimpanzee.

## Chimpanzee

The chimpanzee (Fig. 11-13) is the best known of the great apes (Bourne, 1969–1970). It has a more extensive range in tropical Africa than the gorilla, and some zoologists have recognized several species on the basis of differences in color in different regions. More often these are considered subspecies. However, a smaller species, the pygmy chimpanzee, is found south of the Congo River. Like the gorilla, but more agile, the chimpanzee scurries about swinging by its arms in the trees or progressing on all fours on the ground. In the trees it is capable of brachiation but, descending to the ground to move from one bunch of trees to another, it walks quadrupedally on the outside of its feet and on the knuckles of its hands as well as bipedally on occasion. Jane van Lawick-Goodall (1963, 1965, 1968), who has had wild chimpanzees under observation for longer and at closer range than anyone previously, saw them eating a wide variety of fruits, leaves, seeds, and so forth, but also found that the chimpanzees cherished termites and flesh when they could get it. The chief chimpanzee food is fruit.

The chimpanzees' lips are free, and they can produce a range of facial expression by moving the fine muscles of the face (Fig. 11-14). They can also make a variety of vocal sounds, but cannot really be taught to talk, although several attempts have been made to do so. Recent efforts to communicate with captive chimpanzees use sign language and symbols, under the assumption that part of the problem with past failures in efforts to teach apes to talk has been the limited development of the human type of larynx. Despite the greater measure of success with this "deaf and dumb" communication, most students believe that the chief impediment to speech in the chimpanzee and gorilla is lack of the necessary development of the centers of the brain used in the human type of symbolization of ideas. That chimpanzees have now been taught a much larger vocabulary of word gestures than any ever achieved with spoken words does suggest that the speech area of the human brain which involves hearing and vocalization is undeveloped in chimpanzees.

FIG. 11-13   A mature male chimpanzee. This is the normal "at ease" sitting position.
Photograph by Jane van Lawick-Goodall, © National Geographic Society.

## Relationship of the Living Great Apes to Humans

The great apes resemble humans in the details of most bones, the brain, teeth, and
other parts, and even the blood groups. Furthermore, the close relationship of
humans to the chimpanzee and gorilla is supported by the similarities in their

**165**

FIG. 11-14  Heads of a female and a male chimpanzee at different ages. On the basis of molecular and other evidence the chimpanzee and the gorilla are our closest living relatives. From A. H. Schultz, The size of the orbit and of the eye in primates. *American Journal of Physical Anthropology* 26, 389–408, 1940. Reproduced by permission.

chromosomes (Chiarelli, 1972; Ruffié, 1971) and by the fact that these great apes and we harbor more of the same parasites than we share with any other animal (Dunn, 1966, see Figs. 11-15 and 11-16). Nevertheless, there are a number of respects in which the great apes are more specialized and in which humans more closely resemble the gibbon, Old World monkeys, or more primitive primates. Some monkeys and some great apes have callouslike skin on their bottoms (called **ischial callosities**), which may be an adaptation to sleeping seated, and special sexual skin in the female, which changes according to the stage of the reproductive cycle. Humans and some other monkeys lack these two special areas of skin. W. L. Straus, Jr. (1949), has listed numerous traits of the musculature and skeleton that associate us less with the great apes than with Old World monkeys. Nevertheless, the so-called law of irreversibility of evolution (see Chapter 13) is only a descriptive principle and it is not necessary to assume that the ancestry of humans and the African apes has been separate since before the ancestors of gibbons or Old World monkeys split off from the common lineage (Fig. 11-17). It is preferable to describe such ancestral and descendent species as a *lineage* rather than to refer to these ancestors as "apes" or "monkeys" because, of course, it is illogical to believe that we have descended from any living type of hominoid or cercopithecoid. All other primates have much shorter generations than we do (chimpanzee females start to bear young at about the age of eight), which means that they have gone through even more generations, and hence have had more opportunities for evolutionary change, in the interim since we shared common ancestors many millennia ago. The anatomy of the shoulder and wrist suggests that our ances-

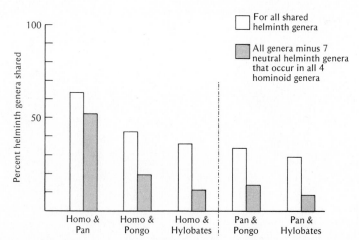

FIG. 11-15   Humans *(Homo)* and the African great apes *(Pan)* share more than 50 percent of their helminth parasite genera. Both share some (but fewer) genera with the orangutan *(Pongo)* and with the gibbon *(Hylobates)*. In this figure Dunn includes both chimpanzee and gorilla in the genus *Pan*. Redrawn from F. L. Dunn, Patterns of parasitism in primates. *Folia Primatologica 4,* 329–345, 1966. Reproduced by permission.

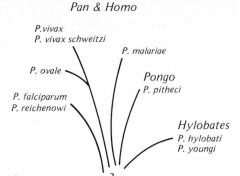

FIG. 11-16   The malarial parasites *(Plasmodium)* of humans *(Homo),* the chimpanzee and gorilla *(Pan),* the orangutan *(Pongo),* and the gibbon *(Hylobates)* apparently evolved from common ancestors together with their hosts. The phylogenetic tree of the parasites is therefore compatible with that of the hominoids that harbor them. In this figure Dunn includes both the chimpanzee and the gorilla in the genus *Pan. P. = Plasmodium.* Redrawn from F. L. Dunn, Patterns of parasitism in primates. *Folia Primatologica 4, 329–345, 1966. Reproduced by permission.*

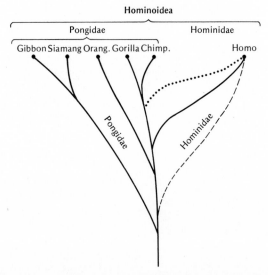

FIG. 11-17   Three views of our relation to the apes: early separation *(dashed line)* at the time the gibbons and siamangs were separating from the great apes; intermediate separation *(solid line)* after the organgutan had separated from the African great apes; and late separation *(dotted line)* at the same time that the gorilla and chimpanzee were differentiating from each other.

tors and those of the African apes could hang by their forelimbs. Then, while we were busy becoming an efficient biped, the African anthropoids, apparently simultaneously, perfected the mechanism for knuckle walking.

Morris Goodman (1963a, 1963b; Goodman et al., 1970, 1972) has prepared antisera that "recognize" certain kinds of protein and that can be used to measure the similarities of primates in respect to their serum proteins. In this way he has been able to show that gorillas, chimpanzees, and humans are similar in respect to some serum proteins (Figs. 5-11 and 11-18). The oragutan and then the gibbon differ somewhat from each other and also (especially the gibbon) from the other apes and us. The Old World monkeys come next and then the New World monkeys show still greater differences from us. The Madagascar lemurs form one distinct group by these tests, the African and Asian lorises another, and the tree shrews a third, with blood proteins more distinct from those of humans than are those of any other primates, but yet in some respects more similar to ours than those of representatives of other orders of mammal, such as hedgehogs and rats. Similar results have been achieved in the comparison of primate serum by Sarich and Wilson (1967; Wilson and Sarich,

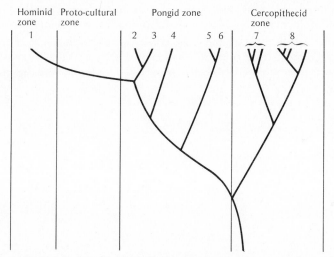

FIG. 11-18  Adaptive and molecular relationships between the Old World monkeys, apes, and humans. This distances between the numbers show the relative closeness to each other of living species in respect to structural and functional adaptation. The depths of the branches show the relative antiquity of common origins as inferred from similarities in response to rabbit anticatarrhine antibodies of blood serum from the various species. Compared with the apes (Pongidae) the designation of the Old World monkeys as a separate family (Cercopithecidae) is justified by molecular differences. The designation of the Hominidae as a separate family is, however, justified only by the wide adaptive differences and lack of any surviving species with an intermediate proto-cultural adaptation. 1, human; 2, chimpanzee; 3, gorilla; 4, orangutan; 5, siamang; 6, gibbon; 7, Colobinae; 8, Cercopithecinae. The data are in part from Simpson (1963) and Goodman et al. (1972).

1969) using a more sensitive immunological test for one serum protein, albumin (see Fig. 5-1). Sarich and Wilson believe that the albumin molecule evolved at a steady rate (a belief that implies that most of the differences are not functionally significant). The assumption of a constant rate of change permits the application of a time scale to the separation of various species. On this basis Wilson and Sarich conclude that we separated from the chimpanzee only four or five million years ago. D. Pilbeam (1968) points out that, if this figure were correct, one would have to exclude *Ramaphithecus* and *Dryopithecus* fossils (which are much older than that—see Chapter 14), from the separate evolutionary lines of humans and great apes respectively, to which they seem to belong. In a recent paper King and Wilson (1975) show that the genetic distance between humans and chimpanzees (calculated on the basis of electrophoretic differences between proteins) is only as great as so-called sibling species, as closely allied species are called, and is less than the differences between any two ordinary species of the same genus in the cases they reviewed. On the other hand, the genetic differences between us and the chimpanzee as measured in this way are some 30 to 60 times as great as those between Black Africans, Japanese and European or American Whites (see Fig. 11-19). Furthermore, King and Wilson do not suggest replacing the anatomical criteria by molecular ones in classifying human and chimpanzee. Crawford (1970) summarizes the general view when he warns that it is premature to depend on one or a few proteins for conclusions about the dates of phyletic separation. It may also be premature to rely on a few pieces of fossil jaws for that purpose.

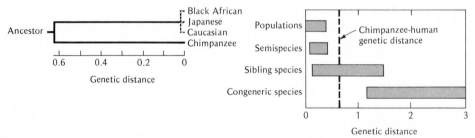

FIG. 11-19  *Left:* Phylogenetic relationship between human populations and chimpanzees. The genetic distances are based on electrophoretic comparisons of proteins. The genetic distances among the three major human populations ($D = 0.01$ to $0.02$) that have been tested are extremely small compared to those between humans and chimpanzees ($D = 0.62$). No human population is significantly closer than another to the chimpanzee lineage. The diagonal hatching of the three human lineages indicates that the populations are not really separate, owing to gene flow. *Right:* The genetic distance, $D$, between humans and chimpanzees (dashed line) compared to the genetic distances between other taxa. Redrawn from M. C. King and A. C. Wilson, Evolution at two levels in humans and chimpanzees. *Science 188,* 107–116. Copyright 1975 by the American Association for the Advancement of Science. Reproduced by permission.

Although there are problems with the timing of divergencies, the qualitative results of molecular biology permit the construction of phylogenetic trees (dendrograms) (Fitch and Margoliash, 1967; Goodman et al., 1970, 1971; Ruffié, 1971). Applied to the primates they confirm the belief of the first modern evolutionists, such as Darwin and Huxley, that we are primates and that our closest affinities are with the anthropoid apes—notably the great apes and more specifically the African great apes: the gorilla and (perhaps even more so) the chimpanzee.

## Summary

The order Primates is divided into two suborders: Prosimii (the lemurs and the tarsier) and the Anthropoidea (monkeys, apes, and humans). The Anthropoidea consist of three families: Ceboidea (the New World monkeys), Cercopithecoidea (Old World monkeys), and Hominoidea (apes and humans). The Ceboidea and Cercopithecoidea are similar to each other in some adaptations but the Cercopithecoidea are more similar to the Hominoidea in those biochemical and other traits that indicate close common descent. Humans (species: *Homo sapiens*) are most closely related to chimpanzee and gorilla, then to orangutan, then gibbon, and then to the Cercopithecoidea (Old World monkeys).

# CHAPTER 12

# BEHAVIOR OF NONHUMAN PRIMATES

The significance of anatomical features lies in their functions. Many of the functions of primates can be classified as *behavior;* that is, besides biochemical and physiological functions of cells or organs there are many actions of the whole animal. Some of these behaviors can be seen in an individual animal. I have already mentioned some, such as feeding, sleeping, and locomotion. Among the primates, however, the behavioral patterns of most significance for different adaptations are usually the interactions between animals, and especially between animals of the same species—that is, social behavior.

A number of popular works have tried to ascribe aspects of human behavior such as aggressiveness and territoriality to our innate biology on the grounds that these characteristics are ubiquitous in carnivorous animals in nature. These accounts are caricatures of natural history. They select evidence here and there from any species that supports the authors' views and they ignore other evidence that does not. Serious studies of animal behavior constitute the science of ethology and they encompass the careful documentation, classification, comparison, and analysis of animal social behavior in the wild. The simplest social question is the physical distance which separates animals. Among primates, for instance, there is a strong tendency to form groups (see

Fig. 12-11) and these groups in turn position themselves with respect to other groups frequently occupying territories or ranges that overlap but spending most of their time in core areas that do not overlap (Fig. 12-1). Primate studies include evidences of cooperation as well as competition. Students of animal behavior use terms such as **agonistic display** to describe threat of combat because terms such as "hostility" may apply only to human feelings. There is

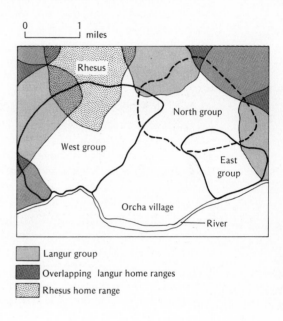

FIG. 12-1  Careful observation of the same groups of primates for many days has enabled field investigators to chart the movements of specific troops. The upper map shows the territories within which such movements of three groups of langurs took place. The territories overlap with each other and with the territories of other groups (including those of rhesus monkeys).

The lower map shows that the core areas of the West, North, and East groups within which the animals spent most of their time do not overlap.

The territories of langurs are small. This is characteristic of tree-living (arboreal), leaf-eating (folivore) forest primates that find ample food for a troop in a small area. A langur is likely to spend its whole life in a five-square-mile area. Terrestrial and semi-terrestrial primates, such as most baboons, often occupy less bountiful habitats in dry regions and have large troops. They therefore range over much larger territories for food. Redrawn from Phyllis Jay: "The common langur of north India," in DeVore (Ed.), *Primate behavior.* New York: Holt, Rinehart and Winston, 1965. Reproduced by permission.

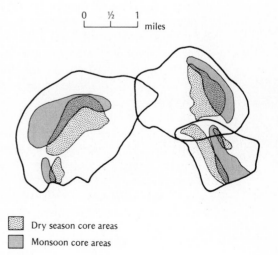

agonistic interaction between primate members of different groups, of course, but it is only very remotely related to human territorial wars (Genovés, 1970). In any case, all groups of primates resolve conflict by a variety of modes of behavior: flight, threat, submissiveness, and so on. Violence is by no means the usual recourse even of "wild animals." The notion that we are "killer apes" and that our aggressiveness is related to the fact that we are the only higher primates who hunt and kill is further refuted by recent evidence (Teleki, 1973) that chimpanzees hunt for meat, sometimes in cooperative groups, but that when the prey has been secured the meat is shared and is not forfeited to more dominant animals by those of lesser rank.

One of the most rapidly expanding subjects of study in anthropology is that of the behavior of primates. Long periods of field observation are necessary and the work of many American and other anthropologists (including numerous students of S. L. Washburn) is now bearing fruit (DeVore, 1965; Jay, 1968; Jolly, 1972; Kummer, 1971).

Social organization is carried to high levels in the primates. Some of the social groups are large—above all those of humans, who now control such destructive weapons that they must have effective social organization on a worldwide level if the species is to survive.

Studies of social behavior of nonhuman primates can be made in two contexts: (1) in the wild, and (2) by experiments in captivity. To investigate a particular species the logical progression is from comprehensive studies of the species in the wild, to studies of special topics concerning some problem that emerges, to experimental studies of the hypotheses these earlier studies suggest.

Washburn and Hamburg (1965) point out that field studies, few of which antedate World War II, are important in discovering the way adaptive behavior functions in the very circumstances under which it has evolved, that is, among free-ranging primates. But experiments disrupting or controlling specific aspects of the social setting or physical environment are often necessary to differentiate between instinctive and learned behavior. As will be discussed below (see p. 186), all cultural behavior is learned. Although not all learned behavior is cultural, the increasing importance of this mode of adaptation in the primates was an essential prerequisite for the evolution of human culture.

## Howler Monkeys

Still among the best accounts of free-ranging primates are the pioneering reports by C. R. Carpenter. In 1934 Carpenter reported a visit to the Barro Colorado Biological Experimental Station in Panama. Barro Colorado Island was formed in 1914 from a ridge of land when the water level was raised behind the Gatun Locks of the Panama Canal. All the animals present at the time the ridge was cut off by the rising water have been isolated in this microcosm, and their descendents form a closed fauna with no immigrants from beyond the precincts of the island. Carpenter found discrete groups or colonies of red howler monkeys (a large New World species with prehensile tails, see Fig. 11-6) on the island, and he could locate each group in the morning when they howled. He then watched them all day.

An average group consisted of 17 animals: 3 adult males, 7 adult females, 3 infants, and 4 juveniles. The age distribution is no doubt chiefly the result of the equilibrium between birth and death rates, but the unequal sex ratio is, at least in part, maintained by the "ostracism" of some males. Such males are forced to live alone and are usually driven away when they approach and attempt to join a group. The proportion of various ages is relatively constant, as is the preponderance of females among the adults. The howler monkeys assume postures, use gestures, and make noises that serve to stimulate other members of the group to specific activities: sexual behavior, movement to a new group of trees, or aggressive deployment to repel another group or a single male. For example, rapid movements of the tongue serve as an invitation to sexual behavior. Agonistic behavior within the howler group is rare. Each group moves about as a unit within a circumscribed territory. They do not defend territory as such; territories therefore overlap widely. However, two groups will not occupy the same part of the overlapping territories at the same time. A group will try to drive other howlers away from where it is. Several students of primate behavior have revisited Barro Colorado Island since Carpenter's original studies and have observed that, although the total howler population has fluctuated and the number of colonies increased, the general pattern of social behavior has remained unchanged (Carpenter, 1965; Chivers, 1969; Collias and Southwick, 1952).

Other kinds of New World Monkeys differ considerably from the howlers; the variations in behavior relate to behavioral adaptation to ecological differences (see Durham, 1971, for instance). Some other studies are analyzed by Jolly (1972).

## Baboons

The baboons (Fig. 12-2) form another group of species that have been studied extensively. Solly Zuckerman's (1932) observations of baboons in captivity raised many questions that could be answered only by further study in the field. In the intervening years Altmann and Altmann (1970), Hall and DeVore (1965), Kummer (1968, 1971), and Washburn and DeVore (1961), among others, have done so. Some of the studies are summarized in a book edited by DeVore (1965; pp. 20–110) and in a series of films by him.

The size of the baboon troop and the nature of the social interaction between its members appear to be dependent on what the environment—forest, savanna, or desert—offers in places to sleep, safety from predators, water holes, and, of course, food. Because it is easier to see animals in open country than in forest, relatively little is known of the forest species (the drills and mandrills).

FIG. 12-2   A fully grown male baboon (left), two females, and an infant. The difference in size between the sexes (sexual dimorphism) is obvious. Photograph courtesy of Dr. I. DeVore.

The mandrills are apparently an extreme form. The males are ferociously aggressive. They are many times the size of the adult females and have longer and more deadly canine teeth than any other monkey.

In the widespread savanna species, troops are highly organized and consist of about 40 animals (8 to 185), always with one or more mature males and usually several mature females. The movement of a troop is between suitable foods (flowers, fruits, seeds, roots, and occasionally insects and animals) and sleeping places (typically in the safety of trees but in some places on cliffs or even in caves). Baboons do not necessarily return to the same sleeping places; members of the troop follow the movement of the large adult males and stay within sight of each other. Since stragglers seem to disappear it is presumed they readily fall prey to large carnivores, whereas an organized group with adult males will drive off even lions. On the move some of the males keep to the front, back, and sides of the troop like the outriders with a covered-wagon train (Fig. 12-3). The dominant males are in the center, however, with the young and the females in heat. If carnivores approach, these males move in the direction of the threat while the other animals beat a retreat. Different troops usually maintain a distance from each other, but at times and in places of scarce water or food, peaceful aggregations of troops occur. There may also be aggregations at sleeping places; occasional fighting between troops has been seen in such situations. Except for a large troop in process of fission, there is probably no ambiguity about troop membership; baboons are apparently born into, and live their whole lives in, the same troop. It is the troop rather than the individual that provides adaptation to the environment, access to adequate food and water, and safety from lions and leopards.

There are usually nearly twice as many adult females as adult males in a savanna baboon troop. This is partly because females are fully adult at five or six years of age, whereas males are classed as juveniles for several more years. There is a clear dominance ranking among the adult males, but several males may act in concert to dominate jointly another to which each singly is subordinate (Fig. 12-4). In specific critical situations that test dominance, the more dominant animal has preferential access to mating with fully adult females in heat, receives gestures of submission from animals lower in the dominance hierarchy of the troop, displays more aggressive behavior, gets first access to food, and assumes a position in the vanguard in the face of potential danger. The agonistic behavior is very noisy, but much of it consists of threatening gestures and chasing rather than actual fighting.

Sexual receptivity of female baboons occurs periodically. In heat they develop tumescent swelling in the perineum. Among the desert hamadryas baboons of Ethiopa and Arabia adult males form permanent harems and the

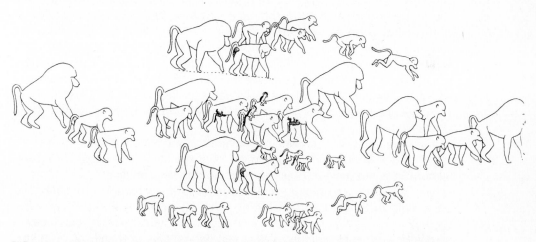

FIG. 12-3  Formation of a baboon troop during group movement. Dominant adult males accompany females with small infants and a group of older infants in the group's center. A group of young juveniles is shown below the center and older juveniles above. Other adult males and females precede and follow the group's center. Two estrous females (dark hindquarters) are in consort with adult males. From K. R. L. Hall and I. DeVore: "Baboon social behavior," in I. DeVore (Ed.), *Primate behavior*. New York: Holt, Rinehart and Winston, 1965. Reproduced by permission.

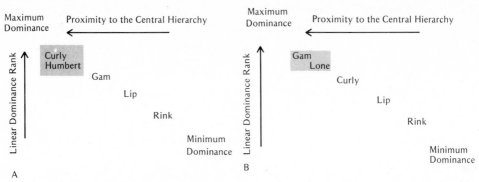

FIG. 12-4 Sometimes an observer has had an opportunity to observe the same group of wild primates after a lapse of time. DeVore (1965) noted changes between July and November 1959 in the dominance hierarchy of the males of a troop of baboons in Kenya. *A,* In July the males called Curly and Humbert jointly dominated the other males although, when alone, Curly is subordinate to Gam. *B,* By November Humbert had disappeared (died?) and a new male (Lone) had joined the group. In the absence of Humbert, Gam had established his dominant status over Curly and, with the new male, was beginning to establish a new central hierarchy. Redrawn from K. R. L. Hall and I. DeVore: "Baboon social behavior," in I. DeVore (Ed.), *Primate behavior.* New York: Holt, Rinehart and Winston, 1965. Reproduced by permission.

females are attacked and "forced" to follow. In other baboons, if only one at a time comes into estrus, the dominant male may monopolize each female when her swelling is most prominent, but if there are several such females, or when the swelling is not at its maximum, other males will mate and even juveniles may attempt to copulate. A male mounts with the hind feet supported on the female's back legs (Fig. 12-7), and a copulation sequence consists of a few rapid thrusts. Other males often threaten them. After copulation the female may run off—sometimes to mate with a different male—but often the same male will mount a whole series of times and the two animals are then described as a "consort pair."

Copulation is often followed by brief mutual grooming, running through the fur with the hands and picking out foreign particles (Fig. 12-5). However, grooming is not limited to periods before and after copulation or to bisexual pairs; it is a very common form of social interaction among all primates, and especially in those, such as baboons, with strong dominance relationships. Frequently subordinate animals groom more dominant ones, but mothers groom their infants, other females groom the mothers, and animals of various statuses may groom each other (Fig. 12-6).

Grooming is only one form of tactile communication. Baboons may nuzzle or bite each other. Numerous forms of vocal communication and gestures are also used. Linguists interpret the wide range of communicative modes in different ways. Some see relatively close analogies to language, and even aspects of what must have been the precursors of human language. Others emphasize the contrast. No abstract symbolism is involved, but baboons and other primates do communicate their attitudes and intentions by facial expressions, body movements, vocalizations, and so on. The constant social interactions of the baboon troop are coordinated by all these types of intercommunication.

The significance of learned behavior among baboons has been demonstrated by experiments with releasing an animal previously kept as a pet, by "provisioning" with food, and by watching responses to other experimentally altered situations. From these it is clear that a large fraction of the behavioral routine is learned rather than innate. The baboon learns by being pushed or pulled by other animals and by seeing the responses of others to a wide variety of stimuli (such as animals of other species). Even sexual activity is inadequately performed by animals that have been deprived of the opportunity to watch as they grow up. The human child can imagine such things from adolescent talk, reading, and pictures; among baboons there is no symbolic communication to permit that kind of sex education (or the learning of other discriminations such as good foods from bad, safe from dangerous, and so on [Fig. 12-7]).

FIG. 12-5   An adult male baboon grooms his consort, who is in estrus. Photograph courtesy of Dr. I. DeVore.

FIG. 12-6 A female baboon with infant is groomed by another female, while a second infant is half hidden between them. Photograph courtesy of Dr. I. DeVore.

## Macaques and Other Old World Monkeys

Comparable studies have now been made of numerous other species of Old World monkeys. Jay (1965), Ripley (1967), and Poirier (1969) have studied the langurs (See Fig. 12-1), and Struhsaker (1967), Gartlan and Brain (1968), and Durham (1969) the vervets. The predominantly ground-living forms, such as the various species of macaques, are best known because they are easiest to observe, however (Imanishi, 1960; Altmann, 1962; Sade, 1965; Simonds, 1965; Southwick et al., 1965; and MacRoberts, 1970). The macaques have been watched in various parts of their range from Japan in the east to Gibraltar in the west (and outside the range by C. R. Carpenter and others on a transplanted colony at Cayo Santiago, a small island off the coast of Puerto Rico). There are many small differences within and between species, but in general the behavior is not very different from that of the baboon. Various amounts of fighting, chasing, presenting, grimacing, grooming, and similar behaviors create a troop with a dominance–submission hierarchy of the same kind in all the species studied (compare Fig. 12-6 with Fig. 12-8). In captivity there is apparently no breeding season among macaques and other higher primates, and this gave rise to the theory that humans owed social organization to the year-round sexual drive they possess as primates. In the wild, however, macaques and other Old World monkeys have specific mating seasons and hence birth seasons related to seasonal climates (Lancaster and Lee, 1965). But the social groups of macaques, like ours, are permanent (except that males will sometimes change groups—with disruptive social effects—and copulate with females of a different group during the mating season [Lindburg, 1969]).

FIG. 12-7   Three examples of primate communication. *Top,* a baboon female presents—a gesture of subordination—to a mother and infant. *Bottom, left,* a juvenile baboon mounts another juvenile. This is a step further in the dominance interaction and does not necessarily have any sexual significance. *Right,* a juvenile and an adult female baboon are involved in an agonistic interaction with an animal out of sight on the right. Note that posture and facial expression are both employed. Top photograph courtesy of Dr. I. DeVore; lower two photographs courtesy of Dr. S. A. Altmann.

FIG. 12-8    A bonnet macaque grooms a mother with infant. Photograph courtesy of Dr. P. E. Simonds.

## Anthropoid Apes in the Wild

C. R. Carpenter (1940) studied the social life of free-living gibbons in Thailand and they have been further studied by Ellefson (1968). These hominoids resemble us in that they live in "families" consisting on the average of one adult male, one adult female with an infant, and about three juveniles. We do not know how permanent gibbon monogamy may be. At times both males and females live alone temporarily. The gibbon family, like the band of the howler monkeys, occupies a specific territory within which it ranges, and the members stimulate responses in each other by the sounds they make and by their movements. Male and female gibbons are of nearly equal size, and the males are not markedly dominant over the females.

The great apes—orangutans, gorillas, and chimpanzees—are difficult to study in their natural habitat. Orangutans (subjects of a continuing study by D. Horr) apparently live alone or in very small groups. No more than six have been reliably reported together and the groups may not be permanent.

Gorillas have recently been studied by Fossey (1970). They travel in groups of 2 to 30. A census of mountain gorillas by Schaller (1963) showed the average group to consist of 17 animals, but in less favorable environments the groups are smaller; there is always at least one old gray-backed male and there may be three or four. There is little serious agonistic behavior towards each other; dominance is maintained by bluff charges which stop short of actual attack. Adult animals do not often bear the scars of past battles so often seen in baboons, but there are probably occasional set-tos. There have been episodes in which gorillas have charged at a man, bitten him, and then run off; perhaps they sometimes react to a strange gorilla in the same way.

Chimpanzees have been extensively studied in the wild, especially by Jane van Lawick-Goodall (Goodall, 1963, 1965, 1968) and Reynolds and Reynolds (1965). The bands apparently are unstable in character and usually small. The bands interact with each other by vocal "calling." Sometimes they aggregate and even exchange members—especially males. Goodall observed some activities of especial significance for comparison with humans. These included predation on other animals and the begging for and sharing of meat. She also observed use of tools, notably leaves used as sponges and twigs used as probes to insert in termites' nests so the termites could be fished out and eaten (Fig. 12-9). Such tools were even manufactured (prepared to an appropriate length) and transported (from a site a short distance from the termite mound). Goodall also observed during the rain a "ritual-like dance"; the chimpanzees repeatedly ran down hill on their hind limbs, breaking off and waving branches in their hands. Another human capacity is a degree of foresight—to the extent that Goodall saw chimpanzees examining termite hills before any possibility of acquiring termites as food; that is, several weeks before the termite migration. The way various activities were learned demonstrates that chimpanzees learn from each

FIG. 12-9   One chimpanzee uses a twig, another a stem of grass to probe a choice termite mound. Photograph by Dr. Jane van Lawick-Goodall. © National Geographic Society.

other, carry the memories for many months, and "plan" activities in a way which must be the closest present day nonhuman approach to human culture.

## Comparative Study of the Structure of Primate Social Groups

In order to gain a wide background from which to view the evolution of human sociality, it is wisest not to depend on a single study (for behavior of members of a primate species varies according to situation) nor to confine attention to a single species (for instance, certain analogies to humans are more persuasively made with baboons than with chimpanzees, and vice versa). Because we occupy so many different ecological situations it is most useful to examine the whole range of primate social relations. Carpenter (1954) was the first to attempt some interspecific generalizations. He hypothesized that:

Primates compose autonomous groups that, for any species, vary in size and in proportional sex and age composition within fixed limits;

The groups occupy limited territories and defend them against other groups of the same species; and

Animals are arranged in order by relative dominance, which determines the extent to which they control the group through signals and behavioral cues.

We now know that the exclusive right to certain parts of the home range at certain critical times of the year when food resources are limited is seen in various species, but otherwise home ranges overlap and in any case are not usually "defended" by overt fighting (Eisenberg et al., 1972).

Recent studies attempt to encompass the social organization of all the primates in a comparative frame of reference by cross-species characterization of a number of ecological variables. They include:

Dietary habits:

frugivore (fruit eating);
granivore (grain and seed eating);
folivore (leaf eating);
insectivore (insect eating);
omnivore (eating of everything);

Habitat:

terrestrial (on the ground);
semiterrestrial (sometimes on the ground);
arboreal (in the trees);

Locomotion:

brachiator (arm-swinging);
semi-brachiator (somewhat arm-swinging);
knuckle-walker;
plantigrade quadrupedal (flat-footed, four-footed);
bipedal (two-footed);

Time of activity:

    nocturnal (at night);
    diurnal (during the day).

These variables are interrelated, of course. In general, small animals have need for high-energy foods such as insects whereas large animals can get along on large amounts of low-energy foods such as leaves. The reason is that the amount of energy needed to maintain body temperature increases only relative to about the square of the animal's length, but the volume of its digestive system increases approximately as the cube of its length and is therefore much bigger in big animals. On the other hand, size influences safety from terrestrial predators, which depends either on escape to the outer branches of high trees or on large size (especially of the males) for defense. Mode of locomotion and time of activity are, of course, also related to these ecological "strategies" of food acquisition and defense.

However, not only are individual characteristics important; the social behavior may be as important to the species as the size and mode of locomotion of its members. The size of the group must be in balance between the needs of food acquisition and safety from predators. Figure 12-10 summarizes some of these interrelationships.

Dispersion (with calls to others when good fruit trees are located) is the best strategy for foraging. On the other hand, herding in large groups—especially if the adult males can stand off carnivores—is the best defense against predation, at least in big terrestrial and semiterrestrial species such as baboons, chimpan-

| | Solitary species | Parental family | Unimale troop | Age-graded male troop | Multimale troop |
|---|---|---|---|---|---|
| Insectivore-frugivore | arboreal (slow loris) | arboreal (marmoset) | | | |
| Folivore | arboreal (*Lepilemur*) | arboreal (*Indris,* gibbon) | arboreal (howler, *Colobus*) | arboreal (howler) | |
| Folivore-frugivore | | | | terrestrial (gorilla) | |
| Frugivore* | | | semiterrestrial (mandrill, *Erythrocebus, Theropithecus*) | arboreal (spider monkey) | arboreal (lemur) |
| Frugivore-* omnivore | | | | semiterrestrial (*Cercopithecus*) | semiterrestrial (macaque, baboon, chimpanzee) |

*The term "frugivore" is used to include gramivore, grain-eating.

FIG. 12-10   Social organization and feeding of a few examples of primates. Modified after Eisenberg et al., 1972.

zees, and gorillas. It may have been such defense rather than hunting that governed the social organization of the evolving human species. The size of the group can vary from one activity to another. For example, desert baboons forage in small groups but come together to sleep, and savanna baboon troops sometimes come together at water holes. Changing group size according to need is obviously an even more complex social system.

The size of the typical primary group depends on the tolerance for each other the members show, and particularly, it seems, the mutual tolerance of adult males (Eisenberg et al., 1972). Figure 12-11 shows one way of classifying by this dimension.

As greater attention is paid to behavior between females and to other aspects of primate social behavior, such as interspecific interaction (Eisenberg et al., 1972), primate societies will require classification into more refined categories or reclassification on the basis of other criteria, and it seems probable that much remains to be learned through this approach.

## Culture, a Human Phenomenon

One of the chief contributions of anthropology to human thought has been the development of the concept of culture. Although the explanation of this concept must be left for works on that subject, it would be impossible to deal with human biology without some attention to culture. On the one hand, evolution has accounted for an animal capable of culture, and the behavior of nonhuman primates must be similar to the starting point of this development. On the other hand, culture provides the milieu within which humans live, and to understand that life, even in biological terms, one must examine their cultural ecology.

Culture denotes the amassing of experience by people from generation to generation, mainly through the use of symbolic speech. All humans, even the most primitive, live in a manner that is learned in this way from their forebears. No other animals do this to anything approaching the same extent, and physical anthropologists as well as cultural anthropologists are virtually unanimous in considering culture to be an essentially human phenomenon (Zuckerman, 1932; Kroeber, 1948; White, 1959). Although chimpanzees can learn to use an arbitrary symbol, only human beings have developed complex systems of symbols of the kinds that allow us to distinguish, for example, public land from private property and holy water from drinking water.

Cultural anthropology includes the study of the religious beliefs, laws, and arts of various peoples. A question for physical anthropology is: what does culture imply in the process of biological evolution? Some would define humans as animals possessing a culture. However, this definition is not adequate if we are concerned with the origin of *Homo sapiens*. The physical anthropologist must also consider humanity's biological status. It may be harder to discover "fossils" of beginning culture of physical remains, and the relationship

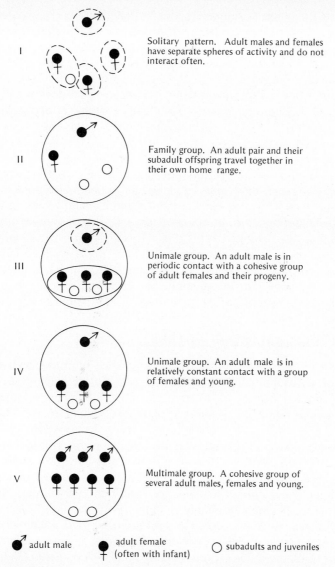

I    Solitary pattern. Adult males and females have separate spheres of activity and do not interact often.

II    Family group. An adult pair and their subadult offspring travel together in their own home range.

III    Unimale group. An adult male is in periodic contact with a cohesive group of adult females and their progeny.

IV    Unimale group. An adult male is in relatively constant contact with a group of females and young.

V    Multimale group. A cohesive group of several adult males, females and young.

⬈● adult male        ● adult female (often with infant)        ○ subadults and juveniles

FIG. 12-11  Several forms of grouping behavior observed in primates. Modified after Eisenberg et al., 1972.

between the state of one and the state of the other is determined by the evolutionary forces within both systems.

Because of this relationship (however tenuous it may be in some situations) and despite the necessary specialization of cultural anthropologists in their own discipline, their data and those of physical anthropology are both necessary for the analysis of the nature and evolution of *Homo sapiens*. Culture is responsible for artifacts (human products made to a culturally determined design). Since artifacts were often made of stone or other durable material they have survived as cultural "fossils." Archaeology and human paleontology therefore both contribute to answer the questions: when, where, and how did *Homo sapiens* originate?

In trying to define the human genus, *Homo,* as one does with any other genus in zoology, on the basis of hereditary anatomical and physiological traits, one sees that *Homo* is marked by the biological traits necessary to create and participate in culture: speech apparatus, manipulative skill, and, above all, the development of the neocortex, the part of the brain used in integrating various sensory inputs, current and remembered. The human way of life—the cultural way—is so distinct, in fact, that virtually all biologists unite the holders of it in a separate family, the Hominidae. All extinct culture-making species of primates, whether ancestral to modern *Homo sapiens* or merely close to our line of descent, also belonged to this family. Despite the close similarity of chimpanzees and gorillas in ways unconnected with the prerequisites of culture, they are not classed as members of the family Hominidae, which has only one living species. We can look to the living nonhuman primates, however, to see to what extent human characteristics are paralleled in other families.

## Social Cohesion as a Prerequisite

Spuhler (1959) has noted that capacity for keen binocular vision, bipedal locomotion, fine manipulation, varied diet, consciously planned sexual activity, vocal communication, and mental association are the biological preconditions for the development of human culture. In addition to the factors mentioned by Spuhler, lengthy maturation and therefore transgenerational social cohesion are biological prerequisites for culture. In his consideration of the "Human Animal," LaBarre (1954) has shown that the living nonhuman primates, although lacking anything like human culture, possess in varying (but always limited) degrees most of the preconditions for culture. Nonhuman primate infants, like human infants, mature slowly (see Fig. 12-12). A slowly maturing animal would be favored in a culture-using ecological niche because the long period of dependence provides a long time for learning from others in the group. LaBarre (1954), borrowing a notion from Freud, believes that provision of a long enough time for cultural learning happened through development of a permanent family in which an incest tabu prevented disruptive sexual competition between the offspring and their parents. Although various species of nonhuman primates lack the incest tabu, young and old males live in the same social groups, and competition for the sexually receptive females is resolved by an established dominance hierarchy or by other mechanisms that permit the continuity of the troop, or other social grouping. The aspects of social behavior that function to preserve social cohesion (cooperative activities and increasing regulation of agonistic behavior through effective modes of communication) may have led to the universal recognition of incest re-

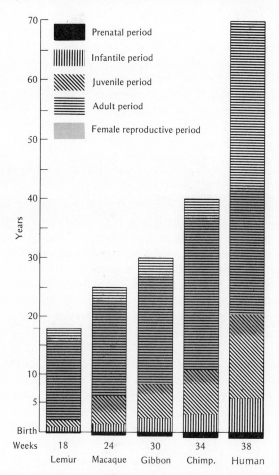

FIG. 12-12 The approximate average duration of the main periods of life in some lower and higher primates. The limits of the infantile and juvenile are based upon comparable stages of dental development. There is a progressive prolongation of the infantile and juvenile periods as one goes from prosimians to monkeys, to apes, to humans. This pedomorphism accompanies an increasing amount and intensity of infant and juvenile care and dependency behavior. Courtesy of Professor A. H. Schultz.

strictions in human mate selection, but the incest tabu could not have been the cause of this regulation of aggression, which is resolved in some way in all species of animals.

The human sexual pattern is biologically distinct. Except for humans, female mammals have a period of heat, called estrus, during which time alone they attract males. Estrus is associated with hormonal secretions that produce changes in smell and appearance. Thus, female chimpanzees, among other primate species, have sexual skin that becomes engorged and provides sexual incentive to males. There is little or no sexual activity at other times. The human menstrual cycle is quite a different matter from estrus, and human beings mate at any time permitted by their cultural codes. The milk-secreting tissue of the human female is surrounded by a prominent fatty breast, whereas in other animals the breasts are conspicuous only when the female has a nursing litter. Women's breasts are considered attractive by men in most cultures. It has been suggested that perhaps breasts are to more constant sexual relations what, in other species, sexual skin is to sexual activity during estrus. In human societies, sexuality and marriage bonds have social significance for the species far more extensive than simply reproduction.

## Playfulness as a Prerequisite

Playfulness, another capacity important in the development of human culture, is also foreshadowed in other primates (Kroeber, 1948). It is doubtful that art, philosophy, and science could have developed solely as planned activities with projected ends. Random activities engaged in for their own sake are certainly pleasurable to the young of many other mammals as well as to humans. In humans, however, and to a lesser extent in chimpanzees, the delay of sexual maturity and the long period of childhood dependence provide extended opportunities for play. Humanity's capacity for "make-believe" is, in fact, a likely stimulus to invention. We might, in this connection, speculate about the wheel. Although it was applied to chariots in ancient times in Asia, before Columbus came to America the only wheels in the hemisphere were on little pull toys (Fig. 12-13). Would American Indians have thought of the cart themselves had it not been for Europeans? Gunpowder was a toy before it was a weapon; was the bow a toy first, too? Kenneth Oakley (1961) believes that *Homo sapiens* played with fire, by plucking burning matter from natural conflagrations, before attempting any purposive fire-using.

However developed or invented, all but the most elementary tools are hallmarks of *Homo sapiens*. Since tool use occurs even in the chimpanzee, however, the fully human brain evolved long after the first use of tools and was no doubt selected for by the developing mastery of toolmaking and tool use. That is, much of the structure of *Homo sapiens* resulted from the developing culture or protoculture of our forebears. A relatively intelligent type of primate, using vocal communication to transmit an increasing array of meanings, would make many uses of social relations, and it is likely that human social life evolved together with biological and cultural development.

## Language as a Prerequisite

Language is generally considered a specifically human activity. Symbolic language is quite a different thing, of course, from the talking of a parrot or a

FIG. 12-13  A wheeled toy of the late classic period (probably 800–1200 A.D.), found near Las Remojadas, central Vera Cruz, Mexico. Several such prehistoric wheeled toys have been found in Mexico but there is no evidence of wheeled vehicles until after the Spanish arrived. This suggests that useful inventions may sometimes start out merely as playthings. Photograph courtesy of the American Museum of Natural History.

mynah bird. In fact, even the most complex communication systems of nonhuman mammals are made up of signals (sounds and gestures that incite to action) rather than arbitrary symbols that convey meanings. Among nonhuman primates the signals are often very complex and are composed of auditory, visual, tactile, and, occasionally, olfactory signs, some of which are quite specific whereas others give only a generalized expression of the emotional state (Washburn et al., 1965). The combinations of communicative modes and intensities can lead to quite subtle influences on social interaction between members of a given species. The study of the nature and origin of language is built upon the comparative study of patterns of signaling in other animals (Sebeok, 1965).

Experiments aimed at teaching chimpanzees to speak have always failed to train for use of more than a few words. With systems using sign language (Gardner and Gardner, 1969) or other symbols (Premack, 1971) a richer vocabulary and rudimentary grammar are possible. This ability is consistent with the relative intelligence of the great apes among the nonhuman mammals, and such experiments may help us understand how language developed. Complex and impressive as the accomplishments may be, however, they also show how much further all human cultures have gone: every human language is readily adapted to the expression of previously unknown concepts, not only by the extension of the proclivity for *naming* and the development of structural *grammar* but also by the capacities to extrapolate through the extension of meanings into generalizations, and to *paraphrase* so that the message is given in different forms (Bronowski, 1969). Furthermore, whereas sign language involves the cerebral correlation of the hands and sight, human speech involves a specialized area of the human brain correlating the speech organs and hearing. This speech area is lacking in other mammals.

Efforts to trace use of language through evolution of the brain as seen in casts of fossil skulls or through development of the jaws and larynx offer no rewards. The best evidence available is in the archaeological discovery of stone tools. Hominids capable of making stone tools to a standard pattern demonstrate that they can impose arbitrary form on materials much as language imposes arbitrary meaning on vocalizations (Holloway, 1972).

Studies of nonhuman primates remain an important channel for the understanding not only of the origin but also of the function of human behavior. Comparative analysis can discover not only the range, but also the interrelationship of factors. Such information is the more useful the wider the spectrum of species studied. For this reason alone, if for no other, it is worth great effort to save from extinction the gorilla, the orangutan, and all other primate species that are now threatened. The effort to save these and other species and to preserve adequate numbers for further study in field and laboratory and for simple appreciation in the wild and in captivity itself must draw heavily on what we know about their biology, psychology, and social organization. Part of the effort of primatology is therefore expended on the conservation of its subjects. Those anthropologists who study humans also devote attention to the conservation of the subjects they study. There was always some awareness of this ethical responsibility. The danger of extermination of species of primates (human and nonhuman) has grown and therefore so has the urgency of efforts to conserve them.

## Summary

Studies of free-living primates give us insight into how their biological traits adapt the various species to their habitats. The behavior of monkeys includes much social interaction. Anthropoid apes forshadow humans in much that they do, including the use and even shaping of simple tools. Their social groupings, sexual relationships, play, and modes of communication suggest the biological preconditions necessary for the evolution of an animal *(Homo sapiens)* with learned culture and symbolic language. Knowledge of these species in the wild feeds back into the effort to conserve them.

# CHAPTER 13

# PALEONTOLOGICAL PRINCIPLES

Paleontology is the study of life of past geological periods. Conclusions concerning the evolutionary relationships and chronology of past organisms depend largely on an examination of fossils and a comparison of the findings with those of studies of living organisms.

Any remains of living forms from the remote past are fossils. Many of them are remains of the animals (or plants) that have been buried under sediments. The soft parts are usually washed away and the teeth and bones gradually turn to stone as they absorb minerals dissolved in the ground water. Only a small fraction of the individuals that die are preserved and only a fraction of those preserved are ever recovered, of course. For many forms, however, there are enough specimens from successive geological deposits to provide records of the course of evolution and to permit the development of theories. In discussing and attempting to interpret the fossil evidence of our evolution and that of our predecessors, anthropologists study the principles developed in work on other lines with more complete fossil records.

## Parallelism and Convergence

Essentially, there are two possible interpretations that paleontologists and anthropologists can use to explain the connection between two related fossil forms or between a fossil form and an extant one. When one of a pair of related fossils is later than the other, it may be reasoned that (1) the later form is directly descended (that is, evolved) from the earlier, or (2) both are descended independently from some still earlier common ancestor. With more than two forms, various combinations of these two interpretations are possible. The two types of hypothesis may be diagramed simply. If A, B, C, and D represent a temporal sequence of related fossils, their family tree may take the form either of a straight palm or of a branched willow (see Fig. 13-1). Evolution in a single line and branching evolution are called **anagenesis** and **cladogenesis** respectively (see p. 138).

The diversity of living species is, of course, testimony to the fact that branching has repeatedly occurred: indeed, all surviving organisms on earth share the same genetic mechanism and code and their precursors seem to have branched from each other at some time. That is why molecular geneticists feel free to represent all living organisms on the same tree. Some fossils must also have been on now-extinct limbs, other ones on the trunk leading to today's species. In the study of human evolution there has, perhaps, been too great a tendency to ignore or underrate the variability of all species and hence the variability at a given place and between places at a given time. Such variability within an evolving species leads to a netlike picture in which within a particular environment there tends to be continuity in adaptation to meet its demands, hence biological continuity in each climatic zone. But there are also

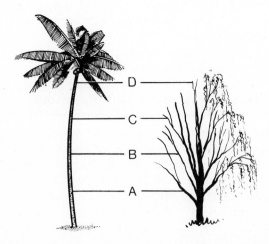

D

C

B

A

FIG. 13-1 It is sometimes uncertain exactly how several fossils are related to each other. An evolutionary tree may be interpreted as taking the form of a branched willow or that of a straight palm. Fossils A, B, C, and D may be related through earlier common ancestors (right) or may all be related as ancestors and descendants (left).

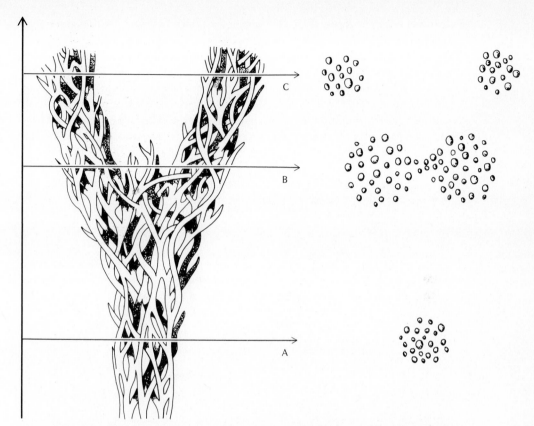

FIG. 13-2    Diagrammatic representation of the process of splitting of a single species (time level A) into two derived species (time level C). The species consist of populations symbolized in the diagram as strands composing a bundle. Some of these strands branch (a population becoming divided into two or more populations), fuse together (merging into single populations), or end blindly (populations becoming extinct). The cross sections shown on the right indicate the situations as seen on three successive time levels, A, B, and C. Redrawn from Th. Dobzhansky: *Evolution, genetics, and man.* New York: Wiley, 1955. Reproduced by permission.

species-wide evolutionary trends that are dispersed throughout the range at any given point in time. The trunk and limbs of an evolutionary tree are thus not simple sticks but are composed of interwoven fibers (Fig. 13-2). In the next three chapters the known fossils are, in general, arranged in chronological sequence insofar as it is known; most of those I discuss are considered as falling into evolutionary lines of ancestors and descendants leading to *Homo sapiens* and other extant species. The lines themselves encompass much species variability between individuals, between the sexes, between geographic locations, and, of course, with time. Some other students of the same material have a narrower concept of species and hence of the lines; they resort to the concept of **parallelism** to indicate that they believe the similarities to depend on earlier common origins followed by similar evolutionary courses.

In other situations it may be believed that the similarities are not the result of being in a line of descent nor of common origin. Thus, organisms, although of different ancestry, may be alike in living habits and appearance; such similar evolutionary development in different forms is termed **convergence** by paleontologists. More specifically, convergence refers to the development of similar

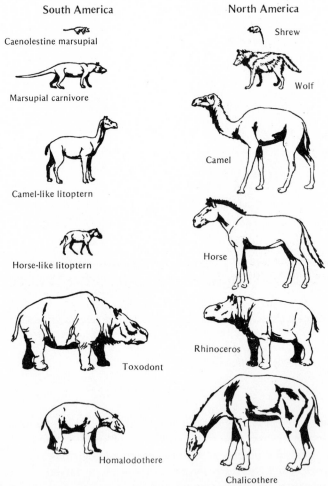

FIG. 13-3  Convergence is seen in animals that are not closely related evolutionarily but that have adapted to the environment in similar fashion. For instance, North and South America were long separated by a strait but convergent forms occurred in both continents. All the illustrated forms except shrew and wolf became extinct in the Americas. From G. G. Simpson: *The meaning of evolution.* New Haven: Yale University Press, 1967. Reproduced by permission.

FIG. 13-4    The convergent evolution of the hummingbird and the hummingmoth is a result of their common search for the same food source.

characteristics in animals that differ in ancestry (Fig. 13-3). The hummingbird and the hummingmoth, for example, have converged in their flying habits as a result of their common search for nectar in flowers as a source of food (Fig. 13-4). Due to their similar environments, the bird and moth developed similar habits even though their respective ancestors differed. Convergence is ordinarily limited to a single or a few characteristics—the whole animal does not converge. Similarities in the retina, the layer of visual cells in the eyes, of some quite diverse night-wakeful (nocturnal) animals are an example. Of the two main types of retinal cells (rods and cones) only rods, which are more sensitive to dim light, are present in some deep sea fish, bats, the armadillo, some lizards and snakes, and probably guinea pigs, whales, some lemurs, and the night monkey; owls, rats, and cats have a high ratio of rods to cones. All these animals differ markedly from each other, however, in respect to other characteristics less directly related to their night life. It is improbable that any instance of evolutionary convergence has been so dramatic and complete as to hide all traces of the diversity of origins.

A number of similarities between tarsiers and humans were once thought to demonstrate that the tarsier, not the great apes, was man's closest living relative. These features, now known to be caused by parallelism, or convergence, involve details of the bones of the skull and of the joints between them. For instance, in many animals the lacrimal bone is largely on the face at the side of the nose, but in us and tarsiers most of it is within the orbit. This is a convergence caused by the fact that we and the tarsier have both evolved large orbits for large eyes, and small noses as less dependence on the sense of smell was needed.

A similar evolutionary development in related forms is called **parallelism.** Parallelism, however, implies a similarity in the biological makeup of the ancestral forms; convergence does not. That is, if the common ancestors of two organisms were not very ancient, and if evolution in the descendant lines followed more or less the same course, the term "parallelism" is used. This term is usually applied to two species of organisms that were similar in origin and that remained similar as they evolved through having some of the same changes occur in both of them after they had become separate species. Thus, some crocodilelike fossils of the age of reptiles descended from the same primitive reptiles as present-day crocodiles, but differences between them indicate distinct evolutionary courses involving similar changes (Kraus, 1964; see Fig. 13-5).

The cause of parallelism is the same as that of convergence. The organisms, in order to survive in similar environments, must adapt the same biological structures. Parallelism, like convergence, is a matter of adaptation under the control of natural selection. The lack of a tail in gibbons, the great apes, and

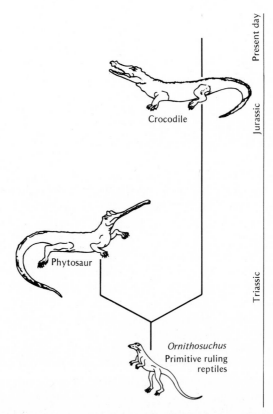

FIG. 13-5 Parallelism in phytosaur and crocodile evolution. The long snout, position of the eyes, and form of the limbs and tail evolved similarly from a common ancestor among the ruling reptiles, as phytosaur and crocodile adapted in a parallel fashion to a similar largely aquatic environment. From B. S. Kraus: *The basis of human evolution.* New York: Harper and Row, 1964. Reproduced by permission.

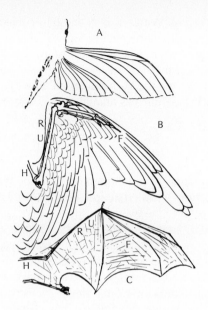

FIG. 13-6   Homology and analogy. The wings of *A,* insect; *B,* bird; and *C,* bat are all analogous in function. The bones of the forelimb: *H* (humerus), *R* (radius), and *U* (ulna) in the two vertebrates are homologous with each other and with the corresponding bones (see Fig. 13-8) in the forelimb of other vertebrates. Note also that homologous bones of the "fingers" *(F)* of the two kinds of vertebrates are not functionally analogous. From G. G. Simpson: *The meaning of evolution.* New Haven: Yale University Press, 1967. Reproduced by permission.

humans is probably a case of parallelism since their common ancestors probably had tails that were lost in a parallel fashion in the separate evolutionary lines after they diverged. We cannot be sure that their common ancestors had more coccygeal (tail) vertebrae than the few short ones present in each of these forms, because no fossil coccygeal vertebra is known. All the monkeys, however, have tails. The Cercopithecidae, the monkeys most closely related to us and the apes, are very varied in tail length and those species with similar tail length are not the most closely related to each other. The tail is a functionally important member used for balance, and very diverse species of Cercopithecidae (the Colobus monkeys and the vervets, for instance) are both highly arboreal and have long tails, probably as a parallel evolutionary adaptation to arboreal quadrupedal locomotion. Likewise the reduction of the tail is probably a response to locomotor requirements that occurred in parallel in response to brachiation and terrestrial life in the gibbons and in the Hominoidea.

## Homology and Analogy

Another way of looking at some of the same phenomena places emphasis on the structures rather than on the processes by which they evolved. In evolutionary biology the term **homology** means similarity in origin, **homoplasy** means similarity in appearance but not in origin, and **analogy** means similarity in function but not in origin (Fig. 13-6). However, as Yount (1967) points out, a statement of homology must give its standard of reference. Thus, the wings of different species of birds are homologous as wings, but there is no homology as wings between those of a bird and a bat. Wings of bird and bat, considered as wings, are merely analogous, but both evolved from parts of the arm, forearm, and hand of four-limbed, five-fingered vertebrates, and as such are homologous as forelimbs, along with seals' flippers and the human upper extremity. The wings of the hummingbird and the hummingmoth, however, are not homologous by any standard (except perhaps as animal appendages); they are analogous as wings.

## Adaptive Radiation

The evolutionary spread and differentiation of the descendants of one type of animal, of whatever level of classification, is called **adaptive radiation.** Unlike parallelism and convergence, which refer to the ways two species of organisms remain similar or become more similar, adaptive radiation refers to the way a species evolves into progressively more and more dissimilar organisms. The descendants of a single species sometimes evolve to take advantage of very varied environments and opportunities. Rapid changes in the external environment may cause new forms of animals to develop from a single ancestral form. The evolution of a trait that opens up many new possibilities may also give rise to adaptive radiation.

Adaptive radiation is well exemplified by the history of the mammals. With the geological revolution that marked the end of the Mesozoic period (the age of reptiles) and the start of the Tertiary, the previous stable climates became more changeable. The dinosaurs did not adapt and so became extinct, while the mammals evolved in many distinct lines. The rodents specialized for gnawing, the carnivores for hunting, the hoofed animals for grazing; the primates and sloths took to the trees; the whales, seals, and sea cows became adapted for life in the oceans; and the bats took to the air. Furthermore, each of these mammalian orders in turn gave rise to sublines that colonized new environments by acquiring new modes of life. Many of today's mammals are far different from their primitive common ancestors of the **Paleocene Epoch.** In addition, various orders and suborders of mammals have undergone further differentiation, branching or "radiating" into types adapted to different habitats (see Fig. 13-7). Thus, as mentioned previously, all the chief groups of primates today include species with contrasting dietary habits. Insect-eating, seed-eating, fruit-eating, leaf-eating, and more or less omnivorous genera recurred in different branches of the primates as these branches departed more and more from the ancestral forms. This adaptive radiation within the branches is thus accompanied by parallelism between the branches and convergence of adaptations toward those of some nonprimate lines. The fact is that all small endothermic animals have relatively large surface area for their weight; they therefore need high-energy food such as insects, and insectivorous adaptations reappear in the small members of many lines. Specializations for use of low-energy, high-bulk vegetation as food reappear in large animals in many evolutionary lines.

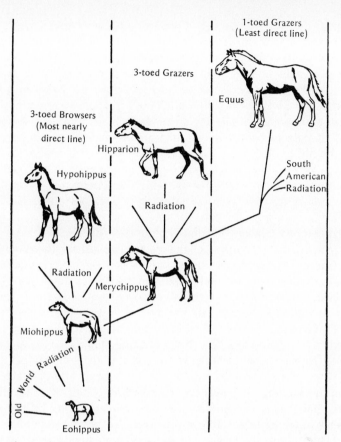

FIG. 13-7    The evolution of the horse family is well known from fossils of numerous species (only a few of which are shown reconstructed above and drawn to the same scale). In contrast to the horse family, the lines of primate evolution are incompletely represented in the known fossil record. Anthropologists rely on the principles developed by studying forms with abundant fossil material, such as the horse, to interpret the nature of adaptive radiation in the primates. From G. G. Simpson: *The meaning of evolution.* New Haven: Yale University Press, 1967. Reproduced by permission.

## Generalized and Specialized Forms

The term "generalized" is sometimes used by biologists to mean "capable of several functions." In paleontology, however, that is true only to the extent that it implies that the anatomical feature or the species as a whole is capable of continuing diversification through evolution by natural selection. Merely to be like ancestral forms is to be "primitive," whereas those structures that serve a variety of functions and preserve the capacity to evolve in a variety of ways are **generalized,** while those that serve a single function and species that can survive only by single restricted ways of life (or that can evolve by further development in only one limited direction) are called **specialized.** The existence, or prospect of development, of diverse functions is a sign of being generalized. By this criterion, we are in many ways generalized mammals. We preserve five digits on each hand and foot and are notably lacking in such specializations as horns, tusks, wings, and hoofs. We are specialized, however, in respect to our unusual hind limbs and in our capacity for rapid movement on them in a manner not duplicated in other animals. This is a specialization, because bipedalism is effective and, although it might evolve to become more so, it is highly unlikely that the hind limbs will re-evolve for quadrupedal locomotion or any other function. It is generally agreed that the retention by humans of generalized features of the upper limb permitted us to manipulate things in our hands, and become toolmakers and tool users. This ability to manipulate is not a specialization because the hand can do several things, and through different behavioral emphasis on one or another of them it would be possible for an animal with such hands to give rise to forms with diverse specializations. Of course, the human hand is capable of very precise manipulations, such as those of the watchmaker and the pianist, but this does not make it "specialized" because the same hands of the same individuals can serve to grip an axe with great strength or a scalpel with great precision. The hand is usually used in one of two ways: (1) in the power grip, all the fingers except the thumb are firmly curled around the object being held; (2) in the precision grip, the thumb, forefinger, and middle finger are used for fine manipulation (as in writing). The hand is also used in other ways: the knuckles in boxing, the flat of the palm in clapping, the nails for removing a splinter. It is the diversity of functions that makes the human hand generalized. The delicately precise movements have not been achieved by loss of all other functions.

It is easier to apply the terms "generalized" and "specialized" to fossil than to living forms. In hindsight one can note that the enormous antlers of the Irish elk are a "specialization," or, since they may have contributed to the extinction of this species, an "overspecialization." But looking ahead it is hard to predict which animals of today will give rise to radiating forms and to say which of their features are generalized and can give rise to diverse new forms. The five-fingered hand is called generalized because we know that it has given rise to forms as diverse as those of the mole and the horse (see Fig. 13-8). The simple mammalian external ear is not usually considered generalized, but it would be so considered if there were some animals that had evolved from external ears new forms of locomotion, touch, or the grasping of food. In the case of the human hand simple diversity of function leads to its classification as generalized. The identification of generalized structures can also be made by comparison with those of specialized descendants.

## Pedomorphism

The evolutionary status of *Homo sapiens* has been characterized not only as plastic and generalized but also as having a third more or less independent property—that of **pedomorphism,** a term meaning "childlike in form." The adult

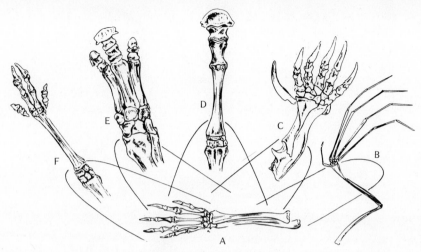

FIG. 13-8   Adaptive radiation in the forelimbs of mammals. *A,* tenrec, a large insectivore with limb structure much like the shrew except for size; *B,* bat wing; *C,* mole; *D,* horse; *E,* rhinoceros; and *F,* deer. (Reduced to similar size.) Each is modified from the primitive form (approximated by the tenrec) by changes of proportion, fusion of parts, or loss of parts. The forms of homologous bones have become modified for flight in the bat, digging in the mole, and walking and running at different rates and supporting different weights in the other animals shown. From E. O. Dodson: *Evolution: Progress and product.* New York: Van Nostrand, 1960. Reproduced by permission.

man or woman displays a number of physical traits that in other animals are seen only in the young or even in the fetus—such features as the rounded form of the forehead and the delay or absence of fusion of certain bones, such as the nasal bones. Adult great apes, on the other hand, show more developed features in these respects, which are referred to as **gerontomorphic** (in the form of old age) (Fig. 13-9). Differences exist in respect to these features in the peoples of different areas: Europeans, for example, show gerontomorphic features of the face, whereas Southeast Asians and South African Bushmen have more bulbous foreheads, flat faces, and other "infantile" characteristics.

What is it about nonfusion of the nasal bones or a bulbous forehead that is adaptively advantageous in humans but not in apes? A brain case bulging in all directions can hold more brains in a smaller package, of course. The nasal bones must represent late development of bones in general and the capacity for continued growth for many years. Prolonged childhood status and postponed reproductive maturity go well with "higher" education. In other words, the aspects of pedomorphism that seem most important have to do with learning and cultural behavior rather than with a "baby face." It is a prolonged social infantilism that keeps the human young at home learning from their parents and that may have aided the development of language and culture.

The extent to which childhood status is prolonged by social custom varies over time. In Elizabethan England children had considerable responsibility and established their own families at a early age. Since the industrial revolution

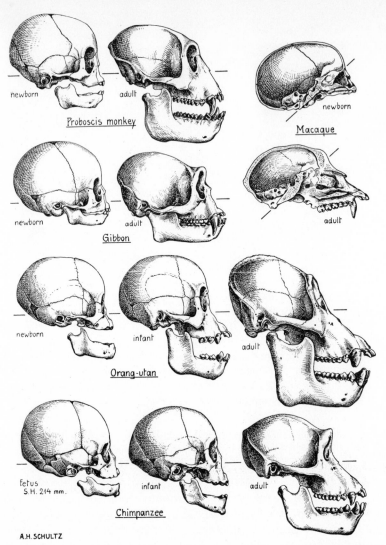

newborn    adult

**Proboscis monkey**

newborn

**Macaque**

newborn    adult

**Gibbon**

adult

newborn    infant    adult

**Orang-utan**

Fetus
S.H. 214 mm.    infant    adult

**Chimpanzee**

A.H. SCHULTZ

FIG. 13-9 Age changes in the skulls of some catarrhine primates, all reduced so that the nasion–opisthocranion (root of the nose to back of the head) is shown as equal. The skulls are shown in the eye-ear plane. The infant chimpanzee skull is that of the 74-day-old daughter of the adult female chimpanzee whose skull is also shown.

Note that during growth the part of the skull in front of the auditory meatus (the ear hole) grows much more than that behind. This is largely the result of the development of the jaws and teeth, and the attachments of the chewing muscles. Jaws and teeth are not well developed in humans. Monkey and ape fetuses and newborn skulls (left) and infant skulls (center bottom) resemble each other and human skulls of all ages but differ in shape from adult monkey and ape skulls (right and center top). In the chimpanzee (bottom row), for instance, the canine teeth overlap and the upper canine teeth of the adult has a large root extending up the face. In monkeys and apes the adult skull is shaped by the muscles at the side of the head. In humans, on the other hand, changes of these kinds do not occur; the retention of infantile characteristics is called pedomorphism. The drawings are the work of, and are reproduced through the courtesy of, Prof. Adolph Schultz.

the duration of childhood has increased. Thus, aspects of social infantilism are cultural rather than biological traits. All human groups maintain long periods of childhood when compared with other primates. There is no reason to believe that the children of those human groups which hold them longer in social childhood mature any more slowly, however. In fact, differences between the rates of social and of biological maturation are a basis of social problems among many, if not all, societies.

## Correlation and Compensation of Parts

Paleontologists once thought that, as knowledge expanded, it would be possible to reconstruct the nature of any whole animal from any small part, such as a tooth. It was argued that the parts are so interrelated as to be mutually determined in detail. In fact, the interrelations are so complex that, for instance, small size of some part may imply either large size of the related part (compensation) or small size of the related part (positive correlation), or it may have no relationship at all.

**Compensation** is a general anatomical principle based on the necessity of some function. For example, two main nerves run to the palm of the hand. Among other functions, they provide for sensations such as touch and pain; one from the thumb side and the other from the fifth finger side. There is considerable variation in the supply to the middle and ring fingers, however. Although the areas supplied overlap, if the one nerve is larger and supplies a more extensive area of skin, the other is generally smaller and runs to a more restricted area. Compensation is also manifest in the two arteries to the same region: if the radial artery to the thumb side is smaller, the function of blood supply to the limb must be met by a relatively larger ulnar artery on the fifth finger side.

Positive correlation is the tendency of related parts to vary together. This is well represented in bilateral symmetry. The structures of the right and left limbs of the same individuals tend to be similar in size and shape. This is true to such an extent that when only one side of a fossil specimen is available paleontologists feel justified in using a photographically reversed image to take the place of the other side; they can readily reconstruct missing parts on the left side of a skull if they have available the corresponding parts of the right.

Positive correlation also expresses itself through general tendencies to influence a whole system or field. Reduction in size of the jaws is likely to be accompanied by reduction in size of the muscles of mastication, hence of the bony attachment of these muscles to the skull. Furthermore, the balance of the head will be affected and in this way reduction in the face will be accompanied by reduction in the neck muscles and in their bony attachments to the skull and to the spine.

The teeth are particularly instructive. There are overall influences on the dentition such as a general tendency to large or small teeth, and there are local correlations of fields (reduction or enlargement of adjoining groups of teeth) so that those rare human beings with four molar teeth in each row usually also have large molars in general and large third molars in particular. Development of teeth takes place in the embryo from a dental ridge that may be large or small in whole or in part.

The upper lateral incisors of man manifest the principle of positive correlation. If a lateral incisor is peg-shaped and reduced in size, it seems to represent a general problem of development of the teeth, and the corresponding tooth of the opposite side is usually also reduced or missing. The principle of compensation may outweigh correlation, however. That is, reduction in size of one tooth may accompany increase in size of an adjacent tooth with the same function (Sofaer et al., 1971). If one upper lateral incisor is absent the adjoining medial incisor tends to be larger than the one on the other side because of the compensatory mechanism.

When one comes to specific fossil material the opposite tendencies of the two principles, correlation and compensation, often make interpretation difficult. General size differences may represent differences in overall size of the organism, and attempts to guess the size of an animal by the size of his teeth have been published. But there are differences within the tooth row. A fossil shark has been estimated to have had a length of 60–100 feet on the basis of huge fossil teeth. New estimates (Randall, 1973), taking into account the decrease in tooth size from front to back of the row in modern white sharks, reduce the estimate to about 43 feet. Differences in proportions of teeth or in the ratio of size of one tooth or group of teeth to another are more likely to represent compensatory functional adaptations through evolution and therefore to represent more significant evolutionary modifications than mere size. The interpretation of **Gigantopithecus** and **Australopithecus** (Chapters 14 and 15) involves evaluation of the significance of overall size and differential size of the teeth.

## Is Evolution Reversible?

In 1893 a Belgian paleontologist, Louis Dollo, published the theory that evolution is irreversible. There are no examples of present forms that have developed independently and that are exactly like some ancient prototype. There are, however, examples of the re-evolution of types highly similar in some particular respects to ancient forms. For example, the extinct flying reptiles, the pterosaurs, developed wings but eventually died out; wings were re-evolved independently in the birds and bats. A change of the natural environment in an exact stepwise reverse order is exceedingly rare; hence, an occasion for reversed natural selection involving a number of factors in a given order would be just as rare. It is hard to imagine that, for instance, a nuclear holocaust would leave human survivors exactly like some of the fossils to be described in subsequent chapters. It is more likely that they would vary in a number of ways, mostly maladaptive, and that if they survived, new relationships with surving flora and fauna would push evolution in a different direction. Other organisms play a large part in the adaptation of any form of life to its natural environment. In order to survive, man, for example, depends upon many other organisms such as cattle, corn, cod, bees, yeast, and pine. If a reversal were to occur in man, it would require that such organisms also be reversing so that past human environments would be recreated. Evolution is irreversible to the extent that true **atavisms** or throwbacks to earlier forms do not occur in detail. Single steps backward, returning to an ancestral condition, sometimes occur in reversed mutations (as has been well documented in bacteria, see Fig. 6-3). That such reversals will not recapitulate a whole sequence is evidence for Dollo's principle. However, according to present knowledge, the following generation is almost as likely to reverse a characteristic as to augment it.

We have no evidence for any force within the organism directing the line of its unfolding evolution (the now discredited idea of **orthogenesis**). Evolutionary trends may be maintained, however, by the process known as **orthoselection.** The climate of the world changes gradually over long periods of time; the advances and retreats of the ice ages, for example, occurred over many thousands of years. Such trends apply continuing selective pressures on organisms—pressures that in turn may give a direction to evolution; in other words, an orthoselection. Since different species form important parts of each other's environment, orthoselection in some organisms would tend to impose orthoselection on others. The trends do not depend on any internal force and may depend on different environmental factors of which climate is only one. Different forces of selection may wax and wane at different times.

## Evolution of Parts and of Wholes

The evolution of a species tends to be inconstant and asymmetrical. That is, it may be rapid at one time, slow at another—in rare cases it may even stop altogether (Fig. 13-10). At one time it may affect the limbs, and at another it may affect the jaws. With a change in the food supply or some other alteration in the environment, running or biting ability, for example, becomes more or less important in natural selection.

This variability in the tempo of evolution of different anatomical structures in the same line (that is, in ancestors and descendants) makes it unwise to draw sweeping conclusions concerning the relationship of two fossil forms on the basis of single characteristics. Instead, it is necessary to follow the evolution of whole functional systems (Washburn, 1951). Since the systems themselves sometimes evolve at different rates, one must also take into account the total morphological pattern of the animal insofar as it is preserved (Clark, 1955). Although all past animals must have been integrated in the same way as living ones, the interrelationships between functional systems in a single fossil animal are not always self-evident. If one knows about the conditions under which it lived it may help interpretation, but often the wisest response to a fragmentary fossil is suspended judgment while one searches for additional material. A few observations or measurements considered out of context can lead the unwary anthropologist far astray.

The evolutionary trends of different organ systems (locomotor system, nervous system, respiratory system, and so on) separately respond to the conditions

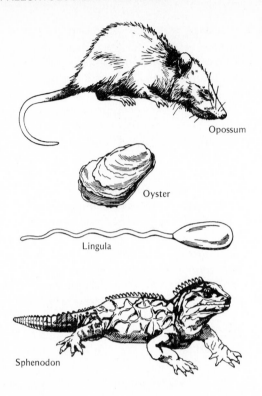

Opossum

Oyster

Lingula

Sphenodon

FIG. 13-10 Some living animals of which we have almost identical fossils over long periods of time. Evolution of these "immortals" seems to have reached a virtual standstill long ago. The opossum, for instance still resembles some of the earliest fossil mammals. From G. G. Simpson: *The meaning of evolution.* New Haven: Yale University Press, 1967. Reproduced by permission.

in their spheres. The systems can therefore sometimes be studied separately. For example, from studies of comparative anatomy and function it is possible to identify some particularly striking hallmarks of *Homo sapiens,* such as the bipedal gait and the relatively large and functionally effective brain. The evolutionary trends toward these characteristics, as they unfold in the fossil record, are referred to as **bipedalization** and **encephalization,** respectively. The evolution of these characteristics was distinct and separate; bipedalism apparently preceded encephalization. Nevertheless the development of a cultural way of life made both advantageous and, in this sense, they are both part of the same process of human evolution. The mosaic pattern of human evolution led first to the evolution of a manipulative apparatus with hand and eye coordination, then to bipedalization to permit use of the hands even during locomotion, but human encephalization was late and rapid. In each case there is a feedback to the earlier established trend: encephalization reinforces the bipedalism and bipedalism permits further evolutionary emphasis on a life niche utilizing exact hand-eye coordination.

## Extinction

In discussing fossil forms one must remember that for evolution it is the species or larger group to which the fossil belonged that is significant. Individuals lived and died and may or may not have left progeny, but the question we want answered is whether the group to which they belonged became extinct or whether it gave rise to some later species.

Relationships between animals that are similar in some respects are often too easily assumed. Some animal forms survive—especially in out-of-the-way places—long after their ancestors have given rise to quite different descendants elsewhere. We may be descended by many lines from one ancestor and by none at all from some of his or her contemporaries. Indeed, it would be sheer chance if any fossil specimen now known were in fact the mortal remains of your very ancestor. With average fertility a person would leave two billion offspring in thirty-one generations, and an average person would be descended about two billion different times by different lines of descent from a single average dweller of the fourth century A.D. About 62 generations ago (if the average parent was just over 25 years old at the birth of each child). Yet the statistics are deceptive because in most cases many lines would reconverge from each ancestor and in other cases no lines continue. No one can claim descent by any line from Saint Agnes, because she had no children when she was martyred about 304 A.D. Furthermore, if there were any direct descendants of **Australopithecus africanus,** they are certainly not from the individual we know by the original fossil skull from Taung; the skull is that of an individual who died well below reproductive age.

Nature produces huge numbers of seeds, eggs, and sperm, and large numbers of young are born. But in stable populations (and all populations sooner or later must stabilize or oscillate around some sustainable number if they are to survive) for each parent the average number of surviving (and reproducing) children must be two. Some individuals have many more, but this is balanced by the many who have less.

Whole populations do not easily become totally extinct—at least extinction is rare in human populations. Even with the overrunning of other lands by Europeans in the last three centuries, Hottentots and Hopis, Polynesians and Pygmies, survive. Although the last pure Tasmanian, a dark, woolly-haired woman called Truganini, died in 1877, and it is often asserted that the Tasmanians have gone the way of the great auk, numerous descendants of Tasmanians (interbred with Australian aborigines and Europeans) survive on Cape Barren Island, Australia (Birdsell, 1948).

In tracing relations between individual fossils we can not imply much about them as individuals. Like the *Australopithecus* fossil from Taung, they may have died childless. We assume, however, that every fossil belonged to a more or less variable population. We merely refer to the taxonomic group in which the individual is classified. Arrows of relatedness on evolutionary charts should be taken to connect groups (that is, populations, species, or even larger categories). Such charts cannot indicate kinship between the former owners of individual skeletons. In the past some anthropologists have, on occasion, emphasized details in their fossil material that may very well represent nothing more than individual idiosyncrasies. Members of any given group will vary to some extent in respect to every feature of every bone. Isolated fossils must be judged in terms of the probable degree of this variability within the population.

Of course, when only one specimen is available, the probable degree of variability can be inferred only from analogous features in other groups of organisms.

## Summary

The study of human evolution, utilizing both living and fossil primates, uses principles derived from other groups of animals to clarify their relationship to each other. Similar fossils of different antiquity may be related as ancestor and descendant, or both may descend from earlier common ancestors. Similar evolutionary developments in different forms is convergence; in related forms it is parallelism. The process by which an evolutionary tree is formed when an evolutionary line splits into species occupying different ecological niches is called adaptive radiation. Species near the base of the tree are generalized; those whose biological endowment restricts them to a limited way of life are specialized. *Homo sapiens* is in some ways generalized. Our species has evolved a tendency to slow individual development. Rapid maturation is the primitive condition, but there is no reason to think that pedomorphy, long maintainance of childlike characteristics, is a specialization.

Large size of some structure, such as a central incisor tooth, may correlate with large size of the teeth in general or it may compensate for absence of the adjacent tooth. Evolution never exactly reverses itself, but its tempo varies greatly and some lines end in extinction. Even when the group survives some individuals leave no progeny, and evolutionary studies therefore focus on populations rather than individuals.

# CHAPTER 14

# EARLY PRIMATES

## The Cenozoic Era

The end of the **Mesozoic Era** saw a geological revolution with upthrusting of the chief mountain systems of today, such as the Rockies. This is inferred from the fact that the Mesozoic rocks of these mountains are much folded on each other, whereas the rock formations of the subsequent **Cenozoic Era** overlie them in more orderly layers. The Cenozoic Era started about 63–66 million years ago (Fig. 14-1). This date has been estimated by means of the clock provided by spontaneous atomic disintegration of radioactive uranium. As uranium gives off its electrons, a stable isotope of lead of atomic weight 206 is left behind, which is distinguishable from common lead of atomic weight 208. The amount of uranium converted to lead 206 per year is always in the same proportion to the amount of uranium present. The conversion of an atom of uranium to one of lead is rare. Though rare, the rate of individual transformation is constant and therefore the number of conversions depends on the amount of uranium present and the length of time that has elapsed. It is therefore possible to calculate from a specimen of lead-uranium ore the approximate number of years it has existed.

| Era (and duration) | Period | Estimated time since beginning of each period (in millions of years) | Epoch | Life |
|---|---|---|---|---|
| | | 0.11 | Holocene (Recent) | Homo sapiens sapiens the only human species |
| | Quaternary | 1.9* | Pleistocene | Modern species of mammals and their forerunners; extinction of many species of large mammals; the great glaciations |
| Cenozoic (age of mammals; about 65 million years) | | 5.5 | Pliocene | Appearance of many of today's genera of mammals |
| | | 26 | Miocene | Rise of modern subfamilies of mammals; spread of grassy plains; evolution of grazing mammals |
| | Tertiary | 37–38 | Oligocene | Rise of modern families of mammals |
| | | 53–54 | Eocene | Rise of modern orders and suborders of mammals |
| | | 65 | Paleocene | Dominance of archaic mammals |
| Mesozoic (age of reptiles; lasted about 165 million years) | Cretaceous | 130 | | Extinction of large reptiles and origin of primates by end of period |
| | Jurassic | 180 | | Reptiles dominant; first birds; archaic mammals |
| | Triassic | 230 | | First dinosaurs, turtles, ichthyosaurs, plesiosaurs |

*The beginning of the Olduvai Event was about 1.9 million years ago. However, the first occurrence of microscopic marine invertebrates of a typically Pleistocene form was about either 0.8 or 1.8 million years ago and this, according to some, is the technically correct date; the Villafranchian land mammals (see p. 232) appeared at very different times from place to place, and some anthropologists set the beginning of the Pleistocene as the onset of the Villafranchian in each area (in France that occurred about 3.2 million years ago).

FIG. 14-1   Geological periods of the Mesozoic and Cenozoic eras. The time estimates are based on the rate of disintegration of radioactive materials found in a number of deposits.

The date of the onset of the Cenozoic (63–66 million years ago) has been estimated from a deposit representing the end of the preceding period, the Cretaceous. The date has been confirmed by dating the first epoch of the Cenozoic, the **Paleocene,** by radioactive isotope methods, especially the potassium-argon method. One of the isotopes of potassium ($^{40}$K), which occurs in volcanic rocks such as basalt, undergoes radioactive decay to a particular isotope of argon ($^{40}$A). Like all radioactive emission this occurs at a constant rate per given amount of the original isotope. Half of it is converted in 1.3 billion years. Potassium 40 is therefore said to have a **half-life** of $1.3 \times 10^{10}$ years. Since the argon gas is trapped within the basalt and can be extracted, measured, and compared to the amount of potassium, the date at which the rock was formed from molten lava can be calculated. In a site near Denver, Colorado, waterborne deposits containing fossils of the earliest Cenozoic types of animals were covered by a flow of lava. The basalt of the flow gives a potassium-argon date of 58 million years ago, and other studies of Paleocene rock by uranium or potassium-argon methods yield dates of 57–59 million years. Since these dates are of Cenozoic rocks, 57–59 million years ago is the latest possible onset of the Cenozoic.

The Cenozoic Era, beginning with the Paleocene, is called the "Age of the Mammals." Cenozoic deposits yield the fossils that demonstrate the adaptive radiation of all the extant orders of mammals, including the primates. Geologists divide the Cenozoic Era into two periods, the Tertiary and the Quaternary. The former is divided into five epochs: Paleocene, **Eocene, Oligocene, Miocene,** and **Pliocene.** The Quaternary is again divided into two, **Pleistocene** and Holocene (or Recent).

The epochs in turn are often divided into three: Early, Middle and Late. These are called "Lower," "Middle," and "Upper," because they are sometimes identified by superposition of later geological strata of waterborne sediments upon earlier ones. Such dates cannot be translated directly into years, but they are very useful because strata often can be traced from place to place by similar appearance of the rock or by having the same species of fossils in similar frequencies. In this way the **stratigraphic sequences** of different sites can be correlated.

## Fossils of Prosimians

By Middle Triassic times (early in the Mesozoic Era) some reptiles showed mammalian features of the teeth, palate, and jaw, and by the Late Triassic, true mammals were already in existence (Romer, 1969).

The chief features that distinguish mammals from reptiles lie in the different modes of reproduction and development. The placenta intimately associating the fetus with the mother is a mammalian development that leaves no trace in the fossil record. The fossils, however, manifest such changes as differentation of the teeth, reduction in number and other changes in the bones of the skull, a secondary palate (the bony roof of the mouth), and simplification of the lower jaw to a single bone. In the typical reptile the teeth are similar to each other; in mammals each tooth in the row has its own distinctive shape. There are four different kinds of teeth in mammals, designated, from the middle of the front of the row to the back on each side of either jaw, as **incisors, canines, premolars,** and **molars.** The list of the number of each kind in each jaw is called the dental formula (see p. 156) and the dental formula can be different in different mammalian species. In most reptiles the nose and mouth are not separated by the palate as in mammals. In present-day reptiles the lower jaw is ossified from several centers; in mammals there is a single pair of jaw bones and the other bones of the reptilian jaw are incorporated into the mammalian organ of hearing as the little bones (ossicles) of the middle ear.

A tooth of what may be the earliest primate fossil, called *Purgatorius,* was found together with bones of six species of dinosaurs in a deposit of the end of the Cretaceous Period in Montana (Van Valen and Sloan, 1965). The genus *Purgatorius* survived into the Paleocene. It was, at least to judge from the teeth, rather similar to some insectivores such as hedgehogs. At that early stage, primate evolution had barely shown itself in some small features of the pattern of the teeth. The typical lower molar tooth has a low area that receives the upper tooth and a high triangular area, the wall of which forms a shears with the upper. These are primitive features. They are found in early **prosimian** primates and are not very different from those of insectivores of the time; in fact, not all paleontologists who have studied the question consider *Purgatorius* to be a primate.

In the following brief Paleocene and longer Eocene epochs a wide variety of prosimian primates evolved. Most of these are grouped into a now extinct superfamily (Van Valen, 1969), but there are also fossils belonging to the superfamilies Lemuriformes and Tarsiiformes. These fossils may include ancestral types of present-day forms. In the Paleocene, North America was joined directly to Europe (Fig. 14-2), and many genera of mammals, including two (perhaps three) of the fossil primate forms, are known in both the Old World and the New. Since all the early prosimians have been found in the Northern Hemisphere it is likely that they were distributed throughout what is now the Artic and that evolution and adaptive radiation of prosimians occurred there during the time when the climate was much milder than now (Simons, 1968a) (Fig. 14-3).

The earliest primate of which a whole fossil skull and much of the skeleton is known is *Plesiadapis* (Fig. 14-4). Fossils of this genus have been found in Paleocene deposits in North America and in France (Simons, 1964a). *Plesiadapis* is a member of a family of rodentlike primates, ranging in size from that of a squirrel to that of the domestic cat. The large front teeth are separated from the cheek teeth by a wide gap and must have been used for gnawing. These and the well-developed nose protruded forward between the eyes, which faced to the sides and were incapable of stereoscopic vision. The orbits also lacked the bar of bone behind the eye **(postorbital bar)** that protects the eyes of animals whose eyes focus forward together.

It should be said at this point that these and other Paleocene primates do not possess many of the diagnostic features of the order (the formation of the bony ear, the postorbital bar, the grasping thumb or great toe with a flat nail) and some scholars therefore relegate them to another order, the **Insectivora,** which serves as a waste basket for unspecialized placental mammals (Cartmill, 1972). *Plesiadapis* is more like a rodent than like an insectivore, however. In fact, the

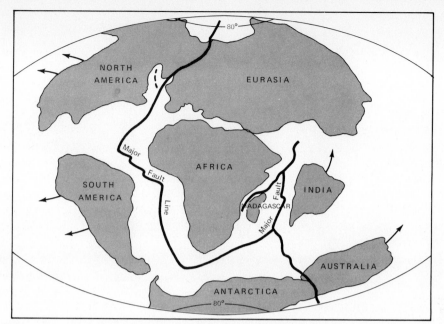

FIG. 14-2   A reconstruction of the world map at the end of the Cretaceous. From R. Pearson: *Introduction to Anthropology.* New York: Holt, Rinehart and Winston, 1974.

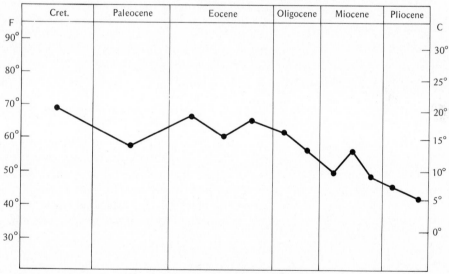

Mean annual temperature latitude 40°- 50° N

FIG. 14-3   In the past the climate was very different from that of today. Temperatures show considerable change from the Paleocene to the Pliocene, with the overall trend being toward cooler climates. In the Pleistocene there was a further drop in temperature and widespread glaciation. However, primate evolution from the late Cretaceous through the Pliocene occurred under milder conditions that those of today. Primate fossils found in Wyoming, for example, lived at a time when that part of the United States had a subtropical climate. Adapted from E. Dorf: "The earth's changing climates." *Weatherwise 10,* 54, 1957. Reproduced by permission.

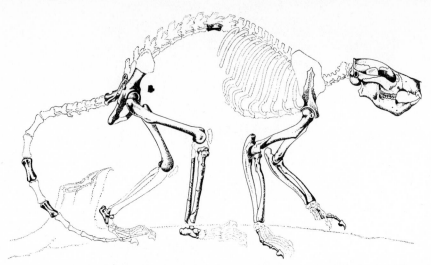

FIG. 14-4    The Paleocene prosimian *Plesiadapis,* reconstructed on the basis of French and North African fossil finds. Bones shown in outline are hypothetical. The characteristic wide gap between this rodentlike animal's cheek teeth and its slanting incisors is evident. From E. L. Simons: "The early relatives of man." Copyright © 1964 by Scientific American, Inc. All rights reserved.

rodents probably evolved from primitive primates and they went through a broad adaptive radiation, displacing prosimians from any adaptive niche that called for continuously growing chisellike incisor teeth (except for the aye-aye of Madagascar, see p. 150).

Another family of prosimians, Adapidae, lived in both hemispheres but several million years after *Plesiadapis.* It shows the direction of evolution in the primates. The Adapidae are well known from *Adapis* in Europe and almost complete skeletons of various species of two North American genera, *Smilodectes* and *Notharctus* (Fig. 14-5). These show forward rotation of the eyes and the associated postorbital bar of bone characteristic of the strong reliance on eyesight of all subsequent primates. These features and the limb bones point to an arboreal way of life. Some members of the Adapidae show close similarities in certain features to living lemuriform and lorisiform prosimi-

FIG. 14-5    *Opposite, top:* The Eocene prosimian *Smilodectes,* several million years junior to *Plesiadapis* (Fig. 14-3) and a far more advanced animal. Its snout is shorter, the front portion of the brain is enlarged, and its eyes are positioned on the skull in a way that permits the visual fields to overlap. Its relatively long hind limbs give *Smilodectes* a remarkable resemblance to the sifaka, a modern Madagastcar lemur. Photograph courtesy of The Smithsonian Institution, negative number 2129.

*Opposite, bottom: Notharctus,* an Eocene lemuroid found in North America, had a small skull about three inches long. Photograph courtesy of the American Museum of Natural History.

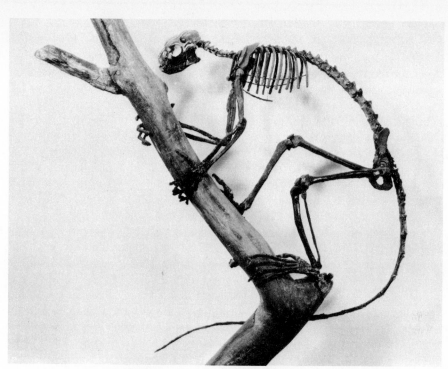

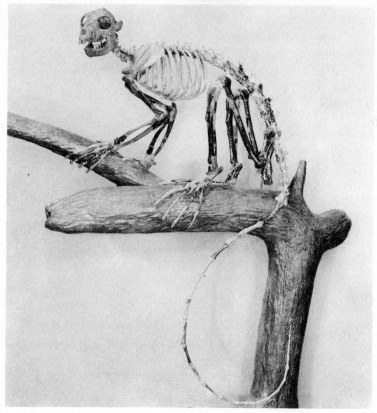

ans (for instance the foot of *Smilodectes* had a widely separated great toe for clutching the upright trunk of trees as in the Indriidae of Madagascar). The actual ancestors of the subsequent Madagascar genera are probably to be found in still unknown or poorly represented Old World genera of the family Adapidae, however. With the southward migration of the equator and the separation of North America and Europe during the Eocene, there was no further sharing of primate genera between Asia and America.

Other Paleocene and Eocene prosimian families show similarities to the other living primates. The tarsier's specialized adaptation of the foot for leaping is already seen in the elongated tarsal (ankle) bones of some of these prosimians, such as *Necrolemur*. This genus also shows more advanced rotation of the orbits to the front as in the tarsier. The dental formula (absence of lower front teeth in *Necrolemur*) is different from that of the modern tarsier, however. Still another Eocene and Oligocene prosimian family, the Omomyidae, shows some close similarities to higher primates and especially to the New World monkeys. The early genera were small and had unspecialized molar teeth. They shared with New World monkeys the same dental formula (2.1.3.3), a reduction in the size of the third molars, and details of molar **cusp** pattern (the arrangement of the little elevations on the biting surfaces of the back teeth). The Omomyidae show progressive enlargement of forward-facing orbits and the movement of the lower incisors away from a jutting comb for fur to the upright position of higher primates. However, there are dental specializations (the lower incisor teeth of the later forms are very large). The relative sizes of the different teeth therefore exclude any but the earliest Omomyidae from consideration as actual ancestors of the South American monkeys.

## New World Primates

By the mid Eocene, Europe and North America were no longer connected. The continents of South America and Africa were closer then than now (the continents of the world have been drifting apart). In the early Tertiary, South America and Africa may have been separated only by a wide strait and been crossed by monkeys on natural rafts. The view that the New World monkeys originated in Africa and crossed by raft has its adherents (Hoffstetter, 1972). The water gap of the South Atlantic was narrow at the time, but the one between North and South America was also narrow and it was apparently easier to cross since there probably were island "stepping stones."

Some South American primate fossils are claimed to date back to the Oligocene epoch. They show some primitive features of the skull, jaws, and teeth and also features of the modern South American monkeys. New World fossils definitely of ceboid monkeys date back to the Miocene epoch in Colombia and Argentina (Olson, 1964). The monkeys were of the type still native to the Western Hemisphere today. The molecular evidence places the Old World monkeys closer to the New World monkeys than to any prosimian. The similarities between the New World **(platyrrhine)** monkeys and the Old World **(catarrhine)** monkeys are better explained by common origin than by convergent or long parallel evolutionary development but does not settle the question of whether they came via North America or across the South Atlantic.

## Oligocene Catarrhines

Almost everything known about higher primates in the Oligocene derives from fossils found in a geological formation in a small area of the Egyptian desert, known as the **Fayum,**\* sixty miles southwest of Cairo. The description and interpretation of the finds and the reinterpretation of the early discoveries are largely due to E. L. Simons (1967a, 1969a, and elsewhere).

The Fayum Oligocene formation is over 730 feet deep and may span 5 to 7 million years. The nine species of six genera of primates that have been found there may therefore not all have been contemporaneous with each other.

Two of the genera (*Apidium* and *Parapithecus*) form a family, the Parapithecidae (from the Greek *para,* "next to," and *pithekos,* "ape"), now known from several scores of fossilized mandibles and a few maxillae; a frontal bone with part of the orbits probably also belongs to *Parapithecus*. The jaws and teeth of *Parapithecus* are very much like those of some modern monkeys of Africa except that they have the typical platyrrhine dental formula (2.1.3.3) rather than that of all contemporary catarrhines (2.1.2.3). However, within a suborder of mammals it is common to have several dental formulae, and this feature in itself can not be used to separate catarrhine from platyrrhine primates in the Oligocene, although it does so today.

Another Oligocene fossil from the Fayum *(Aelopithecus)* foreshadows the later fossil *Pliopithecus* (see pp. 221–222) and the gibbon. *Aelopithecus* has a deep gibbonlike symphysis (the front of the lower jaw) and seems to confirm the belief that the gibbons became distinct from the great apes long before the latter separated from man. Another fossil is called *Propliopithecus* because at the time it was named it was thought to be a forerunner of *Pliopithecus*.

Perhaps the most important find from the Fayum (Simons, 1969a) is the nearly complete skull of *Aegyptopithecus* ("Egyptian Ape") (Fig. 14-6). It dates to about 29 million years ago, and is remarkably like *Dryopithecus africanus* of East Africa (see pp. 222–225) although considerably smaller. It may therefore be the best candidate among the known fossils for a common ancestor of humans and the great apes. The snout and nostrils jut forward and the face is therefore long and narrow. The orbits are closed in back like the Parapithecidae, *Dryopithecus,* and all modern **Anthropoidea** (monkeys, apes, and humans). This is a further development from the postorbital bar of bone of Eocene prosimians.

Still other primate fossils from the Fayum include bones of the arm with a tunnel (the entepicondylar foramen) similar to that which transmits a nerve and artery in many animals, including New World monkeys. And there are well-developed tail bones, which, especially if they come from *Aegyptopithecus,* suggest that the ancestors of apes and humans may have had tails at that time

---

\*Place names in **boldface** will be found in the maps on the end papers.

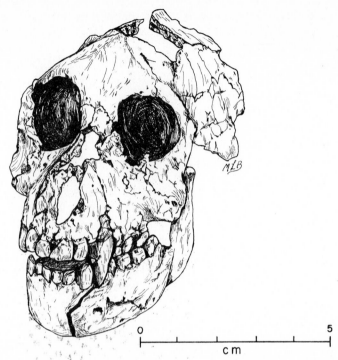

0                                                                5

c m

FIG. 14-6  *Aegyptopithecus zeuxis,* an Oligocene ape species thought to stand near the base of the hominoid radiation. The upper incisors are isolated teeth not found with the skull. The mandible is a composite reconstruction based on two partial lower jaws, and the lower teeth are restored in part from isolated teeth. From C. L. Brace, H. Nelson, and N. Korn: *Atlas of fossil man.* New York: Holt, Rinehart and Winston, 1971. Reproduced by permission. The drawing was made from a photograph furnished by Professor E. L. Simons, Yale University.

(Simons, 1967b). The tail length is very different in some otherwise similar monkeys today, however, so tail length seems to be a variable characteristic.

In general, Simons interprets the evidence as confirming the early tie between Old and New World primate lines and as running against the possibility that the forerunners of today's primates once passed through a tarsier-like stage—a theory formerly advanced by some on the basis of comparative anatomy of present-day forms. As more Oligocene fossils came to light they manifested a considerable variety. Different ones seem to be leading toward different later fossil or present-day forms. They were already well advanced and distinguished from each other (Simons, 1969b). The Old World monkeys are adapted to quadrupedal life in the trees or on the ground; the great apes, sometimes described as semibrachiators, have a very different mode of progression although also quadrupedal; the gibbon is the brachiator par excellence; and we are the only fully bipedal primates.

These features have counterparts in the behavior that must also explain the differences in the skeleton not only of the limbs and trunk but also of the skull and jaws—such as those related to the way the head is carried. It is these critical features we must look for in the fossils. Whether the four separate lines—leading to humans, the African great apes, the gibbons, and the Old World monkeys—were distinct in Oligocene times is still debated, however.

## Miocene Catarrhines

By the Miocene, which started 24 to 26 million years ago, the line leading to gibbons already may have become distinct from that of the monkeys (both cercopithecine and colobine subfamilies were present but only in Africa [Simons, 1970]). Although first discovered in France a century ago, *Pliopithecus* is best represented by some excellently preserved fossils found in a deposit of early middle Miocene at Neudorf, Czechoslovakia. The teeth, narrow snout region, wide-set eyes, and some features of the collarbone and other long bones are gibbonlike or anthropoidal. Many other skeletal features, however, including the spinal column, upper limb, and general body proportions, are

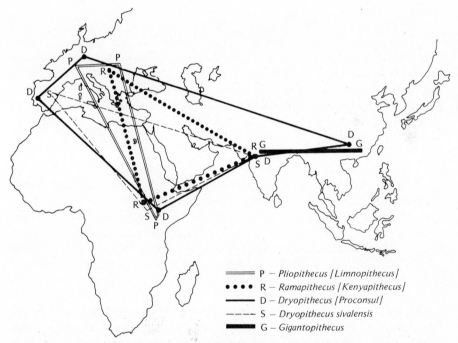

| | |
|---|---|
| ═══ | P – *Pliopithecus [Limnopithecus]* |
| •••• | R – *Ramapithecus [Kenyapithecus]* |
| ——— | D – *Dryopithecus [Proconsul]* |
| - - - - | S – *Dryopithecus sivalensis* |
| ▬▬▬ | G – *Gigantopithecus* |

FIG. 14-7   In the Miocene and Pliocene various genera of hominoids had extensive ranges in Europe, Africa, and Asia. The ranges may well have been even more extensive than shown, as adequate exploration for fossils has been limited to a few sites. The African sites explored are mostly somewhat earlier than the Asiatic and European ones, but the evolutionary radiation of the higher primates is a widespread phenomenon.

those of a monkey. To judge by the relative size of the opening into the sacral canal and the size of its exit from the sacrum, the nerves within the canal in *Pliopithecus* continued into a pendant tail. This is unlike the modern gibbons, great apes, and humans, all of whom lack a tail and have a sacral canal that tapers to a point as the last small nerves to the base of the spine exit from it (Ankel, 1972). Thus some of the features of *Pliopithecus* are more distinctly primitive than those of the gibbon and can be most nearly matched in Old or New World monkeys or even prosimians (Zapfe, 1958).

Similar fossils (also best ascribed to *Pliopithecus)* have been found in Miocene deposits in East Africa. Again they have long gibbonlike canine teeth, and arm bones that are slightly longer (relative to the bones of the leg) than such monkeys as the macaque but shorter than those of the apes. Likewise, the forearm of *Pliopithecus* is intermediate in length, relative to the upper arm, between that of the gibbon and that of the other hominoids. *Pliopithecus* is also known from Pliocene deposits. If *Aelopithecus* and *Pliopithecus* represent a line of precursors of the gibbon extending from the Oligocene through the Miocene and the Pliocene we must conclude that although the differentiation of the line and the characteristic facial and dental features of the gibbon are early, the anatomical modifications for full exploitation of arm-swinging bra- chiation are relatively recent.

Most other Tertiary higher primate fossils of the Old World can be grouped into a single genus, **Dryopithecus** (Pilbeam, 1966). It was first known from some teeth and apelike bits of jaw bone from Miocene and Pliocene deposits of Europe and the **Siwalik Hills of India.** The teeth show the so-called dryopithe- cus pattern, which is found—sometimes in modified form—in the gibbons, great apes, and us, and also in the fossil, *Aegyptopithecus*. The dryopithecus pattern is an arrangement of the cusps of the lower molar teeth (Fig. 14-8). In its simple form three cusps (Nos. 1, 3, 5) are arranged along the cheek side and two (Nos. 2 and 4) along the tongue side. The five cusps are separated by grooves. In the dryopithecus pattern, cusp 3 is separated from 1 and 5 by two grooves that form the forked part of a "Y." The "Y" is completed by a groove between cusps 2 and 4. In us the pattern is sometimes accompanied by a deflecting wrinkle on cusp 2 and Morris (1970) shows that this and a lobe on cusp 3 may be functionally important. The cusps are sometimes smaller or fewer in number and the pattern of fissures may be modified to form a cross ("plus" pattern). The dryopithecus pattern is contrasted with the bilophodont (two-ridged) molar pattern of the monkeys, in which four cusps of each molar tooth are organized as two transverse crests.

*Dryopithecus* was a wide-ranging genus extending from Western Europe to China. Simons (1964a) has shown that various East African Miocene fossils, formerly called "Proconsul," belong to this same genus. The teeth range from smaller than those of a chimpanzee to as large as those of a gorilla. The incisors are relatively smaller, however, than those of the chimpanzee and the gorilla. Fortunately, we have several long bones and one nearly intact skull (Fig. 14-9),

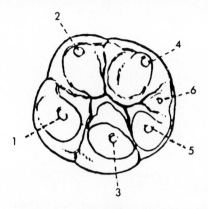

FIG. 14-8 Lower molar tooth showing the dryo-pithecus pattern of grooves. When cusps 2 and 3 are adjacent to each other as in this case the pattern is described as a "Y." Sometimes the pattern is modified and the grooves form a "plus" (+) pattern. The fifth and, especially, the sixth cusps are often absent. Redrawn from W. K. Gregory, *The origin and evolution of the human dentition.* Baltimore: Williams and Wilkins, 1922.

which was discovered in the steep side of a gully by Mary Leakey and extracted by her and her husband, L. S. B. Leakey, who spent most of his life searching for "Adam's ancestors" in his native land, Kenya. The face of *Dryopithecus africanus* is narrower than that of a chimpanzee or gorilla and resembles that of a monkey more closely. The molar teeth, however, have the definite dryopithe-cus pattern; that is, they are apelike and not monkeylike. The chin region of the jaw is heavy. However there is usually no buildup of bone (simian shelf) on the inside of the jaw such as is found in both apes and monkeys today. The simian shelf is also absent in the earlier *Parapithecus* from Egypt, in *Australopithecus,* and in fossil and living humans. From a reexamination of the wrist bones, Lewis (1972) concludes that *Dryopithecus* was well adapted for suspensory arm-swinging locomotion (brachiation) and has evolved in this respect beyond the living arboreal catarrhine monkeys. Perhaps it could hang by the arms rather than brachiate. Other researchers (Morbeck, 1975) interpret the same evidence to indicate an ordinary monkeylike quadrupedal gait. Unfortunately, the bones of the shoulder region (in which we and the apes are similar to each other but very different from monkeys) are not preserved in the fossil record. If the bones of this part of the limb are recovered the issue can probably be resolved.

There are many species of *Dryopithecus,* one of which *(Dryopithecus indicus)* is thought to be in or close to the ancestry of *Gigantopithecus* (Simons and Pilbeam, 1971; and see p. 228). Another *(Dryopithecus africanus)* is thought to be ancestral to the chimpanzee, and another *(Dryopithecus major)* may be ancestral to the gorilla—it has many resemblances to the mountain gorilla and the fossils were found in the same region as this living primate. The date, however, is more recent than that of most of the other African fossils. Still another species, *Dryopithecus sivalensis* (this species was called "Sivapithe-cus" in the older terminology), was once thought to resemble the present-day orangutan. The modern chimpanzee and gorilla are placed in different genera by most (but not all) zoologists, but there must have been a stage (probably that

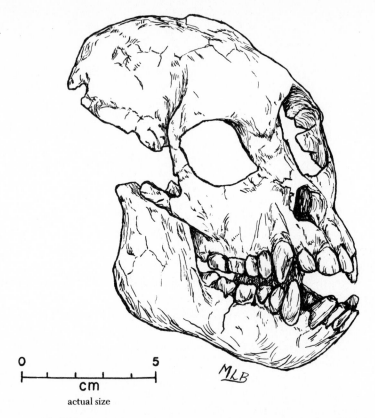

0                    5

cm

actual size

FIG. 14-9 *Dryopithecus* was a widespread genus of the Miocene and Pliocene. It is generally considered to be an anthropoid ape. This species, *Dryopithecus africanus,* is thought to be particularly closely related to the chimpanzee, but the forward thrust of the face and anterior narrowing of the jaw are more like those of a monkey, and the limb bones also suggest that typical ape locomotor habits may not yet have been established. From C. L. Brace, H. Nelson, and N. Korn: *Atlas of fossil man.* New York: Holt, Rinehart and Winston, 1971. Reproduced by permission. The drawing was made from a slide taken by Professor W. W. Howells, Harvard University.

of *Dryopithecus*) when their respective ancestors were members of the same genus; in fact there must have been a stage when the ancestors were the same animals. Branching evolution is well established in principle but it is hard to identify the actual point of separation.

Chimpanzees and especially gorillas are found only in limited areas of Africa, and the orangutan survives only on the islands of Borneo and Sumatra. Fossil orangutans of Pleistocene age are also known from the mainland of Asia, however, and the Tertiary precursors of each of the great apes could have been quite widespread on the mainland from Europe and Africa to the Far East. The distribution of *Dryopithecus* fossils in all of these places points in that direction.

## Ramapithecus

Until the African specimens of *Dryopithecus* were found, all Miocene and Early Pliocene hominoid fossils consisted of teeth and jawbones. One unfortunate effect of this was that a number of different species were erroneously named; in at least one instance the upper and lower jaws of the same species were ascribed to two different species. In 1934 a graduate student at Yale, G. E. Lewis, described one of the maxillary specimens, *Ramapithecus,* as a hominid, but his view was not taken seriously at the time. Simons (1964a and 1964b) reexamined all the material old and new, and concluded that there are two and only two genera in the Miocene to Early Pliocene hominoid material, *Dryopithecus* and *Ramapithecus* (Fig. 14-10). The questions concerning how different *Ramapithecus* is from *Dryopithecus* and how similar *Ramapithecus* is to later hominoids are difficult to answer because so little of the animal is known. The *Ramapithecus* upper jaw is remarkably shortened and therefore does not protrude forward but must have been long vertically. The palate is wider

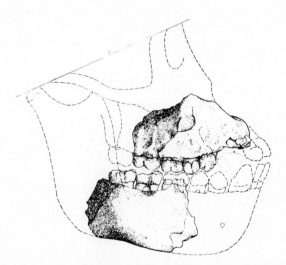

FIG. 14-10   Reconstruction of the face of *Ramapithecus* from the Siwalik Hills of India, based on the maxilla (upper jaw) of one specimen, mandible (lower jaw) in reverse of another, and canine tooth from a third. The face is similar to that of *Australopithecus* (see Chapter 15), but *Ramapithecus* lived some ten million or so years earlier. From E. L. Simons: "On the mandible of *Ramapithecus.*" *Proceedings of the National Academy of Sciences 51,* 528–535, 1964. Reproduced by permission.

behind than in front, a human rather than apelike characteristic, but in this *Ramapithecus* differs little from *Dryopithecus*. The incisors are not known, but are presumed to have been small relative to the back teeth. The teeth show the same kind of wear seen in humans, but *Dryopithecus* teeth show roughly the same pattern and, presumably, rate of wear. On the basis of the short, deep face, some anthropologists conclude that *Ramapithecus* could not have relied on his teeth as weapons to the same extent as *Dryopithecus* (and most subsequent primates other than humans) and must have used his hands for hunting and defense. This further implies that he was specialized for bipedal locomotion to free his hands. Hands used for manipulation rather than walking are one of the most characteristic human anatomical adaptations, and the one thought to have been necessary for the development of tool use. This line of argument has led to the postulate that *Ramapithecus* is the actual ancestor of *Homo sapiens* at that time in human evolution (the Late Miocene). Unfortunately, however, no skeletons are known on which to test this hypothesis.

In 1961, L. S. B. Leakey, among a great many other significant discoveries, described an upper jaw with teeth (including a canine) from a deposit at **Fort Ternan, Kenya, Africa.** The site has since been dated as about 14 million years ago by the potassium-argon method. Leakey recognized in his specimen features that make it a plausible ancestor for *Homo sapiens*. Although he gave it another name ("Kenyapithecus") the specimen differs in no essential way from *Ramapithecus* specimens from India and if it belongs to the same genus it must, according to the international rules of zoological nomenclature, also be officially called *Ramapithecus*. Recently, *Ramapithecus* fossils have been found in Hungary. Thus by the beginning of the Pliocene there was a widespread genus with the small canine teeth one would expect to find in the apelike forerunner of *Homo sapiens*. However, some students of the problem do not believe that the degree of reduction in size of the anterior teeth is sufficient to identify *Ramapithecus* as a hominid (Yulish, 1970; Frayer, 1973). They identify a lower jaw with a simian shelf as belonging to *Ramapithecus* and think that the canine is quite apelike, like a female *Dryopithecus*. A single primate fossil tooth, thought to be at least 7 million years old and more probably 9 to 12 million years old, was said by Leakey to show some affinities (such as a low crown) with "Kenyapithecus" and others with *Homo* and *Australopithecus* (Bishop and Chapman, 1970). However, until the newly discovered limb bones are described and the evidence of locomotion added to that of the jaws, the relation of *Ramapithecus* to us cannot be definitively assessed.

## Oreopithecus

The period after *Ramapithecus*, the Pliocene, has yielded few fossil primates. Some now think that this is because the Pliocene was briefer than is usually believed. Because of the peculiar combination of features, one bizarre Pliocene type, *Oreopithecus*, should remind us not to draw too definite conclusions from a limited number of features. In North Italy, miners have for years found fossils, including primate teeth, in the soft brown coal of **Tuscany.** The molar teeth are generally bilophodont (having the cusps arrayed in two transverse crests like those of monkeys), but also show some primitive features such as a ridge on each tooth near the gumline, the **cingulum.** Most of the earlier reports concerning these *Oreopithecus* specimens were written by scholars who never saw the specimens but relied on casts or previous descriptions. New explorations of the lignite coal fields reveal *Oreopithecus* together with guide fossils (common species of known age) of Early Pliocene date. Re-examination of the available *Oreopithecus* material shows several generalized features of the teeth and jaws, such as small canine teeth, corresponding lack of a gap for upper and lower canines to overlap, and the related shortening of the face (a series of features similar to those of *Ramapithecus*). Hürzeler (1958), who has restudied all the evidence, states that the teeth of *Oreopithecus,* although generalized or primitive, are hominid (of the human family) rather than pongid (of the taxonomic family of the anthropoid apes) or cercopithecid (like Old World monkeys). According to this view, in other words, the teeth belong to animals of the human rather than the ape or monkey taxonomic family, as judged by their proportions, the shape of the lower premolars, and other details. Some features of the skull, jaws, and fragments of limb bones lead to the same conclusion, although the limb bones are generalized and resemble those of monkeys rather than those of apes or humans and the cranium is much smaller than once thought. To add to the mosaic pattern represented by these fossils, the hand was long, a feature shared with arm-swinging apes. The vertebrae at the base of the spinal column are so large and strong, it has been said, as not to exclude the possibility that *Oreopithecus* could walk upright. Furthermore, the sacral canal is tapered so there was reduction of the tail. On the other hand, the diameter of the acetabulum (the socket joint that supports the trunk on the lower limb) is much smaller, relative to other measurements of the pelvis and trunk of *Oreopithecus,* than in us or the great apes (Schultz, 1969), so bipedal locomotion is highly improbable (as one might expect in a swamp ape). A quadruped with its weight supported on four limbs or a brachiator that hangs by its arms does not need a large hip joint to support its weight.

The lignite coal of Tuscany is the remains of a bog. It seems unlikely that any higher primate would be confined to so narrow a habitat, but some authorities believe *Oreopithecus* was strictly a swamp-ape, keeping to the trees and protected from both predators and competition with other primates by the marsh below. Simons notes that the *Oreopithecus* teeth share some details with one of the aberrant Oligocene types from the Fayum, but the time span is immense, and it seems hard to justify such a direct relationship in the face of the other highly advanced features. *Oreopithecus* remains an enigma, and Straus (1963) leaves open the question of whether it is a member of the human family (Hominidae) or needs a separate family by itself.

## Gigantopithecus

In China the teeth of "dragons" are believed to have curative properties, and, to meet the demand, enterprising pharmacists sold "dragon's teeth." These are fossil teeth of almost any kind. The vertebrate paleontologist G. H. R. von Koenigswald, who also retrieved many of the known fossil hominids from Java (see Chapter 16), was aware of this custom and therefore made a practice of visiting Chinese drugstores. Among his purchases were eight enormous molar teeth that have remarkably human cusp patterns (Fig. 14-11). These teeth are about three times the size of human teeth—quite outside the range of any living or fossil human, *Australopithecus,* or even gorilla. What creature these *Gigantopithecus* molars came from was quite unknown.

Without other parts of the skeleton, there could be no certainty as to what relevance these *Gigantopithecus* teeth had for human evolution. From the color of the material that adhered to the teeth, and from other fossil bones of the same color, von Koenigswald inferred that they came from Early Middle Pleistocene cave deposits of Central China. After the communist revolution in China, Pei Wen-Chung (1957), one of the discoverers of Peking man, encouraged the officials of that part of China to report any fossil bones to him and, as a consequence, received 1000 additional teeth. A peasant called Chin Hsiu-huai, who was using cave bone to fertilize his fields, once brought a fossil "dragon" bone to the marketing cooperative to try to sell it as medicine. The officials, realizing that it might be of scientific or cultural value, delivered it to Pei, who identified it as a *Gigantopithecus* mandible. Subsequently, two more such mandibles turned up in the same cave of **Leng-Chai-Shan** in Kwangsi Province where Chin had found the first one.

On the basis of the new evidence, Pei believes that *Gigantopithecus* was contemporaneous with Peking man (see Chapter 16). No stone tools were found at the site and Pei endorses the idea, first advanced by von Koenigswald,

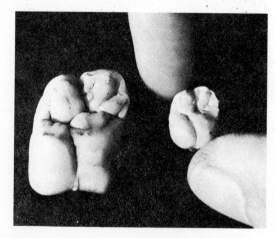

FIG. 14-11  *Gigantopithecus* upper molar (left) compared with the corresponding tooth of present-day man. The similarity in pattern is as marked as is the difference in size. Photograph by F. W. Goro, *Life,* Copyright 1946, Time Inc.

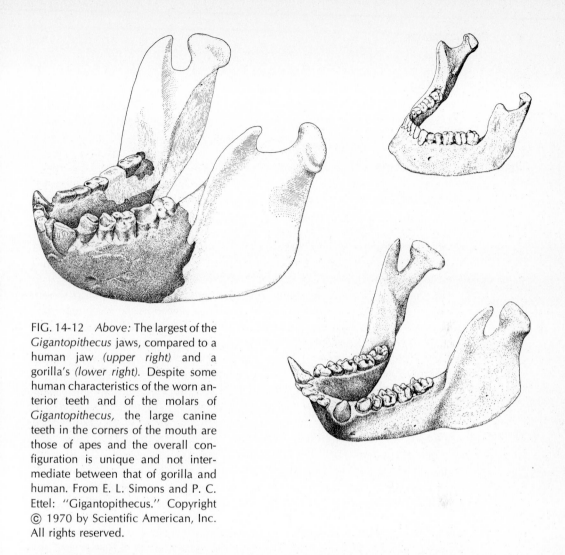

FIG. 14-12 *Above:* The largest of the *Gigantopithecus* jaws, compared to a human jaw *(upper right)* and a gorilla's *(lower right).* Despite some human characteristics of the worn anterior teeth and of the molars of *Gigantopithecus,* the large canine teeth in the corners of the mouth are those of apes and the overall configuration is unique and not intermediate between that of gorilla and human. From E. L. Simons and P. C. Ettel: "Gigantopithecus." Copyright ⓒ 1970 by Scientific American, Inc. All rights reserved.

that *Gigantopithecus* is an ape rather than an apelike fossil human. From the evidence Pei presents, it would appear that the jaw has some human features. The incisors are small and the lower canines short by comparison with those of a gorilla, but the lower first premolars have an elongated crown, an apelike characteristic, although they did not interlock with long upper canine teeth as in monkeys and apes. There is no reason to believe that the animals which possessed the teeth and jaws were gigantic. Garn and Lewis (1958) have shown that there is little correlation between tooth size and body size in modern humans. We therefore need other parts of the skeleton to test the question of whether the big-toothed forms were tall.

Another mandible of *Gigantopithecus* (Fig. 14-12) turned up in North India in association with Middle Pliocene savanna fauna (Simons, 1969a). This pushes back the existence of this form to a considerably earlier date (probably 5 or 10 million years ago). Unfortunately, both *Ramapithecus* and *Giganto-*

*pithecus* have been known only from teeth and jaws. Some anthropologists who believe that we did not separate from the great apes until the Pliocene speculate that, when further parts are described, *Ramapithecus* may prove not to resemble us, closely, whereas *Gigantopithecus* may still prove to be a hominid.

## The End of the Tertiary

The Tertiary saw the evolution of the placental mammals and by its end there must have been (whether we have found their remains or not) separate evolutionary lines leading to all the main groups of such animals known today. In the case of the higher primates we have found traces of most of these lines in fossil forms before the end of the Tertiary and the beginning of the Quaternary (the Pleistocene).

The New World monkeys are represented by a few fossils from South America. The Old World monkeys are only represented in the fossil record of Africa during the Oligocene and Miocene. In the Pliocene and Pleistocene this diverse and widespread group (now ranging from West Africa to the Celebes and from South Africa to the Himalayas and Japan) left fossils variously related to different subsequent forms in all three continents of the Old World (Simons, 1970). The gibbons are foreshadowed by *Pliopithecus*. The orangutan is in some ways similar to one of the *Dryopithecus* species. The molecular evidence suggests that there is approximately as much difference between chimpanzee and gorilla as between either of them and *Homo*. For instance, human and chimpanzee hemoglobins have the same sequences of peptides, but those of gorilla differ slightly, whereas in other proteins gorilla and chimpanzee may be somewhat more similar to each other (see Fig.11-18). It is therefore possible that the lines leading to chimpanzee and gorilla have been separate for as long as those leading to either of them and *Homo*. As already noted, *Rampithecus* was already present in the Middle Miocene and some scholars think that *Ramapithecus* is on the line leading to us. That would mean that our line had separated from the lines leading to chimpanzee and gorilla during or prior to the Miocene.

An early differentiation in respect to molecular details or details of the dental pattern does not mean that gorilla, chimpanzee, and we achieved modern form in the Tertiary, however. The full evolution of *Homo sapiens* of today was yet to come, and this is also likely also true for the apes.

Furthermore, there may have been additional Tertiary evolutionary lines that have no surviving descendants today. That of *Oreopithecus* seems to have been one such, and that leading to *Gigantopithecus* may have been another.

## Summary

Prosimian primate fossils first appear at the end of the Cretaceous Period, about 63–66 million years ago. There was a radiation of diverse prosimian forms in the following Paleocene and Eocene Epochs. Subsequent New World primate fossils are all Platyrrhini. In the Old World, diversification of the Catarrhini is first seen in Oligocene specimens from the Fayum, Egypt. Some of these are of cercopithecoid monkeys (but in some instances with platyrrhine features), others suggest the direction of later evolution to the gibbon, the African great apes, and humans. In the Miocene and Early Pliocene, *Pliopithecus* seems related to the gibbon, *Dryopithecus* to the great apes, and, perhaps, *Ramapithecus* to us. In the Pliocene some fossils of still other Hominoidea occur: *Oreopithecus* and *Gigantopithecus*.

# CHAPTER 15

# AUSTRALOPITHECUS

## Dating the Pleistocene

When the Tertiary Period came to an end there began a time of fluctuating but generally cool climates, the **Pleistocene,** and it included repeated periods of glaciation. The early part of the Pleistocene is identified with certain species of animals that lived then. This *faunal assemblage* is called the *Villafranchian*. Potassium-argon dates of basalt associated with Villafranchian fauna go back at least 3.2 million years and most students of human evolution consider the Villafranchian to span the Pliocene-Pleistocene boundary.

Some of the disputes about this boundary are based on the difficulty of transferring to dry land dates based on deposits under the sea. Marine geologists accept the Pliocene-Pleistocene boundary as the first appearance of a certain cold-water fossil in the sea (Bock, 1970; Emiliani, 1971) and the extinction of warm-water forms found in cores drilled from the ocean floor. By arbitrary agreement, they date the beginning of the Pleistocene from a marine inundation (called a "transgression of the sea") in Calabria, southern Italy. This event has been dated about 0.8 to 1.8 million years ago and was subsequent to the establishment of the Villafranchian fauna on the land.

When the glaciations began is also still uncertain. Evidence of earlier glaciations is largely obliterated by subsequent ones. Geologists used to refer to four (or five) great glaciations of the Northern Hemisphere. There were so many advances and retreats of glacial ice and so many longer or shorter fluctuations in climate that it is almost impossible to identify all such great glaciations, however. The glacial periods lasted for about 2 million years. They began at the time of the Olduvai Event, a normal period of the earth's magnetic polarity within a generally reversed epoch, the Matuyama Reversal Epoch, (Ericson and Wollin, 1968, and see below), and ended (if indeed they have ended) with the last glacial retreat only eleven thousand years ago. The periods of maximum melting of glacial ice seem to have occurred at more or less irregular intervals of about 100,000 years and they lasted for about 10,000 years. There was a warm interglacial period (the Eemian) about 120,000 years ago, and the Holocene Epoch, the last 10,000–15,000 years, may simply be another such cycle. Superimposed on these long cycles are fairly regular but much smaller fluctuations of temperature occurring in cycles of about 20,000 years and these phases in turn are broken up into minor fluctuations of temperature in cycles of about 2,500 years duration. The last cold spell of this minor cycle, sometimes called a little ice age, lasted from about 1430 to 1850 A.D. and caused short growing seasons in the countries of northern Europe. The temperatures from then until the 1940's grew warmer, but the small fluctuations are irregular and it would be difficult to predict what to expect in the years ahead.

The constant radiation from radioactive isotopes, and consequent regular decrease in their proportion relative to their degradation products, provide a whole series of physicochemical methods for geological dating, of which the uranium-lead, the potassium-argon, and the carbon-14 to carbon-12 ratios are examples. Magnetic reversals are a class of occurrences that have left their mark simultaneously throughout the world (Fig. 15-1). These reversals are episodes in which the earth's magnetic polarity is inverted (that is the north pole becomes the magnetic south pole and vice versa). They have occurred a number of times. At any given time in the past, however, the polarity then prevailing is "frozen" in rock that is congealing from lava or in sediments and with an instrument for measuring magnetism one can determine whether such rock was formed during a period with the present polarity or with the opposite one. One reason these magnetic reversals are so important for the study of human evolution is that they were worldwide events and permit one to determine the relative antiquity of fossils and stone tools from different continents. The last magnetic fluctuation was the beginning of the Brunhes Normal Epoch, some 690,000 years ago. Before this there was a long period of reversed polarity, the Matuyama Reversal Epoch (from about 2,430,000 until about 690,000 years ago), interspersed with several brief normal events. The latest of these, called the Jaramillo Event, occurred at about the beginning of Middle Pleistocene times some 950,000 years ago. The exact date of the one before that, called the Olduvai Event, is still debated, but it may have lasted from 1.9 to 1.6 million years ago. Some anthropologists believe that it would

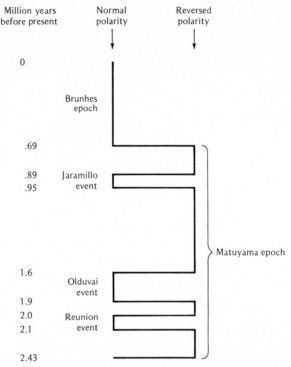

FIG. 15-1   Epochs and Events in the earth's polarity. When the polarity was reversed, the point of the compass that now points north, pointed south. Since the polarity was "frozen" in stone formed at the time, it is often possible to identify geological deposits and their contained fossils with one or another of the Epochs or Events.

be logical to separate the Pliocene from the Pleistocene by the beginning of Olduvai Event and to separate the Lower Pleistocene from the Middle Pleistocene by the beginning of the Brunhes Epoch (Butzer, 1974). The possibilities this may offer for future comparisons over long distances would make them seem desirable (although arbitrary) cutoff points. Ordinarily geological periods are demarcated by changes in the fossil fauna, but since animals arise by evolution, and extinction may be a slow process, paleontological criteria may be less suitable markers than physical events, especially in recent prehistory. Furthermore, with the formation of glaciers (and consequent lowering of sea levels) the old beaches are left far above the high water mark as water is impounded in the ice caps and provide another dating method.

Other methods of geological dating are based on volcanic activity, and astronomical measurements of the position of the earth relative to the sun. Dates from different kinds of evidence do not always coincide but it is often more convenient to give the estimated dates of the fossil Hominidae—the family of *Homo sapiens*—in terms of years before the present (B.P.) than of epochs (such as Early Pleistocene). In any case, evolutionary events are parts of a continuum, and it is not possible to give an exact date for the emergence of the human family.

# A Missing Link?

One cannot properly speak of missing links and known links in evolution, because evolution runs in lines rather than chains and it is always possible to refine one's knowledge as more points on the line become known and the unknown segments between them become smaller. Since the whole line is essential and elimination of any generation would cause extinction, no particular "link" is more important than others for continuation of the line. However, for our understanding, even if not for the process of evolution itself, the stage reached by **Australopithecus** is the most important paleontological evidence of human evolution. *Australopithecus* marks the unquestionable achievement of hominid status in our evolutionary line.

A series of fossils of this genus have been found in Africa. In 1924 a South African quarryman working near a place called **Taung** blasted out a small fossilized skull that he took to be humanlike and so sent it to the anatomist at the University of Witwatersrand medical school, R. A. Dart. Dart (1925) noted a number of resemblances to human skulls that are not shared by chimpanzees or gorillas. His views were immediately challenged by various authorities, but it is now clear that, as Dart indicated, the skull is surprisingly human in many respects. Dart called the species *Australopithecus africanus* (which means "southern ape from Africa" and has nothing to do with Australia).

Despite the unenthusiastic response of others to Dart's announcement, R. Broom (1949), who had made an enviable reputation in paleontology by his study of the South African mammallike reptiles, went to see the skull, became convinced of its importance, and took up the search for more evidence. In the following years Broom and Dart found similar specimens in four other places in South Africa. The lime quarrying at Taung had completely destroyed the deposit from which the first specimen had come, but one of the men who had worked there knew enough about the fossils to recover specimens from a new quarry at **Sterkfontein** of which he was foreman. Two of Dart's students took Broom to the place, and the very next day he secured a specimen of *Australopithecus* (Fig. 15-2). Then one day in 1938 the foreman sold Broom a skull imbedded in limestone of a slightly different color. Broom wheedled from the foreman the name of the place from which he had taken it, **Kromdraai,** in the Transvaal. The search led to a schoolboy, Gert Terblanche, who was at school but out playing. The boy still had in his pocket "four of the most beautiful fossil teeth ever found in the world's history." Before Broom was allowed to take the boy out of class, the principal had the scientist lecture on caves and bones until school was dismissed. The boy then took Broom to a place where he had hidden "a very fine jaw with some beautiful teeth."

Broom had a knack for getting fossils. An American expedition, which had been hunting in South Africa for likely sites and blasting tons of limestone from

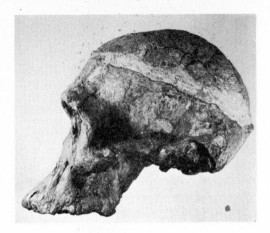

FIG. 15-2 *Australopithecus africanus* from Sterkfontein (Sts 5). This is the best preserved specimen from Sterkfontein and is colloquially called "Ms. Ples." Photograph courtesy of the Transvaal Museum and its director, Dr. C. K. Brain.

several deposits without success, once came to him. He selected for them a promising cave site at **Swartkrans,** only a mile from the Sterkfontein cave. It contained fossil bone cemented together, and within a few days he discovered in it the first of several very large jaws. By now that cave has produced 528 fossil remains representing more than 60 individuals plus 195 stones (mostly quartzite) foreign to the site, of which 30 could be termed artifacts (Brain, 1970). The bone accumulation is thought to be the remains of carnivore meals, and one young *Australopithecus* has two holes in his skull just wide enough apart to be fitted by a leopard's eye teeth. Broom's three sites have yielded the majority of the 1427 hominid specimens of early fossils now known from Africa south of the Sahara. Outside sub-Saharan Africa, there is so far only a tiny bit of definitely pertinent material from Ethiopia and Java.

Dart also continued his discoveries. In limestone from one of the caves at **Makapan,** South Africa, he found enormous amounts of fossil bone. The bones are remains of various species of mammals and include further specimens of *Australopithecus*. Dart thinks that the bone deposits here are the remains of *Australopithecus* meals and, in some cases, are bone clubs and pointed tools manufactured and used by *Australopithecus*.

The specimens from Taung, Sterkfontein, and Makapan are smaller and more gracile (that is, smooth) than most of those from Kromdraai and Swartkrans, and some anthropologists think that there are two or more genera or species, a question to which we shall return. Use of the name *Australopithecus* (with or without the species name *africanus*) in this work subsumes what others have called "Plesianthropus," "Paranthropus," and "Australopithecus robustus."

## Olduvai Gorge

Far to the north, L. S. B. Leakey and his wife Mary explored the steep walls of a dry ravine in Tanzania called **Olduvai Gorge,** where they had found definite evidence of early hominid remains. On July 17, 1959, Mrs. Leakey located, and she and her husband excavated, a much broken but nearly complete skull of *Australopithecus* in situ—that is, where it had lain since death—in a layer that contained stone flakes and tools of the earliest stone-age culture of Africa, the Oldowan (Fig. 15-3). This specimen is sometimes referred to as "Zinjanthropus," the Arabic word for East Africa plus a Greek word for man. It is officially designated Olduvai Hominid 5 (OH 5). It is the most thoroughly studied and described *Australopithecus* skull known (Tobias, 1967).

Olduvai Gorge, which also has yielded other specimens, is part of the great rift of eastern Africa. The northward extension of this rift continues through Kenya and Ethiopia. In southern Ethiopia the rift forms the valley of the **Omo River,** and it is in this dry area that an international team including a French contingent (Arambourg and Coppens, 1967) and an American group under F. C. Howell have explored over 100 fossil locations and found 68 hominid fossils. The fossils there are in sandstone and are soft and poorly preserved, however, so that most of what has remained are teeth plus some fragments of the harder parts of bone.

The Omo River flows into Lake Rudolf, Kenya, only a few miles to the south. In the arid zone behind the eastern shore of the lake (known as **East Rudolf**), R.

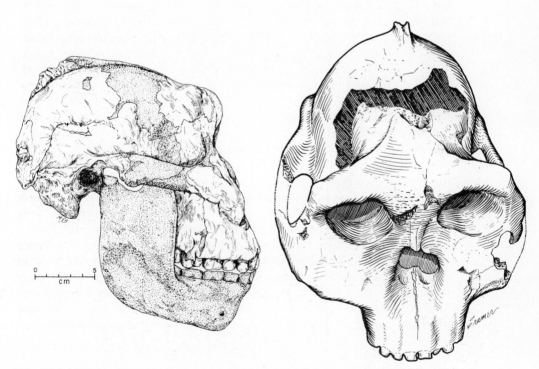

FIG. 15-3   "Zinjanthropus," the robust *Australopithecus* from Olduvai (OH 5). *Left:* Side view of a reconstruction. From C. L. Brace, H. Nelson, and N. Korn: *Atlas of fossil man.* New York: Holt, Rinehart and Winston, 1971. Drawn from a photograph, courtesy of Dr. L. S. B. Leakey and Professor P. V. Tobias. *Right:* Another view. Drawing by D. L. Cramer, courtesy of the Wenner-Gren Foundation Casting Program.

Leakey, the son of the Leakeys of Olduvai fame, has found a series of sites (Leakey et al., 1971, 1972) some of them stratified for a considerable depth, and the preservation of the bones is excellent. Besides over 50 specimens of hominid fossils, Leakey found worked stone implements—both crude choppers and more delicate specimens. Right on the surface and weathered out from surrounding softer rock, Leakey found an almost intact skull (ER 406, Fig. 15-4) identical in all but details to his mother's famous "Zinjanthropus" specimen from Olduvai (Fig. 15-3). Another, smaller skull (ER 732, Fig. 15-4), also almost intact, has been found, as have parts of a maxilla, many mandibles, and various other parts of the skeleton, including one specimen with many skeletal elements preserved. An ankle bone (talus) is quite human. The limbs vary in size from very small to very large. All of the limbs were thick and muscular. At the site where the tools were found there is volcanic material which has been dated at 2.6 million years ago. Correlation of the stratigraphy and comparison of various animal fossils indicate that hominids among the fossils should be dated at about 1 to 2.6 million years ago.

The teeth were the first feature of *Australopithecus* to attract attention. The canine teeth, although pointed, do not project beyond the tooth row, and in this respect resemble *Homo* alone among the higher primates. Many other features of the teeth are also striking. The premolar teeth are unlike those of the great apes; they are not shaped for scissorlike action but meet end to end, as in humans. In fact, some of the baby teeth (deciduous premolars) are extremely human. The rate and order of eruption of the permanent teeth is said to be exactly like that of *Homo,* and not like that of the apes; too much emphasis should not be placed on this resemblance, however, because there are wide variations in the order in both humans and apes.

The front teeth of *Australopithecus* are small, as in *Homo,* while the back teeth are large, often as large as in the gorilla. The upper teeth are in a continuous row unbroken by the **diastema,** the gap that is always found above the large lower canine teeth of monkeys and apes; occasionally there is a diastema in humans (Fig. 15-5). Furthermore, in *Australopithecus* the wear of the teeth tends to be even, and this is said to correspond to a form of the jaw joint similar to the human. In all other primates the upper canine teeth are honed into sharp weapons by wear on the lower teeth. This feature is variable in apes, however. Small canines and flat wear of the posterior teeth (the so-called human type of wear) occurs in an occasional chimpanzee. Certain *Australopithecus* specimens—some from Kromdraai, Swartkrans, Olduvai, Omo, and East Rudolf —have very massive jaws and big molar teeth (Fig. 15-6), but in these the front teeth are as small as the Sterkfontein, Makapan, and other Olduvai, East Rudolf, and Omo specimens.

## One Species or Two?

Because of the differences in the sizes of the teeth and the robustness of the chewing muscles (as reflected by their bony attachments) and for other reasons, some of which we shall mention, many students of the different specimens of

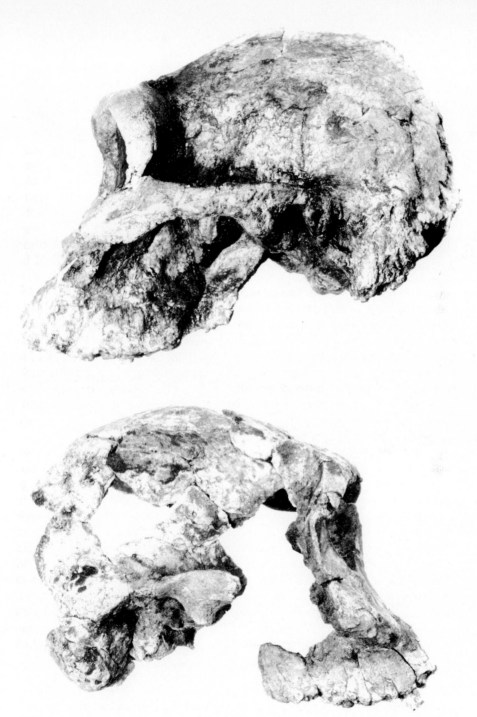

FIG. 15-4   Two *Australopithecus* skulls from East Rudolf. (Top, ER 406; bottom, ER 732.) ER 406 is in many ways the best-preserved *Australopithecus* skull yet found. Photographs courtesy of Richard Leakey.

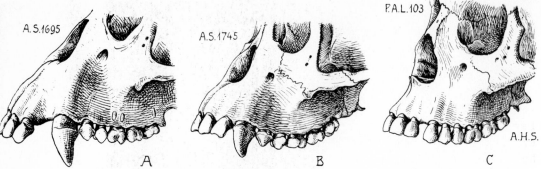

FIG. 15-5  Drawings of jaws of: *A*, adult male chimpanzee with large diastema between the lateral incisor and canine teeth; *B*, adult female chimpanzee with very small diastema; and *C*, human skull with diastema. The diastema is usual in the pongids and is rare in the hominids. From A. H. Schultz: "The relation in size between premaxilla, diastema, and canine." *American Journal of Physical Anthropology* 6(2), 163–179, 1948. Reproduced by permission.

*Australopithecus* have distinguished different species and even genera among them. A common view is that there are two species: *Australopithecus africanus* and "*Australopithecus robustus*." For instance, Washburn and Ciochon (1975) argue that the genus *Australopithecus* can be separated into two distinct groups on the basis of the measurements of teeth.

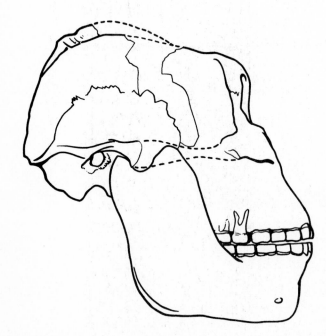

FIG. 15-6  The heavily built *Australopithecus* skull and mandible. Note the level tooth rows without projecting canines. A small sagittal crest is clearly present. (Drawn from a photograph of the Olduvai specimen; the mandible is from Swartkrans.) From B. Campbell: *Human evolution*. Chicago: Aldine, 1966. Reproduced by permission.

In "Zinjanthropus" from Olduvai, the larger specimen from Lake Rudolf, and in some of the specimens from Swartkrans there is a raised **sagittal crest** along the sagittal suture that marks the midline of the vertex or dome of the skull. The sagittal crest occurs in male gorillas (Fig. 15-7), chimpanzees, and other animals with powerful temporal muscles (chewing muscles that cover the temple and side of the head), but does not occur in humans, although the lines of attachment of the muscles sometimes nearly produce one (Riesenfeld, 1955). The sagittal crest is supposed to be characteristic of the male "Australopithecus robustus." Since both supposed species came from the same part of the world they would not have been likely to coexist for long unless they had very different ways of life. For this reason in addition to the anatomical details, J. T. Robinson (1964), who was formerly Broom's assistant, believes that the smaller, more gracile form (found with bones of large mammals at

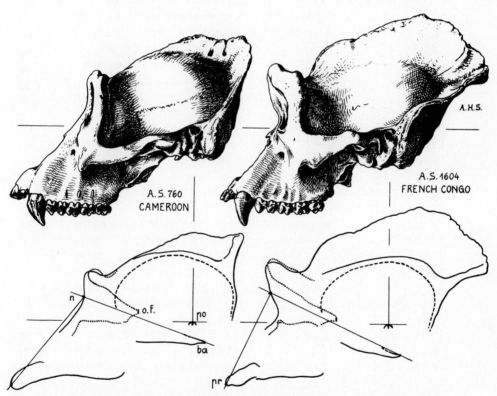

FIG. 15-7   Side views of two adult male lowland gorillas and sections of the same showing variation. Note the greater robustness of sagittal crest and brow ridges of the specimen on the right. The space for the brain is approximately the same in both skulls, however. From A. H. Schultz: Variability in man and other primates. *American Journal of Physical Anthropology* 5(1), 1–14, 1947.

Makapan and elsewhere) was a carnivore and that the larger form with enormous back teeth needed them for his largely vegetarian diet. Swedlund (1974) considers the various forms of interaction between two species of *Australopithecus* that would be possible if they lived in the same areas at the same time and concludes that ecological considerations (especially the small likelihood of two similarly adapted species coexisting for long) argue against the robust and gracile *Australopithecus* having been separate species. Although in historic times humans have been intolerant of other groups in the same territory, and the more successful group often slays, drives out, or absorbs the less successful, other primates are more tolerant and in many places several species coexist. L. S. B. Leakey says he has seen gorillas, chimpanzees, and several kinds of monkeys in an area of five square miles in the eastern Congo, and Jane Goodall watched the interaction of chimpanzees, baboons, and cercopithecus and colobus monkeys in a game reserve in Tanzania. Washburn says that from an ape's eye-view of his habitat, multiple species of *Australopithecus* could easily have existed at the same time and place (but using the resources of the environment differently). The geologists claim that in South Africa the more robust specimens—those from Swartkrans and Kromdraai—are the later. If they are less human and also members of a distinct species and phyletic (evolutionary) line, "Australopithecus robustus" thus would rate as an extinct side line in human ancestry.

The consideration of whether there are several species sifts down to a few points such as the sagittal crests and the size of teeth. However, one view is that the differences are merely those between males and females, but if so, why are they not found together at the same sites? Simons (1967c) states that the best materials of the robust *Australopithecus* taken together do not show more variation than is seen in one species of hominid (*Homo erectus*) or in one species of great ape (*Gorilla gorilla*) (Fig. 15-7). Differences between males and females (called **sexual dimorphism**) are very marked in the gorilla. Simons (1968b) notes that the species of *Australopithecus* are more similar than once supposed, but since hominids are thought generally to show less sexual dimorphism than apes, he concludes that the differences between the robust specimen, "Zinjanthropus," and one of the gracile specimens from Makapan probably do indicate species distinction rather than sexual dimorphism of the same species (see Fig. 15-8). Brace (1971) disagrees, and considers the variations in the South African and Olduvai material to fall in the range of sex differences, a conclusion which Clarke and Howell (1972) reject because they think that some of the robust *Australopithecus* specimens represent the females of that species. A. Mann (1970), however, adds evidence that, in important criteria, specimens of the gracile *Australopithecus africanus* and "Australopithecus robustus" overlap. M. H. Wolpoff (1974) has pointed out that in one of the other specimens from Makapan and in one from Sterkfontein the tops of the skulls are missing but the available parts have converging temporal lines and are therefore much like the corresponding parts of *Australopithecus* skulls of

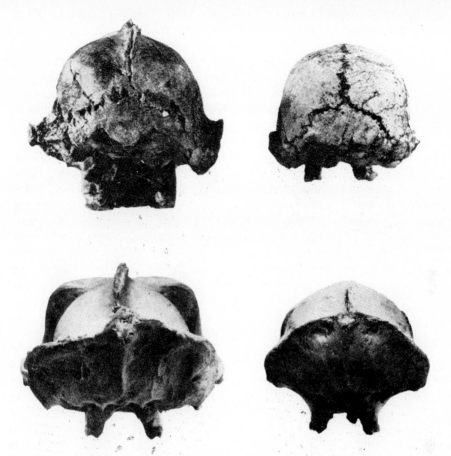

FIG. 15-8 Comparison of (upper left) the "Zinjanthropus" *Australopithecus* with (upper right) *Australopithecus africanus* from Makapan. Below are male and female lowland gorilla skulls. The skulls on the left differ from those on the right in the development of the sagittal crest and other muscular attachments and in the greater development of the mastoid process that contains air cells in the bone. From E. L. Simons: "Assessment of a fossil hominid." *Science 160,* 675. Copyright 1968, American Association for the Advancement of Science.

the robust variety which have a sagittal crest. Brace (1973) thinks that sexual dimorphism has decreased in the course of human evolution and that this factor may account for the great differences found among early hominids, or at least that this hypothesis has not yet been ruled out.

Read (1975), Corrucini (1975), and many others analyse the tooth dimensions and conclude that the robust specimens from East Africa form a separate evolutionary line into which those from South Africa also may fit. Taken together the specimens are too varied to belong to a single, local population at one point in time, but perhaps the long time span may allow all the specimens to be subsumed within a single species.

The skulls of both types of *Australopithecus* are small compared with the large jaws. The skull capacities of normal human beings range from less than a liter (about a quart) to about two and one-half liters. They average about 1.3 liters. The best-preserved *Australopithecus* skulls and endocasts have been measured by R. L. Holloway (1972). They have capacities of 0.404 liter in a child and from 0.428 to 0.530 liter in adults. This means that the brains were about the size of those of gorillas and chimpanzees and smaller than those of normal men and women (Fig. 15-9). Since 0.5 liter is just over a pint, on the basis of brain content these creatures might well be called "pint sized." Some scholars have claimed that some *Australopithecus* brains were larger than those of any gorilla or chimpanzee, but Holloway has carefully remeasured

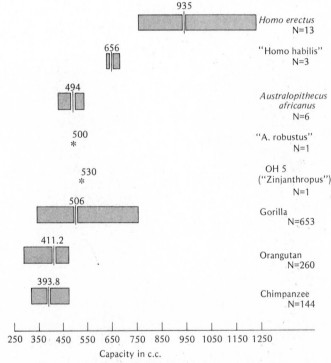

FIG. 15-9   The cranial capacities of available samples of fossil hominids compared with those of extant great apes. The averages are indicated by short vertical lines. Some estimates of the cranial capacity of *Australopithecus* specimens are lower than those given here, but—*relative to estimated body weight*—the brain of *Australopithecus* was in any case larger than those of the great apes. Redrawn from P. V. Tobias: *Brain in hominid evolution.* New York: Columbia University Press, 1971. Reproduced by permission.

several *Australopithecus* specimens and finds their skull capacity to be smaller than previously thought. There is, therefore, no direct evidence for assuming that *Australopithecus* brains were larger than those of great apes. Since *Australopithecus* was smaller than the gorilla, however, relative to body weight the average brain was probably larger than that of any of the living great apes. On the other hand, similar size does not necessarily mean similar intelligence, as there are also qualitative differences between brains.

Efforts have been made to evaluate the surface area of the *Australopithecus* brain (which would correlate with the amount of "gray matter" or cortex) and the sizes of other specific parts such as the frontal area. Such efforts and also the attempt to estimate the number of nerve cells on the basis of a few incomplete and somewhat crushed skulls involve farfetched assumptions and extrapolations. Our best guide to the probable mental capacity of *Australopithecus* remains the interpretation of the archaeological record, the size of *Australopithecus* brains, and the study of the psychology of living primates.

A fair number of bones of the rest of the skeletons are also known. One partial skeleton from Sterkfontein (Sts 14), thought to be of a female, consists of ribs, a nearly complete vertebral column, **pelvis,** and part of a **femur.** Measurements of it indicate that *Australopithecus africanus* was sometimes only about 4 feet 3 inches tall. The shaft of a large femur from East Rudolf indicates that other specimens ranged up to about 6 feet 1 inch tall (McHenry, 1974). A few vertebrae indicate a weight of only 40–50 pounds for some of the smaller individuals (Lovejoy and Heiple, 1970). The vertebrae also show a curve in the lumbar region that is very typically human and is associated with **bipedalism.** There is considerable variation in form as well as in length of the limb bones, but the shapes and proportions are generally close to human ones (Howell and Wood, 1974). However, some features, such as the long necks of the thigh bones (femurs), are unique. These are probably due to a smaller birth canal in these small-brained hominids, so the long neck carried the femur laterally to a position similar to that in human beings. Lisowski et al. (1974) claim that measurements of the talus, the keystone bone of the foot, are also unique.

The limb bone fragments do not help as much as they might in determining the taxonomic position of *Australopithecus,* since humans and apes are quite similar in the form of some parts. The form of the femur and pelvis (Figs. 15-10, 15-11) is compatible with bipedal locomotion, and, considered together, the fragments evidence a bipedal stance.

The probability of upright stance is also evident from the position of the **foramen magnum** (the hole that transmits the spinal cord to the brain through the **occipital bone** at the base of the skull). In *Australopithecus* the foramen magnum is located farther forward than in quadrupeds, although not so far under the skull as in *Homo sapiens. Australopithecus* also has less marked attachments for the neck muscles than, for instance, the gorilla. The position of these muscle attachments indicates that the head was on top of an upright recurved spine. Quadrupeds need to use their teeth or horns for defense, since the forelimbs, even if used in combat, are also needed for standing. "Zinjan-

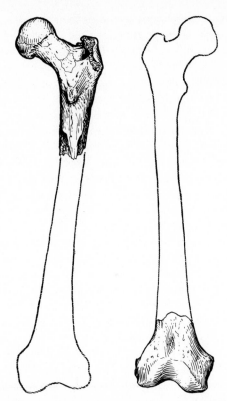

FIG. 15-10 *Left:* Proximal portion of right femur from Swartkrans. *Right:* Distal end of left femur from Sterkfontein. These thigh bones are very similar in shape to those of man today. Drawings by D. L. Cramer. Courtesy of the Wenner-Gren Foundation Casting Program.

thropus'' also has a **mastoid process,** an attachment in humans for a muscle that balances and turns the head. A mastoid process is lacking in nonhuman primates (except for a trace in the gorilla).

The pelvic bones of humans and apes are very different, however, and here the *Australopithecus* specimens (Fig. 15-13) show their closest resemblance to us. They demonstrate that *Australopithecus* had a completely human upright posture. The upper part **(ilium)** is splayed out, as in *Homo sapiens*. The elongation of this part of the pelvis, which is typical of the ape, does not occur in *Australopithecus* (Fig. 15-14), but the ilium is somewhat flatter and broader than in *Homo sapiens* (at least in specimen SK 3155 from Swartkrans). The surfaces of joints between the pelvis and the vertebral column on the one aspect, and the pelvis and lower limb on the other, are small by human standards (McHenry, 1975), but larger than those of any present-day primate except us (Schultz, 1969). Since we distribute all weight on two limbs whereas other primates usually use all four, these joints must carry nearly twice as large a fraction of the body weight in humans compared with the chimpanzee or gorilla, for instance. The acetabulum, the socket for the thigh

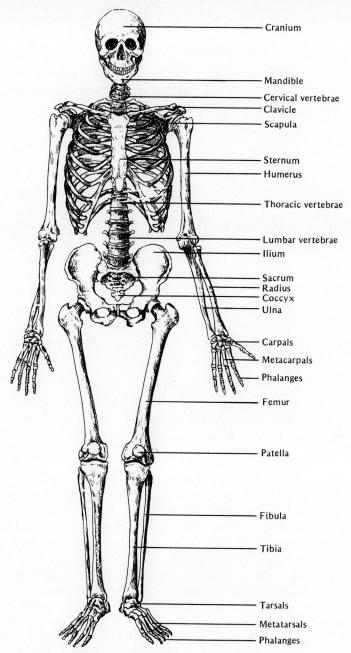

Cranium

Mandible

Cervical vertebrae

Clavicle

Scapula

Sternum

Humerus

Thoracic vertebrae

Lumbar vertebrae

Ilium

Sacrum

Radius

Coccyx

Ulna

Carpals

Metacarpals

Phalanges

Femur

Patella

Fibula

Tibia

Tarsals

Metatarsals

Phalanges

FIG. 15-11  The human skeleton with important bones labeled.

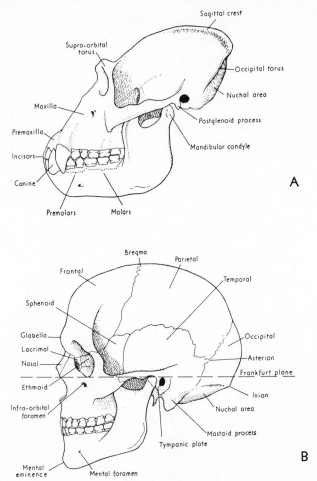

FIG. 15-12 The skull of a male gorilla *(A)* and of modern *Homo sapiens (B)* labeled to show individual bones and anatomical landmarks. From W. E. Le Gros Clark: *The fossil evidence for human evolution*. Chicago: University of Chicago Press, 1955. Reproduced by permission.

bone on the hip bone, of *Australopithecus* is fully as large (in proportion) as that in humans and is larger than that of any other present-day primate (Schultz, 1969). Schultz concludes from this that *Australopithecus* had acquired erect posture. In general the pelves are so human that, had they been found alone, most anatomists would have ascribed them to human beings. As a matter of fact, some of those who have examined the specimens do just that and claim that there was *Homo* as well as *Australopithecus* in the same region at the same time. One hip bone from Swartkrans seems to have some simian characteristics in the lower part (ischium). However, the bone is so badly broken that accurate assessment is impossible. A second pelvis from the site is unbroken and fully

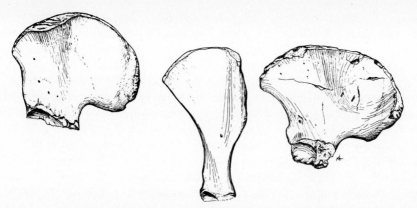

FIG. 15-13 The upper part (ilium) of the hip bone (innominate) of, from left to right, young human, a chimpanzee, and *Australopithecus* (from Makapan). The ilium of *Australopithecus* is essentially human in form. From R. A. Dart: "Innominate fragments of *Australopithecus prometheus. American Journal of Physical Anthropology* 7 (3), 301–332, 1949. Reproduced by permission.

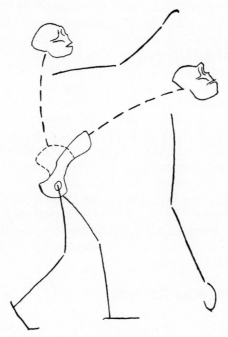

FIG. 15-14 The difference in posture between *Australopithecus* (left) and a great ape (right) are associated with differences in the ilium. Drawing by S. Washburn.

human. Napier (1964) concludes that the two forms of *Australopithecus* differed in gait: the gracile form was fully bipedal but the robust form waddled. Almost all primates are agile and a waddling gait is not plausible. Other authors find no differences in gait between the various specimens of *Australopithecus*.

W. Leutenegger (1974) argues that evolution of the human pelvis has involved a compromise in natural selection between a good strut for use of the lower limb and a large bowl for ease in childbearing. Since the head of the newborn *Australopithecus* was small compared with that of a newborn human, the problems of childbearing would have had less influence than in primitive human populations. The selective pressures for effective locomotor adaptations compared with those for obstetrical adaptations would therefore have been greater in *Australopithecus*. He therefore concurs with J. T. Robinson's (1972) view that *Australopithecus africanus* was at least as well adapted to bipedal locomotion as modern human beings, among whom, in women at least, the demands of reproduction adversely affect maximum locomotor efficiency.

Although many quadrupeds are faster than human beings on short sprints, a man jogging all day can cover as great a distance as any of them. If he can keep it in sight (and bipedal running helps in that respect also) a human hunter can wear down and overtake a fleeter animal. It is hard to believe that our predecessors ever had an inefficient gait: chimpanzees can move rapidly on all fours and even the initial bipedalism of *Australopithecus* must have marked a further advance. The advantages would have caused a rapid evolutionary change, and intermediate stages seem to be absent from the fossil record.

There is really one variable type of pelvis and one general type of skull and dentition. If there was a long time span involved, the existence of two very similar species is unlikely. All African *Australopithecus* fossil specimens should be assumed to belong to the same species unless new evidence to the contrary suggests that we separate them. If there was only one type of hominid present, the evidence of deliberately worked stone tools in the deposits at Swartkrans and Olduvai and the suggestion of bone tools at Makapan point to *Australopithecus* as the toolmaker. Upright stance would permit simultaneous holding of tools in the hands while running or walking, a stance that is possible for an animal with pelvis and femora of the kind seen in *Australopithecus* (Fig. 15-14). Furthermore, the increasing use of tools and weapons would have created conditions favorable to the evolution of adaptation to bipedalism. In this way behavior often determines the direction evolution will take. The propensity for behaviors is in turn dependent on evolved characteristics inherited from predecessors. Such a feedback mechanism must have worked in the evolution of the unique human mode of locomotion.

## The Dating of Australopithecus Deposits

The deposits at Olduvai consist of a series of *beds*, as successive geological strata silted out from bodies of water are called. Starting at the bottom there are two significant beds, a lower Bed I and an upper Bed II. Between them there is a discontinuity that represents a span of time. The discontinuity can be located in various parts of the fossil deposits at Olduvai. There are also three later beds (III, IV, and V) above them. Bed I has been dated by the **potassium-argon method** previously described, and its base yielded a date of 1.85–1.90 million years ago. Pumice from Bed I just above the level containing the "Zinjanthropus" skull gives a date of 1.76 million years.

The bed has also been dated by counts of the tracks that spontaneous atomic fission of uranium 238 leaves in glass. Suitably treated and examined the minute permanent trails of atomic particles can be seen and counted. The number of fission tracks per amount of $^{238}U$ is proportional to the age. Natural volcanic glass from Bed I gives a date of 2.03 plus or minus 0.28 million years—consistent, within the limits of accuracy of the method, with the potassium-argon date. The marker bed between I and II has been dated at 1.6 million years old, but the top of Bed II can not be dated by the potassium-argon method. A large *Australopithecus* milk molar was found in Bed II over 100 feet higher up the Olduvai canyon wall, so it is claimed that the "Zinjanthropus" type lasted over a very long time span.

No comparable dating method can be applied to any of the South African *Australopithecus* sites. Their relative dates are based on climatic and fossil evidence. A higher proportion of extinct fossil species in the *Australopithecus*-bearing deposits of Sterkfontein and Makapan than in those of Swartkrans and Kromdraai suggest that the latter sites, with their robust specimens of *Australopithecus*, were the later. The dates of South African deposits cannot be tied into the East African sequence, however, since climate may have differed. Pending more information, there is no good reason to accept any great gap in age between South and East African *Australopithecus* materials.

The findings of "Zinjanthropus" in Tanzania greatly increased the known range of *Australopithecus* and encouraged further search in East Africa and elsewhere. In 1961 Y. Coppens reported a skull from Chad in the Sudan (Coppens, 1966). In 1964 one of the Leakeys' assistants, Kamoya Kimeu, discovered a huge, almost complete mandible with all the teeth in place at a place called **Peninj,** west of Lake Natron in Tanzania. This mandible is a little smaller than the upper jaw of the "Zinjanthropus" skull, but must have belonged to a similarly robust individual. The Peninj jaw is believed to be about the age of Bed I at Olduvai.

Other specimens from East Africa point to still earlier dates than those at Olduvai. B. Patterson and W. W. Howells of Harvard (1967) describe a fragment of an *Australopithecus* humerus from sediments dated at 2.5 million years ago by potassium-argon analysis of overlying lava. Still further to the north (in Southern Ethiopia) Arambourg and Coppens (1967) have reported a mandible that can be compared to *Australopithecus africanus* but associated with fossils older than those of Bed I at Olduvai. In April 1969 a party led by F. C. Howell (1969) found two jaws and many teeth belonging to the genus *Australopithecus* in the same region. Like the Peninj jaw, the more massive jaw of Howell's specimens closely fits the upper jaw of the "Zinjanthropus" skull.

Potassium-argon dates are said to give the jaws an age of about two million years, but some of the loose teeth, of somewhat smaller size, are said to go back about 3.75 million years. In 1974 C. D. Johanson found numerous fragments of all parts of a skeleton further north in Ethiopia and estimates the date at more than 3 million years ago, but no description has yet been published. An *Australopithecus* specimen, a mandibular fragment from **Lothagam Hill,** Kenya, is said to have lived 5.5 million years ago (Patterson et al., 1970) and is thus of Early Pliocene date.

Discovery of early specimens of *Australopithecus* are important because, whether or not there were eventually two or more species (some of them outside the human line of descent), at least the early members of the genus must have been our direct ancestors.

## Summary

The first fossils of the Hominidae (human family) are apparently about 5.5 million years old. Most *Australopithecus* fossils in Africa occur in association with Villafranchian fauna and are of Pliocene and Early Pleistocene date. Fossils of the genus *Australopithecus* are well represented by many specimens from various places in Africa. The face is short but large, the front teeth small, the skull capacity very small by human standards but large for a small ape, and the skeleton—especially the pelvis—is similar to that of *Homo* in respect to those features which go with bipedal locomotion. Crude stone tools appear by about 2.6 million years ago. Some scholars think that there were at least two species of *Australopithecus*, a gracile and a robust species; others, that the variations are merely differences between local populations, between different times, or between the sexes. In either case, at least the early members of this genus were ancestral to our species.

CHAPTER **16**

# EARLY MEMBERS
# OF THE GENUS HOMO

**"Pre-zinj"**

In 1961 L. S. B. Leakey reported finding in Bed I at **Olduvai Gorge** parts of the skull and jaw of a juvenile hominid (see Fig. 16-1) different from "Zinjanthropus." Since they came from lower in the deposit, the remains (OH 7) were called **"Pre-zinj."** Some juvenile hand bones were found together with the juvenile skull fragments.

The skull is said to be larger in capacity than those of *Australopithecus,* but it was badly broken and the estimates are not exact. Other estimates do not place it outside the size range of *Australopithecus.* Nevertheless, the back teeth are smaller and much narrower side to side (called "bucco-lingual," cheek to tongue) than are the teeth in the "Zinjanthropus" and **Peninj** jaws. Because the dental and other features are comparable to later fossils and modern teeth and bones, Leakey, Tobias, and Napier (1964) created a new species. They ascribed it to the human genus and called it **"Homo habilis"** (handyman). It is not certain whether the foot bones of OH 8 (see Fig. 16-2), from the same approximate time, belonged to the same species. They were not from the same individual as OH 7. B. A. Wood (1974) has compared one of these bones,

FIG. 16-1 The original Pre-zinj "Homo habilis" mandible (OH 7). The front teeth are larger and the back teeth narrower and smaller than those of the robust East African *Australopithecus* mandible. Photograph courtesy of Dr. Phillip V. Tobias.

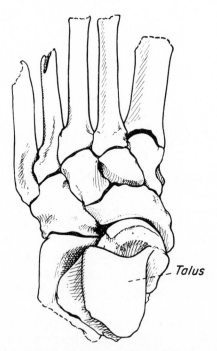

FIG. 16-2 Drawing of the "Homo habilis" foot bones (OH 8). They are nearly identical with those of *Homo sapiens* and are completely consistent with effective bipedal locomotion at a stage in human evolution when the brain was the size of that of a chimpanzee or gorilla. From W. E. Le Gros Clark: *History of the primates* (ed. 9). London: Trustees of the British Museum (Natural History), 1965. Reproduced by permission.

the talus, with tali from **Kromdraai, East Rudolf,** and modern humans. Wood concludes that the East Rudolf talus belonged to *Homo* rather than *Australopithecus,* but that the other two specimens, though similar to each other and more human than apelike, also come from a biped, but perhaps one that lacked the striding human gait. Wolpoff thinks that if Wood had examined some American Indian skeletons he would not have reached that conclusion. Leakey had also found various other fragmentary remains in Beds I and II at Olduvai. To some of them he had given colloquial names such as "George" (OH 16) and "Cinderella" (OH 13) in order to avoid prematurely ascribing them to a species. Leakey et al. (1964) placed these also in "Homo habilis." Some students of the problem believe that the degree of variation in size from one group of teeth to another (or in a particular tooth from one dimension to another) seen between *Australopithecus* and "Homo habilis" occurs only between genera.

Tobias (1969), while conceding that "Homo habilis" probably occupies in East Africa the morphological and ecological niche occupied by gracile *Australopithecus africanus* in the South, refers to "Homo habilis" as "ultra-gracile" and to "Zinjanthropus" as "hyper-robust." Others (see, for instance, Brace et al., 1971) call attention to the fact that the size of teeth can vary greatly even within a species; they consider "Pre-zinj" as *Australopithecus* and the later "George" and "Cinderella" as probably transitional between *Australopithecus* and **Homo erectus.**

## "Telanthropus"

Long before these "Homo habilis" remains had been found at Olduvai, J. T. Robinson had discovered at **Swartkrans** a mandible with teeth (Sk 15) that was more human than the comparable parts of most of the other Swartkrans material. Robinson (1953) called this mandible (together with another piece of mandible, a maxillary fragment (Sk 80), a loose tooth, and a piece of bone from the forearm) **"Telanthropus,"** and considered it a true human. Subsequently he and others have reclassed "Telanthropus" as *Homo erectus* (pp. 259 ff.). "Telanthropus" seems to fit into the same grade (that is, the same level of evolutionary development) as "Cinderella," the *Homo* specimen from the upper part (Bed II) of the Olduvai deposit, and with the more rugged specimens of *Homo erectus* from Java (see p. 265). In fact, recent work by C. K. Brain shows that the original "Telanthropus" mandible probably is much later in time than the other Swartkrans specimens. In 1967 F. C. Howell said that there are two lines (Fig. 16-3). One is that of *Australopithecus africanus* (from which he excluded the rugged specimens), which emerged from still unknown precursors and gave rise to a succession of species of the genus *Homo* including Olduvai hominids 7, 8, 9, 13, and Swartkrans 15. The other is that of "Australopithecus robustus" (including "Zinjanthropus," Peninj, Swartkrans 46, 48, etc., and Kromdraai specimens), a distinct species which also extended throughout Bed I and much of Bed II. Howell said that culturally patterned behavior was clearly present by 2 million years ago when "Australopithecus robustus" and

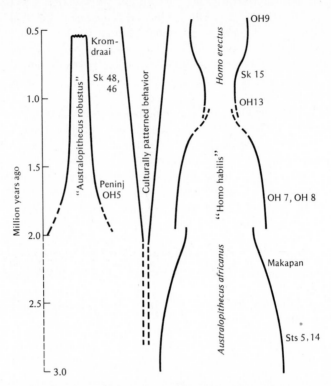

FIG. 16-3   In the diagram on which this is based, Howell (1967), who is conducting research in the Omo valley of Ethiopia, stresses the long duration of culturally patterned behavior (especially stone tools) and the fact that we cannot associate them with particular fossils. He also shows "Australopithecus robustus" as a separate line of long duration that eventually became extinct. Views similar to Howell's are widely held by well-informed students of the question, but some others think that there was only one—very variable—species at a time. The approximate dates are indicated. *OH*, Olduvai hominid; *Sk*, Swartkrans; *Sts*, Sterkfortein.

*Homo* were on the scene in both East and South Africa, but did not commit himself as to who made the tools.

One of the "Telanthropus" specimens from Swartkrans (Sk 80) is now known to have belonged to the same individual as several fragments of a skull (Sk 246, Sk 247) formerly ascribed to "Australopithecus robustus" (Clarke et al., 1970). Now that the whole specimen is pieced together it is seen to be rather gracile, however, and the jaws and their musculature must have been relatively small. On the other hand, M. H. Wolpoff (1968b, 1970) thinks that this and other specimens of "Telanthropus" are within the plausible range of variation of *Australopithecus* at the site and that only one species was present.

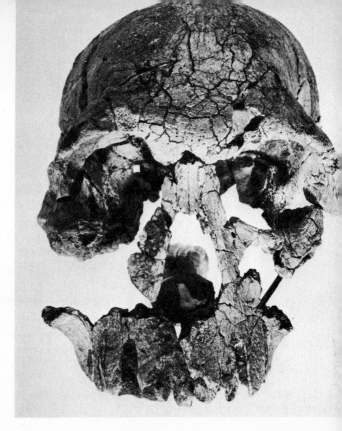

FIG. 16-4 Richard Leakey's ER 1470, the "Third Hominid Model" from east of Lake Rudolf, Kenya. The deposit in which it was found has been dated as approximately 2.6 million years old. It is in some ways remarkably human. As can be seen in the photographs, some parts are missing and considerable reconstruction is necessary. Full evaluation will have to wait further scientific study of the specimen and interpretation of its relation to other fossils. Photographs courtesy of Richard Leakey and the National Museums of Kenya.

0 _____ 5
CMS

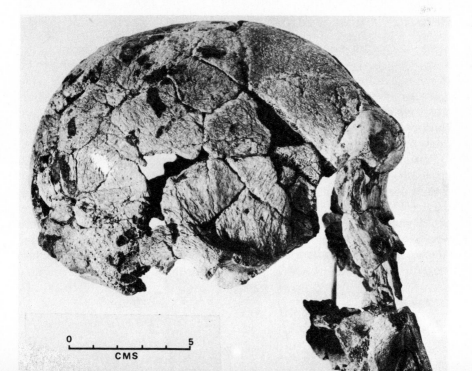

0 _____ 5
CMS

257

## Third Hominid Model

At a recent meeting of the Zoological Society of London, Richard Leakey (1973), who is among those who believe that he already has evidence of two distinct types of early hominid from East Rudolf, showed casts of fossils he ascribes to a "Third Hominid Model," from deposits possibly older than 2.6 million years. A preliminary description of this skull (ER 1470, Fig. 16-4) has now been published (Day et al., 1975). The formation has been dated by radio-active isotope methods as 2.61 ±0.26 million years B.P., and this is roughly confirmed by paleomagnetic studies that give an antiquity of about 2.7–3.0 million years to the deposit. The skull has been pieced together from a great many fragments. R. L. Holloway prepared an accurate latex mold of the interior and estimates the cranial volume to be 0.770 to 0.775 liters. The brow ridges are less prominent than in *Homo erectus* (see below). The exact relationship of the parts of the face and of a little bit of the foramen magnum to the skull will probably remain topics for debate, but it seems probable that, however constructed, the skull capacity is larger than previously measured *Australopithecus* and "Homo habilis" skulls. The face is very large; the post-orbital constriction is moderate; there is no sagittal cresting. The palate is said to be horseshoe shaped, the teeth and sockets show that all of them, both front and back, were probably very large. A number of other specimens from East Rudolf have been ascribed to our own genus *(Homo)* rather than to *Australopithecus* (Leakey and Woold, 1973; Day and Leakey, 1974). Although the analysis is far from complete, at least one of the three mandibles (ER 992) falls within the range of size and form of *Homo erectus* (Olshan, 1975). Pebble tools and stone chips have also been recovered.

Among the fossils collected during the 1971 and 1972 expeditions to East Rudolf there are numerous other specimens that Leakey and his colleagues (Leakey and Wood, 1973; Day and Leakey, 1974) provisionally classify as human (genus, *Homo;* species, not determined). Most of these specimens are limb bones (two femurs and parts of a tibia, a fibula, and a third femur—the names of the bones of the skeleton are given in Fig. 15-11) and have been described by Day et al. (1975). As may be seen in Fig. 16-5, the two femurs are essentially complete, a rarity in the early hominid fossil record. They are consistent with a human upright stance. They are very varied, however, ranging from small to truly massive dimensions.

Two questions remain to be answered. First, were the specimens unambiguously associated with geological material of so early a date? And second, if so, are any of the anatomical features so different from the corresponding parts of previously known ancient fossils of comparable or subsequent date that they could not have belonged to the same species? The burden of proof is on those who would answer both questions in the affirmative. In the meanwhile the simple view is to classify together all specimens that *may* belong together. Answers to similar questions about other specimens in the past have rarely been universally agreed upon even after years of study and discussion by

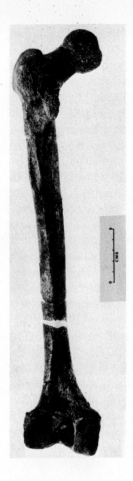

FIG. 16-5 Left femur ER 1481 from East Rudolf. Two femurs and a fragmented tibia were recovered during 1972 from horizons below the KBS tuff. The femurs compare closely with those of *Homo sapiens*. Photographs courtesy of Richard Leakey and the National Museums of Kenya.

competent scholars. At best, there always seems to be room for debate. In any case, those who believe there has been a long history of true humans have new fossil candidates for the honor and those who argue that there is only one line in hominid evolution have further evidence of great variability within the line.

Whether "Telanthropus," "Pre-zinj," and some specimens from Lake Rudolf were female *Australopithecus*, a distinct gracile species of *Australopithecus*, or belonged to the genus *Homo*, all students of the matter agree that they conform with what human ancestors must have been like at the time. In fact, virtually all anthropologists place them in the human lineage.

## Homo erectus

Shortly after the exposition of evolutionary theory in Darwin's *Origin of Species*, Thomas Huxley (1863) published *Evidence as to Man's Place in Nature*, in which he demonstrated the similarities between us and the great apes. This led to the search for "missing links" between the apes and humans. In 1891 and 1892, during a search on the island of **Java** for such a "missing link," or ape man, Eugene Dubois, a young scholar who had become a colonial Army surgeon specifically so he could undertake the search, discovered what he was looking for—some fossilized teeth, a fossil human thighbone (femur) and a skull cap. The teeth are large and much worn so that interpretation of their significance has been difficult. The femur (which may not have belonged to the same time period as the skull) has an unusual osteophyte (tumorlike growth of bone) protruding from its normal contour; otherwise it looks like that of a modern human. The skull cap, however, is intermediate between those of humans and *Australopithecus* in size and shape. It is low and narrow, especially just behind the forehead region, and there is a horizontal ridge of bone (supra-orbital torus) extending over both eye sockets. The brain, or more exactly the cranial cavity, is small by modern human standards, but far exceeds in size that of any known ape. Dubois gave this fossil the name "Pithecanthropus erectus," the erect ape man. The name has since been modified to *Homo erectus,* upright man, because, now that much more hominid fossil material is known, the degree of difference from *Homo sapiens* is seen to separate them as two species of the same genus and not as two genera.

Subsequently, additional material of *Homo erectus* has been discovered in Java, much of it due to the efforts of G. H. R. von Koenigswald (Figs. 16-6–16-8). The *Homo erectus* materials from Java consist of parts of ten skulls, six femurs, a number of facial fragments including those of five mandibles, and teeth.

The skulls are all incomplete but estimates of their capacity range from 0.7 to nearly 1.1 liter. The smallest is that of an 8- or 10-year-old child from **Modjokerto,** but this specimen is much more ancient than most, if not all, of the others. In any case, except for this specimen the skull capacities are well above those observed in *Australopithecus* or "Homo habilis," but only very rarely is the skull capacity of normal human skulls today as small as that of the largest specimens of *Homo erectus* from Java. All the skulls have the same general conformation (Jacob, 1966). Compared with modern humans the skull is low and "pinched" behind the **orbits,** features that merely reflect the small brain case associated with a prominent supraorbital **torus** (see Fig. 15-12). At the back of the skull there is a corresponding occipital torus extending backwards and associated with an enormous crest above the **mastoids** to make a reinforced frame and to give attachment to powerful neck muscles. The back of the occiput is also shelved to give wide attachment to some of these muscles. The mastoid process itself has large irregular cells that in life were air sinuses. Mastoid processes give attachment to a muscle, the sternomastoid, that runs to the clavicle (collarbone) and sternum (breastbone). This muscle is especially well developed in us to help hold up the head in the human erect position. In quadrupedal animals it helps turn the head but is relatively less important. Although there is sometimes a rudimentary mastoid process in adult gorillas it is never seen in the young of any living nonhuman primate. There is, however, a mastoid process on the Modjokerto skull.

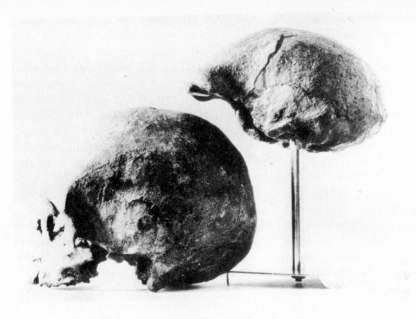

FIG. 16-6 *Top:* The skull of *Homo erectus*—the specimen II from Java (upper right) compared with that of *Homo sapiens*—a recent skull of an Australian (left). Note the much greater size of the brain case in *Homo sapiens* than in *Homo erectus. Bottom:* Posterior view of the same skull of *Homo erectus,* which is very similar to the other adult skulls from Java. Note the large browridges, narrowness of the upper part of the skull, and generally robust appearance of *Homo erectus.* Photographs courtesy of Prof. G. H. R. von Koenigswald.

Among von Koenigswald's material there is also a lower jaw and, with one of the skulls, an upper jaw. Both jaws are large and robust. The teeth are large but not enormous like some of those of *Australopithecus*. The elevations on the biting surfaces, the cusps, are of human pattern; where the cusps are worn off, there are signs of a characteristic human type of wear toward a plane surface higher next to the tongue and lower at the cheek. The **canine teeth** overlap somewhat, the lower meeting a small gap **(diastema)** between the upper canine and lateral incisor teeth in at least one instance. Such a diastema of larger size is frequent in modern apes but, as we have already noted, absent in *Australopithecus* as well as in humans. In the lower jaw there is no chin, and the mental foramina, the openings in the bone near the chin for the passage of small nerves and blood vessels, are multiple as in most apes. Nevertheless, the jaws are definitely more human than *Australopithecus*-like, in size and proportions and in the teeth they carry. The additional femurs, like the first one, are also entirely human, but their antiquity is equivocal (Day and Molleson, 1973).

## The Antiquity of *Homo erectus* from Java

The Java fossils of *Homo erectus* come from two different strata: the Trinil of Early Middle Pleistocene age and the Djetis, which extends back into the Lower Pleistocene (Fig. 16-9). The majority of the fossils, including the original specimens, come from the later Trinil deposits. One of the adult skulls, all but one of the mandibles, a maxillary bone, and the Modjokerto child remains, apparently come from deposits of the earlier (Djetis) beds. The area of central Java where the Trinil and Djetis deposits occur was never glaciated, but there were a series of deposits showing climatic changes and volcanic eruptions during the Pleistocene. The Solo River and its tributaries have eroded these deposits and it is in the natural terraces of these streams, not in cave deposits, that all the material has been found. The chief basis for dating the deposits has been the association with remains of Pleistocene animals—the so-called Sivo-Malayan fauna ("animals of the **Siwalik Hills** and Malaya") of Middle Pleistocene date (Movius, 1949). A test for the amount of fluorine in tiny specimens taken from fossils confirms that the proportion of this element (hence the degree of fossilization and in a rough way the age) is the same in the *Homo erectus* femurs as in other fossils of the Sivo-Malayan fauna. Furthermore, a series of potassium-argon dates for basalt specimens from the Trinil (see Fig. 16-9) is beginning to give an idea of the absolute age. The hominid specimens in the Djetis beds are apparently somewhat more robust than those of Trinil age and have sometimes been ascribed to the separate species (on grounds that are not justified when one considers the range of variation possible within a single species). No evidence of tools, stone or otherwise, has been found with the Java *Homo erectus*, but the lack is not surprising since the fossils were not discovered where the individuals lived and died, but among the gravel of river deposits where they had apparently been washed.

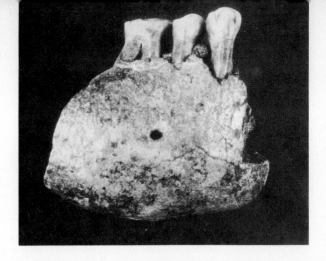

FIG. 16-7 *Left:* The original mandibular fragment of "Meganthropus" from Java. This is a massive specimen and led some students to the conclusion that the genus *Homo* was descended from gigantic predessors. To the extent that the conclusion refers only to the size of the jaw, it is supported by much additional evidence. Photograph courtesy of Prof. G. H. R. von Koenigswald.

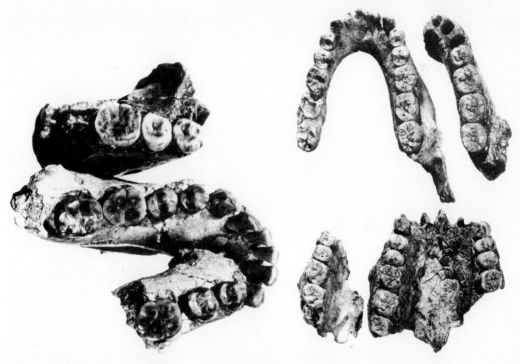

FIG. 16-8 *Left:* The mandible of "Meganthropus" from Java (top) compared with that of the Bed I "Homo habilis" from Olduvai Gorge in Africa (OH 7). Despite the great distance between the sites, the jaws are in many ways similar, as pointed out by Tobias and von Koenigswald (1964). *Right:* Remains of *Homo erectus* specimens from Java (right of each pair) compared to the Bed II "Homo habilis" from Olduvai Gorge (OH 13). The teeth and jaws of the African specimens are extremely close in morphology to those from Java but the brain cases are very different (that of Sangiran 4 from Java is almost double in size that of OH 13). OH 13 is not as similar to the Pre-zinj "Homo habilis" OH 7 as was formerly thought. Photographs courtesy of Professor G. H. R. von Koenigswald.

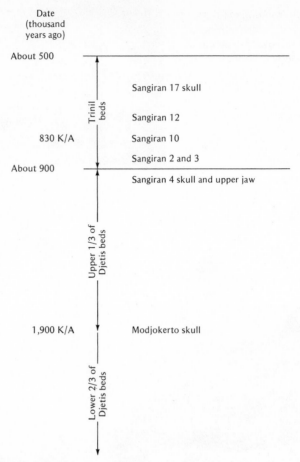

FIG. 16-9   The dating of Java hominids. The Sangiran material is all classified as *Homo erectus*. The status of the Modjokerto child is debated. K/A dates have been determined by the potassium-argon method.

## "Meganthropus"

At one location of the earlier Djetis beds, von Koenigswald also recovered a jaw fragment of truly massive proportions which he called "Meganthropus," "large man" (Figs. 16-7, 16-8). It has larger teeth and especially larger supporting bone than the *Homo erectus* specimens, but the forms of the teeth are the same. Two other mandibular fragments from the same place have also been ascribed to "Meganthropus." Franz Weidenreich, the anthropologist who studied Peking *Homo erectus* (see below), believed that there was a succession from "Meganthropus" to *Homo erectus* and that they properly belong to the same genus.

When the materials from Java and some of those from Africa were directly compared by two of the scholars most familiar with these remains (Tobias and von Koenigswald, 1964) they found nothing in the Java jaws as large and primitive as those of "Australopithecus robustus." "Meganthropus" they found to fit in well with the Pre-zinj specimen but the teeth of the former were a little larger (Fig. 16-8). Another so-called "Meganthropus" maxilla from Tanzania, Africa, however, is probably *Australopithecus*.

The other remains from the Djetis beds in Java—the more robust jaws of *Homo erectus*—correspond very closely to the hominid remains of "Cinderella" from the lower part of Bed II at Olduvai. The original "Telanthropus" specimen from Swartkrans is possibly of the same level of development and may have been contemporary.

Unfortunately, the direct comparisons made by Tobias and von Koenigswald when they got together in June 1964 did not include examples of the more gracile South African *Australopithecus africanus,* but many students of the subject believe that *Homo erectus* derived from *Australopithecus africanus*

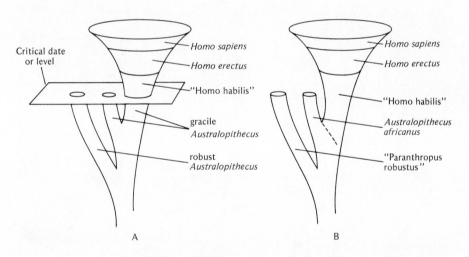

FIG. 16-10  Two ways of classifying the same traditional view of the phylogency of the family Hominidae. These figures are derived from Reed's (1967) redrafting of P. V. Tobias' schema, as modified by Reed in a personal communication in 1972.

   *A*  If one classifies by grade—that is, by degree of evolutionary development—everything below a certain critical level or before a certain critical date is classed as *Australopithecus* and everything beyond that level (or after that date) as *Homo*.

   *B*  If one classifies by lineages (clades) the separation between *Australopithecus* and *Homo* is placed at the fork (dashed line) and robust *Australopithecus,* if it is considered separate, may be designated as a distinct genus, "Paranthropus."

and that the so-called "Homo habilis" (and hence also "Meganthropus" from Java) are local (and perhaps temporal) variants.

C. A. Reed (1967) shows that, in part, the conflicting views concerning the names of these fossils stem from the use of two systems of classification: by grades and by clades (Fig. 16-10). When fossils are scarce there is a tendency to classify by grades, general levels of organization. When there are fewer gaps in the fossil record, however, the lineages can be identified and there is a tendency to shift from a horizontal (grade) type of classification to a vertical (clade) one in which ancestral and descendant individuals are grouped together. Thus, if the lines had become extinct long ago and there were no *Homo erectus* and *Homo sapiens* to follow, the Pre-zinj Bed I "Homo habilis" from Olduvai and "Meganthropus" from Java would certainly have been called *Australopithecus* rather than *Homo*.

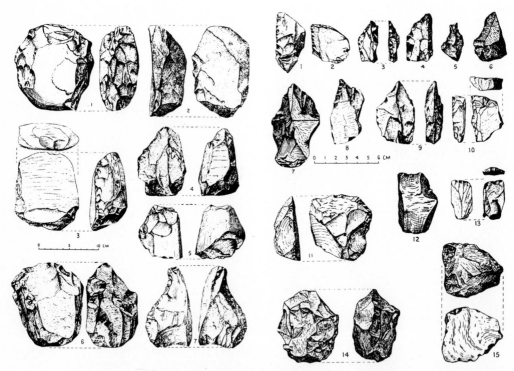

FIG. 16-11   *Top: left:* Choppers and chopping tools from Locality 1 at Choukoutien. The paleolithic stone tools associated with *Homo erectus* in the Far East are of the chopper type rather than the Chelles-Acheul hand-axe type of Africa and Europe (see p. 273 and Fig. 16-18). *Right:* Flake implements and cores from Locality 1 at Choukoutien. Chips from the making of such stone tools led to the excavation and discovery of Peking man at Choukoutien. From the Cenozoic Research Laboratory of China.

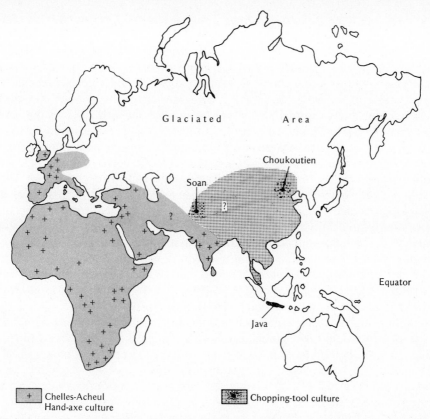

Fig. 16-12   The distribution of Lower Paleolithic hand-axe and chopping-tool cultures. Redrawn from Movius, 1949.

## *Homo erectus* in China

In 1921, J. G. Anderson, a Swedish geologist working in North China, noticed chips of quartz—apparently not native to the place—in the limestone filling of a Pleistocene cave at the town of **Choukoutien,** some thirty miles west of Peking (Fig. 16-11). The implication was that the quartz must have been brought by prehistoric humans. Excavations soon revealed a human tooth, the first of a number of finds. Davidson Black (1927), a Canadian anatomist who was then teaching at a Chinese medical school, recognized from details of its shape that the tooth was "human" and believed that it belonged to a distinct genus, which he called "Sinanthropus pekinensis." Subsequent specimens demonstrate that this is only a variant of *Homo erectus,* the original specimens of which had already been discovered in Java. But Black's finding was of major importance since no hominid fossils of comparable antiquity were then known in association with stone tools. The tools are flakes and choppers, and none of the hand-axe types of Europe, Africa, and Western Asia are found in the Far East (Fig. 16-12).

Shortly after describing the first of the remains, Black died. Franz Weidenreich, a Jewish refugee from Nazi Germany, went to China and examined and described the various finds of Peking man in four monographs (Weidenreich, 1936, 1937, 1941, 1943; on the lower jaws, teeth, long bones, and skull respectively) and in numerous shorter reports. In the first days of the war between the United States and Japan, all the original specimens were lost.

The skulls of Peking man are of fully human size, the capacity ranging from 0.9 to 1.3 liters (Fig. 16-13). They are also much like the skulls from Java, notably in having marked bony bulges fore and aft (supraorbital and occipital **tori**). The skulls are wide at the base, and at the top they are keeled (narrow to a ridge). It is not the elevated sagittal crest of the gorilla and some of the *Australopithecus* specimens, built up when the two temporal muscles meet each other at the midline of the top of the skull, but merely that the highest part of the skull is angular rather than globular, giving the skull a gabled, rooflike appearance. The face protrudes, and the nose is broad. The teeth, like those from Java, are large and set in large jaws. There is no chin. The mental foramen, as in most apes and as also in *Homo erectus* from Java, is always multiple.

Weidenreich has called attention to a few features that the Peking hominids shared with modern Mongoloid peoples, including the present-day Chinese (Fig. 16-14). The midline ridge or "keel," already referred to, is one of these. There is also an overgrowth of the bone of the lower jaw—the so-called mandibular torus (Fig. 16-14), common in Eskimos and also occurring occasionally in Europeans and others. The molar teeth have large pulp cavities *(taurodont, "teeth like a bull's")*, a feature rare in primates but pronounced especially in Neanderthals and, to some extent, in some modern Mongoloid peoples. The

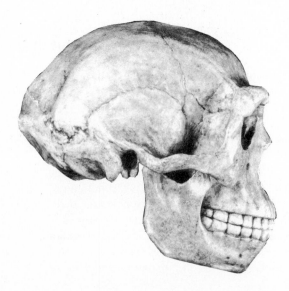

FIG. 16-13 Peking man. Cast of a reconstruction of the skull. These fossils from Peking have been assigned to the species *Homo erectus*, but the cranial capacity is larger than those of the specimens from Java, and Peking man was probably more advanced. Courtesy of the American Museum of Natural History.

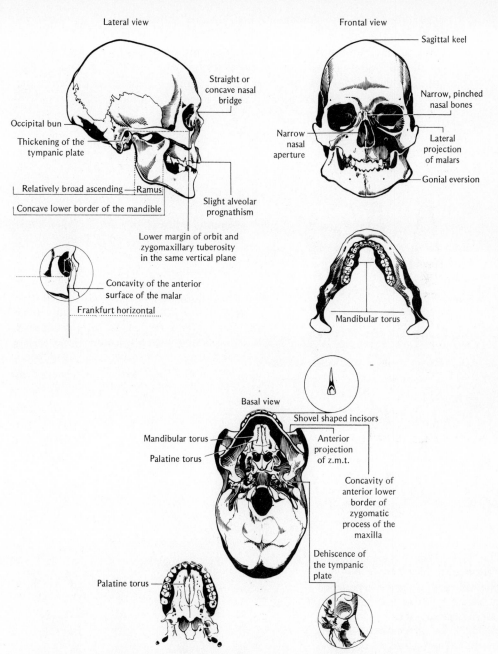

Lateral view

Straight or
concave nasal
bridge

Occipital bun

Thickening of the
tympanic plate

Relatively broad ascending —Ramus

Concave lower border of the mandible

Slight alveolar
prognathism

Lower margin of orbit and
zygomaxillary tuberosity
in the same vertical plane

Concavity of the anterior
surface of the malar

Frankfurt horizontal

Frontal view

Sagittal keel

Narrow, pinched
nasal bones

Narrow
nasal
aperture

Lateral
projection
of malars

Gonial eversion

Mandibular torus

Basal view

Shovel shaped incisors

Mandibular torus

Palatine torus

Anterior
projection
of z.m.t.

Concavity of
anterior lower
border of
zygomatic
process of the
maxilla

Dehiscence of
the tympanic
plate

Palatine torus

FIG. 16-14  Variant anatomical traits frequently observed in Eskimo skulls—in this case from the Mackenzie Delta (Kittigaguit). These include some of the "Mongoloid" features Weidenreich noted in the Peking skulls: the sagittal keel, shovel-shaped incisors, and mandibular torus. From O. Oschinsky: *The most ancient Eskimos*. Ottawa, Canada: The Canadian Research Centre for Anthropology, 1964. Reproduced by permission.

upper front teeth are concave behind. These "shovel-shaped" incisors (Figs. 16-15, 16-16) are present in most Mongoloid individuals (including East Asians, Eskimos, and American Indians) and occur in less pronounced form in occasional individuals of all human populations. Weidenreich concluded that, although these traits suggest affinities with modern peoples in the same part of Asia, this would not preclude ancestral relations with modern *Homo sapiens*

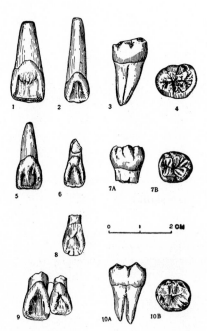

FIG. 16-15 Comparison of teeth of Peking *Homo erectus (1–4)* with Upper Pleistocene human teeth found in Shansi Province *(5–7)* and the Ordos Desert *(8)* of China and modern Chinese *(9–10)*. The central incisors *(1, 5, 9)* and the lateral incisors *(2, 6, 9, right)* are all shovel shaped. The lower second molar teeth *(3, 4, 7, 10)* all show the dryopithicus pattern but vary in degree of taurodontism, crown shape, and other features. From Kwang-chih Chang: "New evidence on fossil man in China." *Science 136,* 749–760. Copyright 1962 by the American Association for the Advancement of Science.

FIG. 16-16 Shovel-shaped maxillary incisors with thickening of the marginal ridges. This feature is common in Aleuts and other Eskimos and in East Asiatics and American Indians in general. It is another feature that Weidenreich believed links Peking man to the Mongoloid peoples. From C. F. A. Moorrees: *The Aleut dentition.* Cambridge: Harvard University Press, 1957.

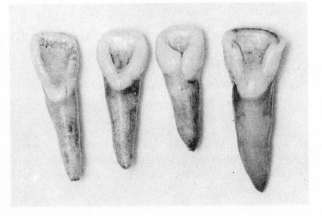

in general. The great time span (since the Middle Pleistocene) and the pre-
· sence of non-Mongoloid humans in the same place subsequently (as attested by
the three skulls of the Upper Cave at **Choukoutien**—see p. 307) make a direct
and separate descent of the Mongoloids from Peking man unlikely. In any case,
Peking man is much less like the modern Chinese than he is like *Homo erectus*
of Java. The latter is little more primitive than Peking man not only by reason
of its probably somewhat earlier date, but also in respect to a few features:
smaller skull, lower and flatter forehead region, larger jaws, and diastema.

Despite the tragic loss of the original material, we are fortunate to have
photographs, drawings, and descriptions of the originals and some excellent
casts of some of it made by the Chinese technicians in Peking. Some additional
new material has also turned up subsequently. There are, for example, two
teeth in a collection of fossil bones from Choukoutien that turned up in a fossil
collection at Uppsala, Sweden, and a few more fossil teeth of the type (but
slightly larger) that von Koenigswald had bought in a Chinese apothecary shop.

The present government of China has encouraged further searches. Excavations at Choukoutien have yielded an additional five teeth, two fragments of
limb bones, several mandibles, and the remaining portion of a cranium first
recovered many years ago. (Woo, 1956; Woo and Chao, 1959). Furthermore,
two places at **Lantian,** in Shensi Province, yielded, together with some stone
tools, a mandible, a skull cap with facial bones, and teeth. The skull is said to
be about 700,000 years old (Aigner and Laughlin, 1973) and very much like
that of the earlier Djetis *Homo erectus* from Java (Chang, 1968). Dr. Woo Ju-
Kang estimates the cranial capacity of the Lantian skull to be about 0.78 liters,
so it fits in with the earlier and more primitive Java skulls in this respect also. The
mandible is thought to be perhaps 300,000 years old. Both its third molar
(wisdom) teeth are congenitally absent and such reduction in the number of
teeth, common today, is usually thought of as "advanced." Since congenital
absence of third molar teeth is common in East Asiatics and American Indians,
some anthropologists use this feature of the Lantian skull to relate it to the
"Mongoloids." On the other hand, this characteristic is present in all modern
populations and is never present in a majority of individuals, so a definite
conclusion is not possible.

## Olduvai Hominid 9 and "Atlanthropus"

At Olduvai near the top of Bed II an expedition led by L. S. B. Leakey
discovered Olduvai Hominid 9 in 1960 (Fig. 16-17). It is the larger part of a
thick skull, but lacks the base and face. Like the Java skulls of *Homo erectus* it
is broadest down in the temporal region rather than up on the parietal bones,
but the supraorbital torus is bigger than in any specimen from the Far East and
the skull is not keeled. It is larger than any of the Java skulls and Tobias
estimates the cranial capacity as one liter.

At the level where the skull was found, as well as at numerous places in

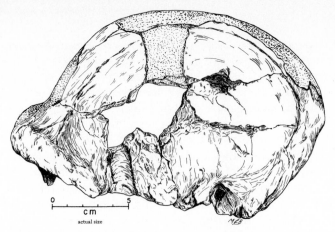

FIG. 16-17 Olduvai hominid 9 (OH 9) is an African *Homo erectus*. The specimen was formerly called "Chellean man" because of the Chelles-Acheul type "hand-axe" tools found at the same level at Olduvai Gorge. The distribution of *Homo erectus* in Africa as well as Asia (and probably Europe) suggests a satisfactory adaptation of this species to a variety of situations. From C. L. Brace, H. Nelson, and N. Korn, *Atlas of fossil man*. New York: Holt, Rinehart and Winston, 1971. Reproduced by permission.

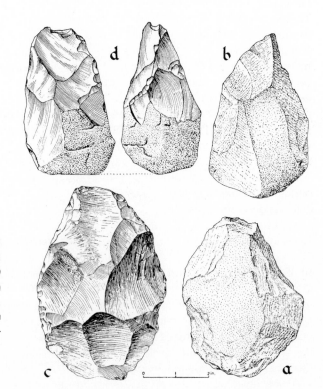

FIG. 16-18 Hand-axes from *(a)* Olduvai Gorge; *(b)* Morocco; *(c)* Chelles-sur-Marne, France; and *(d)* Caversham, England. From Kenneth P. Oakley: *Man the toolmaker*. London: The Trustees of the British Museum, 1950. Reproduced by permission.

Europe, Africa, and Western Asia, Middle Pleistocene deposits have yielded a type of human stone tool in which a stone has been sharpened by knocking big chips off both sides. This instrument is sometimes called a hand-axe, although we have no certainty that it was used in the way the term suggests (Fig. 16-18). The general term for these stone tools is the **Chelles-Acheul Industry,** after the places in France where two types of hand-axe were first found. Such hand-axes are numerous in the open Middle Pleistocene terraces of the rivers of Europe and elsewhere, but fossil remains of their users have been scarce. Olduvai Hominid 9 has been called "Chellean man" because the tools at that level at Olduvai are of Chellean type, but L. S. B. Leakey, who believed that there were several distinct kinds of hominids evolving simultaneously over long periods of time in the Gorge, cautioned against the careless assumption that this was necessarily the maker and user of the tools.

At **Ternifine,** Algeria, C. Arambourg (1955) pumped out the water from the deeper levels of a sand pit in what must have been the floor of a lake in Pleistocene times. Together with animal bones of species of the Early Middle Pleistocene he discovered three extraordinary mandibles (Fig. 16-19) and the side of a cranium. He also found flakes of stone and stone tools of the Chelles-Acheulian "hand-axe" or biface type. The jaw bones themselves, one particularly heavy, conform in shape to those of "Meganthropus" but are not so large. The chin region is not developed at all. The teeth are taurodont and similar to those from Peking and to SK 15 from Swartkrans. Despite these similarities, Arambourg assigned to the jaws to a new genus, "Atlanthropus." Part of another mandible, collected in a gravel pit at Casablanca, Morocco, in 1954, has also been ascribed by Arambourg and Biberson (1956) to the same species. It is reminiscent of Peking *Homo erectus* and is also associated with Acheulian tools. In this case, however, the tools are of a more developed type, and the site has been dated by a raised beach 100 feet above the present level of the sea. Arambourg believes that this beach was contemporary with the next to the last great glaciation.

These mandibles form a morphological link with and between the Java and Peking hominids and "Telanthropus." No Chelles-Acheul type tools were found with *Homo erectus* in the Far East (the Chinese tools are chips). Furthermore, Acheul-type tools were found with a more developed *Homo* in Europe (see Swanscombe, p. 299). Therefore, until the finding of *Homo erectus* with Chelles-Acheul tools in North and East Africa, the possibility that *Homo erectus* made them was pure speculation. It seems more likely that any humans have always used any available kit of tools. Today, for instance, every group of people readily borrows the design for any type of tool that will lighten their work. Thus one is not justified in making assumptions about the species or type of *Homo* from tools that are found without fossils; one is likewise not justified in assuming what type of culture some fossil form had unless one also recovers material evidence of the culture, such as stone tools.

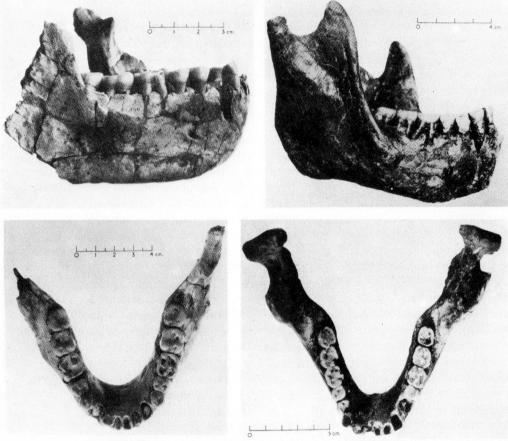

FIG. 16-19 The mandibles from Ternifine, Algeria. Comparison with *Homo erectus* mandibles from Java and China show similarities. The Ternifine specimens are a little more massive than is typical for the Asiatic specimens, however. Photographs courtesy of Professor C. Arambourg and the Institut de Paléontologie, Paris.

## Did *Homo erectus* Inhabit Europe?

In 1907, deep in a sandpit at **Mauer,** near Heidelberg, Germany, workmen discovered a mandible in a layer that has since been ascribed (on the basis of other fossils) to the latter part of the first interglacial period—that is, some 450,000 years ago. The jaw itself is very massive (even by comparison with the earlier and more robust Java specimens) and it lacks a chin, but the teeth are relatively small and resemble those of Neanderthals (Chapter 17) rather than those of *Homo erectus*. Calling the Heidelberg mandible *Homo erectus* rests largely on the fact that it is thought to have been contemporary with members of that species in Asia and Africa. Although much has been said about the Heidelberg find, not much can be determined except that it belongs to some species of the human genus.

The search in Europe for other evidence bearing on *Homo erectus* continued with no success for many years. Finally, in 1965, a Hungarian site, **Vertesszöllös,** yielded human fossils with an early pebble tool industry (similar to the industry at Choukoutien). The specimens represent two individuals. The teeth of one are similar to those of Peking *Homo erectus.* The other is represented by an occipital bone (the back of the skull). Wolpoff (1971) believes that all the features of this specimen are compatible with it being *Homo erectus.* The skull must have been relatively big, however, and the capacity was well within the range of modern *Homo sapiens.*

A new and very promising discovery has been made in the floor of a cave, **Arago,** near Tautavel in the eastern Pyrenees Mountains in France (H. and M.-A. de Lumley, 1971). A human facial skeleton, two mandibles, teeth, bones of several species of extinct rodents, wolf, and horse, and hand-axes and points of worked stone of Tayacian culture (a type of coarse stone implements considered to be the last type of the Lower—that is, early—Paleolithic) have been found together and are claimed to be of the beginning of the next to the last great glaciation, about 200,000 years ago. Preliminary accounts refer to massive eyebrow ridges, remarkably flat forehead, narrow and pinched behind the browridges, indicating a narrow, elongated, small brain. The teeth of one mandible are of modern human size, those of the other are said to be twice the size of those of modern humans in certain respects. Depending on the extent of these features, they could be traits of a transitional stage between *Homo erectus* and *Homo sapiens neanderthalensis* (Fig. 16-20). Photographs of the specimen show that the mandible is similar in shape to one from **Montmaurin,** France, discovered in 1949 in association with stone tools of a type more ancient than those of Neanderthal man. Vallois (1956) states that the Montmaurin mandible presents a combination of characters of the Neanderthal and Heidelberg fossils. The same may be provisionally suggested for the jaw from Arago. In the Arago specimen there is also a facial skeleton, so removal of the encrusted matrix—the surrounding stone—in which it is imbedded is awaited, and scholars look forward to photographs, casts, descriptions, measurements, and comparisons. A skull from **Petralona,** Greece, is also supposed to be of considerable antiquity and of *Homo erectus,* but again the specimen has not been prepared nor studied. If the European fossils are *Homo erectus,* they are the most recent examples. Since Europe is constantly being explored it is surprising that we have not found more definitive evidence of *Homo erectus,* especially since early stone tools of Chelles-Acheul types are abundant.

*Homo erectus* is distinct from our species *(Homo sapiens),* but there is a tendency to exaggerate the differences. Even if one ignores transitional or otherwise hard to classify specimens and limits consideration to the Java and Peking populations, the range of variation of many features of *Homo erectus* falls within that of modern *Homo sapiens* (Garn, 1963). Most fossil skulls are thick; so are some of those of living men and women. Teeth of *Homo erectus* were large; Garn says that tooth sizes in contemporary American Whites encompass the fossil range (with the exception of the early Java specimens). The eruption of second premolar teeth through the bone of the jaw before the second molar has erupted is called the "fossil sequence," but it is not always present in fossil specimens and occurs in 38 percent of contemporary Whites according to Garn. Height and breadth of the front of the jaw (symphysis) are supposed to be large in the fossils, but, "Meganthropus" aside, are not. Only one or two of the fossils fall outside the range of a small series of American White subjects in these features, although differences in cranial size and form are significant. Although not convinced of a major gap between fossil and modern humans, Garn considers the increased size of the *Homo sapiens* cranium to be significant.

## Summary

In East Africa, at Olduvai, there are fossils of a hominid more gracile than "Zinjanthropus" from the same place. The gracile fossils have been ascribed by some to a separate species, "Homo habilis," but the early ones, "Pre-zinj," are more rugged than the later ones. Considering the long time span, it is possible that "Pre-zinj" and "Zinjanthropus" belong to a single, very variable species.

In South Africa, too, there are specimens called "Telanthropus," in some

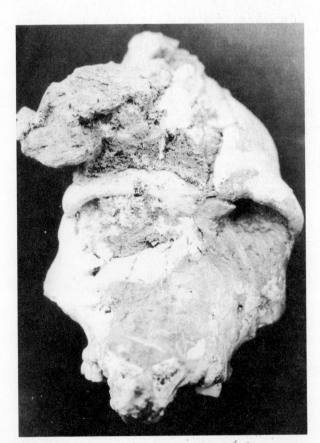

FIG. 16-20 The skull from Arago, France, still in matrix. The supraorbital torus and the prognathism are marked. Photograph courtesy of Professor Henri de Lumley.

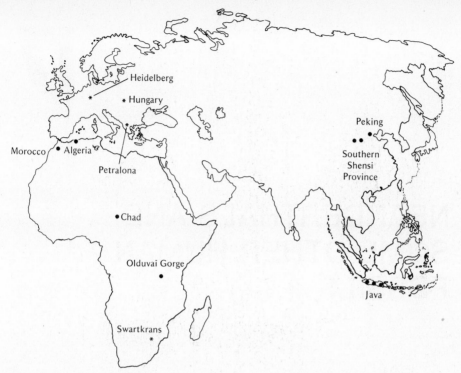

FIG. 16-21   Locations where *Homo erectus* specimens have been found. The specimens from sites indicated by asterisks in this diagram (Heidelberg, Hungary, and
Petralona in Europe and Swartkrans in South Africa) are not included in this species by
some students of human fossils, however.

ways more human than those typical for *Australopithecus*. They are now
considered by many to be of the genus *Homo* but others see no specific
difference from the rugged *Australopithecus* specimens with which they were
found. Some other newly found early East African specimens are also said to be
more like *Homo* than like *Australopithecus*.

By Early Middle Pleistocene (possibly 900,000 years ago) *Homo erectus*
occurs in Java. This has a low skull and powerful jaws but is of human, not
*Australopithecus*, type. The skull capacity is intermediate and the thighbone is human. Some other specimens from Java ("Meganthropus") are earlier
than most of the *Homo erectus* specimens and, like "Pre-zinj" and "Telanthropus," seem intermediate in some respects between *Australopithecus* and
*Homo erectus*. *Homo erectus* is also well known by fossils from Choukoutien,
China, and Africa (Olduvai Hominid 9, and also North Africa) and perhaps
Europe. In Europe the only specimens that seem to belong are in need of further
study; specimens from Vertesszöllös in Hungary, Arago in France, and Petralona in Greece may be transitional forms between *Homo erectus* and *Homo
sapiens*. In China and Africa *Homo erectus* is found in association with well
formed stone tool types.

# CHAPTER 17

# NEANDERTHALS AND SOME OTHER HUMAN FOSSILS

**Neanderthal** man (the name refers to the valley of the Neander River near Düsseldorf, Germany, where the first specimen was found) is a well-known and generally consistent form of hominid represented by skeletons found in caves throughout much of Europe: Germany, France, Belgium, Gibraltar, and Italy (Fig. 17-1). Additional, possibly somewhat less typical, specimens have been found in Yugoslavia, Germany, Czechoslovakia, Italy, North Africa, Israel, Iraq, and Uzbekistan in Central Asia.

To describe fossil specimens somewhat like Neanderthal but not identical, scholars have added the suffix "-oid" meaning "-like." Hence, Neanderthaloid means Neanderthal-like, just as anthropoid, the name for the great apes, is the "-oid" compound of the Greek root for human being, "anthrop." The term "anthropoid" does not include humans, and "Neanderthaloid" does not include the classic Neanderthal. A considerable variety of fossil specimens have been found that resemble the Neanderthal only in part and are thus classed as Neanderthaloid.

The Neanderthals have no better claim to being ancestral to modern populations than have some of their Neanderthaloid contemporaries. Indeed, some anthropologists consider the Neanderthals an extinct primitive sideline that was later replaced by more advanced people from elsewhere. Precisely be-

FIG. 17-1   The location of some of the Neanderthal and Neanderthaloid discoveries: *1,* Neanderthal; *2,* Spy; *3,* La Chapelle-aux-Saints, La Ferrassie, Le Moustier, and La Quina; *4,* Cariguela a Piñar; *5,* Gibraltar; *6,* Krapina; *7,* Saccopastore and Monte Circeo; *8,* Skhūl, Tabūn, and Amud; *9,* Shanidar; *10,* Teshik Tash; *11,* Mapa; *12,* Solo; *13,* Haua Ftea; *14,* Broken Hill, Rhodesia; *15,* Saldanha.

cause of the significance of this question, and the special interest and great number of known remains of human fossil in Europe, the "Classic" West European Neanderthal (represented, for instance, by the almost complete skeleton from **La Chapell-aux-Saints,** France, and the skulls from **La Ferrassie,** France, and **Monte Circeo,** Italy) will be considered first and used as a standard for comparisons with other fossil remains of the period (Figs. 17-2 and 17-3).

All of the known Neanderthal skeletal remains in Europe that can be dated come from deposits of the last glaciation or the preceding last interglacial. The dates for Neanderthal man listed by K. Oakley (1966), in the most comprehensive list of the kind, range from 35,000 to 70,000 years ago. Although the characteristic Mousterian tools have been found in later deposits, there is no direct evidence that the Neanderthals survived. In some sites in Russia and the Middle East late Mousterian tools are associated with bones of a modern type of human being.

The combination of features of the Neanderthal skulls is at the extreme limit or outside the range of *Homo sapiens* skulls of living and recent populations.

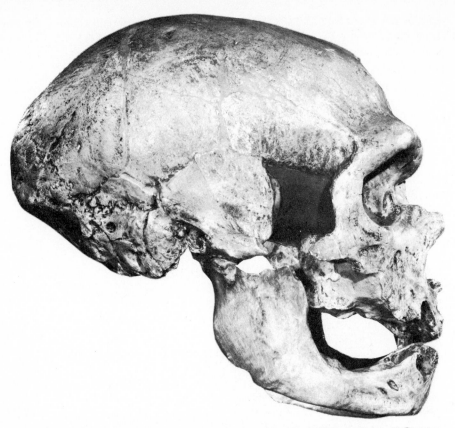

FIG. 17-2 A cast of the skull of "the old man of La Chapelle-aux-Saints." Courtesy of the American Museum of Natural History.

Although, as in all populations, there is considerable variation, in general Neanderthal skulls are flattened down and have a large mound-shaped frontal **torus** over the orbits. At the back of the head there is a backward extension of the occiput and an occipital torus. The **foramen magnum** transmits the spinal cord from head to neck further back on the skull base than is usual in people now; this is associated with long single spines on the vertebrae of the neck—a sign of more powerful back muscles than are found in modern humans. The face is long and wide, with jutting jaws **(prognathism).** By contrast, today, people with large brow ridges, notably Australian aborigines, usually have short faces. Neanderthal teeth are large and set in large jaws, but the teeth are completely human. The pulp cavities of the molars, however, are exceptionally deep (taurodont) in a way rarely found in modern humans. The chin is absent in the earlier specimens and the jaws are robust with a wide area for attachment of the chewing muscles.

One of the salient features of the Neanderthal skull is its large cranial capacity. Cranial capacity is especially interesting because larger capacities are generally associated with larger brains. It is well to bear in mind, however, that the measurements are not as accurate as the estimates might seem to imply and, in any case, intelligence is not dependent on the exact size of the brain. The La Chapelle skull has a cranial capacity of about 1.622 liters, large even for today; the skull from La Ferrassie, about 1.681 liters (Heim, 1970). Furthermore, a Neanderthal skull found at **Amud,** Israel, has a larger cranial capacity of about 1.75 liters (Suzuki and Takai, 1970). And a skull of an eight- or nine-year-old Neanderthal child from **Teshik-Tash** in Uzbekistan in Soviet Central Asia has a cranial capacity of 1.5 liters, which presumably would have increased slightly if the child had lived. Some Neanderthal skulls thus seem to have contained brains large by comparison with modern European populations (for whom averages of 1.30 to 1.45 liters are usually accepted). Other Neanderthal cranial capacities range down to about 1.2 liters, however, and it is

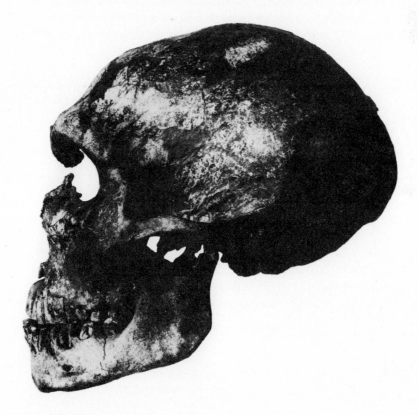

FIG. 17-3   The La Ferrassie I skull is that of a classic Neanderthal. It was found in a rock shelter in association with Mousterian stone implements. H. V. Vallois is engaged in a thorough study of the specimen. Photograph courtesy of Dr. Vallois.

unwarranted to assume that Neanderthal individuals were in general significantly more brainy than later ones. On the other hand, there is no evidence that they were deficient in some specific part of the brain such as the frontal lobes (another unjustified interpretation of the past).

The Neanderthal face is set forward on the skull so that instead of being under the brain case the face can be said to be somewhat in front of it. The angle between the frontal part of the skull base (the roof of the face) and the back part of the base is very obtuse (Fig. 17-4). In later skulls, including those modern ones with low flattened vaults, the angle at the base of the skull is somewhat more acute, so that the face is brought back farther under the frontal part of the brain. In fact, the modern human head is high, the back of the crown is short, and the small basal angle makes it seem, by comparison with Neanderthal skulls, as if the whole back of the skull were pushed up under the front part.

H. V. Vallois (1969) has placed emphasis on the distinctiveness of several features of the temporal bone of the Neanderthal skulls. This is the bone at the side of the skull that contains the mastoid process, houses the organs of hearing and balance, and articulates with the mandible. In these skulls the mastoid is

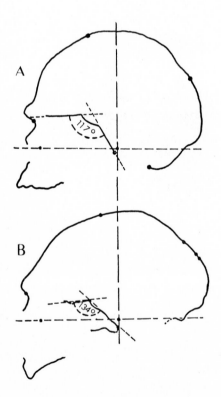

FIG. 17-4 Midsagittal sections of: A, a Neanderthaloid skull from Israel (Skhūl V); and B, a Neanderthal skull from Italy (Monte Circeo I), to show the decreasing angle of the base. From F. C. Howell: The place of Neanderthal man in human evolution. *American Journal of Physical Anthropology 9, 379–416, 1951.*

small, there is little depression of the area in which the head of the mandible rotates and glides, and the petrous part of the temporal bone, which contains the inner ear, has an angle (it is almost straight in modern humans).

These features reinforce for Vallois the view he had previously supported on the basis of the distinctive shape of the shoulder blade and other features: "Homo neanderthalensis" should be considered a separate species from *Homo sapiens,* the present human species. There are, however, intermediate forms, with some characteristics of each, from various parts of the world. It seems best, therefore, to classify the Neanderthal fossils in our own species. It can be designated as a subspecies, *Homo sapiens neanderthalensis.* Such a taxonomic decision is based on the assumption that this is a distinct subgroup, but could interbreed with modern humans and would have done so if both were present at the same place at the same time. Pilbeam (1972) prefers not to use the term *Homo sapiens neanderthalensis* and calls all the ancient members of our species "archaic" or "early" *Homo sapiens,* whereas he calls modern humans "*Homo sapiens sapiens.*" He does this so as to include other fossils in his archaic group. So-called "races" are not as distinct as the subspecies. Thus, the subspecific differences through time are recognized as greater than the geographic differences today. The distinctive features of Neanderthals also had a geographic basis, however. Western Europe during the last ice age was a marginal zone at the edge of human occupation and it apparently had a somewhat distinct population. Marginal areas may afford possibilities for distinctive characteristics of a discrete population to persist.

## Reconstruction of the Neanderthals

Reconstructions of the Neanderthals usually picture them as standing stooped forward with knees bent. The basis for this supposition is the position of the foramen magnum, the angle at the base of the skull, and especially the rugged limb bones with bent shafts and enlarged joints. The bowed shaft of the bones of the thigh and leg and the direction of the joints of the bones of the leg and foot have suggested to some authors a characteristic and somewhat apelike bent-knee gait. Bowing of leg bones is sometimes caused by a vitamin-deficiency disease, rickets. In Neanderthals it may simply be associated with large, powerful limb muscles. The limb bones of the old individual from **La Chapelle-aux-Saints** are in some respects distinct from those of modern adults Straus and Cave (1957) reexamined them and concluded that the individual suffered from a severe disease of the joints. Other fragments of Neanderthal limb bones, such as those from **Amud** and **La Ferrassie** are less distinctive. Furthermore, the six fossil thighbones from **Java,** parts of seven from Choukoutien, and as we shall see, the limb bones from **Solo** and **Broken Hill,** and the **Skhūl** fossils are of essentially modern type. Although the Neanderthal skeletons present some distinctive features, none of these contradict the possibility of a human upright posture. The bones of the hand show it to have been a squat, powerful grasping organ, but, again, variations in modern individuals are known to be compatible with delicate control of fine movements.

Another feature of the attempted reconstructions of Neanderthal man is the invariable presence of copious body hair. We have, of course, no evidence whatever concerning hair, except the fact that Neanderthal man lived at the height of the last glaciation, and that some of his contemporaries, the woolly rhinoceros and the woolly mammoth, had plenty of hair. On the other hand, modern human arctic populations are not particularly hairy today. Hairy or not, Neanderthal man was probably well protected by the hair of his contemporaries—that is, the fur of animals. Bones of many species are found together with Neanderthal stone tools, which are the characteristic forms collectively referred to as the "Mousterian Industry" (Fig. 17-5). One of the common types of this class of flint tool is of a shape that would serve well for scraping, as in preparing pelts.

Neanderthal bones were buried together with red ochre, an iron pigment. This had led to the assumption that they thought about death and afterlife. Several skulls of Neanderthal man as well as those from Choukoutien and Solo have been found without other parts of the skeleton and have had the bottom of the skull broken open. This suggests that the brains were removed for ritual cannibalism, of a kind subsequently practiced in Melanesia and Borneo (Blanc, 1961). The burials, ashes from hearths, bones of prey, and stone tools are all found together in limestone caves and grottos of Europe. From them we can infer a rugged hunting way of life and a society of small family groups.

As noted earlier (p. 191) it has been claimed that one of the reasons people can speak but chimpanzees can not is the difference in the anatomy of the vocal tract. Human beings have a large pharyngeal space between the vocal cords and the mouth, whereas this part of the pharynx is much smaller in chimpanzees and cannot be used to "shape" human vowel sounds. The anatomical differences between the human and chimpanzee vocal tracts have been described by Dubrul (1958), who associated the changes with the assumption of the erect human posture. Hill (1972) argues that the changes in posture began long ago and that the earliest origins of true language might be several million years old. Crelin et al. (1972), however, note great anatomical similarity in the vocal tract of the chimpanzee and the newborn infant. The angle at the base of the Neanderthal skull (see p. 282) is similar to that of the chimpanzee and the newborn human, and Crelin and his colleagues have reconstructed the soft parts and concluded that, like newborn infants and chimpanzees, the Neanderthals had a range of vocalization too limited for the development of proper language. This deficiency is in turn used to explain the slow progression in stone tool types from the time of *Australopithecus* to the Upper Paleolithic compared with the rapid growth in material culture in the last few millennia.

This has been challenged by LeMay (1975), who notes that adult humans with a condition called platybasia (flat base of the skull) and as much facial

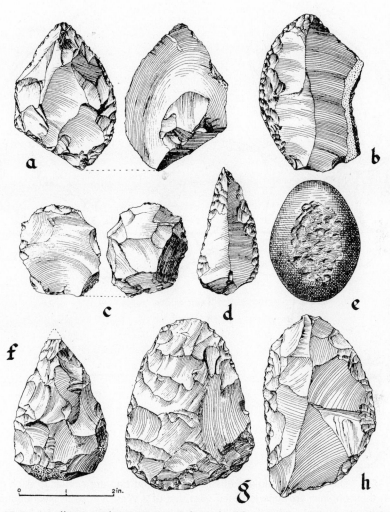

FIG. 17-5    A collection of Mousterian tools: *a, b,* side-scrapers *(racloirs), c,* disc-core, and *d,* point, from rock-shelter at Le Moustier near Peyzac (Dordogne); *e,* small anvil- or hammerstone (pebble of feruginous grit), Gibraltar caves; *f,* hand-axe from Le Moustier; *g,* hand-axe (chert); and *h,* oval flake-tool (flint) from Kent's Cavern, Torquay, England. This collection of Mousterian tools shows that Neanderthals were capable of making a wide variety of specialized implements. It also shows the continuity from one tradition to another. Thus, there are hand-axes worked on both sides as in the Acheulian tradition and flake tools struck off from a larger block with a single blow after the shape had been prepared by preliminary chipping in the Lavalloisian tradition. From K. P. Oakley: *Man the tool-maker.* London: British Museum (Natural History), 1950. By permission of the Trustees of the British Museum.

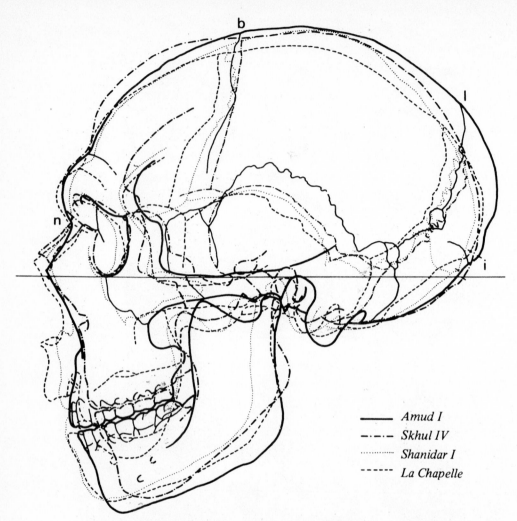

FIG. 17-6   The Neanderthaloid skulls from Israel and Iraq are similar to each other. When their outlines are superimposed with that of a West European Neanderthal (La Chapelle) the general similarity can be seen, but of these the La Chapelle skull has the most forward jutting jaw and the most receding forehead. From H. Suzuki and F. Takai: *The Amud man and his cave site.* Tokyo: The University of Tokyo, 1970. Reproduced by permission.

prognathism (see p. 316) as Neanderthal man are able to enunciate ordinary language well. However, if the argument about the vocal tract does not apply to Neanderthal man it is hard to see how it could be decisive in the case of earlier evolution, as Hill (1972) claims. Instead the development of the brain seems to me to be critical. It was still small in all Lower Pleistocene hominids but in Neanderthal man it was large and modern, insofar as one can tell, in respect to parts important for speech (LeMay, 1975).

Since changes in all anatomical systems and development of language and other cultural manifestations were undoubtedly continuous processes during human evolution, the interrelationship between them is bound to remain speculative. Even substantive issues about human evolution continue in dispute and one should not expect a final answer to fascinating but rather intractible questions such as the origin of language.

## Early Hominids from Israel and Iraq

Among the most interesting specimens of Neanderthaloid fossils are the remains from Mount Carmel in Israel. These were excavated between 1929 and 1934 from two caves (**Tabūn** and **Skhūl**) by members of a joint British and American expedition. The skeletal materials were described by T. D. McCown and Sir Arthur Keith (1939). The Tabūn skeleton is dated at about 41,000 years ago. The Levalloiso-Mousterian tools (a skillfully made variant of the Mousterian) and the fauna persuade some authorities to date Skhūl the same or a bit later; others date it much later (28,500 B.C.). One difficulty in dating these remains by the cultural associations is that at Tabūn there were stone blade tools (an even more advanced type) antedating the Levalloiso-Mousterian flakes of the Neanderthaloid level. In Western Europe, blades are always Upper Paleolithic and follow the Mousterian. The best-preserved Tabūn skull is slightly less robust than those of typical European Neanderthals. The more rounded occiput is usually explained as being the female type of occiput (less robust neck muscles), in a population in which a protruding occipital "bun" is found in the males. In any case, the occiput does not exclude the Tabūn specimen from consideration with the Neanderthals because, like the European specimens, the Tabūn mandible lacks a chin and has very prominent bony ridges above the eyes. If this had not been thought to be a member of the same population as the Skhūl skeletons, it would probably have been called Neanderthal. In fact, a fragment previously found at the northeastern end of the Sea of Galilee was so classified.

The Skhūl specimens are variable but more like modern man (Fig. 17-7). They have a forehead that, although it is marked with large brow ridges, is rounded and also high. These ridges, unlike those of the West European Neanderthals, are divided in the middle, as in contemporary individuals who have prominent brow ridges (especially some Europeans and aboriginal Australians). In the Skhūl specimens the back of the skull is rounded, the facial skeleton is more delicate, and there is a definite chin. The long bones are not appreciably different from those of modern humans.

Eight skeletons from Jebel Qafzeh near Nazareth have not yet been described in detail. They seem to be similar to Skhūl, with well-rounded foreheads and occiputs. One of the skulls that has been pictured is lacking the

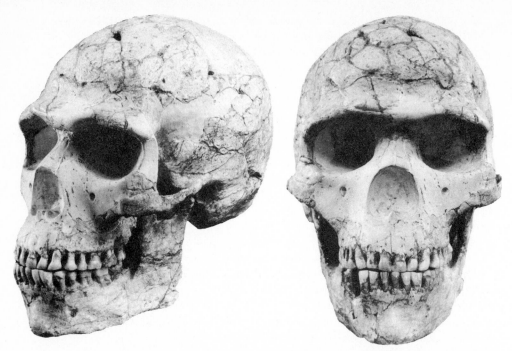

FIG. 17-7  One of the Skhūl skulls (Skhūl V) in the reconstruction by Hillel Burger. Photographs by Hillel Burger. Courtesy of the Peabody Museum, Harvard University.

prognathic forward jut of the middle face seen in Skhūl, and in this is even more like subsequent Near Eastern and European populations.

The **Amud** specimen, also from Israel, was found in a cave on the northwestern shore of the Sea of Galilee (Suzuki and Takai, 1970). It is similar in general to other Neanderthaloid remains from the same general region. It was tall (to judge by the bone lengths) and had a very large head (Fig. 17-8). Most specific traits are similar to those of either Skhūl or Tabūn or are intermediate between these.

The Skhūl and Tabūn remains were found near each other and were formerly thought to be contemporary with each other. Some anthropologists therefore explained the variation as the result of hybridization between races or even between species. Ascribing such variation to hybridization is based on the largely incorrect assumption that racially composite populations are more variable than relatively isolated ones. The range of variation in human fossils in Israel is more easily viewed as occurring over a span of time in successive populations rather than in terms of presumed mixture of classical Neanderthal with a more modern-appearing form. Howells (1974) places considerable emphasis on the differences between these populations and does not see in them any sign of a steady transition from earlier Neanderthal to later "modern" characteristics. In one study he concluded from a statistical analysis of the measurements that the Skhūl skulls show significant differences both from Neanderthal and from modern forms and do not represent an intermediate hybrid but could be a primitive form of our own species (Howells, 1970). Other authors believe that all the Near Eastern specimens are transitional.

Six hundred miles to the north and east of Mount Carmel is a cave in the **Shanidar Valley** of northern Iraq; here an American expedition led by R. S. Solecki (1963) excavated a perpendicular wall of deposit 40 feet deep. Remains of the skeletons of seven individuals were found in association with Eastern Mousterian tool types. Some of the higher human fossil remains at Shanidar are from a level dated at 46,900 ± 1,500 years before the present. Several others are even older. The skeletons themselves are of essentially Neanderthal type, with long faces and small mastoid processes, but have a few divergent features including separate brow ridges rather than a continuous supraorbital torus (Fig. 17-9). From the crushed condition and the position of

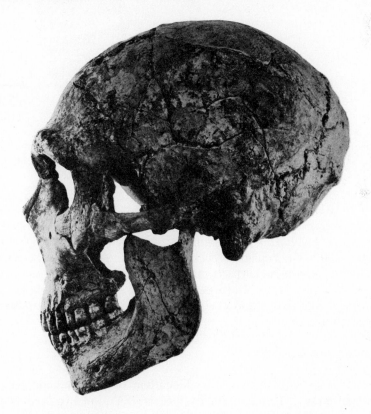

FIG. 17-8    The Amud skull, that of a tall, large-brained Neandethaloid from Israel. From H. Suzuki and F. Takai: *The Amud man and his cave site.* Tokyo: The University of Tokyo, 1970. Reproduced by permission.

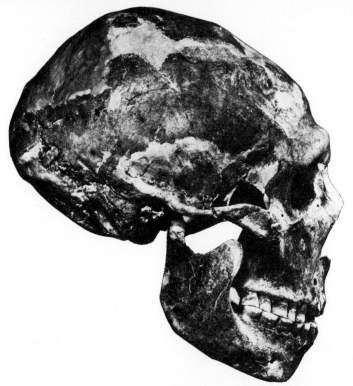

FIG. 17-9  Neanderthaloid skull from Shanidar, Iraq (Shanidar 1). Note the general similarity in shape of the forehead, back of the skull, and so on, to the Neanderthal skull from La Chapelle (Fig. 17-2). The outlines are superimposed in Fig. 17-6. Photograph courtesy of the Smithsonian Institution.

some of these bones it appears that they belonged to individuals who had been killed by collapse of parts of the ceiling of this large cave. One individual had a withered arm of which the lower part had been amputated during life. Perhaps he was obliged to stay behind during hunts and was to some extent cared for by others or had some special tasks. If so, this is one of the earliest pieces of evidence of these characteristic aspects of human social organization: care for incapacitated individuals and occupational specialization. (One *Australopithecus* recovered from a broken leg. Was he also cared for?)

## Dating by Radioactive Carbon

The Shanidar remains were dated by the **carbon-14** ($^{14}$C) **method.** Tree, plant, and animal remains permit dating by measuring the relative amount of this carbon isotope. It has the advantage of being independent of other techniques and of giving an approximate date in "years before present" (B.P.) that can be directly translated into a "B.C." or "A.D." date. The basis for this method is the discovery that the carbon of the organic compounds of living matter always has the same ratio of ordinary carbon ($^{12}C$) to the radioactive isotope ($^{14}C$). The atmosphere contains nitrogen isotope ($^{14}N$) atoms that are bombarded by cosmic rays to produce the isotope $^{14}C$, each $^{14}N$ atom yielding one $^{14}C$ atom and a proton. This $^{14}C$ combines with oxygen (O) to form radioactive carbon dioxide ($^{14}CO_2$), which, when it reaches the earth's surface, is absorbed by plants in their life processes. In turn, animals get $^{14}C$ from the plants or from other animals they eat. All living things, regardless of their age or location on the earth, therefore have a fixed ratio of $^{14}C$ to $^{12}C$. When they die, however, $^{14}C$ is no longer absorbed, and the radioactive $^{14}C$ slowly and spontaneously changes back to $^{14}N$. The rate of this change would lead to loss of one half the originally present $^{14}C$ atoms in 5,730 years; this fact allows computation of the age of the sample by comparing its ratio of $^{14}C$ to $^{12}C$ with that in fresh organic material today. For example, wood from ancient bristlecone pine trees of various ages during the last 8,000 odd years has been studied. The annual rings gained their carbon from the air thousands of years ago and now have a ratio of $^{14}C$ to $^{12}C$ that gives this wood an antiquity of approximately the same age as that indicated by counting the annual rings. That is, counting the rings more or less confirms the age calculated from the carbon isotope ratio (Ferguson, 1968). There is a consistent discrepancy, however; the $^{14}C$ dates are younger than the tree ring dates, so it can be concluded that the amount of $^{14}C$ in $CO_2$ from 800 B.C. or before must have been lower than today. At 4,000 to 4,500 B.C., $^{14}C$ dates are about 750 years more recent. Historically dated samples from ancient Egypt are intermediate between the $^{14}C$ dates and what they would be if corrected for the discrepancy with the bristlecone pine tree dates.

With these cautions, the $^{14}C$ method can be used for estimation of dates as long ago as 70,000 years. For the older dates the proportion of radioactive carbon is very small; since it is reduced by half in every 5,730 years, the earlier dates are less accurate. Carbon, unless charred, is often lost in the process of fossilization; the best opportunities for use of the method therefore usually occur when charcoal or burnt bone is available for analysis. Errors in counting are estimated from sample counts and reported plus or minus ($\pm$) an amount of time in years which would span the calculated date about two times in three. These standard errors refer only to the error in counting and do not include the effects of errors in the assumptions of the investigator or from contamination of the specimens (either by more recent carbon such as roots of plants, or more ancient carbon such as carbonates from ground water). Despite these problems in application, the $^{14}C$ method has permitted numerous relatively consistent determinations.

## African Neanderthaloids

Two Neanderthaloid skulls and a juvenile mandible were discovered in a mine at **Jebel Irhoud,** Morocco, together with Middle Paleolithic flake stone tools. Several mandibular fragments of general Neanderthaloid type have also been found in Morocco and North Africa. Among them are two from a cave at **Haua**

**Fteah** in Cyranaica, Libya, that were associated with Levalloiso-Mousterian tools and have been dated by [14]C method to 40,700 ±500 B.P. They seem more similar to other African fossil jaws and those from Israel than to European Neanderthals.

The term "Neanderthaloid" has also been extended to cover the human remains blasted from a quarry at **Broken Hill,** Zambia (formerly Rhodesia), in 1921. The name "Rhodesian man" is still sometimes used for these. The supraorbital torus extends to the outer edges of the orbits and is larger than in any other known form of human fossil; in fact, it is comparable in size to that of the gorilla (Fig. 17-10). The upper jaw also is enormous. The face is flat but protruding. The skull is flattened down, and the occiput has a torus. All these characteristics have been mentioned before as "Neanderthal," but the Broken Hill skeleton also has distinctive features. Coon (1962) sees *Homo erectus* elements in it, a suggestion supported by the recent evidence that it is more ancient than once believed (Klein, 1973). The supraorbital torus, forehead, and cranial breadth are somewhat like the Solo hominid (p. 296) and the Petralona skull (p. 294), but, like other fossils of *Homo,* the pelvis and limb bones are indistinguishable from those of men today. Incidentally, the robust jaw contained diseased teeth: dental decay and dental abscesses also occur occasionally in *Australopithecus,* however, and in living nonhuman primates. An upper jaw (maxilla) from another individual was found in the same place at Broken Hill and is apparently of the same antiquity. It is considerably smaller and is somewhat hollowed above the canine teeth, and in this respect is comparable to the big-boned types of today.

A few years ago near **Saldanha,** about 90 miles from the southernmost tip of Africa, a large number of fossil bones (about 20 percent of them of extinct forms) were found together with many stone tools, including hand-axe types. Besides teeth of giant wart hogs and horns of buffaloes with a spread of a dozen feet, the fossils include a human skull cap and a fragment of mandible. The skull cap is almost exactly the shape of that of Broken Hill. However, it is a bit smaller.

Tobias (1971) has described a mandible from Cave of the Hearths, one of the many caves at **Makapan** in the Transvaal. It is associated with African Acheulian stone artifacts and is dated as being about 55,000 years old. Tobias sees both *Homo erectus* and Neanderthaloid resemblances. This mandible has also been matched with the upper jaw of the Broken Hill skull.

## Other African Finds

In Africa there are some specimens of more or less modern configuration with claims to considerable antiquity. At **Florisbad** in the Orange Free State in South Africa, T. A. Dreyer (1947) found a skull with large brow ridges, together with Middle Stone Age tools and fossils of extinct animals, in a spring. The Florisbad specimen, however, is assigned by virtually all authorities to our own species, and probably would have received little attention were it not for the fact that it

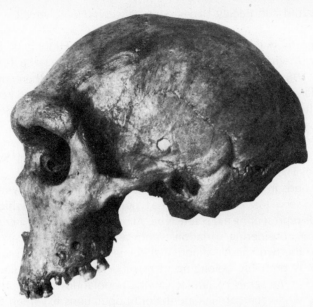

FIG. 17-10  The skull from Broken Hill has huge brow ridges, upper jaw, and area for attachment of the neck muscles. These features are large by Neanderthal standards, and Coon (1962) believes that this skull should be classed as *Homo erectus*. The skull capacity is large for *Homo erectus* (about 1.3 liters) and the general shape of the skull is similar to that of European Neanderthals. For these reasons the designation Neanderthaloid is more appropriate. Photograph courtesy of the trustees of the Bristish Museum (Natural History).

seems not to be similar to any of the people of that part of Africa today. Association with an African Middle Stone Age culture (that is, contemporary with the end of the Mousterian and Levalloisian traditions of Europe, the Near East, and North Africa) and $^{14}$C tests (which, however, may have been contaminated with coal) lead to a date of about 35,000 to 44,000 or more years ago. The skull is said to resemble the second (maxillary) fragment from Broken Hill, and to be somewhat Neanderthaloid. At least superficially it seems more like North African or even East European *Homo sapiens sapiens* fossils, our own subspecies.

L. S. B. Leakey has described a piece of mandible from a place called Kanam on the shore of Lake Victoria, which he thought was associated with the Early Pleistocene fauna and crude stone tools of the site. Other anthropologists have described the jaw as modern in form and doubt its great antiquity. Uranium isotope dating also gives it a Later Pleistocene age. Tobias (1962, 1971) examined all these and other African fossils and concluded that in all of Africa features similar to *Homo erectus* survived until nearly the end of the Middle and even the Upper Pleistocene, and that in the Upper Pleistocene there is a

Neanderthaloid subspecies transitional between *Homo erectus* and *Homo sapiens*.

Further north, in the **Omo** River region in Southern Ethiopia, R. E. F. Leakey (1970) found remains of three individuals that he says may be 100,000 years old. Day (1969) compares these skulls with several others that will be described later in this chapter and in the next. To anticipate a bit, however, Day considers the best preserved of the Omo skulls to resemble that of Broken Hill as well as *Homo erectus,* and, especially, the **Solo** skulls. Another of the Omo skulls, although contemporaneous with the first, is more modern in general form and can reasonably be compared with those from **Skhūl** and **Swanscombe** (see p. 299). The variability at Omo, like that in Israel, is thus of the kind and extent one finds in modern populations. The study of variation within populations should serve to warn one against a typological approach, which sees each specimen as representing a discrete type. At best, types provide a crude frame of reference for considering variation within and between populations. Instead we can see the two slightly different specimens at Broken Hill and the three from Omo as probably belonging to members of single populations. There must have been a series of similar varying populations running the length of East Africa, while general Neanderthaloid populations extended to Palestine, Iraq, and beyond in Asia, and to Libya and Morocco in North Africa. In addition, of course, a group of Neanderthal populations existed in the then tundra environment at the front of the last great glaciation in Western Europe.

## Petralona, Steinheim, Ehringsdorf, and Mapa Skulls

One skull, found in association with remains of the great Ice Age cave-bear at **Petralona** in Thessalonica, Greece, in 1959, was formerly thought of as Neanderthaloid. It still has not been cleaned of adhering material and properly studied but it is now thought to be considerably more ancient than the Neanderthal remains and perhaps should be compared with *Homo erectus*. The skull is small. It has straight rather than bulging sides—like the less Neanderthaloid Omo skull—and in this and other respects is reminiscent of the Broken Hill skull. Stringer (1947) says that overall it most closely resembles the Broken Hill and Jebel Irhoud skulls but that the face is massive like Peking *Homo erectus* and the jaw is the largest yet found in Europe. If one looks beyond Western Europe one sees considerable variety of Neanderthaloid forms. This may be truer of Europe, too, than would be admitted by those who exclude from the Neanderthal category any specimen that does not resemble their typological ideal.

One such specimen is the **Steinheim** skull (Fig. 17-11) (unfortunately badly deformed and somewhat broken) found in Germany in 1933. This skull was in the same gravel deposits as fossils of extinct warm-climate animals and is therefore ascribed to one of the warm interglacial periods antedating the last glaciation. It is often considered to belong to the great penultimate interglacial. No stone tools were found with it. The skull itself is low, a Neanderthal

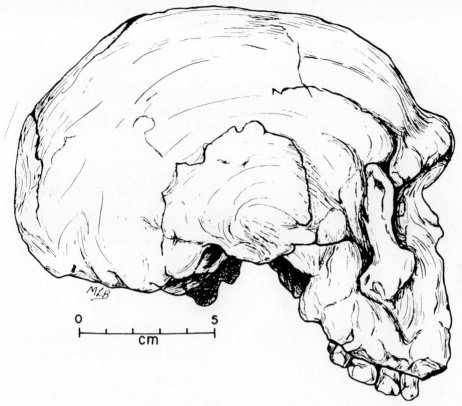

FIG. 17-11 The Steinheim skull resembles the Neanderthal in having heavy brow ridges and a wide nasal opening, but the skull is small. Its affinities remain in doubt. From C. L. Brace, H. Nelson, and N. Korn: *Atlas of fossil man.* New York: Holt, Rinehart and Winston, 1971. Drawing of a cast. Reproduced by permission.

feature, and exhibits massive brow ridges (though these have been described by some as of the type occasionally found in moderns). Although the skull is small, the forehead is somewhat rounded. Furthermore, the region around the ear does not differ greatly from that of modern individuals.

Another skull from Germany was excavated at **Ehringsdorf** near Weimar in 1925 and described by Weidenreich (1927). The skull conforms well with that from Steinheim. It was found in a stratified deposit overlying a river terrace. From the geology and from the associated fauna it seems probable that the Ehringsdorf skull dates from the last part of the last interglacial. A radioactive isotope method (protoactinium/thorium ratio) dates associated rock as 60 to 120 thousand years old. The stone tools are said to be more primitive than those of the West European Neanderthals. The skull itself is fragmentary; it has a well-developed mastoid process of modern type and large brow ridges.

FIG. 17-12   One of the skulls of Solo man (Solo VI). It is low, and the supraorbital torus at the front (right) is large but not separated from the forehead by a groove, as in, for example, Neanderthal skulls. Photograph courtesy of the American Museum of Natural History.

More recently a fossil skull has been found at **Mapa** in Kwantung, China, which, to judge from a preliminary description and photographs (Woo and Peng, 1959), is similar enough to the European Neanderthal specimens to be classed as Neanderthaloid. The skull fragment was found together with fossil animals of the end of Middle or the beginning of Late Pleistocene times. The skull vault is as low as that of some Neanderthal skulls. The frontal torus resembles those of Neanderthal skulls in some respects and of **Solo** (see below) in others. The orbits are rounded as in Neanderthals. This specimen is so far the only one of the kind found anywhere in the Far East.

## Another Fossil Type from Java: the Solo Specimens

In other parts of the world a number of skulls have been described as Neanderthaloid, but their resemblances to Neanderthals are not close. Java has yielded, besides "Pithecanthropus," a series of eleven skulls and two shinbones (tibias) found at a place called Ngandong in a Late Pleistocene terrace of the **Solo River,** twenty meters above the present water level. The skulls of Solo man, as he is called, are of small capacity and are widest low on the vault (Fig. 17-12). They have marked supraorbital tori, but the foreheads slope away from these rather than being separated by a depression, as is usual in Neanderthal skulls. The occipital torus is marked; the cranial vaults are low; and the skulls are unusually thick. They are certainly not the modern type, but seem to be intermediate between Javan *Homo erectus* and Neanderthal in many respects. In two cases the base of the skull is preserved. Unfortunately, this part is present in very few other fossil specimens, so that direct comparison is not possible; but Solo man seems distinct from both modern and Neanderthal specimens in this region of the skull.

In these skulls the direction of the temporal bone that holds the inner ear is angulated somewhat like that of the gorilla (a feature also of a Neanderthal temporal bone from **La Quina,** France). The leg bones, like so many fossil limb bones already discussed, are essentially like those of modern humans. Although an overall statement is of dubious value, in skull configuration Solo man is more "primitive" than the European Neanderthals and Neanderthaloids (Fig. 17-13). Although the skulls have been thought of as late, T. Jacob (1973) reports that a skull from Sambugmachan which is in all respects like the Solo skulls comes from a Middle Pleistocene formation (that is, very early). Howells (1974) says this affirms the affinity of the Solo remains with *Homo erectus* rather than Neanderthal.

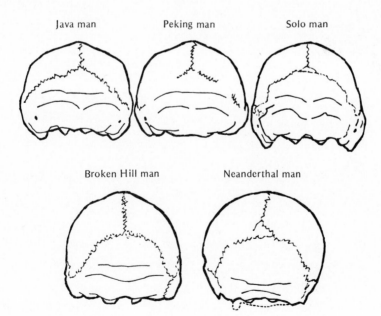

FIG. 17-13   Comparative rear views of fossil man (after Weidenreich). Note the development of the brain case and shape of the skulls.

## Summary

Neanderthal and Neanderthaloid skulls have a wide distribution in Europe, Asia, and Africa. Some of the early members of this variable group are what we would expect of human ancestors. The Neanderthals, in the broad sense, are thus on the main line of human ancestry. The West European Neanderthals, however, were limited in time and space. They are best thought of as a sub-species of *Homo sapiens*. Some anthropologists attempt to trace specific features of modern Europeans back to the Neanderthals of the same area, but most ancestors of the present population of Europe probably immigrated from elsewhere.

Neanderthal *Homo sapiens* dates from the last period of glaciation (70,000 to 35,000 years ago), according to $^{14}C$ tests. The cultural association is usually with Mousterian Industry. The skull capacity and the face are large, and there is a supraorbital torus. Some specimens from Israel (Skhūl and Amud) are more modern in form.

Broken Hill and other finds from Africa are at the Neanderthaloid evolutionary level with huge supraorbital tori. Neanderthal skulls from Eastern Europe are also atypical. Solo man from Java combines some primitive and advanced features.

# CHAPTER 18

# THE QUESTION OF
# THE ORIGIN OF
# *HOMO SAPIENS*

As I have said, the interpretation of any fossil rests on whether it antedates all more modern-appearing forms and could be ancestral to them. A few anthropologists still argue that modern man *(Homo sapiens sapiens)* has been on earth for a long time and that Neanderthal man *(Homo sapiens neanderthalensis)* was a side branch which became extinct without contributing to later evolution. This argument is based on a few fossil skulls and requires that considerable emphasis be put on a few of their features. What is that evidence?

## Swanscombe and Fontéchevade

At **Swanscombe,** England, in 1935 and 1936, A. T. Marston (1937) found several pieces of a skull deep in a stratified deposit of the 100-foot terrace of the Thames River. The circumstances of the find were investigated and confirmed by a committee of the Royal Anthropological Institute. The associated stone tools are of Middle Acheulian type (hand-axes and flakes) (Fig. 18-1). The bones found with the human skull are of animals that lived during the long second interglacial period. Furthermore, fluorine analysis of the human bones indicates a degree of fossilization comparable to that of the Middle Pleistocene

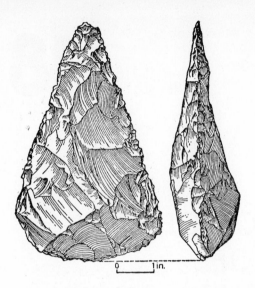

FIG. 18-1   Flat side and edge views of a Middle Acheulian hand-axe from the Skull layer, Middle Gravels 100-ft terrace, Swanscombe. Reproduced by permission of the Trustees of the British Museum.

animal bones from the same 100-foot terrace. Here we have claims for an antiquity greater than that of any of the Neanderthal or Neanderthaloid specimens known. Unfortunately, however, the Swanscombe specimen is only a small fragment of the skull vault, pieces of parietal, and a part of the occiput. As far as these go, it is distinguished by unusual thickness and by a large area for neck muscles. There is little to class them with modern skulls except the lack of an occipital torus. The skull, however, belonged to a young adult, perhaps twenty years old (Fig. 18-2), and, by comparison with those of an old male Neanderthal, the occipital and parietal parts of the skull of a weak young Neanderthal would have more closely resembled those of *Homo sapiens sapiens*. A crest behind the mastoid process is similar to that in Neanderthal skulls and may, therefore, have been associated with a Neanderthal type of mastoid process and a Neanderthal type of frontal torus. Furthermore, M. R. Drennan (1956) states that the shape of the Swanscombe skull corresponds remarkably with that of the Broken Hill skull. After a number of unsuccessful attempts, additional bits of the same skull were found. These match the old bits like pieces of a jigsaw puzzle, representing the counterparts of the earlier bones—that is, coming from the other side of the same skull. Unfortunately, therefore, they add little to our knowledge.

In 1947, at **Fontéchevade,** France, G. Henri-Martin excavated parts of two skulls from the deposit outside the mouth of a cave (Vallois, 1949). The cave roof must have extended over this part at the time these individuals lived, because the layer was completely sealed off by an overlying layer of stalagmite from the former ceiling of the cave. Above the stalagmite were strata containing stone tools of Mousterian type (the Neanderthal culture) and later Paleolithic types. The stone flakes found at the level of the skulls are of the coarse type called Tayacian, ascribed to the Lower Paleolithic. The animal fossils are of forms associated with a warm to temperate climate, hence consistent with a date of the last interglacial period. Fontéchevade I is a specimen consisting of a small piece of frontal bone from the glabella (the middle of the forehead between the brows). The brow ridges are said to be of feeble development, such as occur in European women today, but Wolpoff (1971) says the glabella region can be matched in the Neanderthal specimens from **Gibraltar** and Le Moustier, France. It might have belonged to an adult Neanderthal rather than to an adult of modern form.

Fontéchevade II is a larger piece of bone from the crown of another individual (Fig. 18-3). It also has a part of the frontal present; this shows a dent that has been taken to be the frontal sinus. On the basis of the shape of the preserved part some have argued whether there was or was not a protruding frontal torus in the missing part. What we would need to answer the question is a little bit more of the skull. The occiput is also lacking. What there is of the skull is thick and broad at the rear, as in the Swanscombe skull. Drennan points out that the contour of Fontéchevade II is not very different from that of a young Neanderthal man. It may be, however, that the frontal region, especially of the first specimen, was of more modern configuration.

The evidence for *Homo sapiens sapiens* antedating *Homo sapiens neanderthalensis* in Europe—that is, principally the Swanscombe and Fontéchevade

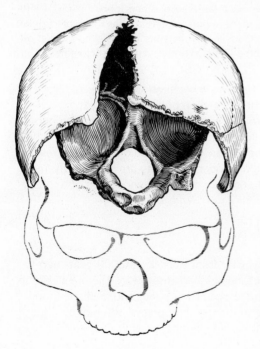

FIG 18-2 The Swanscombe skull fragments. The face in conjectural. Drawing by D. L. Cramer. Courtesy of the Wenner-Gren Foundation Casting Program.

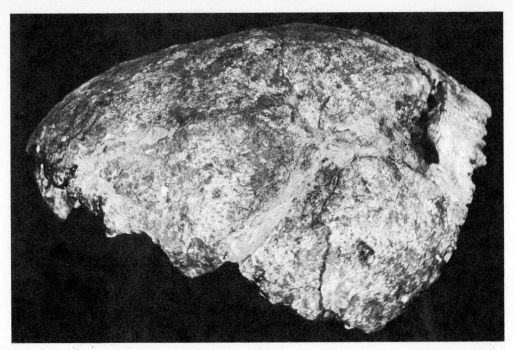

FIG. 18-3   Fontéchevade II. This skull cap was found with a fragment of the frontal region of another individual. They were under a stratum of stalagmite and thereby sealed into a layer with an early pre-Mousterian type of stone tools. Vallois (1949) considers the skulls to be presapiens and places much emphasis on the traces of a frontal sinus, but some others believe they could be the remains of a Neanderthal type. Photograph courtesy of Dr. Vallois and the Director of the Musée de l'Homme.

finds—is thus very limited. If the distinction is between subspecies of the same species (as the names we have used implies) then one would not expect a clear distinction in all features and one would expect that among earlier members of the species some individuals would resemble the later norm more, while others would resemble it less. Perhaps Swanscombe and Fontéchevade resemble it more. That does not imply that modern humans are necessarily more closely related to these forms than to other of their contemporaries or to Neanderthal, however.

## Upper Paleolithic *Homo sapiens sapiens*

Although the last great glaciation was far from over, by 30,000 years ago the *Homo sapiens neanderthalensis* subspecies had disappeared and the *Homo sapiens sapiens* subspecies occupied Europe. Their bones and teeth are thought by some to be essentially like those of modern Europeans. Some other anthropologists stress features in which these specimens are intermediate between Neanderthal and modern skeletons.

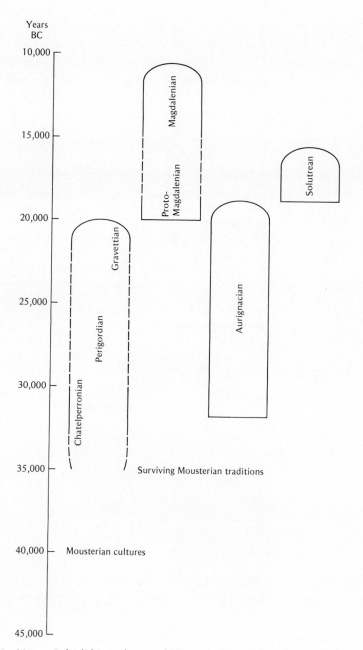

FIG. 18-4   Upper Paleolithic cultures of Western Europe based on [14]C dates (After Oakley, 1966).

Some show signs of disease, and estimates of the ages of death show that most of them died young. In fact, to judge by the evidence of aging of skeletons (eruption and wear of the teeth, closing of growth centers in bones, wear and tear of joints), there was only a slight increase of life span throughout human prehistoric and historic experience until the last two centuries. Up until then the average age of death in Europe was 40 years or less (Angel, 1947, 1969). Associated with fossils of cold-weather fauna, including the woolly mammoth, archaeologists have found the cultural remains of a series of Upper Paleolithic cultures with the characteristic bone and pressure-flaked stone tools of Chatelperronian, Perigordian, Aurignacian, Gravettian, Solutrean, and Magdalenian types (see Fig. 18-4).

At **Combe-Capelle** in France a long-headed narrow-faced skull dated about 34,000 years ago ushers in *Homo sapiens sapiens*. It seems to have been similar to that of modern Europeans—certainly so by the standards of anything that preceded it. Near the towns of **Brno, Pavlo, Mladeč,** and **Predmost** in Moravia, Czechoslovakia, archaeologists excavated similar heavy-featured, strong-jawed skeletal remains of some 26,600 years ago and earlier (Fig. 18-5). These are associated with earliest Upper Paleolithic cultural remains. Brace et al. (1971) refer to the large brow ridges, heavy attachments for neck muscles, and large teeth of some of these specimens as being signs of recent evolution from a Neanderthal ancestry. Contemporaneously, or almost so, in Moravia and in France there were other individuals whose skulls are lower and who had short faces.

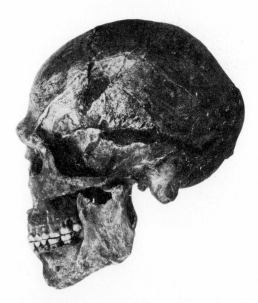

FIG. 18-5 Predmost III, discovered in a collective grave in a large open-air site in central Czechoslavakia. Photograph courtesy of the American Museum of National History.

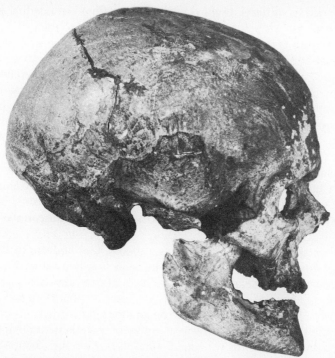

FIG. 18-6   Cro-Magnon man. The skull and skeleton of the "Old man of Cro-Magnon" were discovered in 1868. It is thus one of the longest known and hence most discussed of the skeletal remains of Upper Paleolithic age. The brow ridges are large but of modern type, and the facial features are little different from those of Europeans today. Photograph courtesy of H. V. Vallois, Institut de Paléontologie Humaine, Paris.

One of the first discovered, hence most discussed, examples of this sort is from **Cro-Magnon** in the Dordogne Region of France. There, in 1868, L. Lartet found in a rock cleft the remains of at least five individuals. For a description of the skulls Lartet called on Paul Broca, better known for his study of the human brain—especially the area for speech. Broca assigned the skulls to a new Cro-Magnon "race." The best-preserved skull, that of an old man who had lost his teeth (Fig. 18-6), has the facial features of a European of today. His brow ridges were large but were of the divided modern type and within the size range of those of today. To judge by the length of the bones he was relatively tall.

Numerous similar specimens have been found with characteristic bone and pressure-flaked stone tools, particularly of the Magdalenian culture period (15,000–10,000 B.C.). The men and women of the Upper Paleolithic periods of Europe were all *Homo sapiens sapiens*. Those most similar to the "old man" are usually grouped collectively under his name as "Cro-Magnon man." Those which diverge in some respects are often given other designations. It was formerly believed that there was a sharp break between the Neanderthals and the Cro-Magnons in Europe. Variation at early sites such as Mladeč shows that, in Europe as in Israel, there was a transition from Neanderthal to *Homo sapiens sapiens.*

Two European Upper Paleolithic finds are of special interest because some anthropologists have believed them comparable with non-European modern races. In 1901, in a cave on the Riviera, L. de Villeneuve unearthed two burials in the Aurignacian layers. One is that of a child; the other, to judge from the skull, is that of an adult woman. These **Grimaldi** skeletons, so-called from the name of the ruling prince of Monaco, patron of the study, show some features resembling those of modern Africans. The proportions of the limb bones, especially the relatively long forearm, are part of the resemblance. In addition, the skull is **prognathic:** the region of the upper jaw bone between the nose and the mouth tends to shelve slightly forward as in Africans and some East Indians. This may in part result from the way the skull has been repaired, and such African skeletal features as the low, flat, wide nose are lacking in the Grimaldi woman.

The other skull of special interest is called **Chancelade** from the site in Dordogne, France, where it was found in 1888 in a deposit of Magdalenian age. The Magdalenian culture, last of the Paleolithic sequence, is characterized by bone tools: needles, harpoons, and fish hooks. Stone tools are small and include such types as engravers to etch decorations in bone. All artifacts greatly resemble the corresponding native equipment of the Eskimo. Perhaps this fact influenced those anatomists who see Eskimo features in the Chancelade skull. It is certainly a narrow skull with a broad face and strong jaws like the Eskimo, but this characterizes most Upper Paleolithic as well as Eskimo skulls. One special feature is a **palatine torus,** a longitudinal ridge along the roof of the mouth (see Fig. 16-13). A palatine torus is rarely seen in human fossils, but it is common in Lapps, Icelanders, and North Europeans as well as in Eskimos; at least a small palatine torus occurs in about 20 percent of adults in the United States. The Chancelade skull is not very different from other Upper Paleolithic specimens; there is no special reason to believe it related to the Eskimo. When a British anthropologist, G. M. Morant (1930–1931), took the measurements of all the then available Upper Paleolithic skulls of Europe, including Grimaldi and Chancelade, he found that they are not very variable; on the contrary, they conform to each other as closely as measurements of skulls from a single English cemetery.

In general, the principal characteristics that differentiate continental populations today are not well reflected in the skeletons. In the same way, Upper Paleolithic skulls from diverse regions lack marked racial features and display instead a common set of characters such as ample jaw, narrow head, and large but divided brow ridges—that is, the hallmarks of Upper Paleolithic skeletons in Europe.

The physical characteristics of the living population group in any part of the world today cannot be matched exactly with those of a group of predecessors in the same region ten thousand or more years ago. There is considerable evidence that large migrations took place in prehistoric as well as historic times. The newcomers, whether peaceful immigrants or conquering warriors, virtually always mingled with, rather than merely superseded, the indigenous people. Furthermore, changes within groups have occurred in relatively recent postglacial times and continue today; evolution is not something that happened once a long time ago and created once and for all the variations we see today; factors making for evolutionary changes have continued since the Pleistocene.

The reliably dated early skulls from North Africa, for example, are not Negroid. In Algeria, French anthropologists found more than 50 skeletons in a rock shelter at **Afalou** on the coast. Many of the skulls had prominent brows and strong muscle markings. The front teeth were knocked out during life so the faces are curiously shortened but they would not have been prognathous like Blacks in any case. This is hardly surprising as, racially, modern North Africans fit in most closely with Europeans. But south of the Sahara, too, the earliest skulls are often described as resembling large versions of those of Bushmen or, in some cases, even of Australians. Many, however, look like robust Blacks.

In the Near East, as in North Africa, the Upper Paleolithic remains as well as the modern inhabitants are physically similar to those of Europe. More or less typical Upper Paleolithic forms of skulls have been found in Western Asia. The skeletons excavated by C. S. Coon from a cave at **Hotu,** Iran, and described by J. L. Angel (1951) are, except for the great height of the skull, not different in any important respect from European specimens of the period.

## Three Skulls from the Upper Cave

At **Choukoutien,** the home caves of Peking man, there is an upper cave that was occupied at a later date. It contained **Mesolithic** tools including a bone needle. Weidenreich (1939) examined three skulls from the upper cave and saw similarities between one of them and Eskimos, between another and Europeans, and between the third and Melanesians. The first is not specifically Eskimo; in fact, it is hardly safe to call it Mongoloid, even in the widest sense, but it does have a wide, flat, midfacial region and a narrow skull. The second, thought to be the only male of the three, was described as Protomongoloid by Weidenreich; it is a big, rugged skull with short face and large brow ridges. Such a skull type occurs today among Europeans, aboriginal Australians, and the Ainu of the northern islands of Japan. This is a generalized Upper Paleolithic man but the proximity of China to Japan suggested an Ainoid designation. The third skull is marked by a protrusive face, a feature of the Oceanic Melanesians; but one feature that may have influenced Weidenreich in his classification is that the skull is very high. It has been crushed, which makes its exact shape uncertain, but it may have been *artificially deformed* during life. Some more recent peoples, such as the Aymara Indians of Bolivia and Peru, used to

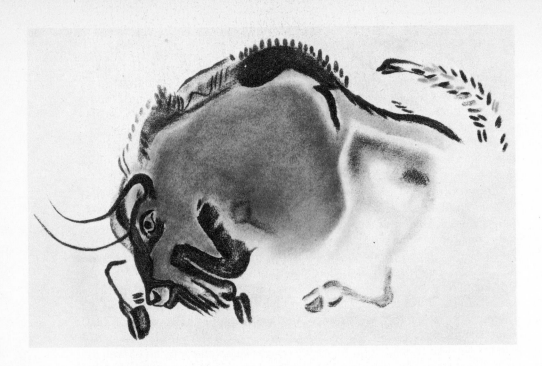

FIG. 18-7   Among the artifacts of Upper Paleolithic culture are the well-known (and in some cases superbly executed) examples of cave art. *Upper left:* A bison, from the cave at Altamira, Spain. *Lower left:* A reindeer from the cave at Font-de-Gaume, France. *Above:* A cave painting from Les Trois Frères, France, of a man dressed in a deerskin. It is believed the purpose was to perform a magical dance to secure an abundance of game. Courtesy of the American Museum of Natural History.

bind the head during infancy. This practice produces an elongated head shape. One or another form of head binding was formerly used by many American Indians to strap their babies to the cradle board.

Joseph B. Birdsell (1951b) dismisses the implication of Weidenreich's discrete racial designations and considers the skulls to show a mixture of Mongoloid and European features. Although living contemporaneously (some suggest as husband and wives) in the confines of a small cave, they are about as diverse as the Upper Paleolithic types of Europe.

Other Upper Pleistocene skulls from China have also been called Protomongoloid, but this is largely a geographic statement. They tend to have rather wide flat faces and noses but, in a general way, so do European Cro-Magnons. The characteristic shovel-shaped incisors (see Fig. 16-12) do, however, seem to mark both early and recent populations of East Asia.

## The Peopling of the Americas, Borneo, and Australia

Many claims have been made that one or another discovery in the Americas dates back to before the last phase of the Pleistocene. A. Hrdlička, virtually the father of physical anthropology in the United States, successfully demonstrated the weakness of all such claims. Many of those made subsequently are equally insubstantial. As the carbon-dating method has reduced our previous estimate of the time span since the last glaciation in Europe, however, it has increased the established antiquity of the stone tools of the first human beings in the New World. Only a shallow channel, the Bering Strait, separates Alaska from Siberia. The sea was lower during the glacial periods, and America and Asia were repeatedly connected by land. From carbon dates of land and marine specimens that indicate the height of the seas at various times in the past, we know that the last land bridge from Asia to America existed from about 25,000 years ago until about 10,000 or 11,000 years ago (Hopkins, 1959). America was discovered during that period if not earlier. Some of the known American skeletal remains may, therefore, pertain to the same period as the Upper Paleolithic in the Old World, but there is nothing in any of them to suggest Neanderthal or earlier features (Stewart, 1960).

The earliest date we have for New World human skeletal material is an occipital bone found near the **Los Angeles** International Airport in 1936 and dated at more than 26,000 years by a $^{14}$C analysis by R. Berger. The specimen provides no significant information about the appearance of the individual, however (Merbs, 1971). Other relatively old dates for skeletal remains from the New World include 12,000 B.P. for **Guitarrero Cave** in Peru (Lynch and Kennedy, 1970), about 11,000 B.P. for **Tepexpan** man (Fig. 18-8) from Mexico (de Terra et al., 1949), about 10,000 B.P. for **Arlington Springs,** California (Orr, 1962), and about 8,670 B.P. for a skeleton of American Indian affinities, discovered at **Midland,** Texas, beneath a stratum containing an American type of Upper Paleolithic tool, the Folsom point (Wendorf et al., 1955).

In general, these American skulls of considerable antiquity are somewhat, but not markedly, "Amerindian," as anthropologists sometimes call the American Indians. The degree to which populations may be considered Amerindian (or more generally, Mongoloid) can be calculated on the basis of the frequency and degree of shovel-shaped incisors and other features of the crowns of teeth (Turner, 1969). Unfortunately the incisor crowns are often missing, as in the Guitarrero Cave and Tepexpan specimens. Some of the early skulls have big brow ridges and prominent jaws. However, these are merely the common features of early *Homo sapiens sapiens* skulls almost wherever they are found. The early American skulls most closely resemble those of later Amerindians, but also show resemblances to skulls of East Asians.

Wallace, the co-discoverer with Darwin of the principle of natural selection, thought that the caves of **Borneo** would be a good place to search for prehistoric hominids. Finally, in 1957, T. Harrison found paleolithic-like artifacts at the level dated 38,000 ±1,000 B.P. by ¹⁴C. Buried, and therefore only possibly belonging with this level was a skull of an adolescent boy. It has been described as *Homo sapiens sapiens* and most closely resembling a Tasmanian aborigine. The Borneo boy and the Tasmanian aborigines had short but rugged faces and long skulls, but these features were also common in Cro-Magnons of distant Europe.

Some anthropologists believe that the best fossil representatives of the ancestors of the Australian aborigines are two rugged skulls from Wadjak, **Java,** discovered there by Eugene Dubois. In Australia itself, radiocarbon dates associated with artifacts show that people were there at least some 12,900 years ago. In fact, Birdsell (1972) states that ¹⁴C dates associated with similar tools go back to 26,300 years ago and a cremated skeleton from **Lake Mungo** has an antiquity of 32,000 years—a time at which New Guinea, Australia, and Tasmania were connected by land. The earliest skeletal materials so far giving much information about what their possessors were like, are less than 9,000 years old and most of them are not very different from modern Australian aborigines (Macintosh, 1967). These aborigines have short faces like Cro-Magnons. In this they also resemble the Tasmanians, mentioned before, but the Australians are bigger and more rugged and thus quite similar in skeletal characteristics to Upper Paleolithic Europeans.

## Summary

Some essentially modern skull fragments are ascribed to considerable antiquity. The Swanscombe skull in England consists only of some thick and not very distinctive parts of the skull but is apparently associated with an early geological setting containing stone tools of the pre-Mousterian Middle Acheulian type. From Fontéchevade, France, came fragments of two skulls of possibly modern form with pre-Mousterian Tayacian stone tools.

About 34,000 years ago in Western Europe there was a transition from Neanderthal to modern types of skeletal remains, such as Combe-Capelle and Cro-Magnon and Upper Paleolithic cultural remains. The variations are not

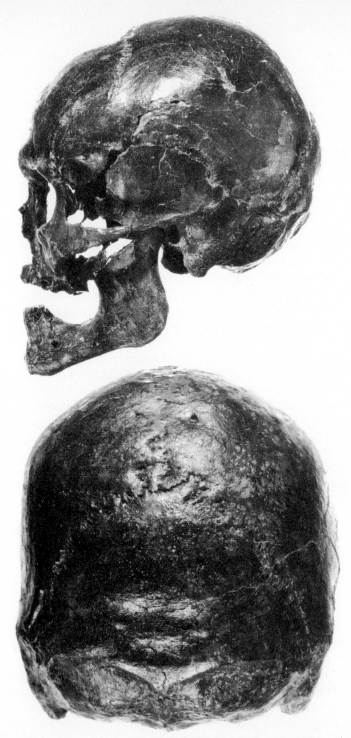

FIG. 18-8 The Tepexpan skull (side and back views) after restoration, showing its essentially modern form. Photographs courtesy of Depto. de Antropologíca Física, Instituto National de Antropología e Historia, Mexico.

readily ascribed to racial differences, because there are broad similarities in many parts of the world, but to local differences within Europe and even within a single site such as the Upper Cave of Choukoutien, China.

America was first peopled at about this time; the earliest available remains are not very different from later American Indians, but somewhat resemble East Asiatics and, for that matter, Upper Paleolithic skeletons from elsewhere. Early remains from Borneo and Australia also have resemblances to later peoples from the same parts of the world and, in a way, to Upper Paleolithic *Homo sapiens sapiens* elsewhere.

Our subspecies, *Homo sapiens sapiens*, is thus over 30,000 years old. It has always been variable but there is no evidence of greater differences between regions in antiquity; hence modern populations cannot be considered mere mixtures of ancient races. Furthermore there has been a general trend to less massive facial features, so most Upper Paleolithic skeletons seem very rugged and the jaws and browridges large by comparison with those of modern individuals.

# CHAPTER 19

# ANTHROPOMETRY

Physical anthropology got its name and its status as a science by its application of "physical" measurement to anthropology and the standardization and application of such methods. So far I have been concerned with the problems of physical anthropology and with some of the findings, but I have had little to say about its methods. Methods and concepts are both applicable to other fields of knowledge, but it is the methods of physical anthropology that may be most useful to the attack of new problems outside the field, such as those of medicine and dentistry. One reason for slighting the subject of method is that most of the techniques of physical anthropology are held in common with other disciplines. Furthermore, this introduction is intended to give an insight into the nature of physical anthropology rather than to help train professional practitioners—a task beyond the scope of a brief introduction. Nevertheless, a description of some of the traditional methods of the field, especially of those peculiar to physical anthropology, should help give an appreciation for the prospects as well as the findings to date, and some introductory courses in physical anthropology include laboratory exercises to help students realize what is involved (Swedlund and Wade, 1972).

The first writings on physical anthropology consisted of descriptions and classifications of distant peoples (see Count, 1950). Johann Friederich Blumenbach (1752–1840), the father of physical anthropology, classified human beings into five races: Caucasian, Mongolian, Ethiopian, American, and Malayan. Dissection of primates had already been undertaken by Edward Tyson (1650–1708) and Louis-Jean-Marie Daubenton (1716–1799). By the early 1800s taxonomy and comparative anatomy were established methods in physical anthropology and the use of measurements had begun. In Germany, Rudolf Virchow, a famous anatomist, pathologist, anthropologist, and statesman, tried to get his colleagues to standardize their anthropometric methods, while in France, Paul Broca, a neuroanatomist and anthropologist, set himself a similar task.

Anthropometry (literally, the measurement of humans) greatly enhanced the appreciation of subtle differences in size and (when several measurements are considered together) form. In 1860 Anders Retzius, a Swedish anatomist-anthropologist, demonstrated that the ratio of maximum length to maximum breadth of the head (the **cephalic index**) varies between populations. A similar measurement on the skull yields a *cranial index*. The cranial index averages about two units higher than the cephalic index but if allowance is made for this, one can compare the head shape of present and past populations. Retzius also considered the degree of **prognathism**—the protrusion of the face. This can be gauged by the facial angle.

Description of variables such as the cephalic index, the facial angle, the upper facial index, and the nasal index require a few anatomical landmarks.

Milan Dokládal (1965), of Brno, Czechoslovakia, places the cephalic index in wide context. He demonstrates that after some fluctuation of the index in the fetal skull, the relative breadth (that is, the cephalic index) greatly increases in the first half month after birth and then decreases rapidly for a month, then more slowly until adulthood. Among nonhuman primates the skull is relatively very narrow (called hyperdolichocranic) in most prosimians, narrow to medium (dolichocranic to mesocranic) in monkeys, and often broad (brachycranic) in anthropoid apes. *Australopithecus* is dolichocranic; Neanderthaloid skulls range from relatively very narrow to medium and early *Homo sapiens sapiens* skulls are in the same range. Dokládal thus confirms the view that human antecedants were generally **dolichocephalic** and that **brachycephalization** (a **pedomorphic** tendency) is characteristic of the human phylogenetic record. Nicole Heintz (1964) emphasizes that this infantilization of the human head form (also seen in other dimensions, Heintz, 1966) is the result of a later age of retardation in growth in breadth of the skull, relative to length, in our species compared with the anthropoid apes.

The following are some of the more important landmarks and measurements in anthropometry of the head and face:

*Maximum head breadth* is the transverse diameter between euryon and euryon (euryon being the most lateral point over the parietal bone).
*Maximum head length* is the caliper distance from *glabella,* the prominent point between the brows, to *opisthocranion,* the point furthest back in the midline of the skull (Fig. 19-1, left).

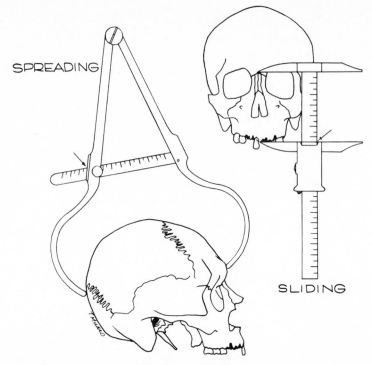

SPREADING

SLIDING

FIG. 19-1   Sliding and spreading calipers; two of the most frequently used instruments in anthropometry. Source: National Museum of Man, National Museums of Canada, Bulletin No. 221, *The human skeleton* by J. E. Anderson, 1962. Reproduced by permission of Information Canada.

*Cephalic index* is $\dfrac{\text{Maximum head breadth} \times 100}{\text{Maximum head length}}$.

*Nasion* is the junction of the nasal and frontal bones in the median plane.

*Basion* is the anterior margin of the foramen magnum in the median plane. It can be seen only on the skull or on carefully posed lateral X-rays, and, cannot be used for direct measurement of the living.

*Prosthion* is the point of bone between the upper central incisor teeth.

*Facial angle* is the angle between nasion-basion and prosthion-basion lines.

*Eye–ear* or *orbital–meatal* or *Frankfurt* plane was accepted as the standard for orienting the skull or the head by a meeting of anatomists at Frankfurt, Germany, in 1879. It consists of a plane through the top of both ear holes and the lower margin of an orbit. In this orientation the maximum height of the skull above the plane is seen to be notably lower in *Homo erectus* and Neanderthals than in most populations of *Homo sapiens sapiens,* past or present (see Fig. 13-9).

**Prognathism** is the forward jut of the upper jaw. It is measured by the extent to which prosthion lies in front of a perpendicular frontal plane through nasion when the skull is in the eye-ear plane (see Fig. 19-2). Regional differences are marked. There is notable prognathism in most African populations south of the Sahara and to some extent in South and East Asiatic and American Indian peoples. Choukoutian Neanderthal and some other fossils also manifest considerable prognathism.

*Upper facial height* is the nasion–prosthion distance (Fig. 19-1, right).

*Bizygomatic breadth* is the transverse distance between zygion and zygion, the most lateral points on the zygomatic arches.

*Upper facial index* is $\dfrac{\text{Bizygomatic breadth} \times 100}{\text{Upper facial height}}$. Regional differences in height of the face have been documented. In general, high faces seem to go with tall stature; not always, however—for instance, Cro-Magnon were tall but relatively low faced.

*Menton* is the tip of the chin.

*Total facial height* is the nasion–menton distance.

*Total facial index* is $\dfrac{\text{Bizygomatic breadth} \times 100}{\text{Total facial height}}$.

*Nasal breadth* is the maximum distance between the wings of the nostrils.

*Nasal height* is the distance from the inferior aspect of the nasal spine to nasion.

*Nasal index* is $\dfrac{\text{Nasal breadth} \times 100}{\text{Nasal length}}$.

On the skull, however, only the opening for the nose (the piriform aperture)

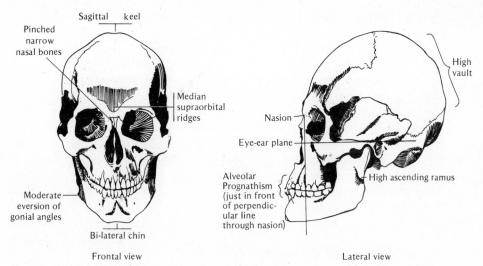

Frontal view                    Lateral view

FIG. 19-2   Some features of a prehistoric Indian skull from Ontario. The sagittal ridge or "keel" and the prognathism are traits present in Peking man. From O. Oschinsky: *The most ancient Eskimos.* Ottawa, Canada: The Canadian Research Centre for Anthropology, 1964. Reproduced by permission.

remains. The nasal breadth is the maximum breadth of this aperture and the height is the distance from the lower margin of this aperture to nasion. Both measurements are smaller on the skull, but the breadth is especially reduced. It is therefore possible to compare nasal indices on the living with those on the skull only in a very general way.

Many other measurements of the head, the skull, and of the constituent bones of the skull have been devised. Also, there are many measurements of the limbs and limb bones and the trunk. The standard works on anthropometry (Martin, 1928; Martin and Saller, 1957), list the way measurements on the skeleton and on the living are to be taken. They are in German, but other manuals of physical anthropology (Comas, 1960; Weiner and Lourie, 1969) give these in English and, for measurements of the living, Garrett and Kennedy (1971) give the different definitions and list many results. Nevertheless, there is constant need to devise new measurements. Those designed to answer a particular question about form and its relationship to function often serve better for that purpose than the standard methods listed in the anthropometric handbooks.

Some dimensions, such as those of the dental arches and the teeth, have immediate practical applications to the health sciences by providing answers to such questions as whether there is room enough for the teeth to erupt into well-formed dental arches or whether, if braces are not applied, the teeth are likely to be crowded and to force each other out of a regular row. Likewise, X-ray measurements of the female pelvis and the fetal head may determine if there is adequate room for normal delivery or if a cesarian operation is needed. Only the cruder direct measurements are made in most cases, however, since exposure of mother and fetus to X-rays should not be undertaken without a good cause.

Stature and body weight can be reliably determined by persons with little training and have been widely applied. Since other dimensions tend to correlate with these, all sorts of information concerning biological status can be inferred from the voluminous data on these two variables.

Mean measurements of various peoples of the world differ. Since these differences are consistent, it is easy to see why the early anthropologists thought that if they standardized their methods adequately, examined adequate samples, and considered enough dimensions, they could trace the origins of peoples. Sometimes more emphasis was placed on definition of a measurement so that two practitioners could achieve the same result than on questioning whether the measurement meant anything. Most measurements are of bones or of bony parts of the intact body because the rigidity of these lend themselves to precise measurement (and of course because only the skeleton usually survives long after death).

Karl Pearson (1896), an English mathematician, following leads of Francis Galton and others, developed the science of *biometry* (measurement and the quantitative comparison of biological variation). Pearson studied partial dependence of variables—that is, **correlation.** In anthropology empirical anthropometry led to a decreased emphasis on types and an increased awareness of the overlapping range of possible shapes of body, head, and face between each people and its neighbors. Statistical analysis of probability, now applied in every field of science, found some of its first successes in anthropometry.

One of the obvious results of the application of statistics to a series of measurements is the demonstration that, on the average, men differ from women in almost every dimension. In studies of the skeleton the sex is sometimes known from artifacts the archaeologists find with it. More often, however, it is left to the physical anthropologist to determine the sex. Working from skeletons of known sex, they have shown that many kinds of observations and measurements (and, especially, formulae combining them) give correct sex determinations in most (but unfortunately never quite all) cases. The chief features stem from the fact that males tend to have more marked raised rough areas on the bone, where muscles attach, and larger joint surfaces, even relative to overall size. Females have, in addition, some specific features of the pelvis (Fig. 19-3). Natural selection has seen to it that the birth canal of the female pelvis is larger than the corresponding part in males, and this means that the pubic bone of the pelvis is longer, both absolutely and relatively, in females than in males.

Besides establishing the sex of specimens the physical anthropologist usually wishes to know their ages at death (Stewart and Trotter, 1954). Features that reflect age include the stage of ossification achieved (including the state of fusion of the bones of the skull), microscopic changes in bone, eruption of teeth, and even the wear of the teeth (a feature relied on for judging age by horse traders).

On the basis of closure of cranial sutures and tooth eruption, Vallois (1961) has estimated that, of 22 specimens from Peking, 15 died before age 15 and only 1 lived beyond age 50; of 39 Neanderthal specimens, again, only 1 lived beyond age 50, and of 76 Upper Paleolithic Eurasians 2 did (see p. 304). The rarity of old individuals must have had profound implications for the transmission of traditional knowledge.

Anthropometry is useful also in reconstructing the stature of skeletons. We know more about the influence of various factors on stature than on other measurements of the living, and reconstruction of stature permits the application of this knowledge to interpreting the past. The method has been to use bones of individuals of known stature and to develop formulae from their limb bones that most accurately predict their stature. Details of the various procedures for sex, age, and stature estimations on skeletons are given in the handbooks of physical anthropology, such as Martin (1928) and Comas (1960).

Development of biometric methods has had other influences on physical anthropology. It permitted demonstration of the falsity of the assumption of fixity of bone dimensions in the living individual (see Chapter 9). It also permitted the development of quantitative human genetics. Correlation and other methods of analysis of quantitative data have been applied to pairs of relatives such as parents and their offspring. This permits the partitioning of the variation into the fraction within the pair of relatives (due to the common genetic inheritance and any common environmental factors) and that between random individuals. Besides being applied to parents and children, and brothers and sisters, such methods have been applied to twins (see p. 350). Studies of the degree of similarity between related individuals in respect to various body dimensions permit estimates of the extent of environmental and genetic influences on those body dimensions.

## Constitution

There are other uses of anthropometry, too. For example, it has been known since at least the time of Hippocrates that persons with particular body forms tend to be prone to particular diseases. The study of constitution has been handicapped by its long reliance on subjective overall impressions. Sheldon et al. (1940) introduced the use of standardized nude photographs (thus allowing independent verification) and linear scales. They devised a system called *somatotyping* by which any individual is scored in respect to various "components."

These components are related to constituents of body composition, and numerous investigators have attempted to devise methods for measuring the absolute and relative amounts of bone, muscle, fat, and other constituents (Brožek and Henschel, 1961) and to relate these to such other variables as age, sex, origin, diseases, fertility, and mortality.

FIG. 19-3   Some differences between the bony pelves of men and women:

| *Adult male pelvis* | *Adult female pelvis* |
|---|---|
| 1. The inner surface of the sacrum is vertical. | The inner surface of the sacrum is angled back below, enlarging the exit of the birth canal. |
| 2. The sacroiliac *(a)* and the lumbosacral joint surfaces *(b)* are larger. | The joint surfaces are small, but the sacral wings are wide. |
| 3. The pubis *(a)* is short relative to the ischium *(b)*. | The pubis averages almost as long as the ischium. |
| 4. The sciatic notch is narrow. | The sciatic notch is wide. |
| 5. The subpubic angle *(a)* is acute, and the pelvic cavity *(b)* is deep. | The subpubic angle is obtuse and the pelvic cavity is shallow. |
| 6. The ilia *(a)* tend to be vertical and the pelvic outlet *(b)* is constricted (ischial spines and coccyx project inward). | The ilia tend to flare out, and the pelvic outlet is more open (ischial spines are less prominent and project less; the coccyx is more mobile). |
| 7. The pelvic inlet is usually more constricted. | The pelvic inlet is wide (side to side) and round. |

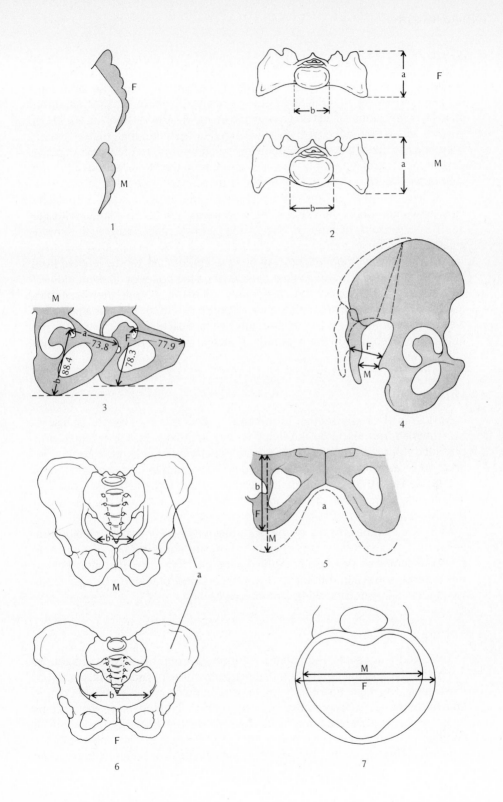

1

2

3

4

5

6

7

## Bone

The skeleton of a cadaver can be weighed, of course, either intact or just the mineral component after the fat has been chemically removed. Such measurements will reveal the effects on growth and aging of various factors in the life of the individuals studied, especially their diet. Furthermore, the relative dimensions and density of a skeleton can be measured on X-rays. A few days of acute starvation can lead to mobilization of calcium from the bones, so that although their outer dimensions are not altered bone density decreases, and in this sense the skeleton is by no means fixed and immutable. In fact, X-rays (especially those of women) show the cavities of the bone shafts to become larger with age and this resorption of bone is one of the reasons older individuals have a greater susceptibility to fractures.

Seen in this way, measurements of bone tell more than can be learned from the outer dimensions alone. Differences between the bones of different individuals measure other aspects besides genetic differences. Bone density studies may give insight into human biological response to diet, disease, or a period of weightlessness. In fact, assessments of this kind are useful in the appraisal of the ill and may even help in the handling of mineral balance problems in individual patients.

## Muscle

Muscle is obviously subject to increase or decrease by exercise or disuse. Measurement of muscle on the living is only approximate. For example, it is possible to distinguish superficial fat from underlying muscle and muscle from bone on an X-ray of a limb and to record muscle width as a percentage of total width (see Fig. 19-5). By assuming a section of limb to be cylindrical one can estimate the percentage of the total volume taken up by muscle (Garn and Shamir, 1958).

Muscle and other tissues of the body are involved in active metabolism. Since fat has a very low rate of metabolism, for some studies of metabolic processes it may be significant to estimate the total amount of nonfat tissue. For this purpose some anthropometrists use the concept of *lean body mass* (body weight less the estimated weight of fat, see below).

## Fat

Total body fat can be estimated by a formula using height and weight. So estimated, the amount of fat has long been known to depend on the amount of food eaten. The exact distribution patterns of body fat are only now becoming known, however. In some human groups, such as the Hottentots, there seems to be a special tendency for fat to deposit on the buttocks (producing a condition called steatopygea) and on the thighs. There are also characteristic differences, in general, between male and female fat distribution patterns: men usually have relatively more of their fat on the abdomen, whereas women have more of theirs on the thighs, arms, and breasts.

Much of the body fat is deposited just beneath the skin. Subcutaneous fat plus skin can be measured simply by picking up a fold and measuring the *skinfold* with a suitable caliper under specified pressure (Fig. 19-4). Another

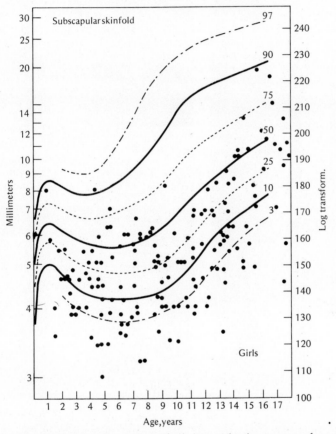

FIG. 19-4   The thickness of a double fold of skin and subcutaneous fat at the lower corner of the shoulder blade (measured at constant pressure by a pair of calipers that close with a spring). Only 3 percent of British girls had values below the lowest line, only 10 percent below the next higher (solid) line, 25 percent below the next (dashed) line, 50 percent below the next (solid) line, 75 percent below the next (dashed) line, 90 percent below the next (solid) line, and 97 percent below the highest line. The dots on the chart represent individual girls from the island of Tristan da Cunha in the middle of the South Atlantic. Note that in this population 36 of the 160 girls (22.5 percent) are as thin or thinner than the leanest 3 percent of British girls. Skinfolds can, of course, be measured on other parts of the body, such as the back of the arm or the abdomen. Redrawn from W. A. Marshall: "Anthropometric measurements of the Tristan da Cunha islanders." *Human Biology 43*, 133, 1971. Reproduced by permission.

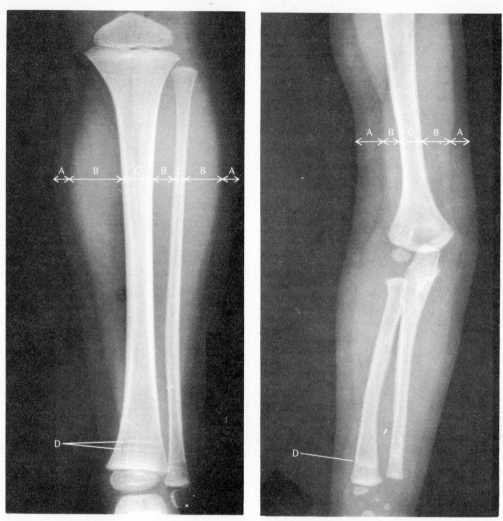

FIG. 19-5   *Left:* X-ray of leg of a three-year-old girl, showing *A,* subcutaneous fat; *B,* muscle; and *C,* bone. *D,* transverse lines from arrest of growth. *Right:* X-ray of arm and forearm, showing same body components. *D* indicates radiopaque lines following lead poisoning. From S. M. Garn, F. N. Silverman, et al.: "Lines and bands of increased density: Their implication to growth and development." *Medical Radiography and Photography 44,* 58, 1968. Reproduced by permission.

way to measure the thickness of skin plus subcutaneous fat is by the cross section of this tissue shown in an X-ray (see Figs. 19-5 and 19-6). The reason subcutaneous fat is less opaque to X-ray than muscle, and hence is distinguishable, is that fat is less dense than muscle and other tissues. In fact, the specific gravity of most tissues is just slightly higher than that of water (1.0), but human fat has a specific gravity of approximately 0.9.

By use of the Archimedes principle (weighing under water) it is possible to determine the human volume (the difference between body weight in air and under water in kilograms equals the volume of displaced water, hence of the body, in liters). From this one can calculate the specific gravity (weight per volume) and estimate the proportion of fat (Fig. 19-7). Such estimates involve

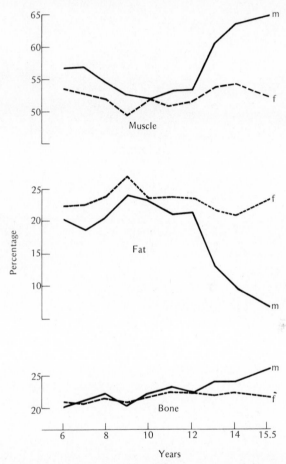

FIG. 19-6   The relative thicknesses of the different tissues of the arm in school-age children. In females (dashed lines) the width of the X-ray shadows of muscle and of bone are relatively constant fractions of the total width—although each increases with age. In males (solid lines) the muscle width increases markedly relative to total width during adolescence and the fat width decreases proportionately. Bone width also tends to increase relative to total width with age in males. These kinds of changes with age in body composition are not uniformly present in all individuals. Both genetic and environmental factors influence the amounts and the distribution in various parts of the body of fat and other tissues. Redrawn from F. E. Johnston and R. M. Malina: "Age changes in the composition of the upper arm of Philadelphia children." *Human Biology* 38, 1–21, 1966.

FIG. 19-7 Underwater weighing device at Medical Nutrition Laboratory, Fitzsimmons Army Hospital, Denver, Colorado. The difference between weight in air and weight in water gives the volume. Weight in kilograms per volume in liters is the specific gravity. From J. Brožek and A. Henschel (Eds.): *Techniques for measuring body composition.* Washington, D. C.: National Academy of Sciences–National Research Council, 1961. Reproduced·by permission.

assumptions concerning the specific gravity of lean body mass and of fat. Furthermore, one must also measure or estimate the volume of air in the lungs and allow for it, too. Results from density determinations can be compared with combinations of various measurements including skinfolds. The latter alone can then be used for estimating the amount of body fat (Damon and Goldman, 1964).

The amount and proportion of fat is directly related to nutrition. Leaner individuals have an increased incidence of pulmonary tuberculosis, certain mental diseases, and other conditions. Individuals who are heavy for their height have an increased likelihood of heart and vascular diseases, kidney ailments, and diabetes, and fat adults have an appreciably reduced expectation of life. The relative importance of fat and total body size in causing these differences is not fully understood. Likewise, the role of physical condition, the differential distribution of the fat in different parts of the body, and the nature of the fat itself (there are different kinds) remain to be explored in detail. But these are just the kinds of questions which modern anthropometry and other studies may combine to help answer. Long-range studies of individuals examined and then followed for years are especially informative. These yield only statistical conclusions, of course, but they permit one to assess probabilities.

For instance, Damon et al. (1969a) applied somatotyping and a series of body measurements (including skinfolds) to a study of proneness to heart diseases. After age, blood pressure, and serum cholesterol had been partialled out, there were distinct differences in average physique between those who did and did not later have one kind of heart ailment. Coronary heart disease without myocardial infarction was positively associated with weight, chest depth, arm girth, skinfold below the shoulder blade (but not on the back of the arm), and with fat, muscle, and boniness as assessed by somatotyping. These are only statistical estimates of risk, of course. Anthropometry can only establish that certain physical attributes, such as increased weight, are associated with greater risks, just as cigarette smoking is associated with increased risk of lung cancer. More studies would be needed, however, to show whether weight reduction reduces the risk of these kinds of heart disease in the way that quitting smoking seems to reduce the risk of lung cancer.

## Summary

Traditional anthropometry involves standardized measurements between defined points on the skull and other parts of the skeleton (or equivalent points on the living). Head dimensions and proportions, such as cephalic index, and limb measurements are determined in this way. Populations vary in respect to standard anthropometric measurements. Functional questions often require special measurements. Stature and weight reveal a good deal because they measure the whole body and because of the large amount of comparative data. Measurements of the jaws and the pelvis are of direct value in orthodontics and obstetrics respectively. Studies of body constitution and of body composition (by X-ray, underwater weighing, pinch calipers, and so on) reveal the relative amounts and distribution of fat, muscle, and bone, which are related to age at death and to coronary heart disease and other diseases.

# CHAPTER 20

# GROWTH AND
# DEVELOPMENT

Most of the early biologists took a predominantly static view of their subject. Anatomy and, after the invention of the microscope, histology—the study of tissues—were initially largely descriptive sciences. Physical anthropology, however, except for an early exercise in describing the peoples of the world, has always been a dynamic subject concerned with the "fourth dimension," change through time. The chief focus has been on evolutionary change, but the short-term changes that constitute growth and development have also received attention.

Biological changes go on throughout life (Table 20-1). The term *development* is usually used for the changes of form associated with the acquisition of new functions during embryonic life. The term *growth* refers to changes in size and is usually applied to the period from birth to physical maturity. The term *involution* is sometimes used for the process of aging in late adulthood. Changes go on all the time, however, even during the plateau of mid-adulthood, and the changes virtually always involve both change in size and change in form. Even during youth the changes are not all towards increase in size and development of functions. Reduction in size of some part and loss of its function often accompanies acquistion or enlargement of other structures with different functions.

These processes go on from "womb to tomb" (in S. M. Garn's phrase, "from sperm to worm"). Human development is a continuous process encompassing both prenatal and postnatal changes.

The process of birth involves an appreciable risk of death in the perinatal period, especially under conditions of poverty and deprivation. Even under the best conditions, however, there are deaths at this age caused by hereditary defects that prevent the individual from living without a **placenta.** At birth the individual shifts from dependence on the placenta for oxygenation of **hemoglobin** and nutrition to breathing air and suckling its mother. These critical changes cause a few days interruption of the gain in size, but normally within a week or two the weight at birth is regained. The birth weight of the average live-born White in the United States is 3.32 kilograms (7.3 pounds). By world standards this is heavy but it is very similar to the average in European countries (Meredith, 1970). Birth weight is several billion times the weight of the fertilized ovum, so there is much opportunity for the prenatal growth to be influenced by a variety of conditions. Lighter birth weight may in part be accounted for by: (1) shorter duration of pregnancy (in fact "prematurity" is often arbitrarily defined as a birth weight less than some fixed amount, such as 2.5 kilograms); (2) birth order (the first born are usually the lightest, and average birth weight increases with parity); (3) sex (females are lighter); (4) nutrition (deficient food or protein or lack of supervision of the health and diet

**TABLE 20-1    Stages in the life span**

| Period | Approximate age | State |
|---|---|---|
| Germinal | First 7 days | |
| Embryonic | 8 days to 6 weeks | |
| Transitional | | Placenta, body form and internal structures mostly present |
| Fetal | 8 weeks to 40 weeks | |
| Birth | | |
| Neonatal | First 2 weeks | Postnatal weight loss regained |
| Infancy | 2 weeks to 14 months | Habitual upright posture achieved |
| Childhood | 14 months to 14 years | |
| Puberty | Variable | Menarche, change of voice, axillary and pubic hair |
| Adolescence | May be early (14–16 years) or late (17–20 years) | |
| Maturity | Variable | Reproductive period |
| Old age | Variable | |

of mothers is associated with lighter birth weight); (5) climate as measured by latitude (in tropical zones the newborn are lighter than in temperate zones); (6) racial origin (for example, South Asian, African, and Oceanic infants are light); (7) altitude (at high altitudes—such as those of some communities in Colorado—the newborn are significantly light); (8) twins and other multiple births tend to be light; (9) the economic status of the father is involved, perhaps through several of the previous variables (the poorer the lighter, of course); (10) some specific genetic and other influences are known (members of families tend to run to similar birth weights; low birth weight is the rule in some birth defects, while diabetic mothers tend to have heavy infants at birth). The range of birth weights must be maintained by natural selection. Light weight at birth would be selected against by the higher mortality of underweight infants. Very large and heavy newborn are also selected against; large infants with large heads make for difficulties in delivery through the mother's birth canal and raise the possibility of the child or the mother dying.

Body weights can of course be followed throughout life. Growth in weight is often delayed and sometimes even reversed by a particularly severe illness or deprivation. Since it measures growth of all parts of the body and is responsive to health and nutrition, weight (and change in weight) is a particularly sensitive anthropometric index of the health status of an individual.

Overall body length provides another general measure of growth. **Embryos** and **fetuses** are usually measured from the head to the rump (crown–rump length) because the flexed limbs do not lend themselves to a linear measurement comparable to stature. Crown–rump length is, in fact, the most generally used measurement of the degree of development of an embryo. It is possible also to determine the stage of ossification. All bones start as cartilage or membrane. Then they begin to calcify from ossification centers such as those in the shafts and ends of the long bones. Each calcified center has a more or less characteristic time of appearance (Fig. 20-1). For example, two ossification centers form in the membrane that is to become the **clavicle** (collar bone) during the sixth week of embryonic life. An embryo that had no calcified bones except for these centers would thus be at this earliest stage of ossification. The jawbones (**maxilla** and **mandible**), those of the arm and forearm (humerus, radius, and ulna), the thighbone (**femur**), and the **tibia** also ossify in the embryo during the second month of pregnancy.

When the developing individual reaches a crown–rump length of 30 millimeters it is called a fetus. This occurs at about the eighth week of pregnancy. From then until birth, during the fetal stages, many additional ossification centers are formed. The formation of centers and fusing together of those that will later form a single bone is a continuous process and continues into adulthood. Stages are therefore somewhat arbitrary.

The relationship of the crown–rump length to the stage of bony development provides a possible method for the study of growth in size versus progress in development and hence of the influences of prenatal conditions during this

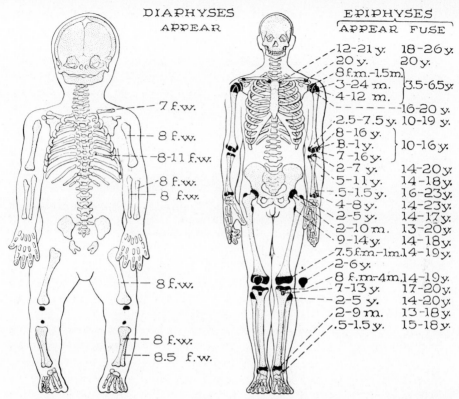

DIAPHYSES
APPEAR

EPIPHYSES
APPEAR    FUSE

12-21 y.    18-26 y.
20 y.        20 y.
8 f.m.-1.5m.
3-24 m.    3.5-6.5y.
4-12 m.

- - - - - -16-20 y.
2.5-7.5 y.  10-19 y.
8-16 y.
B.-1 y.      10-16 y.
7-16 y.
2-7 y.       14-20 y.
5-11 y.      14-18 y.
.5-1.5 y.    16-23 y.
4-8 y.       14-23 y.
2-5 y.       14-17 y.
2-10 m.    13-20 y.
9-14 y.      14-18 y.
7.5 f.m.-1m. 14-19 y.
2-6 y.
8 f.m.-4m. 14-19 y.
7-13 y.      17-20 y.
2-5 y.       14-20 y.
2-9 m.      13-18 y.
.5-1.5 y.    15-18 y.

7 f.w.

8 f.w.

-8-11 f.w.

8 f.w.

8 f.w.

8 f.w.

8 f.w.

8.5  f.w.

FIG. 20-1    First appearance of the shafts (diaphyses) and joint ends (epiphyses) of the appendicular skeleton (f.w., fetal weeks; f.m., fetal months; m, months; y, years). From G. G. Robertson: "Developmental anatomy." In B. J. Anson (Ed.), *Morris' human anatomy* (ed. 12). New York: McGraw-Hill Book Company, 1966. Reproduced by permission. These times are based on anatomical studies a number of years ago. Recent X-ray data on U.S. populations give slightly different values.

period. At birth, crown–rump length is about 33 centimeters and represents about two thirds of the total body length of the newborn infant.

Young infants cannot stand. Instead of estimating their height anthropologists therefore ordinarily measure their recumbent body length instead. In older persons recumbent length exceeds standing height somewhat, because lying down straightens and lengthens the back. When the length (or height) of an individual is plotted on a graph by age, it is seen that there are certain periods of very rapid growth and certain periods of slower progress (Figs. 20-2 and 20-3). The first spurt normally follows the first week of life and continues at a gradually decreased rate for the first four years or so. Growth then slows, but speeds up again in the period before sexual maturity (puberty). During the interval, girls, who on the average are smaller at birth than boys, briefly exceed

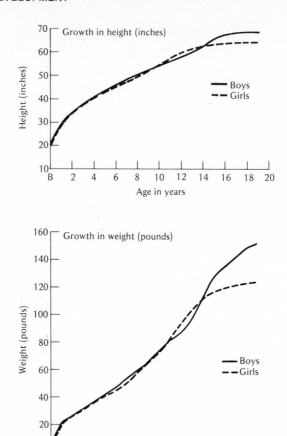

FIG. 20-2   Growth in height and weight of American boys and girls. Note that during the age range 10–14, girls (dashed lines) are first taller, then heavier on average than boys (solid lines), but that the boys eventually spurt past them. Based on data from H. Stoudt et al. *Human Biology 32,* 331–341, 1960.

the boys in average height, usually between the ages of 9 and 12. The growth of girls slows down after puberty, and their stature reaches stability several years later. Boys reach puberty later than girls and most of them continue to grow into their twenties.

The above description is very general. There are considerable differences that depend on genetic origins and environment, both among populations and, especially, among individuals. Growth curves based on groups of different ages, such as all the children of a certain school, show considerable fluctuations and, if the time intervals are short, even occasionally an apparent downward trend. These fluctuations are recognized as biologically meaningless and merely the result of the limited size of the samples studied. They would occur, for example, when the set of individuals measured at one age happen by chance to be somewhat smaller for their age than the other set of individuals measured at an earlier age.

Information and conclusions concerning individual differences in the growth process can be derived only from remeasuring the same individuals repeatedly. Such a growth study is called longitudinal, while surveys employing only one examination of each individual, and comparing different individuals of various ages, are called cross-sectional.

The first recorded instance of a systematic attempt to follow the growth of an individual longitudinally was undertaken between April 11, 1759, and January 30, 1777 (Scammon, 1927). During this period, Philibert Gueneau de Montbeillard, a French country gentleman, measured his son's height twice a year (Fig. 20-4). On the basis of these data his friend, the celebrated French naturalist Georges Louis Leclerc de Buffon, noted that growth is greater in summer than in winter. Buffon also was the first to state that stature tends to decrease during the day and increase after a night's rest.

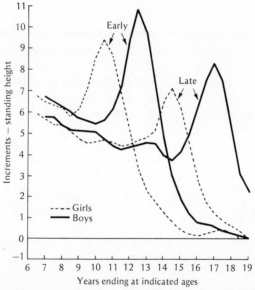

FIG. 20-3  The amount of increase in height per year of early-maturing and late-maturing girls and boys. Although late-maturing girls show the peak rate of growth almost two years later than early-maturing boys, they still reach this stage nearly two and a half years before late-maturing boys reach the same peak velocity of growth. The curves of growth for height and weight are related to the maturation of the skeleton. This in turn is related to maturation in general (including the hormonal changes associated with sexual maturation). Redrawn from N. B. Henry (Ed.): *Adolescence*. Forty-third Yearbook of the National Society for the Study of Education, Part I, 1944. Reproduced by permission.

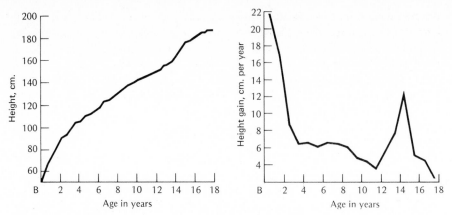

FIG. 20-4   Growth in height of de Montbeillard's son from birth to 18 years (1759–1777). *Left:* Height attained at each age; *right:* amount of growth in each year (incremental, or velocity, curve). Redrawn from J. M. Tanner, *Growth at adolescence.* (ed. 2). Oxford: Blackwell Scientific Publications, 1962. Reproduced by permission.

## Adolescence

One conclusion from longitudinal studies is that the pubescent growth spurt is much sharper than appears from cross-sectional data, but that variations in the age at which the spurt occurs make it appear more gradual when data from different individuals are averaged. This suggests that chronological age may not be the best way of evaluating growth progress. In girls the pubescent growth changes are more closely related to the time of the first menses (called *menarche)* than they are to age. The development of such secondary sexual characteristics as body hair, breasts, and, in boys, the change of voice occur in relationship to each other and to the stage in the growth process (as marked, for instance, by the time of the maximum spurt in the rate of increase in stature); among different individuals, in different groups, and between the two sexes these events may all tend to occur at a somewhat earlier or a somewhat later age.

Furthermore, these developmental changes occur at an earlier age now than they formerly did. In the fourth century A.D., Oribasius observed (Amundsen and Diers, 1969), "In the majority the menses begin around the fourteenth year, in a few around the thirteenth or twelfth, and in many, later than 14 years." The same statement would have been true a generation ago. However, recent studies in the United States give an average age of menarche of 12.9 years—that is, in the thirteenth year—but with considerable individual variation. There has been, on average, a decrease of one and one-half years between young women today and their own mothers (Damon et al., 1969b). This is apparently the result of improved nutrition, because later average age of menarche has been observed regularly in populations with poorer nutrition: tropical Africans, New Guineans, Andean highlanders, and Europeans and

Americans of previous periods. Within a population there is also considerable variation, lower socioeconomic groups maturing later on the average. Girls increase in weight the fastest just after the age of 12, when they weigh about 86 pounds on the average; menarche usually follows this growth spurt in 6 to 12 months (Frisch and Revelle, 1969).

The late occurrence of adolescence is a peculiarly human trait, and all other primates reach maturity at much younger ages than do human youths (see Fig.

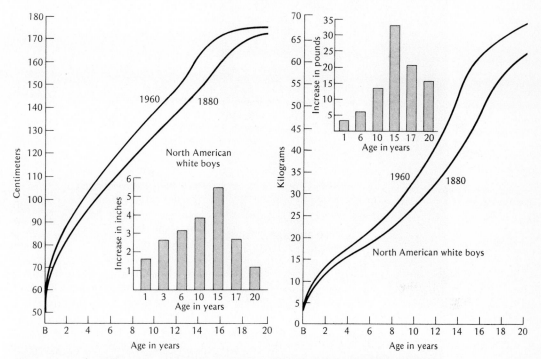

FIG. 20-5   *Left:* Differences in growth in stature of American boys between 1880 and 1960. Note that the curve showing the average in 1960 is always well above that for 1880. The bar graph (below) shows the increase during those 80 years in inches at various ages. Note that the growth in 1960 accelerates up to 15 years of age and then slows sharply. At 20 years of age the young man of 1960 averaged slightly over an inch taller than one in 1880. Some evidence suggests that the tendency for sons to exceed their fathers in height has now come to an end. To judge by some data concerning similar secular changes in England, the difference would be still less in 30-year-old men.

*Right:* The curves of secular trend in weight show that boys in 1960 were heavier than their age mates of 1880. The bar graph shows the tendency to be considerably heavier continues after age 15 and is still considerable at age 20. Other evidence shows that adults today are heavier on average at all ages than adults of earlier periods.

Redrawn from H. V. Meredith: "Change in stature and body weight of North American boys," In L. P. Lipsitt and C. C. Spiker (Eds.): *Advances in child development and behavior,* Vol. 1. New York: Academic Press, 1963. Reproduced by permission.

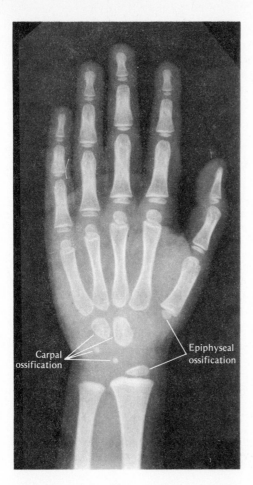

Carpal ossification

Epiphyseal ossification

FIG. 20-6   X-ray of hand and wrist of a four-year-old girl showing epiphyseal and carpal ossification. From S. M. Garn, F. N. Silverman, et al.: "Lines and bands of increased density: Their implication to growth and development." *Medical Radiography and Photography 44,* 71, 1968. Reproduced by permission.

12-12). Schultz (1949) describes the period of postnatal growth as lasting approximately 20 years in man, 11 years in great apes, and only 3 years in lower primates. How then do we account for the trend toward early maturation of modern youths? Late maturation must have been selectively advantageous for man in the past. In recent times and in places with adequate food resources the need for the long delay has disappeared. Evolution may not merely be selecting for early maturation, however. It is more probable that it has already established a degree of plasticity (see Chapter 9). This may work through a hormonal mechanism which, when a certain stage of growth is reached, feeds back to retard growth and trigger the onset of maturity.

T. W. Todd (1937) studied the ages at which various bones ossify and their component parts fuse. He examined the process of transformation of cartilage and membrane to bone as seen by X-ray and related this skeletal maturation to the postnatal growth process. The number and state of epiphyseal and carpal ossifications progresses with age (Figs. 20-6 and 20-7). Todd and others published atlases of typical X-rays of children of different ages (Greulich and Pyle, 1959; Todd, 1937). The X-ray of a child is compared with those in the atlas, which gives the "bone age" of the X-ray nearest the same state of development. The difference between this "bone age" and the chronological age is considered to be the degree of maturational acceleration or retardation.

A refinement of the method involves studying the transformations of each different ossification center separately. The stages through which the bone must pass in every individual become *maturity indicators* (Acheson, 1966). They can be separately rated and studied or averaged to give a "bone age." The set of standards based on the analysis of maturity indicators in 5,000 X-rays of the hands of British children (Tanner et al., 1959 and 1962) is the most widely used by anthropologists in comparative studies of the acceleration or retardation of bone development. Since such indicators show how far along its course the growth process has gone, formulae taking bone age into account are helpful in predicting the adult stature of older children. Roche et al. (1975) use the recumbent length of the infant and the stature of the parents for predicting adult stature of infants up to four years of age. For older children they use stature instead of recumbent length and add weight and then bone age (determined from X-rays of the hand and wrist) to achieve the best prediction formulae.

Bone age, like overall growth, is retarded by adverse conditions such as inadequate food. In fact it is the delay in stages of ossification of the bones of the lower limbs and the vertebrae that accounts for the delay in the spurt in growth. Specific periods of disease and malnutrition leave their mark on the bones (lines of arrested growth) and these can be seen in X-rays (Fig. 19-5) of living individuals and ancient bones.

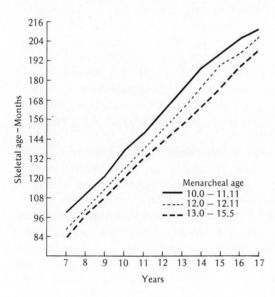

FIG. 20-7   Skeletal age (the degree of ossification of the bones of the wrist or other parts of the skeleton) is advanced in children who mature early (solid line) and is retarded in children who mature late (heavy dashed line). That is, girls with earlier than average onset of menstruation also tend to undergo skeletal maturation at early ages, and vice versa. After Simmons and Greulich (1943).

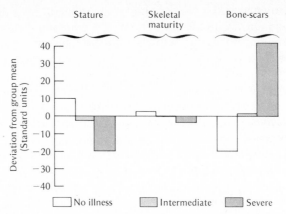

FIG. 20-8 Children who have had no illness are somewhat taller and have fewer "bone scars" showing arrested growth than average. Children who have been severely ill (for more than 6 weeks) are shorter than average and have more than average bone scars. Skeletal maturity, however, is little affected by illness and is largely genetically determined. Redrawn after R. M. Acheson, in J. M. Tanner: *Third symposium on human growth*. New York: Pergamon, 1960. Reproduced by permission.

## Relative Growth

Most of the postnatal growth of long bones occurs through ossification in the epiphyseal growth zone of cartilage between the shaft and epiphyseal center. Because in the process of growth these centers ossify and fuse with the shaft at different and characteristic times, periods of rapid and slow growth alternate, and there are differences in the amount of growth in different segments of the body and even at the two ends of segments spanned by a single bone.

The most notable feature of this relative growth is the precocious growth of the head, which, although it continues to grow, represents a constantly decreasing fraction of stature (Fig. 20-9). The trunk also completes its growth earlier than the limbs and the upper limb is precocious relative to the lower. Growth is thus asymmetrical in a way analogous to the asymmetry of evolution (Fig. 20-10). The ears and nose have cartilaginous "skeletons" and continue to grow throughout life.

The tissues of the body as well as the segments show different growth patterns (Fig. 20-11). Lymphatic tissue and the thymus gland develop early in childhood and actually regress considerably in adulthood. The brain and other nervous tissues also develop early, and their growth rapidly decelerates in early childhood. On the other hand, the gonads (ovaries and testes) and the secondary sexual tissues such as breasts develop very little at first but suddenly spurt ahead at puberty. Most other body tissues show an intermediate type of growth that reflects general growth: they show infantile and pubescent spurts and more moderate growth rates between these times. A growth curve of muscle or bone is similar to one of stature or weight.

## Facial Growth

Numerous other applications of precise body measurements to the healing arts have called on the skill of anthropometry. One of these, measurement of facial growth in relation to the shape of jaws and position of teeth, has called for collaborative efforts of anthropologists and orthodontists (dentists specializing in straightening the teeth). Especially among Europeans and peoples of European culture, wherever they live and whatever their origin, there is a large proportion whose teeth are maloccluded and seem too big for their jaws or whose jaws seem unmatched to each other. While some consider these disharmonies inherent, others have demonstrated situations in which dietary and other habits are largely responsible. The teeth may be rotated or crowded out of the tooth row, and upper teeth may fail to meet the lower ones or may do so in an unsatisfactory manner.

C. L. Brace and P. E. Mahler (1971) traced the reduction in size of the area of the crowns of the teeth during the course of recent human evolution and related it to the development of cooking. Since Mousterian times and even within the last 5,000 years, especially recently, as boiling water with hot stones

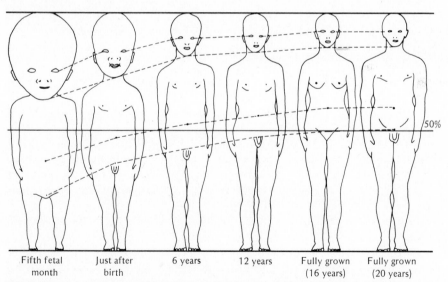

| Fifth fetal month | Just after birth | 6 years | 12 years | Fully grown (16 years) | Fully grown (20 years) |

FIG. 20-9 Progressive growth pattern. Note the changing proportions with age due to the relatively great early growth of the head and late growth of the limbs. Redrawn from A. A. Abbie: *Papers and Proceedings of the Royal Society of Tasmania 98*, 65, 1964. Reproduced by permission.

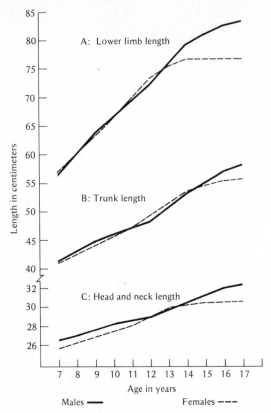

FIG. 20-10   Growth of the different segments of stature (*A,* lower limbs; *B,* trunk; and *C,* head and neck) proceeds in a way generally resembling stature, that is, with a spurt in the preadolescent period, first in girls (dashed lines), then in boys (solid lines). Note, however, that in length of the trunk females exceed males on average for a longer period than in the other segments, and that the difference in trunk length between the sexes is absolutely and proportionately less as they approach adulthood. These trends in relative growth provide the average female with a large abdominal area for the accommodation of the fetus and placenta in the gravid womb, as well as for the organs of digestion and reproduction. Redrawn from H. V. Meredith: Length of head and neck, trunk and lower extremities of Iowa City children aged seven to seventeen years. *Child Development 10(2),* 129, 1939. Reproduced by permission.

in skins and then boiling in pottery were introduced, teeth have evolved to smaller sizes—presumably because, in the absence of positive adaptive advantage, any structure tends to be reduced. The muscles for biting and chewing and their bony attachments have also been reduced.

Furthermore, with well-cooked food, malocclusion is no longer a fatal disease as it once would have been, and the chief drawback of malocclusion now is that it may be considered unattractive. To correct these malformations, orthodontists move the teeth in the jaw by the application of mechanical forces. Orthodontists need accurate data concerning the measurement of growth of the face because unless they can predict the amount of future growth of the jaws of children, the process of correction may be inadequate or may overcompensate and produce other maladjustments.

To obtain adequately accurate measurements of growth potential, anthropologists and radiologists have devised a number of techniques to X-ray the head under standardized conditions that permit the restudy of the same individual under identical conditions later. In this way the changes can be studied. These techniques of *cephalometry* consist of taking a true lateral view, by inserting plugs in the ear holes and aligning the two plugs with the central beam of the X-ray. The junction of the nasal bones with the frontal bone (nasion) and other bony landmarks can be identified on the X-ray films, and changes in dimen-

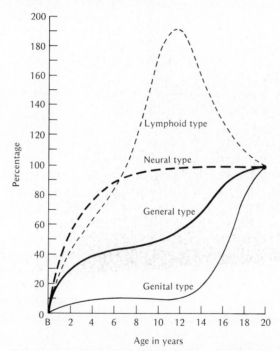

FIG. 20-11　The four basic curves of postnatal growth. *Lymphoid type:* thymus, lymph nodes, intestinal lymphoid masses; *neural type:* brain and its parts, dura, spinal cord, optic apparatus, many head dimensions; *general type:* body as a whole, external dimensions (with exception of head and neck), respiratory and digestive organs, kidneys, aorta and pulmonary trunks, spleen, musculature as a whole, skeleton as a whole, blood volume; *genital type:* testis, ovary, epididymis, uterine tube, prostate, prostatic urethra, seminal vesicles. Redrawn from M. J. Baer and J. E. Harris: "A commentary on the growth of the human brain and skull." *American Journal of Physical Anthropology 30,* 39–44, 1969. Reproduced by permission.

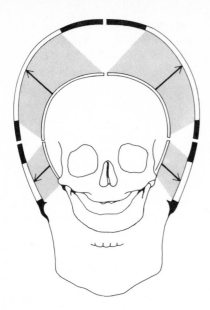

FIG. 20-12   The bones surrounding the brain and the sutures between them form a cerebral capsule. The early growth of this cerebral capsule accompanies growth of the brain. The individual bones are passively carried outward (arrows) but bone forms along the sutures (black areas) to keep adjacent bones approximated to each other. In this way the bones ossify successively larger areas of the cerebral capsule. Redrawn from M. L. Moss and R. W. Young: "A functional approach to craniology." *American Journal of Physical Anthropology 18,* 281, 1960. Reproduced by permission.

sions and angles can be determined with millimeter accuracy (as precise as most caliper measurements of actual bones).

Arbitrary landmarks for the study of facial growth, such as the center of the seat of the pituitary gland *(sella turcica),* suffice for the orthodontist to orient and superimpose outlines from X-rays of the same patient taken on different visits and to measure the change. For a more fundamental understanding of where the growth occurs, however, experimental methods are necessary. A growing animal can be injected with a dye (such as alizarin red S) that stains growing bone but not already formed bone (Baer, 1954). Studies by this and other methods demonstrate that growth of cranial bones is controlled by the contained structures: the brain case by the brain (Moss and Young, 1960—see Fig. 20-12), the orbit by the eye (Washburn and Detwiler, 1943), the tooth-supporting part of jaws by the erupting teeth, and so on. Each edge of cranial bones, where they meet each other at sutures, responds by independent growth to meet the need for expansion at that locus, but the response is limited by innate capacity and terminates when the adjacent bones fuse together (synostose) at the suture between them. After that there can be only appositional growth, on the surface under the scalp for instance (Mednick and Washburn, 1956). Such appositional growth includes raising of lines of attachment for the tendons of active muscles. Structures such as the **sagittal crest** in those animals in which it occurs are produced by appositional growth of bone. There also is resorption of bone allowing for the remodelling of the general shape or for maintenance of the shape as the individual bones grow at the sutures. Resorption also causes loss of the raised bony attachments for muscles when the muscles are paralyzed (Washburn, 1947).

The comparative study of growth processes thus has great significance for evolutionary studies. Schultz (1949) has made extensive comparative studies of growth and development in the primates. These place the great apes nearest to humans, but we continue to grow to a greater age and larger in those traits that are most characteristic of our species. An understanding of the human growth process and its evolution also has direct applications to medicine and dentistry.

## Summary

The size of a human infant at birth is already the result of a long period of intrauterine development. Birth weight is influenced by the length and influences of gestation. Overall postnatal growth is measured by longitudinal studies of changes in weight, height, and other anthropometric dimensions. Puberty is marked by a spurt in growth rates and by a series of adolescent developmental changes such as voice change in boys and menarche in girls. The age at which these events occur tends to be positively correlated with developmental changes in ossification.

Different structures grow fastest at different times. Differences in growth of the face and eruption of teeth, for instance, are of concern to the practice of orthodontics, which must deal with these disharmonies. Growth of the face and head may be followed by X-ray cephalometry. Bone markers, such as intravital dyes, provide other methods for the study of growth.

# CHAPTER 21

# RACE

The great variability of mankind in respect to genetic polymorphisms has already been noted (Chapter 5). Furthermore, because of this, the different populations of the world are characterized by different gene frequencies. This is what is meant by race differences. A race is a subdivision of a species; it consists of a population that has a different combination of gene frequencies than do other populations of the species. The hereditary component of characteristics that have not been successfully analyzed as "genes" is also racial, of course, but it may be difficult to apply racial analysis to such partially inherited traits as stature and cephalic index.

Since a race is a population, membership in a race is membership by descent. The physical characteristics generally used to ascribe people to a race do not do so unless they acquired them from their ancestors who belonged to that population. For broad racial groups it may be possible to recognize many persons as belonging, but there are always many ambiguous cases. There are two reasons for this. First, since different populations of the same species can and do interbreed, the "boundaries" of populations are indefinite and there are always individuals who could be classed in more than one race or in a race all to themselves. Second, since there is a great deal of genetic variation within every human population as well as differences between populations, the genetic characteristics of some members of a population may be very unusual for that racial group. In fact, the characteristics may be less unusual in some other populations. Thus, one can define the general concept "race" in a straightforward way. Furthermore, one can see racial differences among individuals. The scientific study of specific races is, however, a very much more difficult matter, with only limited usefulness in studies of the origins of peoples and with virtually no applicability in the matter of behavioral genetics, where statements such as that "all peoples have the same mentality" or "different races have different mentalities" are both without scientific foundation. To learn much of the biological history of peoples or of their mentalities and the genetic basis for mental characteristics requires reframing of the concepts of race and mentality.

A great deal has been written about race since 1775, when Blumenbach described the human species as divided into five races: White, Yellow, Black, Red, and Brown. Unfortunately only a tiny fraction of these publications contributes to our understanding of human variability. The rest, even when based on conscientious research, are purely descriptive or historical in orientation and generally do not analyze the dynamic basis of human variation. Some of the earlier studies treated nonbiological linguistic or other cultural phenomena as criteria of racial membership.

Until about the time of the Second World War there were many racial studies that classified individuals into typological races. In these studies the effort was made to divide mankind into a number of racial classes, each of which was characterized by a number of distinguishing physical features. E. A. Hooton and C. W. Dupertuis (1955) reported an anthropometric survey which had been conducted before the war of nearly 10,000 Irish men. More than half the individuals failed to fit the chief ideal types: for example, only 55 were called "Pure Nordic," only 33 "Pure Mediterranean," and there were no "Pure Alpine." The majority were ascribed to several hyphenated types such as "Nordic-Mediterranean" and "Nordic-Alpine." Terms such as "mixed races" have sometimes been used even when there was no evidence of breeding between populations—merely because of a failure to meet the classifier's idea of a "pure" type.

All individuals can be ascribed to some typological "race" but only if enough categories are created or if the categories are very broadly defined. However, E. E. Hunt (1959) has reanalyzed the same data on the Irish males and shown that if hair color, eye color, cephalic index, nasal index, and stature were completely independent of each other—in other words were not part of a "racial package"—the proportion of intermediate combinations belonging to one "race" in one respect and another "race" in another respect would be only slightly higher than actually observed. For example, although there is some tendency for individuals with light hair to have light eyes and for tall individuals to have long heads, these tendencies are of a low order of association. Hunt makes clear—as had earlier been pointed out by M. S. Goldstein

(1956) in his review of the Hooton and Dupertuis book—that the genetic mechanism does not lead to inheritance of racial type; both parents might be ascribed to one "race" and their children to another. That is, both parents might be of modest height and have brown hair, relatively broad heads, and so on, and be classed because of all these physical characteristics within the "Nordic-Alpine" race. But because of the way stature, hair color, and cephalic index are inherited and modified according to environment these parents may have children who are tall, blond, and dolichocephalic, for instance, and who would have been classed as "Pure Nordic" in type.

After the Second World War, S. L. Washburn organized a series of seminars of then-youthful physical anthropologists under the auspices of the Wenner-Gren Foundation for Anthropological Research (formerly called The Viking Fund). J. B. Birdsell and M. T. Newman presented the shortcomings of the typological as against the genetic concept of race, and the issue was hashed over and resolved for most of those in attendance (see Kaplan et al., 1946). This view is presented in a little book by Coon, Garn, and Birdsell (1950), in which the term "race" is applied only to populations rather than to individuals and is specifically limited to those aspects of human biology that are genetically transmitted. Since that time few anthropologists have tried to create or use ideal typologies, although naive views are, of course, still current among the uninformed.

Because of the different ways in which the term "race" has been used and because they see no scientific value in such overall terms even when they are restricted to breeding populations, some anthropologists prefer to avoid use of the term "race" altogether. Two biological factors support their view: (1) to the extent that human beings find their mates in genetically different, or distant populations, there is no isolation into a series of discrete populations. Inherited biological traits usually form a geographic continuum along which there is a gradient (**cline**) from higher to lower frequency of the defining criteria; and (2) since genetic information is carried on the forty-six chromosomes and the chromosomes assort independently in **meiosis** (and parts of them cross over), genetic characteristics do not clump into racial types; each gene has its own independent transmission.

On the other hand, clines are not always gradual and Coon (1966) has pointed out that in our cosmopolitan cities there are no recognizable clines for skin color. In a cosmopolitan city there are people of very different skin color, for instance, and one cannot make a meaningful map showing gradual change from light-skinned to dark-skinned zones since individuals with different characteristics live in the same neighborhood—in fact they may be members of the same family. The same argument has been advanced against the concept of the cline in nonurban areas. In rural places also, biological groups are separated by other features as well as by geographic distance. People select their mates by language, religion, and social class as well as by where they were born. Nevertheless, people can be divided into a number of "races" that are apparent and can sometimes tell you something about where at least some of their ancestors probably came from: Mongoloids from the Orient, Whites from Europe, and Blacks from Africa.

Among neighboring peoples, however, purely racial criteria are not useful even for such deductions about their history. Even persons very familiar with the Far East would make errors in sorting out Japanese from Chinese according to purely biological criteria. Racial traits are of virtually no use in distinguishing among French, German, English, and Irish individuals. Although, on the average, European nationalities differ slightly from one another in most racial characteristics, individuals within each of these countries vary much more. In selecting agents for espionage within each other's boundaries European nations never have needed to pay much attention to racial traits.

Some human differences can be called "racial." The difficulty is that all individuals differ from all others, if a sufficiently wide variety of characteristics is considered. Even within a single nation, tribe, or limited breeding population, there are usually many differences in the color of the skin, eyes, and hair, the form of the head and face, the shape of the nose, the quantity of beard and body hair, and the proportions of the body. In some cases, however, the same criteria that separate some human groups may unite others: skin color, for example, distinguishes all but a very few Europeans from all but a very few tropical Africans, but skin color does not distinguish various peoples of East Asia, Polynesia, Micronesia, the Near East, North Africa, and the Americas from each other—although these groups may be distinguished on other grounds.

Furthermore, the number and the nature of races defined by different classifiers vary greatly. There is no single consideration equivalent to the criterion of noninterbreeding in the classification of species. If **alleles** are studied, different investigators discover the same classificatory system and achieve the same results in applying it. This is much less true of overall racial designations. One classifier will put more emphasis on hair color, another on facial features, and it is unlikely that the two will reach similar results.

Races change all the time. F. S. Hulse (1962) refers to race as an "evolutionary episode." Among 32 local races so designated by Garn (1970), 4 are less than a score of generations old: "North American Colored," "South African Colored," "Ladino," and "Neo-Hawaiian." At best, racial classifications look back at the relatively recent past.

Instead of a single crude overall term, analytic methods permit the study of population variability along a large number of different dimensions, with prospects of more helpful answers even to purely historical questions about origins.

Racial designations are, however, widely used by laymen in multiethnic societies. These concepts are referred to as "social race" in contrast to "biological race." Charles Wagley (1971) points out that the designation of social race may be based on any of several different theories: in some societies, such as those of the highlands of Central and South America, terms having biological etymologies such as "White," "Mestizo" (mixed), and "Indian" refer to such cultural criteria as whether a person wears shoes and speaks Spanish or wears sandals and speaks a native language; in others, such as those of the Caribbean Area where many African slaves were imported, specific physical features are used, but a rich person with dark skin, "bad" hair, thick lips, and a flat nose may be classified in a higher social race than that in which these traits would otherwise place him; in other societies, such as those with strongly Europe-based ties, there may be an almost pathological interest in genealogy, and the child of a "mixed" marriage is ascribed to the group with the lower social status. For example, in the Republic of South Africa today, and in Nazi Germany a generation ago, there have been legalistic arguments over whether any one grandparent or great grandparent so classified makes his descendant "colored" or "Jewish" respectively. Race is a term that has been much abused by persons who would emphasize human differences for the sake of maintaining a superior economic and social position.

These considerations lead me to use the word "race" rarely and then chiefly to describe population entities of past times when there was somewhat less human migration and mixture. It is true that some problems of historic interpretation concerning the origins and movements of peoples cannot be solved solely by genetic analysis; biological traits that cannot yet be successfully analyzed in that way also distinguish some geographic groups; if they predominate in some groups more than in others, they may be useful in reconstructing the history of populations. It is often convenient to apply the adjective "racial," even though there are no discrete categories to which one can apply the noun "race." Racial characteristics (such as the coarse straight black hair, eyelid folds, pronounced cheek bones, and shovel-shaped incisors of so-called "Mongoloids") are certainly genetic entities, although the mechanism of their inheritance is not always fully known and they may be modified by nongenetic influences. With each new trait that is subjected to satisfactory genetic and ecological analysis, an added fraction of human difference can be removed from the class of purely superficial **phenotypic** differences and added to our store of material for analytic anthropology. The need to rely on the somewhat misleading classification of whole individuals into races thus diminishes as we increasingly use the methods of population genetics and experimental analysis of the features of human adaptation.

J. S. Weiner (1964, p. 236) says:

> The notion that mankind comprises three or four "primary" or major races is from the ecological point of view, almost devoid of biological meaning. I have tried to show that the basic entity is the eco-system and that "fitness" or successful survival requires a complex response in physiological and genetic terms. Any large region, a region as large as a continent, must by its very nature produce a multiplicity of overlapping eco-systems and, therefore, local variation in patterns of adaptive response. The broad labels Caucasoid, Mongoloid, Australoid, can convey nothing of this variety or complexity of adaptation; and at the same time these terms obscure the basic similarity throughout *Homo sapiens* of the

adaptive responses available, though differing, of course, in expression. In fact, as we have seen, and we should not be surprised by it, in every continent or race the range of skin colour or of physique or of head shape for that matter, is always very wide indeed.

# Race and Behavior

The chief issue about race is not whether there are differences between populations in color of the skin or form of the hair (which all would acknowledge). It is not even whether some peoples have developed specific adaptations to conditions of climate, work, nutrition, and disease. We are gaining knowledge of these adaptations and finding out to what extent particular adaptations are more marked in specific populations. Although there may be some differences in interpretation of the significance, most investigators of the subject report that individuals inherit somewhat different capacities of these kinds and that some of the inherited capacities are (but usually only slightly) differently distributed in different populations.

The most socially important question about race is whether there are significant inherited differences in such behavioral characteristics as temperament and intelligence.

| Genetic and nongenetic relationships studied | | Genetic correlation | Range of correlations | Studies included |
|---|---|---|---|---|
| Unrelated persons | Reared apart | 0.00 | | 4 |
| | Reared together | 0.00 | | 5 |
| Foster-parent—child | | 0.00 | | 3 |
| Parent—child | | 0.50 | | 12 |
| Siblings | Reared apart | 0.50 | | 2 |
| | Reared together | 0.50 | | 35 |
| Twins | Two-egg | Opposite sex | 0.50 | 9 |
| | | Like sex | 0.50 | 11 |
| | One-egg | Reared apart | 1.00 | 4 |
| | | Reared together | 1.00 | 14 |

FIG. 21-1    A summary of correlation coefficients compiled by L. Erlenmeyer and L. F. Jarvik from various sources. The horizontal lines show the range of correlation coefficients in "intelligence" between individuals of various degrees of genetic and environmental relationship. The vertical lines show the averages. There is a general tendency for those pairs of individuals who are most similar genetically to be most similar in intelligence. Nevertheless there is also a clear tendency for individuals of the same degree of relationship who are reared apart to reflect their different environments in greater differences in intelligence. From I. M. Lerner: *Heredity, evolution, and society.* San Francisco: W. H. Freeman and Company. Copyright © 1968.

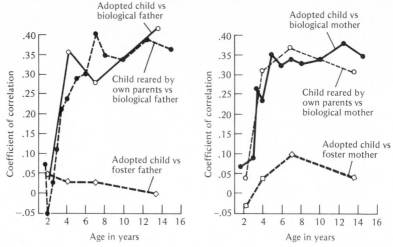

FIG. 21-2   One way of estimating the extent to which intelligence is hereditary versus the extent to which it is determined by environment is to compare the IQ test scores or educational attainments of relatives. Thus, the scores of biological parents and their children are correlated and tend to be similar, but foster parents and their foster children show little tendency to vary together. A survey of the literature of heritability shows wide variation in the findings of different studies but suggests that perhaps 25–65 percent of the IQ score is determined by heredity, some 15–55 percent by environment, and in most studies about 20 percent cannot be allocated between them. The greater the variation in environments, the less the heritability, of course, since these are relative measurements. From I. M. Lerner: *Heredity, evolution, and society.* W. H. Freeman and Company. Copyright © 1968. (From M. Honzik, and M. Skodak and B. M. Skeels.)

## Behavioral Genetics

Since *race* is limited in scientific discourse to inherited biological aspects of human populations, one cannot discuss possible racial differences in mental functions until one has demonstrated what aspects of these functions are genetic and to what degree.

One strategy for determining the relative role of genetics in mental character-istics is the study of multiple births; twins and triplets. Twins are of two types: **monozygotic** (one-egged) or identical twins, formed from a single fertilized ovum and having identical genes, and **dizygotic** (two-egged), formed from two ova separately fertilized. Dizygotic twins are genetically no more closely related to each other than ordinary brothers and sisters and are therefore sometimes referred to as fraternal twins. In 1937, H. H. Newman and his associates published a study of 119 pairs of twins. As one might expect, the identical twins were much more similar to each other in physique than were the fraternal pairs. In tests of intelligence, the identical twins were also more similar than the fraternal pairs, but the contrast was somewhat less marked. The most interesting finding, however, pertained to nineteen pairs of monozygotic twins who had been separated shortly after birth and reared apart in different social and physical environments. These pairs showed greater differences than the monozygotic twins reared together in respect to weight and especially in respect to scores on intelligence tests, but not appreciably in respect to eye color and pattern or size and shape of ears, nose, head, and face.

In a chapter on hereditary factors in psychological variables, S. G. Vandenberg (1967) reviewed the results of the comparison of monozygotic with dizygotic twins. He found an appreciable degree of hereditary control of perception, motor skill, personality, and temperament. Methods that would pinpoint the inherited aspects and permit their effective separation from environmental influences have not yet been developed, however. Since environmental influences are important in all these variables, and since critical environmental differences probably occur in every comparison one can make, acceptable evidence of genetic differences of these kinds between populations is limited to such discrete but relatively rare genetic conditions of the nervous system as color blindness and infantile amaurotic idiocy **(Tay-Sachs disease).** The genes responsible for color blindness and infantile amaurotic idiocy occur with very different frequencies in different populations. This does not mean that the same would necessarily be true for the still unknown genes for minor variations in perception and cognition, however.

It is true, of course, that persons of different nationality, language, and religion may respond quite differently to the same event or circumstance. Nationality, language, and religion, however, are facets of culture that are learned by individuals. Within a cultural group exposed to similar cultural stimuli, psychologists may identify differences in mental capacity or temperament that are presumably innate, but, even within the same family, no two people have been subjected to *exactly* the same cultural learning experiences, and, between individuals of different culture, hence with different aspirations and habits of thought and speech, there is no satisfactory way to measure differences in innate intelligence. One can say, therefore, that all groups seem to have some bright and some dull individuals but that if group differences in innate capacity exist, they have not been demonstrated under conditions of identical or equivalent culture. Even with members of a Stone Age culture, the Australian aborigines, tests in which the importance of language is minimized show that when the unfamiliarity with the test situation is taken into account, the aborigines' response is generally little if at all inferior to that of Whites. In tests scored on speed or memory their performance is poor, presumably, at least in part, because the test conditions are not relevant to the aborigines' culture and experience.

Tests of American Blacks and Whites, such as the intelligence tests administered by the Army during the First World War, show many Blacks scoring higher than some Whites and some Blacks higher than most Whites, although Whites usually have a slightly higher average score. In view of the wide differences in educational opportunities, these scoring differences cannot be considered proof of an inherent difference. On the contrary, Klineberg (1935), in a series of studies of Black children born in the South but living in New York

City, showed that success in intelligence tests was greater the longer the children had been in New York. Klineberg also analyzed the school records of Blacks in the South and showed that those who later migrated did no better in school than those who stayed behind. Thus, the better scores of Northern than of Southern Blacks is not a matter of selection; young Blacks who later went North were no brighter than others who remained in the South. The higher scores on intelligence tests after migration thus reflect the changed circumstances of life. Furthermore, how would one account for the generally lower scores of Southern than Northern Whites if not on the basis of differences in opportunity to learn the kinds of skills that were rated in these tests?

One difficulty in refining behavioral genetics is that there are undoubtedly many different perceptual and intellectual traits and that genetically determined neurological structures determine them to different extents. Psychologists and geneticists have not yet been able adequately to define the units of behavioral genetics. When they do, some population differences are to be expected, but we have no assurance as to which populations will be better endowed than which others. Since most of the evolutionary history of all human groups has been lived under similar primitive conditions, specific adaptations of neurological functions to urban life may not have developed. The inherited capacities may not vary much between groups. The small differences that may be found could well be in favor of groups that only now are beginning to lead the life of the "advanced" nations.

A recent survey of studies of the weight of the brain and the size of its parts notes that although there are three studies of brains of Whites who died suddenly without prior disease, no such study exists for Blacks, and the brain weight of healthy Blacks is unknown (Tobias, 1970). A further conclusion is that there is no acceptable proof that the cortex (grey matter) of the brains of Blacks is thinner in whole or in any of its layers than that of the brains of Whites. There is thus no good anatomical evidence to form a basis for an inherent difference in mental capacities between Whites and Blacks.

A recent review of the literature on race differences in intelligence (Loehlin et al., 1975) surveys the various studies that have attempted to assess the genetic and nutritional components of intellectual abilities and the distribution of those abilities in children of different ethnic groups in the United States. Their conclusions are very limited and do not justify the dogmatic assertion of either racial or pure environmental determination of intelligence. They state (pp. 238–239):

> 1. Observed average differences in the scores of members of different U.S. racial-ethnic groups on intellectual-ability tests probably reflect in part inadequacies and biases in the tests themselves, in part differences in environmental conditions among the groups, and in part genetic differences among the groups. It should be emphasized that these three factors are not necessarily independent, and may interact.
>
> 2. A rather wide range of positions concerning the relative weight to be given these three factors can reasonably be taken on the basis of current evidence, and a

sensible person's position might well differ for different abilities, for different groups, and for different tests.

3. Regardless of the position taken on the relative importance of these three factors, it seems clear that the differences among individuals *within* racial-ethnic (and socioeconomic) groups greatly exceed in magnitude the average differences between such groups.

Let us emphasize that these conclusions are based on the conditions that have existed in the United States in the recent past. None of them precludes the possibility that changes in these conditions could alter these relationships for future populations. It should also be noted that the probable existence of relevant environmental differences, genetic differences, and psychometric biases does not imply that they must always be in the same direction as the observed between-group differences.

On the whole, these are rather limited conclusions. It does not appear to us, however, that the state of the scientific evidence at the present time justifies stronger ones.

If all individuals were the same there would be no need for equal opportunity or at least no profit to society from it. As Th. Dobzhansky has repeatedly emphasized, the function of equality of opportunity is precisely to take advantage of the existence of biological differences and to allow those with greater ability in particular ways to develop in those directions to the ultimate advantage of the whole polytypic species. Since the significant kinds of diversity may be related to diverse habitats and to diverse cultural adaptations to the environment, preservation of variation in environments and cultures as well as genetic diversity is potentially valuable to the species. Ecocide (destruction of habitats) and ethnocide (extermination of cultures) as well as genocide (killing of members of a racial group) decrease the variability—perhaps impossible to replace—on which future adaptation of the whole species depends.

## Summary

Some people have tried to classify individuals by their physical traits into types. Such typological races are poor biological tools because different characteristics are independently inherited and children may be of different types from their parents. The term "race" must be limited to a partially isolated population of a species which has a different combination of gene frequencies than other populations. Biological race must be kept distinct from "social race" ascriptions using biological terms but making sociocultural distinctions. Genetic, ecological, and historical analysis of specific biological characteristics is becoming relatively more important than racial studies in physical anthropology.

Differences in mentality and temperament exist among individuals, and by twin studies it can be shown that such differences are in part hereditary. Differences among groups in these respects exist, but so many culturally determined factors enter into the measurement of intelligence, for example, that it is not certain which racial groups, if any, are better endowed with inherited capacity. Since most of the evolutionary history of all human groups has been lived under similar primitive conditions, adaptation to those conditions on the part of different groups is probably similar. Urban life is so new in terms of biological evolution that differentiation of groups by reason of adaptation to the city would be expected to be slight. In any case, true equality of opportunity best utilizes the human variability that exists.

# CHAPTER 22

# PHYSICAL ANTHROPOLOGY AND THE FUTURE

The story of our changing place in nature has led us into several scientific asides. Nevertheless it has brought a partial answer to the question of the origin of the human species. We have seen the changing forms of our fossil ancestors and their collateral kinsmen achieving the traits that—later and further developed—made us human. More significant still, we have learned much about the nature of human evolution—the genetic processes by which such endowments have been transmitted and altered in the past and may be transmitted and altered in the future. We thus have a frame into which we can fit the picture manifest by fossils now known or still to be unearthed.

In establishing this framework we came at last to the question of race. Racial characteristics, it is clear, are any hereditary characteristics that vary in frequency from one group of people with common ancestry to another. Some such variations in traits may result from the fact that those traits are advantageous for life under only certain conditions (although this is usually difficult to establish) but other variations are more plausibly explained as the result of historical events unrelated to any such advantage. In any case, traits advantageous to members of a particular group today are the property of the whole human species tomorrow. There is enough interbreeding, at least between neighboring groups, for genetic endowments eventually to spread to all peoples who follow a way of life in which the traits would confer advantages for survival. The genetic diversity of the human species is thus clearly an asset for our descendants. Those who inherit our good points, and in whom someone else's good points are substituted for our bad, may naturally be chosen.

How does any of this fit in with humanity today and with predicting or planning for the future? I do not pretend that a physical anthropologist's view of these matters is more trustworthy than those of nonanthropologists, or that other physical anthropologists would see the prospects for the future the way I do. The value judgments involved in one's hopes for the future do not stem from science as such, although philosophy may be informed by science. However, the long view of human evolution as a fact and the theories of how the evolution has worked should influence views of the future. Our principal problems are in a sense unprecedented, however. If there were precedents there would also be well worked out responses, for cultural development like biological evolution has been adaptive.

To me the three principal threats to continued human existence are, in order of seriousness: (1) unrestricted world war; (2) the population explosion; and (3) pollution.

An unrestricted world war with nuclear weapons could conceivably be precipitated at any instant through simple miscalculation, or by someone having access to the button who regards some plausible eventuality as being "worse than death."

The population problem is a principal threat not because we shall be standing on each others' heads—the very principles enunciated by Malthus assure us that at some point deaths must rise to equal births. As that point approaches, however, some will say "fewer of *them*," pointing away, and the cry of *Lebensraum* will increase the peril of unrestricted war. The fuse of the population bomb is burning short. It used to be said that a fool is born every minute. That may be so, but today 150 or so infants are born every minute. That is, as many individuals are now born in a year as was the estimated world population at the beginning of the Neolithic period. And life expectancy has doubled or more, especially through the reduced mortality rates among infants, children, and young adults during the last two centuries. J. L. Angel (1947, 1969) has shown that in Greece, for example, even though the count of those who died before adulthood is probably underestimated for the earlier period, the estimated average length of life has doubled since the Byzantine era. Ascadi and Nemeskéri (1970) present data that show an expectation of life of 13 years in *Homo erectus*, 21 years in Upper Paleolithic peoples, and 25–35 years in Roman times. Dumond (1975) believes that the Upper Paleolithic deaths did not balance natural fecundity and that fertility control was regularly practiced until the prevalence of agriculture. In his view the population explosion was well under way long before the sharp decline in death rates at the beginning of the present century. In any case, in recent decades in all parts of the world the number of years in which the population doubles has become smaller and smaller until it now increases seven- or eightfold per century! It is heartening to note that recent surveys indicate that, in some areas at least, attitudes are now favorable for a move to halt the further growth of population (Barnett, 1970).

If, beginning now, all the people in the world would begin to practice zero population growth, the population of the world would still continue to grow for some time to come. This is so because zero population growth is usually taken to mean that the next generation will be no bigger than the present one, but there is an overlap between generations and the overlap is increasing. So long as the average length of life continues to increase, as it has done in all countries for the last two centuries, more individuals of our parent's generation will, so to speak, continue to live into our generation and into those of our children and grandchildren. Even if the generations are equal in numbers the average family will have more generations alive simultaneously and thus the world population will continue its growth. An increase in a population is simply more births and immigrants than deaths and emigrants. For the world as a whole immigration and emigration have no effect so only births and deaths count. Ultimately everyone dies so births and deaths will be equal, but for very long periods of time births can exceed deaths and that is what we have been experiencing.

Furthermore, even if the population were completely stable and birth rates and death rates equal, some findings of physical anthropology indicate that the food needs of the population would still increase greatly. That is because the average individual would be bigger and need more food. With the aid of a former student (Lasker and Womack, 1975) I made some rough calculations of the size and body composition of an average resident of the United States (to represent developed nations) and of an average Mexican (to represent developing nations). Whereas the population of Mexico is 24 percent of that of the United States, we estimated that the body weight of all Mexicans is only about 17 percent of that of the total U.S. population. The lean body mass (see p. 322) of all the people of Mexico is only about 18 percent of that of all the people of the U.S. The smaller size of the average Mexican is because a much higher proportion of Mexicans are children and also because members of each age and sex group in Mexico are smaller on average than those of the corresponding age and sex in the U.S. Since lean body mass is roughly proportional to metabolism and hence to food needs, if Mexicans were our age and size they would need over 30 percent more food even if there were no change in the size of either population. In Mexico the average length of life (hence average age) of individuals has been increasing and the average size for age has also, and with further improvement of economic conditions these trends will continue for some time to come (Fig. 20-5). Thereafter, a marked increase in the amount of food will be needed for Mexico (and for all other similar developing nations of the world) even if growth of population ceases completely. The extent is probably not as great as our crude estimates might suggest because children would be decreasing in relative numbers and, per unit of lean body mass, children need more calories in their diet than do adults. Furthermore, the difference in size between the adults of developing and developed nations is not likely to disappear; only part of the difference in size is a response to malnutrition and other effects of economic and health conditions that can be improved dramatically. Nevertheless, a spread of the U.S. standard of living will add very greatly to world food needs even if there is no further increase in numbers. The goal of an equitable world with ample to eat requires not zero population growth, but a rollback.

The third threat to our existence is pollution, which is still largely an unknown entity. It consists of a series of problems, all of them exacerbated by the growing density of the population. Perhaps when our ancestors acquired the use of fire and exposed themselves to its combustion products in their shelters they gradually became somewhat adapted, and we may have inherited a greater resistance to smoke pollution than would otherwise have been the case. Theoretical considerations suggest that within a few hundred years natural selection might make an appreciable difference. The examples of spread and then decline in sickle-cell hemoglobin, reduction in tooth size, depigmentation in high latitudes, and increase in color blindness suggest that selection pressures in man are felt within a few score generations. But the large number of forms of evironmental pressures from pollution today make it a biologically complex problem against which natural selection would take long periods of time to adapt. This is because an individual who carried a mutation toward hereditary ability to resist leukemia from ionizing radiation, for instance, would simultaneously be exposed to other agencies, such as hormone residues in meat or insecticide adhering to fruits, and it would be his greatest weakness, not his inherited resistance, that would determine his survival or death. Evolution can hardly work rapidly enough to meet the environmental problems at the rate we have been creating them. But we already have built-in resistances to various conditions from our wide range of diets and ways of life (including, for example, populations in dairying zones in which adults produce lactase to digest milk). This heritage from the past suggests that we will probably not pollute the whole species off the face of the earth in the next several generations—a length of time greater than that allowed us to solve the problems of overpopulation and war.

The solutions to all these problems, if they are to come, lie in the necessary social attitudes and political processes. Science (in part responsible through what it has made possible) will have to be called upon in seeking the solutions and scientists will have to be educated broadly enough in social concerns as well as in technology. But scientists as such are not alone responsible for deciding if the solutions will be implemented. It is my impression that scientists in general are prepared to accept their share of responsibility. In this, physical anthropology can play its small role by the perspective it obliges one to apply. Thus, physical anthropology's role is similar to that of history, whose accounts of revolutions temper the revolutionary, and whose accounts of martyrdom fortify the righteous. The evolutionary perspective gives us scale. We can envision what time will work. But the basic decisions will have to be those of the body politic and so the role of physical anthropology in this decision will be through general education.

There are not likely to be biological panaceas. Eugenics is the deliberate breeding of desirable qualities. The deliberate choice of mates, or the decision whether to reproduce or not, is a part of its concern. Eugenics so far has had little effect in eliminating hereditary diseases or otherwise modifying future generations. Some writers believe that its practice may be dehumanizing (Kass, 1971). In any case, in anthropological perspective we see the difficulty of knowing what traits are good and we see the good in diversity of traits—perhaps our present best hope of survival as a species.

At present the quantitative problem seems more imminently threatening than any biological qualitative one. A sense of responsibility for the future embodied in any system of social ethics must avert war and limit population. In 1961 I wrote: "Today the effects of planned parenthood in such countries as the United States seem to be to bring the number of offspring of families close to a generally accepted idea of a normal family (one with three or four children). Furthermore, although some parents of offspring with hereditary (usually recessive) defects show reproductive restraint, others tend to compensate for births of defective children by deciding to have further children." Already the norm (the number of children people think it would be good to have) is dropping toward one compatible with zero population growth (2.2 per couple) and, in addition to family planning, the need is seen for policies concerning marriage, birth control, abortion, adoption, economic or other rewards for family limitation, and so on. The purpose would be to encourage attitudes and acts leading to reproductive restraint.

It should be recognized, however, that some past social arrangements led to unequal numbers of offspring for different individuals: for example, under a system of polygamy some men had many wives and children, other men none (Neel, 1970). To the extent that these inequalities were associated with any hereditary factors they created conditions for rapid evolution. Population policies that encouraged not only small but equally small families would tend to minimize opportunities for further evolutionary changes in the species. A population policy aimed only at reproducing "the best" might also tend to reduce variability. For example, the spread of artificial insemination and even possibly "cloning" (reproduction of individuals from cell nuclei without sexual reproduction and **meiosis**) could lead to large numbers of similar or identical individuals and loss of human variability. Thus, long-run population policy will best aim at zero growth or even a rollback in numbers but not at an equal number of surviving offspring per individual (perhaps by favoring an equal number of births rather than an equal number of surviving offspring per couple). The variable rate of survival would, of course, permit some play of natural selection along the many unknown directions of human adaptation. A voluntary planned parenthood policy that, at present, does little to discourage parents of genetically defective children from having further offspring who may have the same defect can be replaced by one using methods of prenatal diagnosis already known in order to permit elective abortion of certain kinds of defective embryos. The choice by parents of children with hereditary diseases to have further offspring involves not only purely private risks for the family but also involves the risk of huge social costs to the community.

Neel (1970) refers not only to the problems of numbers and of genetic disease; he also adds two others: increased mutation rates and the creation of an environment in which various genotypes can find harmonious expression. He cites the need for protection against damage to the gene pool from radiation and also from known or still unknown mutagenic agents that are inserted into our food, air, and water. He estimates that artificial radiation alone now adds from 500 to 1,000 defective infants (with all the tragedy this implies) for every million births in the United States.

The search for harmonious environments in which individuals of varying genetic potential can live their lives together in happiness, however defined, is beyond the scope of this work. It is not beyond the responsibility of every student, however, and such humanistic goals can be reasonably set only on the basis of knowledge of the nature of man, the facts of his past and present evolution, and his potentialities and prospects for the future. The biological value of biological variety is paralleled by the comparable value of cultural variety.

The status of the human species in its changing environment seems to me not greatly different from the way I saw it in 1961. I wrote then:

> There is no assurance of human "progress." The impact of human activities which can release toxic substances and radiation into the air we breathe and the food we eat, may outstrip natural or deliberate selection. Natural history, too, imposes new conditions: Changes in the animals, plants, things, and climate that surround us. And man goes on changing his relationship to his environment. The world is rapidly becoming one in which the immediate surroundings and resources are losing the direct influence they have had on human evolution through the selective process man shares with the animal world. Not only is more of the environment man-made, but the local environment becomes almost inconsequential for continued human evolution as man's world becomes more mobile and his larger environment makes new demands on body and mind. This calls for a high degree of plasticity in responding to different natural and artificially produced conditions. Space travel and living on other planets may add another dimension to the environment in which man must be able to function in order to survive. At least he must leave his offspring equipped with the essential capacities for effective mastery of the total environment.

This account of human evolution has covered great spans of time through analysis of the fossil primates. Emphasis has also been given to the evolution that is going on in us today. But whether through the long-term changes seen in the fossil record or through the short-term changes of population genetics, the key to understanding evolution in the future lies in an analysis of the processes involved. Whatever you think of past evolution, you had best be aware of its present potentiality.

Furthermore, in such a time as ours, progress along the established lines however great it has been in the recent past, cannot be held to meet the need for new knowledge. There is needed also a new vigor in approach to both old and new problems. The best evidence that physical anthropology possesses this vigor, lies in the uncompromising directness with which so many of its practitioners are attacking complex problems. Without abandoning the rigor of proven methods, or the painful accumulation of detailed additions to knowledge that has been so fruitful in the past, they are willing to re-examine the concepts that may no longer suffice to explain the multitude of collected data, and to explore new hypotheses—sometimes suggested by an excursion into the realm of an allied scientific discipline—that would account for a wider range of facts. They are creating a theoretical basis of physical anthropology in close harmony with the now rapidly changing conceptual structure of the universe and of man's place in it.

In physical anthropology there are branches in which, as has been shown, general theory and methodology are sufficiently far advanced to permit considerable specialization, both in further research and in application to such problems as the epidemiology of specific diseases. The greatest need and the greatest opportunity for the development of the science is to be found, however, in the search for comprehensive understandings: of the origin of the human species, of its responses to the environment, and of its great variability and evolutionary potential.

# GLOSSARY

ABIOGENETIC   Possessing the property of originating from substances that are neither living nor the products of living things.

ACCLIMITIZATION   Modifications in physiological function in response to climatic conditions. Reversible changes adapting individuals to the immediate environment.

ACHONDROPLASTIC DWARFISM   A type of dwarfism involving short limbs and inherited as a *dominant.**

ADAPTATION   Adjustment to the prevailing environmental conditions: *1*, by responding to the immediate circumstances; *2*, by developing appropriately under the influence of environmental factors; or *3*, by *natural selection* of adapted individuals.

*AEGYPTOPITHECUS*   The "Egyptian ape," which lived about 29 million years ago and may have been close to the common ancestor of the great apes and man.

---

*Terms given in italics are cross-references to other concepts in the glossary.

AGGLUTINATION    Clumping of red blood cells by an *antibody* reacting with *antigen* on their surface.

AGONISTIC DISPLAY    An animal's gesture of threat. Among primates, communication of intention to attack usually leads to appropriate submissive behavior, which aborts the overt aggression and prevents fighting.

ALBINISM    Lack of ability to synthesize melanin pigment in skin and hair. Albinism is a *recessive* genetic condition.

ALBUMIN    The most abundant protein in blood serum. Some albumin variants are *polymorphic* in American Indians.

ALLELE    Any of several *genes* determining alternative characteristics. Alleles occupy the same *locus* on *homologous chromosomes.*

ALLEN'S RULE    Cold-adapted animals tend to have short extremities because, of two animals of the same size, the one with short extremities has less surface area for dissipation of body heat.

AMINO ACIDS    The building blocks of proteins. The 20 which are essential for building proteins (see Fig. 4-9) are aligned in various sequences in peptide chains.

ANAGENESIS    Evolutionary changes within a single thread or line in which a single *species* succeeds a single ancestral species.

ANALOGOUS    Having the same function but different evolutionary and developmental origins. The wings of birds and insects are analogous.

ANAPHASE    Stage of cell division in which the *centromere* of each *chromosome* divides longitudinally, thus completely separating the two *chromatids* from each other. The chromatids move under the influence of the spindle fibers toward opposite poles of the cell. Upon completion of the anaphase stage, a complete set of chromatids lies at one pole of the cell and an identical set at the other.

ANEMIA    A disease of deficient capacity to transport oxygen in the *hemoglobin* of red blood cells. See *G6PD deficiency, sickle-cell trait,* and *thalassemia.*

ANTHROPOIDEA    The suborder of the *primates* that includes the monkeys, apes, and human beings. The Anthropoidea are divided into the *Platyrrhini* or *Ceboidea* (New World monkeys) and the *Catarrhini* (Old World monkeys, apes, and hominids).

ANTHROPOMETRY    The techniques for measuring human beings.

ANTIBODY    A serum protein that reacts with foreign proteins.

ANTIGEN    A substance, usually protein, which, when introduced into the body of a vertebrate, stimulates production of antibodies to it.

APE   A member of the Pongidae, the family of mammals most closely related to the human family.

ARBOREAL   Living in trees.

ASSORTATIVE MATING   Preferential selection of a mate with a particular *genotype*. Preference for a mate of the same genotype is "positive assortative mating"; preference for a spouse of a different genotype is "negative assortative mating."

ATAVISM   A throwback to an extinct *phenotype*. There are no true atavisms in evolution, since evolution is irreversible, except for an occasional reverse mutation or the re-emergence of *recessively* inherited traits.

*AUSTRALOPITHECUS*   An extinct *genus* (often divided into two or more species) of *Hominidae* (the human family) of the *Pleistocene* and *Pliocene* epochs. It gave rise to the human genus. Some specimens are considerably more robust than others; however, the validity of all but the one species, *Australopithecus africanus,* remains to be demonstrated.

AUTOSOME   A *chromosome* other than a sex chromosome.

BACTERIOPHAGE   A virus that is a parasite of bacteria and causes their lysis (dissolution).

BERGMANN'S RULE   Cold-adapted animals tend to be large because, of two animals of the same shape, the larger has relatively less surface area for dissipation of heat relative to its mass.

BIPEDALISM   Two-legged locomotion.

BLOOD GROUPS   Blood *polymorphisms,* characterized by different *antigens* on the surface of red blood cells, and demonstrated by *agglutination* of the red cells by *antisera.*

BRACHIATION   Locomotion by hand-over-hand swinging suspended by the arms; a mode of locomotion of the gibbon and, to a lesser extent, the chimpanzee.

BRACHYCEPHALIC   Having a head width 80 percent or more of the head length. Hence having a *cephalic index* of 80 or above.

BREEDING POPULATION   A group of adults that share potential descendants and among whom mates are found.

BRUNHES NORMAL EPOCH   The present period of normal polarity of the earth. It began about .69 million years ago, at the beginning of the Middle *Pleistocene.*

CANINE   The eyetooth. In monkeys and apes the canine teeth (one in each quadrant) are usually large and project beyond other teeth in the row. In *Homo* they are much reduced.

CARBON-14 METHOD    A method for dating organic material by measuring the extent to which it has lost the radioactive *isotope* carbon-14 by transformation into carbon-12.

CARNIVORES    In general, animals that live on meat, but in zoology an order of mammals that includes the cats, dogs, and bears.

CARRIER    A person who is *heterozygous* for an abnormal *gene* and its normal *allele,* but who appears normal.

CATARRHINI    The Old World monkeys, apes, and hominids.

CEBOIDEA    The New World monkeys; also known as the *Platyrrhini.*

CENOZOIC ERA    The last 63–66 million years or so: the Age of Mammals. It is divided into the following 7 epochs: *Paleocene, Eocene, Oligocene, Miocene, Pliocene, Pleistocene,* and Recent.

CENTROMERE    The point of attachment of two *chromatids* to each other and of the whole *chromosome* to the spindle structure.

CEPHALIC INDEX    $\dfrac{100 \times \text{head breadth}}{\text{head length}}$

CHELLES-ACHEUL    A tradition of stone toolmaking beginning perhaps as many as 1.4 million years ago in Africa and characteristic of the Middle *Pleistocene* of Africa, Europe, and Western Asia. The characteristic types of tool (called "hand-axes") were made by knocking chips off both sides.

CHIASMA (*pl.:* CHIASMATA)    Connecting point along the length of a bivalent *chromosome.* These points at which the two *homologues* are held together are the points at which exchange of genetic material or *crossing-over* has occurred during *meiosis,* and are known as *chiasmata.* The number of chiasmata is generally proportional to the length of the chromosomes, but there are exceptions. The chiasmata in most species begin a movement, tending to reduce their number, which consists of their displacement along the length of the chromosomes from the *centromere* toward the ends. This displacement of the chiasmata is called terminalization.

CHROMATID    Each of the two identical strands into which the arms of a *chromosome* divide.

CHROMOSOMES    Rod-like bodies in the *nucleus* of a cell which contain the *DNA* responsible for inheritance. Each chromosome consists of two long, thin, parallel strands *(chromatids)* connected at the *centromere.* During *meiosis* pairs of *homologous chromosomes* come together and parts may cross at *chiasmata* and replace the corresponding part of the sister chromosome.

CINGULUM    A horizontal ridge of enamel near the gum line of some teeth. It is a feature of some primitive primate teeth.

CLADOGENESIS Evolution in which multiple forms derive from common ancestors—branching like a candelabrum or a tree. Compare *anagenesis*.

CLAVICLE Collar bone.

CLINE A slope. Within a species the progressive change in the frequency of a biological characteristic in geographically successive places. Used chiefly of a gradient in *gene* frequencies.

CODON A *triplet* of three sequential base pairs in a *DNA* or *RNA* molecule that determines a specific *amino acid* at a specific locus in a peptide chain.

COEFFICIENT OF INBREEDING *(F)* The probability that an individual has received both *genes* of a homologous pair from an identical ancestral source; the average of such probabilities in a population.

COLOR BLINDNESS Inherited inability (or difficulty) in distinguishing colors. The most common form is an inability to distinguish between red and green. Because it is caused by one of several *sex-linked recessive* genes, color blindness is much more common in males than in females.

COMPENSATION The antomical principle that if one structure is abnormally small its function will be assumed by enlargement of another structure.

CONCORDANCE The presence of the same trait in both of a pair of individuals (especially twins).

CONVERGENCE Evolution of similar *adaptations* in unrelated organisms.

CORRELATION The extent to which two measurements vary together. Association of the two measurements is positive correlation. Dissociation is negative correlation. The coefficient of correlation measures the degree of covariation on a scale from $-1$ to $+1$, with 0 indicating no correlation.

CRANIAL CAPACITY The volume of the skull, hence that of the brain plus other contained structures. It is usually measured by the amount of water or other substance it takes to fill the skull.

CROSSING OVER The exchange of genetic information between *homologous chromosomes* by means of *chiasmata* formed during cell division.

CULTURE The amassing of experience through use of symbolic language, and the products of this uniquely human activity.

CUSP A point or projection on the biting face of a tooth.

CYTOPLASM The cellular substance outside the cell *nucleus*. It contains *ribosomes*, tiny *organelles* on which protein synthesis takes place.

DENDROGRAM Evolutionary tree showing *phylogenetic* branching.

DERMATOGLYPHICS The patterns of the ridges on the skin of the fingers, palms, toes, and soles.

DIABETES    More correctly diabetes mellitus, a disease of sugar *metabolism* caused by inability of the body to synthesize adequate amounts of a hormone, insulin. Diabetes is now customarily treated by administering insulin.

DIASTEMA    A gap between two adjacent teeth, especially the space between the upper lateral *incisor* and the upper *canine* teeth, which interlocks with the lower canine tooth of most monkeys and apes.

DIFFERENTIATION    The process in *embryological* development by which tissues come to differ from each other in characteristic ways. It occurs because daughter cells may acquire new properties.

DISCORDANCE    The posession by one member of a pair of individuals (especially twins) of a certain trait that the other member of the pair does not possess.

DIZYGOTIC (FRATERNAL) TWINS    Twins who are formed from two ova separately fertilized, hence as different genetically from each other as other pairs of *siblings*.

DJETIS BEDS    Early *Pleistocene* deposits in Java in which robust specimens of Java *Homo erectus,* the Modjokerto child's skull, and the "Meganthropus" mandible were found. One place in the bed has been dated at 1.9 million years ago by the postassium-argon method.

DNA    Deoxyribonucleic acid. The principle genetic material. The molecule of DNA is a long loop that forms a double spiral, with sugar (ribose) on the outside and bonds between pairs of bases on the inside. The order of the bases determines the genetic message.

DOLICHOCEPHALIC    Having a head width less than 75 percent of the head length. Hence having a *cephalic index* below 75.

DOMINANCE    A tendency in certain animals, such as the macaques, to social ranking. Fighting and threats lead to priorities in access to food or space that are recognized within the group but are, of course, subject to change in time. Also, in Mendelian genetics, *alleles* that are expressed in the phenotypes of *heterozygous* individuals. When two or more alleles are so expressed they are called co-dominant.

*DRYOPITHECUS*    A genus of *Miocene* and *Pliocene* fossil *Hominoidea* ancestral to the African great apes and perhaps also to the orangutan and to the *hominids*. Specimens have been found in China, India, Europe, and Africa. Also the characteristic pattern of lower molar teeth of this genus and of other Hominoidea.

ECOCIDE    The destruction of environments.

ECOLOGICAL NICHE    A way of life of an *organism* in a particular habitat. Also, the characteristics of the habitat that permit a particular kind of life within it and thus select against other adaptations, channelize evolution, and define the terms of competition for survival.

ECTOTHERMIC   Cold-blooded, so that the body temperature varies with the temperature of the outside environment. Fish, amphibia, and reptiles are, in general, ectothermic.

EMBRYO   The developing individual during the first part of gestation (about the first eight weeks).

EMBRYOLOGY   The study of *embryos* and *fetuses*. The biology of development up to the time of birth.

ENCEPHALIZATION   The evolutionary trend towards having a large, functionally complex brain.

ENDOGAMY   Marriage within the social group.

ENDOTHERMIC   Warm-blooded, so that the body temperature is different from that of the environment and is controlled internally by the animal's physiology. All mammals and birds are more or less endothermic. Endothermy first evolved in some dinosaurs.

ENZYME   A substance within or secreted by cells that serves to catalyze a biochemical reaction.

EOCENE   The second epoch of the *Cenozoic Era,* during which *prosimian* primates underwent much of their adaptive *radiation*. Approximately 37–38 to 53–54 million years ago.

ERYTHROBLASTOSIS FETALIS   Hemolytic disease of the newborn: *anemia* of the newborn infant resulting from immunization of the mother to the red cell *antigens* of her fetus. The immune *antibodies* formed by the mother cross the *placenta* and destroy the fetal red cells carrying the specific antigen.

ETHNIC GROUP   Those people who share the same culture.

ETHOLOGY   The scientific study of animal behavior.

EUGENICS   The effort to improve the human species by deliberate breeding (positive eugenics) or by discouraging breeding (negative eugenics) of different *genotypes*.

EUTHERIAN MAMMALS   Those mammals that produce a *placenta* for attachment of the *embryo* to its mother.

EVOLUTION   A continuous change over generations in frequencies of genetically determined characteristics.

EXOGAMY   Mating with a person who is not a member of the same social group; the opposite of *endogamy*.

FAUNA   The animal life of a particular time and area.

FAVISM   A disease (an *anemia*) caused by the reaction of some individuals with *G6PD deficiency* to the broad bean ("fava" in Italian).

FEMUR   The thighbone, the longest bone of the human body. It is a major component of body height, and its length is often used in estimating stature from the skeleton.

FERTILITY   The number of offspring produced (in contrast to "fecundity," the capacity to produce offspring). Birth rates measure fertility.

FETUS   The developing individual during the later part of gestation, from about the eighth week of pregnancy until birth.

FIBULA   The long thin bone on the lateral aspect of the leg.

FINGERPRINT   A method for running electrophoresis and chromatography in two dimensions to separate the components of a protein such as *hemoglobin;* also, of course, *dermatoglyphics* on the fingers.

FITNESS   In *natural selection,* the ability to have offspring who survive to reproduce. Darwinian fitness has no necessary connection with being in good condition, so-called physical fitness.

FORAMEN (*pl.:* FORAMINA)   Natural perforation through a bone, usually for the transmission of a nerve or blood vessel. **Foramen magnum:** large foramen at the base of the skull for transmission of the spinal cord. **Mental foramen:** foramen near the chin *(menton).*

FOSSILS   Remains of *organisms* of past ages.

FOUNDER EFFECT   When new *breeding populations* are established by the fission of old ones there is a tendency for the number of founders to be small and unrepresentative of the old in genetic endowment. This is a special case of *random genetic drift* caused by the fact that new populations are often established by closely related individuals.

G6PD DEFICIENCY   Glucose-6-phosphate dehydrogenase deficiency. A deficiency of a red blood cell enzyme. The deficiency is caused by a sex-linked *recessive gene.* Deficient individuals react in specific ways to certain drugs and other substances. The deficiency may cause *anemia* but is thought also to give an individual some degree of resistance to malaria.

GAMETE   Germ cell; sperm or unfertilized ovum. These cells, since they are the product of *meiosis,* contain only one of each pair of *chromosomes.*

GAMMA GLOBULIN   A class of blood serum proteins characterized by slow or negative electrophoretic migration. The immunoglobulins *(antibody* proteins) are among them.

GENE   The unit of inheritance. The inherited material responsible for the nature of a morphological or functional trait.

GENE FLOW   Change in *allele* frequency in a population, caused by immigration and intermating.

GENE POOL   All the genes of all members of the population. In a more restricted sense: in a population, all the *alleles* at a particular *locus*.

GENERALIZED   Of a trait, capable of use in several ways (such as both fine manipulations and power grasping of human hands) or capable of evolving for use in different ways (such as the five-fingered hand of earliest vertebrates). Opposite of *specialized*.

GENETIC CODE   The system by which *triplets* of three sequential bases in *DNA* or *RNA* determine which *amino acid* will be laid down in a *polypeptide* chain. Also, certain "three-letter words" or *codons* initiate or terminate syntheses.

GENETIC DRIFT, RANDOM   Changes in *allele* frequency in a population caused by chance variations from generation to generation. The effect is greater in proportion to the smallness and isolation of the population.

GENOTYPE   The genetic constitution of an individual in respect to the *alleles* at one *locus*. Also, by extension, the genetic constitution in its entirety.

GENUS *(pl.: GENERA)*   A subdivision of a biological family. A group of related *species*.

GERONTOMORPHIC   Having the form or features of old age. The opposite of *pedomorphic*.

*GIGANTOPITHECUS*   A genus of fossil pongid of the *Pliocene* of India and the *Pleistocene* of China, known from huge jaws and teeth. It has some more-or-less human features.

GLOBULIN   Blood plasma protein.

HABITAT   The kind of environment in which a species of animal lives.

HALF LIFE   The time it takes for half of one *isotope* to become another.

HAPTOGLOBIN   A serum protein that combines with *hemoglobin*. There are *polymorphic* haptoglobins in some populations, including a variant, ahaptoglobinemia, that results in the total lack of observable haptoglobin.

HARDY-WEINBERG LAW   The principle that, under *random mating,* the frequencies of the *genotypes* will achieve and maintain equilibrium at the values of the square of the sum of the gene frequencies: gene frequencies $p + q$ yield genotype frequencies $p^2 + 2pq + q^2$.

HEMOGLOBIN   An iron-containing protein of the red blood cells that enables them to transport oxygen from the lungs to the body tissues. Hemoglobin consists of four *polypeptide* chains of several principal varieties.

HEREDITABILITY *(H)*   The extent to which some characteristic (usually a quantitative one determined by many genes) is inherited. One measure is the variance in dizygous twins *(dz)* less that in monozygous twins *(mz)*, $(H^2 = dz^2 - mz^2)$

HETEROZYGOUS (HETEROZYGOTIC)   Having different *alleses* at a given *locus* on two *homologous chromosomes*.

HOMINID   Pertaining to the human family, Hominidae, which includes the genera *Australopithecus* and *Homo*. A member of our taxonomic family.

HOMINOID   Pertaining to the Primate superfamily Hominoidea, which includes the gibbons (Hylobatidae), great apes (Pongidae), and the *hominids* (Hominidae).

*HOMO*   The zoological genus to which human beings belong.

*HOMO ERECTUS*   A fossil species of the human *genus* characterized by supraorbital and *occipital tori,* low and small brain case, and other features. The species prevailed in Java, China, Africa, and probably Europe. It lasted for most of the last million years.

"HOMO HABILIS"   A term applied to certain *hominid* fossils from Olduvai Gorge that are believed by some to consitute a distinct *species* of the genus *Homo*. Others class the pre-Zinj specimen as *Australopithecus* and the later specimens as *Homo erectus*.

HOMOLOGOUS   Having the same developmental or evolutionary origin.

HOMOLOGOUS CHROMOSOMES   Chromosomes that are paired in the sex cell during *meiosis,* and that participate in *crossing over.*

*HOMO SAPIENS NEANDERTHALENSIS*   A subspecies of the modern human species that lived from about 70 to about 35 thousand years ago. It is characterized by large brow ridges and other special features. Like all subspecies, the decision as to which *fossil* specimens are subsumed within it is rather arbitrary.

*HOMO SAPIENS SAPIENS*   The present human subspecies.

HOMOPLASY   Similarity in appearance but not in origin.

HOMOZYGOUS (HOMOZYGOTIC)   Having the same *alleles* at the corresponding *loci* of a pair of *homologous chromosomes.*

HYBRID   Progeny whose parents are of two different *species* or of two different inbred lines. It is sometimes inaccurately used to describe human offspring of parents from different subpopulations.

HYPERCALORIC DIETS   Diets containing too many calories; in contrast to hypocaloric (starvation) diets.

ILIUM   The superior part of the *pelvis*. The iliac crest is the bony part one can feel at one's side just below the waist.

IMMUNIZATION   The production of *antibodies* by the introduction of foreign *antigens* by blood transfusion, pregnancy, or injection.

INBREEDING   See *coefficient of inbreeding*.

INCEST   Mating with close relatives.

INCISOR   A front tooth. In monkeys, apes, and human beings there are normally four upper and four lower more-or-less chisel-shaped incisors.

INSECTIVORES   An order of insect-eating placental mammals that evolved early and is very diverse today. It includes the hedgehogs and the shrews.

INTERGLACIAL PERIODS   The periods between major glacial advances during the *Pleistocene epoch*. These fluctuations are now known to have been less discrete than was formerly thought; there were numerous minor fluctuations in climate.

INTERPHASE   The "resting stage" of *mitosis* or *meiosis*. The condition in which the cell is found before beginning division and to which it returns after division is completed.

ISCHIAL CALLOSITIES   In certain monkeys and apes, the hardened skin covering the ischial tuberosities.

ISCHIAL TUBEROSITY   Each of the pair of bony parts of the *pelvis* on which one sits.

ISOLATE   A subgroup that does not mate with outsiders. Human isolates are usually small populations bound together by religion or other cultural factors, in which almost all marriages are between members.

ISOTOPE   One of several forms of the atom of an element that has a different atomic weight. Isotopes are designated by their mass numbers, such as carbon 12 ($^{12}$C) and carbon 14 ($^{14}$C).

KARYOTYPE   The *chromosomes* of an individual cell cut out from a microphotograph and displayed according to size and other characteristics.

KNUCKLE WALKING   Quadrupedal locomotion in which the hand is used as a fist and the metacarpal bones transmit the weight. Chimpanzees, gorillas, and, rarely, orangutans walk in this way.

LIFE   The possession of the abilities to grow, reproduce and evolve, *metabolize* and excrete.

LINEAGE   An evolutionary line of ancestors and descendants.

LINES OF ARRESTED GROWTH    Discs of denser bone that are formed in long bones during periods when growth has been slowed by malnutrition or disease. They can be seen as lines in an X-ray.

LINKED GENES    Two genes near to each other on the same *chromosome* are said to be linked, since they are inherited together unless separated by *crossing over*.

LOAD OF MUTATIONS (GENETIC LOAD)    The frequency of harmful *genes* in the population (usually recessive genes in *heterozygous genotypes*).

LOCUS    The position a *gene* occupies on a *chromosome*. The area of a chromosome within which different genes are *alleles*.

MALOCCLUSION    Failure of lower and upper teeth to interlock in a regular way. Malocclusions are especially frequent in recent *Homo sapiens sapiens*. They are more frequent in domestic animals than in wild ones.

MANDIBLE    The lower jaw bone.

MARSUPIALS    A subclass of mammals in which the young are born at an early stage of development and then spend a period of time in a pouch in the mother's abdomen, where they can suckle and develop further. Opossums and kangaroos are marsupials.

MASTOID PROCESS    A bony protuberance of the skull behind the ear. It contains air cells and it gives attachment to the sternomastoid muscle (important in balancing and turning the head).

MATURITY INDICATORS    Detailed traits of ossifying bones that mark the stages of development of the skeleton.

MATUYAMA REVERSAL EPOCH    A period of reversed polarity of the Earth extending from about 2.43 to about .69 million years ago.

MAXILLA    The upper jaw bone.

"MEGANTHROPUS"    A fossil mandible from Java that is similar to the Pre-zinj mandible from Olduvai Gorge in Africa.

MEIOSIS    A process of cell division similar to *mitosis*, but in which the number of *chromosomes* per cell is halved by loss of one of each *homologous* pair. It consists of two divisions of the nucleus: the first is a reduction division and the second is essentially the same as a mitotic division. The end result is the formation of sex cells *(gametes)*: sperm in males and ova in females.

MENARCHE    The onset of menstruation. Age at menarche is an index of the state of development.

MENDELIAN POPULATION    See *Breeding population*.

MESOLITHIC   The middle stone age. A brief transitional period of prehistory between the *Paleolithic* and the *Neolithic*.

METABOLISM   Storage and release of energy by cells.

METAPHASE   Stage of cell division in which the *chromosomes* lie in the equatorial plane of the cell between the two opposed halves of the spindle.

MICROEVOLUTION   Changes in gene frequencies within a *breeding* or *Mendelian population* from generation to generation.

MIOCENE   The fourth epoch of the *Cenozoic,* approximately 7–26 million years ago.

MITOSIS   Cell division into two daughter cells, each with *chromosomes* identical to those of the parent cell. The stages are *interphase, prophase, metaphase, anaphase,* and *telophase.*

MOLAR   Cheek tooth. These are the grinding teeth. In most monkeys and apes they constitute the last three teeth on each side of each jaw. The same is true of human beings, but the third molars (wisdom teeth) are sometimes lacking.

MONGOLOID   A term applied to peoples of the Far East and to Amerindians because of certain traits that are frequent or ubiquitous among them.

MONOTREME   A mammal that lays eggs. The duckbill platypus and the spiny anteater are the only Monotremes surviving today.

MONOZYGOTIC (IDENTICAL) TWINS   Twins formed from a single fertilized ovum.

MUTAGEN   Any substance or force that increases the *mutation rate.*

MUTATION   Changes in the nature of single *genes,* or segments of *chromosomes,* which are then passed on from cell to cell. Refers to totally new genetic manifestations not received from antecedents, but which can be passed on to descendants.

MUTATION RATE   The rate at which *mutations* occur at a given *locus.*

NATURAL SELECTION   Selection that takes place naturally, without intention or control by any outside agency. The process in which some organisms have inherited characteristics that better equip them to leave more offspring.

NEOLITHIC   The new stone age. The prehistoric period extending from the beginnings of agriculture, animal husbandry, and use of pottery until the introduction of metal working.

NORMALIZING SELECTION   *Natural selection* against extremes. This kind of natural selection selects against those that differ greatly from their parents. Some deviants fail to survive or reproduce their kind, thus slowing evolutionary change.

NUCLEUS (*pl.:* NUCLEI)    A central structure in most cells. It contains the *chromosomes.*

OCCIPITAL    Pertaining to the bone of the skull at the back and part of the base of the brain case.

ODONTOLOGY    The study of teeth.

OLDUVAI EVENT    A normal event interrupting the *Matuyama Reversal* of the magnetic polarity of the earth. The Olduvai Event occurred between 1.6 and 1.9 million years ago. Since this was a worldwide event some anthropologists use its onset to define the boundary between *Pliocene* and *Pleistocene* Epochs.

OLIGOCENE    The third epoch of the *Cenozoic,* about 26 to 37–38 million years ago, during which the principal adaptive radiation of the *Anthropoidea* seems to have occurred. Our knowledge of this is largely derived from a single locale, the Egyptian Fayum.

ORBIT    Bony eye socket.

*OREOPITHECUS*    The so-called fossil swamp-ape from Tuscany, Italy. Whether it is properly a member of the human family, of the ape family, or of a family of its own is under dispute.

ORGANELLES    Structures within cells, having characteristic forms and functions. One type of organelle is the *ribosome,* on which proteins are synthesized.

ORGANISM    An individual possessing *life.*

ORTHOGENESIS    The idea that some force drives *evolution* in a straight line. No such force exists within organisms, however, and orthogenesis is discredited except to the extent that there may be long-range trends in the environment to which the organism continues to *adapt (orthoselection).*

ORTHOSELECTION    *Natural selection* in a straight line caused by a gradual change in the environment in a consistent direction.

OSTEOLOGY    The study of bones.

PALEOLITHIC    The old stone age. It is usually divided into three major parts: Lower, Middle and (most recent) Upper. Stone tool types of the Lower Paleolithic include pebble tools, *Chelles-Acheul* so-called "hand-axes" and the flake tools that accompanied them, and Tayacian points and flakes. The Middle Paleolithic comprises principally the Mousterian Industry (the tool types found with Neanderthals). The Upper Paleolithic had many types of industry and numerous kinds of stone, bone, and antler tools, all associated only with *Homo sapiens sapiens.*

PALEONTOLOGY    The study of living forms of the past, hence, especially, the study of *fossils.*

PALEOCENE   The first epoch of the *Cenozoic,* approximately 54–59 to 63–66 million years ago.

PARALLELISM   Similar course in two evolutionary lines after their divergence from earlier common ancestors.

PEDIGREE   Graphic representation of the occurrence of a genetic characteristic in a family.

PEDOMORPHIC   Having features in the adult like those of a child (such as open cranial *sutures*).

PELVIS   The hip bones and the sacrum. The part of the skeleton that transmits the weight of the body from the vertebral column to the thigh bones. In females, it contains the birth canal.

PENETRANCE   The frequency with which a *gene* is expressed in the *phenotype.* When a *genotype* is expressed in less than 100 percent of the cases the trait exhibits reduced penetrance.

PHAGE   Short for *bacteriophage,* a virus that infects bacteria.

PHENOTYPE   The visible, measurable, or testable characteristics of an individual, determined by both *genotype* and environment.

PHYLOGENY   Line of evolutionary descent.

PHYLUM *(pl.:* PHYLA)   A subdivision of an organic kingdom. The phylum Chordata consists of the animals with a notocord at the back and brain in the head.

PLACENTA   An outgrowth from the mammalian *embryo* that attaches to the wall of the mother's uterus and provides for absorption of food, supply of oxygen, and dissipation of waste.

PLASTICITY   Ability of the individual to be adaptively modified by response to the environment during growth.

PLATYRRHINI   The New World monkeys; also known as the *Ceboidea.*

PLEISTOCENE   The last epoch of the *Cenozoic.* A geologic epoch of cool climates that started about 1.9 million years ago, and ended with the retreat of the last glaciation about 11,000 years ago.

PLIOCENE   The geologic epoch of the *Cenozoic* that preceded the *Pleistocene.* There are few fossil deposits and the epoch may have been of shorter duration than approximately 2 to 7 million years ago, the span usually assumed.

POINT MUTATION   A genetic change resulting from modification of a single *locus,* or *codon* (assumed to be a specific triplet in the *DNA*) of a *chromosome.*

POLYMORPHISM   The occurrence of an *allelic gene* in at least 10 percent of some populations. A genetic variant occurring at too high a frequency for occurrence to be explained by repeated *mutation* or *random genetic drift.*

POLYPEPTIDE    A chain of *amino acids* held together by peptide bonds. Protein molecules are composed of one or more polypeptide chains.

POLYSOME    In the cytoplasm of a cell, a *ribosome* plus attached messenger *RNA;* this unit determines the nature of the protein peptide that is being synthesized.

POLYTYPIC SPECIES    *Species* that contain different varieties and vary from place to place. *Homo sapiens* is polytypic.

POPULATION    See *Breeding population* and *Mendelian population.*

POTASSIUM-ARGON DATING    Some volcanic rocks can be dated by the proportion of a certain *isotope* of argon that has been formed in the period since the rock was molten.

PREMOLAR    A tooth between the *canine* and *molars* in the row. In New World monkeys there are normally three in each quadrant, in Old World monkeys and apes and in humans there are normally two. In humans they have two *cusps* and are also called "bicuspids."

PRIMATE    A member of the order of mammals to which we, the apes, monkeys, tarsiers, and lemurs belong.

PROGNATHISM    Forward jut of the jaws and anterior teeth.

PROPHASE    First stage of *mitosis* (following *interphase*) during which the threads seen in the *nuclear* matrix become shorter and thicker, best described as short rods. These rods are the chromosomes.

PROSIMIANS    The premonkeys, all the primates except the *Anthropoidea.* All primate fossils prior to the *Oligocene* are classed as prosimians, and the lemuroids, lorisoids, tarsioids, and tree shrews of today are also included. Some authorities question the inclusion of the tree shrews.

PUBIS    One of the paired anterior bones of the *pelvis.*

RACE    A conceptual term meaning a variety reproductively partly isolated from other members of the *species;* formerly sometimes applied to groups of people who resemble each other in appearance, but now, when used by an anthropologist, confined to meaning a *breeding population* whose members share a higher degree of common inheritance than they share with other members of the species.

RADIATION, ADAPTIVE    The branching into many species with different ways of life, which usually follows any major evolutionary innovation.

*RAMAPITHECUS*    A genus of the *Miocene* and *Pliocene* epochs. Some believe that it is a *hominid;* others think that it is little (if at all) different from the Pongid, *Dryopithecus.*

RANDOM GENETIC DRIFT   See *Genetic drift.*

RANDOM MATING   Selection of a mate without regard to *genotype.* The opposite of *assortative mating.* In a randomly mating population, the frequencies of the various matings are determined solely by the frequencies of the genes concerned.

RECESSIVE GENE   In Mendelian genetics, an allele whose effect is not expressed unless *homozygous* (present in both of a pair of *homologous chromosomes*).

RECOMBINATION   The formation of new combinations of *linked genes* by *crossing over* between their *loci.*

REDUCTION DIVISION   The first *meiotic* division, so-called because at this stage the *chromosome* number per cell is halved.

RIBOSOME   A cell *organelle,* composed of protein and *RNA,* that moves along messenger RNA and reads the coded message into a *polypeptide* chain, thus synthesizing protein.

RNA   Ribonucleic acid. A class of compounds that can, like *DNA,* bear specific genetic messages, coded by different *triplets* of four bases in a long chain. One of its functions is to determine the exact nature of proteins synthesized. RNA is similar to DNA but contains uracil rather than thymine. **Messenger RNA** (mRNA) carries the complementary coded message transcribed from the DNA on which it is formed. **Ribosomal RNA** forms with protein the *organelle* on which protein synthesis takes place. **Transfer (soluable) RNA** (sRNA) picks up individual *amino acid* molecules and transfers them to the developing *polypeptide.*

ROULEAUX FORMATION (PSEUDOAGGLUTINATION)   Red cells stacked like a pile of coins, thus appearing (falsely) to be agglutinated.

SAGITTAL   Pertaining to a vertical plane that divides the body into right and left halves. **Sagittal crest:** a raised crest on the top of the skull formed by marked development of the attachment of the temporal muscles on each side.

SECULAR TREND   The tendency for periodic cycles of long-term changes. Gradual changes in average stature over several decades or more are called "secular changes."

SEDENTES   Nonmigrants. People who have not left their country of birth.

SEGREGATION   The separation of *allelic genes* at *meiosis.* Since allelic genes occupy the same *locus* on *homologous chromosomes,* they always pass (segregate) to different gametes.

SELECTION   See *Natural selection.*

SEX CHROMOSOMES   Chromosomes responsible for sex determination.

There are two kinds, X and Y. Among vertebrates the genotype XX is that of the normal female and XY that of the normal male.

SEX LINKAGE   Inheritance by *genes* in the *sex chromosomes,* especially on the X-chromosome.

SEXUAL DIMORPHISM   Anatomical differences—particularly of size—between males and females of the same population or species.

SIBLINGS   Brothers and sisters. The term "sib" is sometimes misused for "sibling."

SICKLE-CELL TRAIT   Having red blood cells capable of taking certain bizarre forms under particular circumstances. This is caused by possession of a variant *hemoglobin* (hemoglobin S) as well as hemoglobin A. The individual has the genes *HbS* and *HbA.* Persons with the trait are more resistant to one type of malaria, but if they mate with each other some of the children may have sickle-cell *anemia,* a serious disease caused by *homozygous* occurrence of the gene *HbS.*

SPECIALIZED   Highly evolved for a specific function and conceived of as capable of further evolution only for the same function. The front teeth of the beaver are specialized for gnawing wood. Compare *generalized.*

SPECIES   A group of closely related *organisms,* designated by the same binomial scientific name. Among sexually reproducing organisms in the same place and time, species are defined as reproductively isolated populations of animals or plants capable of having descendants in common. Under other conditions species are identified by analogy with such genetic species.

STRATIGRAPHIC SEQUENCE   The relative position of geological deposits. Since later waterborne and windborne geological beds are interposed sequentially on top of earlier beds, the stratigraphic sequence dates the deposits relative to each other.

SUTURE   Literally: stitch. The juncture between two flat bones of the skull.

SYSTEMATISTS   Those biologists who are concerned with the relationship of organisms to each other. The naming of organisms, *taxonomy,* is a branch of systematics.

TAXONOMY   The science of classification of organisms according to their relationships.

TAY-SACHS DISEASE   Infantile amaurotic idiocy, a hereditary disease causing blindness and severe mental deficiency.

"TELANTHROPUS"   Specimens from Swartkrans now thought by some to be of the genus *Homo,* by others, of *Australopithecus.*

TELOPHASE   The stage of cell division that begins when the daughter *chro-*

*mosomes* reach the poles of the dividing cell and lasts until the two daughter cells take on the appearance of *interphase* cells.

TEMPORAL LINE   Marking or ridge on the skull vault where one of the muscles of mastication, the temporalis, attaches. The line encompasses a larger area when the muscle is powerful and the two lines come together and form a *sagittal crest* in animals with small skulls and large jaws.

THALASSEMIA   *Anemia* caused by a hereditary defect in the synthesis of *hemoglobin*.

TIBIA   The bone of the leg that transmits almost all of the weight to the foot. The shin bone.

TORUS (*pl.:* TORI)   A raised mound of bone. **Occipital torus:** a transverse raised bar of bone at the back of the skull where the neck muscles attach. **Palatine torus:** a mound or ridge on the midline of the bony palate. **Supraorbital torus:** brow ridges extended over both eye sockets.

TRANSFERRIN   A beta *globulin*. This serum protein combines with iron, an essential ingredient of *hemoglobin*. Many *polymorphisms* of transferrin occur in monkeys, apes, and humans.

TRINIL DEPOSITS   Fossil-bearing deposits in Central Java, dated at about 500,000 to 900,000 years ago, in which most of the Java *Homo erectus* fossils have been found.

TRIPLET   In molecular genetics, a unit of three successive bases in *DNA* or *RNA*, coding for a specific *amino acid*. A *codon*.

VIVIPAROUS   Live-bearing, as in the *placental (eutherian)* mammals, rather than egg-laying.

X-LINKAGE   *Sex linkage*. Genetic traits transmitted by *genes* on the X chromosome.

WAHLUND EFFECT   Inbreeding effect resulting from *endogamous* mating within subgroups of a population that differ from each other in *gene* frequency.

ZYGOSITY   Whether or not an organism is *heterozygous* or *homozygous* for a particular gene.

# REFERENCES

Abbie, A. A.  1964  The factor of timing in the emergence of distinctively human characters. *Papers and Proceedings of the Royal Society of Tasmania 98:* 63–71.

Acheson, R. M.  1960  Effect of nutrition and disease on human growth. In J. M. Tanner (Ed.), *Third symposium on human growth.* New York: Pergamon.

Acheson, R. M.  1966  Maturation of the skeleton. In F. Falkner (Ed.), *Human development.* Philadelphia: Saunders, pp. 465–502.

Adams, M. S., and J. V. Neel  1967  Children of incest. *Pediatrics 40:* 55–62.

Aigner, J. S., and W. S. Laughlin  1973  The dating of Lantian man and his significance for analyzing trends in human evolution. *American Journal of Physical Anthropology 39:* 97–109.

Aldrich-Blake, F. P. G.  1968  A fertile hybrid between two *Cercopithecus* spp. in the Budongo Forest. *Folia Primatologica 9:* 15–21.

Allison, A. C.  1954  Protection afforded by sickle-cell trait against subtertian malarial infection. *British Medical Journal 1:* 290–294.

Altmann, S. A.  1962  A field study of sociobiology of rhesus monkeys, *Macaca mulatta. Annals of the New York Academy of Science 102:* 338–435.

Altmann, S. A.  1967  *Social communication among primates.* Chicago: University of Chicago Press.

Altmann, S. A.  1970  Baboon ecology in Amboseli. *Bibliotheca Primatologica 12.* Basel, Switz.: S. Karger.

Altmann, S. A., and J. Altmann   1970   *Baboon ecology.* Chicago: University of Chicago Press.

Amundsen, D. W., and C. J. Diers   1969   Age of menarche in classical Greece and Rome. *Human Biology 41:* 125–132.

Anderson, J. E.   1962   *The human skeleton.* Ottawa: National Museum of Canada.

Angel, J. L.   1947   The length of life in ancient Greece. *Journal of Gerontology 2:* 18–24.

Angel, J. L.   1951   The human skeletal remains from Hotu Cave, Iran. *Proccedings of the American Philosophical Society 96:* 258–269.

Angel, J. L.   1969   The bases of paleodemography. *American Journal of Physical Anthropology 30:* 427–437.

Ankel, F.   1972   Vertebral morphology of fossil and extant primates. In R. Tuttle (Ed.), *The functional and evolutionary biology of primates.* Chicago: Aldine-Atherton, pp. 223–240.

Arambourg, C.   1955   A recent discovery in human paleontology: Atlanthropus of Ternifine (Algeria). *American Journal of Physical Anthropology 13:* 191–201.

Arambourg, C., and P. Biberson   1956   The human fossil remains from the Palaeolithic site of Sidi Abderrahman (Morocco). *American Journal of Physical Anthropology 14:* 467–489.

Arambourg, C., and Y. Coppens   1967   Sur la decouvert dans le Pléistocène inferiéur de la vallée de l'Omo (Éthiopie) d'une mandibule d'Australopithecien. *Comptes Rendus de l'Académie des Sciences* Paris, *265:* 589–590.

Ascádi, Gy., and J. Nemeskéri   1970   *History of human life span and mortality* Budapest: Akademiai Kiadó.

Ashton, E. H., and S. Zuckerman   1951   The influence of geographic isolation on the skull of the green monkey *(Cercopithecus aethiops sabaeus),* III and IV. *Proceedings of the Royal Society,* London, series B, *138:* 354–374.

Avery, O. T., C. M. McLeod, and M. McCarty   1944   Studies on the chemical nature of the substance inducing transformation of pneumococcal types. *Journal of Experimental Medicine 79:* 137–158.

Avis, V.   1962   Brachiation: The crucial issue for man's ancestry. *Southwestern Journal of Anthropology 18:* 119–148.

Azen, E. A.   1972   Genetic polymorphism of basic proteins from parotid saliva. *Science 176:* 673–674.

Azevedo, E., H. Krieger, and N. E. Morton   1969   Ahaptoglobinemia in Northeastern Brazil. *Human Heredity 19:* 609–612.

Baer, M. J.   1954   Patterns of growth of the skull as revealed by vital staining. *Human Biology 26:* 80–126.

Baer, M. J., and J. E. Harris   1969   A commentary on the growth of the human brain and skull. *American Journal of Physical Anthropology 30:* 39–44.

Baker, P. T.   1960   Climate, culture and evolution. *Human Biology 32:* 3–16.

Baker, P. T.   1969   Human adaptation to high altitude. *Science 163:* 1149–1156.

Baker P. T., and M. A. Little (Eds.) In press *Man in the Andes: A multidisciplinary study of high altitude Quechua.* Stroudsburg, Pa.: Dowden, Hutchinson and Ross.

Bakker, R. T.   1972   Anatomical and ecological evidence of endothermy in dinosaurs. *Nature 238:* 81–85.

Barnett, L. D.   1970   Education and religion as factors influencing attitudes toward population growth in the United States. *Social Biology 17:* 26–36.

Barnicot, N. A.   1951   Physical anthropology. *Science Progress 153:* 124–131.

Barnicot, N. A.    1964    Anthropology and population genetics. *Genetics Today*. Proceedings of the XI International Congress of Genetics.

Benoist, J.    1964    Saint-Barthélemy: Physical anthropology of an isolate. *American Journal of Physical Anthropology 22:* 473–487.

Bernstein, F.    1924    Ergebnisse einer biostatistischen zusammenfassenden Betrachtung über die erblichen Blutstrukturen des Menschen. *Klinische Wochenschrift 3:* 1495–1497.

Bernstein, I. S.    1968    Social status of two hybrids in a wild troop of *Macaca iris. Folia Primatologica 8:* 121–131.

Bernstein, I. S.    1974    Birth of two second generation hybrid macaques. *Journal of Human Evolution 3:* 205–206.

Beutler, E.    1959    The hemolitic effect of primaquine and related compounds: A review. *Blood 14:* 103–139.

Birdsell, J. B.    1948    The racial origin of the extinct Tasmanians. *Records of the Queen Victoria Museum 2* (3). Reprinted in *Yearbook of Physical Anthropology—* 1950, pp. 143–160.

Birdsell, J. B.    1951a    Some implications of the genetical concept of race in terms of spatial analysis. *Cold Spring Harbor Symposia on Quantitative Biology 15:* 259–314.

Birdsell, J. B.    1951b    The problem of the peopling of the Americas as viewed from Asia. In W. S. Laughlin and S. L. Washburn (Eds.), *The physical anthropology of the American Indian*. New York: The Viking Fund.

Birdsell, J. B.    1957    Some population problems involving Pleistocene man. *Cold Spring Harbor Symposia on Quantitative Biology 22:* 47–69.

Birdsell, J. B.    1972    Review of *The Original Australians* by A. A. Abbie. *American Anthropologist 74:* 149–152.

Bishop, W. W., and G. R. Chapman    1970    Early Pliocene sediments and fossils from the Northern Kenya Rift Valley. *Nature 226:* 914–918.

Black, D.    1927    On a lower molar hominid tooth from the Choukoutien deposit. *Palaeontologica Sinica, Series D, 7:* 1–28.

Blanc, A. C.    1961    Some evidence for the ideologies of early man. In S. L. Washburn (Ed.), *Social life of early man. Viking Fund Publications in Anthropology*. Vol. 31, pp. 119–136.

Boas, F.    1910    Changes in bodily form of descendants of immigrants. Senate document 208, 61st Congress, 2nd Session. Washington, D.C.

Bock, W. D.    1970    Hyalina baltica and the Plio-Pleistocene boundary in the Caribbean Sea. *Science 170:* 847–848.

Bonné, B.    1963    The Samaritans: A demographic study. *Human Biology 35:* 61–89.

Bourne, G. H. (Ed.)    1969, 1970    *The chimpanzee*. Vols. 1 and 2. Basel, Switz.: Karger.

Bowles, G. T.    1932    *New types of Old Americans at Harvard and at eastern women's colleges*. Cambridge: Harvard University Press.

Boyce, A. J., C. F. Küchemann, and G. A. Harrison    1967    Neighbourhood knowledge and the distribution of marriage distances. *Annals of Human Genetics 30:* 335–338.

Boyd, W. C.    1950    *Genetics and the races of man*. Boston: Little, Brown.

Boyd, W. C.    1964    Modern ideas on race in the light of our knowledge of blood groups and other characters with known mode of inheritance. In C. A. Leone (Ed.), *Taxonomic biochemistry and serology*. New York: Ronald, pp. 119–169.

Boyer, S. H., A. N. Noyes, C. F. Timmons, and R. A. Young    1974    Primate hemoglobins: Polymorphisms and evolutionary patterns. *Journal of Human Evolution 1:* 515–543.

Brace, C. L.   1964   The fate of the "classic" Neanderthals: A consideration of hominid catastrophism. *Current Anthropology 5:* 3–34.

Brace, C. L.   1971   Sex, inadequacy and Australopithecine identity conflicts. *American Journal of Physical Anthropology 35:* 274 (Abstract).

Brace, C. L.   1973   Sexual dimorphism in human evolution. *Yearbook of Physical Anthropology-1972,* 16: 31–49.

Brace, C. L., and P. E. Mahler   1971   Post-Pleistocene changes in human dentition. *American Journal of Physical Anthropology 34:* 191–203.

Brace, C. L., H. Nelson, and N. Korn   1971   *Atlas of fossil man.* New York: Holt.

Brain, C. K.   1970   New finds at the Swartkrans Australopithecine site. *Nature 225:* 1112–1119.

Bronowski, J.   1969   On the uniqueness of man. *Science 165:* 680–682.

Broom, R.   1949   The ape-man. *Scientific American 181:* 20–24.

Brožek, J. (Ed.)   1956   *Body measurements and human nutrition.* Detroit: Wayne State University Press. Reprinted from: *Human Biology 28:* 109–273 (1956).

Brožek, J., and A. Henschel (Eds.)   1961   *Techniques for measuring body composition.* Washington, D.C.: National Academy of Sciences–National Research Council.

Brues, A.   1954   Selection and polymorphism in the ABO blood groups. *American Journal of Physical Anthropology 12:* 559–597.

Brues, A. M.   1963   Stochastic tests of selection in the ABO blood groups. *American Journal of Physical Anthropology 21:* 287–299.

Buettner-Janusch, J.   1961   Transferrin differences in chimpanzee sera. *Nature 192:* 632–633.

Buettner-Janusch, J.   1973   *Physical anthropology: A perspective.* New York: Wiley.

Burrell, R. J. W., M. J. R. Healy, and J. M. Tanner   1961   Age of menarche in South African Bantu girls living in the Transkei Reserve. *Human Biology 33:* 250–261.

Butzer, K. W.   1974   Geological and ecological perspectives on the Middle Pleistocene. *Quarternary Research 4:* 136–148.

Calvin, M.   1956   Chemical evolution and the origin of life. *American Scientist 44:* 248–263.

Campbell, B.   1966   *Human evolution.* Chicago: Aldine.

Carcassi, U., R. Ceppellini, and F. Pitzus   1957   Frequenza della talassemia in quattro popolazione sarde e suoi rapporti con la distribuzione dei gruppi sanguigni e della malaria. *Bollettino dell'Istituto Sieroterapico Milanese 36:* 206–218.

Carpenter, C. R.   1934   A field study of the behavior and social relations of howling monkeys *(Alouatta palliata). Comparative Psychology Monographs,* Vol. 10, No. 48. Baltimore: Johns Hopkins Press.

Carpenter, C. R.   1940   A field study in Siam of the behavior and social relations of the gibbon *(Hylobates lar). Comparative Psychology Monographs,* Vol. 16, No. 5. Baltimore: John Hopkins Press.

Carpenter, C. R.   1954   Tentative generalizations on the grouping behavior of non-human primates. *Human Biology 26:* 269–276.

Carpenter, C. R.   1965   The howlers of Barro Colorado Island. In I. DeVore (Ed.), *Primate behavior.* New York: Holt, pp. 250–291.

Cartmill, M.   1972   Arboreal adaptations and the origin of the order Primates. In R. Tuttle (Ed.), *The functional and evolutionary biology of primates.* Chicago: Aldine-Atherton, pp. 97–122.

Chakraborty, R., M. Shaw, and W. J. Schull   1974   Exclusion of paternity: The current state of the art. *American Journal of Human Genetics. 26:* 477–488.

Chang, Kwang-chih   1962   New evidence on fossil man in China. *Science 136:* 749–760.

Chang, Kwang-chih   1968   Archaeology of ancient China. *Science 162:* 519–526.

Chiarelli, A. B.   1972   Comparative cytogenetics in primates and its relevance for human cytogenetics. In A. B. Chiarelli (Ed.), *Comparative genetics in monkeys, apes and man.* New York: Academic Press, pp. 273–308.

Chiarelli, A. B.   1973   Check-list of Catarrhina primates. *Journal of Human Evolution 4:* 301–303.

Chivers, D. J.   1969   On the daily behavior and spacing of howler monkey groups. *Folia Primatologica 10:* 48–102.

Clark, W. E. Le Gros   1955   *The fossil evidence for human evolution.* Chicago: University of Chicago Press.

Clark, W. E. Le Gros   1965   *History of the primates* (ed. 9). London: British Museum (Natural History).

Clarke, C. A.   1959   Correlation of ABO blood groups with peptic ulcer, cancer, and other diseases. *Journal of Medical Education 34:* 400–404.

Clarke, R. J., and F. C. Howell   1972   Affinities of the Swartkrans 847 hominid cranium. *American Journal of Physical Anthropology 37:* 319–335.

Clarke, R. J., F. C. Howell, and C. K. Brain   1970   More evidence of an advanced hominid at Swartkrans. *Nature 225:* 1219–1222.

Clegg, E. J., G. A. Harrison, and P. T. Baker   1970   Impact of high altitudes on human populations. *Human Biology 42:* 486–518.

Collias, N., and C. Southwick   1952   A field study of population density and social organization in howling monkeys. *Proceedings of the American Philosophical Society 96:* 143–156.

Comas, J.   1960   *Manual of physical anthropology.* Revised edition. Springfield, Illinois: Charles C Thomas.

Coon, C. S.   1939   *Races of Europe.* New York: Macmillan.

Coon, C. S.   1962   *The origin of races.* New York: Alfred A. Knopf.

Coon, C. S.   1966   The taxonomy of human variation. *Annals of the New York Academy of Science 134:* 516–523.

Coon, C. S., S. M. Garn, and J. B. Birdsell   1950   *Races: A study of the problems of race formation in man.* Springfield, Illinois: Charles C Thomas.

Coppens, Y.   1966   Le Tchadanthropus. *L'Anthropologie 70:* 5–16.

Corruccini, R. S.   1975   Multivariate analysis of *Gigantopithecus* mandibles. *American Journal of Physical Anthropology 42:* 167–170.

Count, E. W.   1950   *This is race.* New York: Schuman.

Crawford, M. H.   1970   Trends in genetics and biological anthropology: 1966–1968. In B. Siegel (Ed.), *Biennial Review of Anthropology.*

Damon, A.   1968   Secular trends in height and weight within Old American families at Harvard, 1870–1965: I. Within twelve four-generation families. *American Journal of Physical Anthropology 29:* 45–50.

Damon, A., S. T. Damon, H. C. Harpending, and W. B. Kannel   1969a   Predicting coronary heart disease from body measurements of Framingham males. *Journal of Chronic Diseases 21:* 781–802.

Damon, A., S. T. Damon, R. B. Reed, and I. Valadian 1969b Age at menarche of mothers and daughters. *Human Biology 41:* 161–175.

Damon, A., and R. F. Goldman 1964 Predicting fat from body measurements: Densitometric validation of ten anthropometric equations. *Human Biology 36:* 32–44.

Daniels, F., P. W. Post, and B. E. Johnson 1972 Theories of the role of pigment in the evolution of human races. In V. Riley (Ed.), *Pigmentation: Its genesis and biologic control.* New York: Appleton.

Dart, R. A. 1925 *Australopithecus africanus:* The man-ape of South Africa. *Nature 115:* 195–199.

Dart, R. A. 1949 Innominate fragments of *Australopithecus prometheus. American Journal of Physical Anthropology 7:* 301–332.

Darwin, C. 1859 *On the origin of species by means of natural selection.* London: Watts, 1950.

Darwin, C. 1871 *Descent of man and selection in relation to sex* (2nd ed., revised and augmented). New York: Appleton.

Davis, A. E., and T. Bolin 1967 Lactose intolerance in Asians. *Nature 216:* 1244–1245.

Day, M. H. 1969 Omo human skeletal remains. *Nature 222:* 1135–1138.

Day, M. H., and R. E. F. Leakey 1974 New evidence of the genus *Homo* from East Rudolf, Kenya: III. *American Journal of Physical Anthropology 41:* 367–374.

Day, M. H., R. E. F. Leakey, A. C. Walker, and B. A Wood 1975 New hominids from East Rudolf, Kenya: I. *American Journal of Physical Anthropology 42:* 461–475.

DeVore, I. (Ed.) 1965 *Primate behavior.* New York: Holt.

Dobzhansky, Th. 1937 *Genetics and the origin of species.* New York: Columbia University Press.

Dobzhansky, Th. 1955 *Evolution, genetics, and man.* New York: Wiley.

Dobzhansky, Th. 1962 *Mankind evolving.* New Haven, Conn.: Yale University Press.

Dobzhansky, Th. 1969 Evolution of mankind in the light of population genetics. *Proceedings of the XII International Congress of Genetics 3:* 281–292.

Dodson, E. O. 1960 *Evolution: Progress and product.* New York: Van Nostrand.

Dokládal, M. 1965 Die Schädelform im Laufe der phylogenetischen und historischen Entwicklung des Menschen. *Anthropologie* (Prague) *2:* 19–35.

Dolinow, P., and V. Sarich (Eds.) 1971 *Background for man: Readings in physical anthropology.* Boston: Little, Brown.

Dollo, L. 1893 Les lois d'evolution. *Bulletin de la Société Belge de Géologie 7:* 164–166.

Doolittle, R. F., and G. A. Mross 1970 Identity of chimpanzee with human fibrinopeptides. *Nature 225:* 643–644.

Dorf, E. 1957 The earth's changing climates. *Weatherwise 10:* 54.

Drennan, M. R. 1956 Note on the morphological status of the Swanscombe and Fontéchevade skulls. *American Journal of Physical Anthropology 14:* 73–83.

Dreyer, F. T. 1947 Further observations on the Florisbad skull. *Soölogiese Navorsing van die Nasionale Museum 1:* 183–190.

DuBois, E. F. 1948 *Fever and the regulation of body temperature.* Springfield, Illinois: Charles C Thomas.

Dubrul, S. L.    1958    *Evolution of the speech apparatus.* Springfield, Illinois: Charles C Thomas.

Du Chaillu, P. B.    1861    *Explorations and adventures in equatorial Africa.* London.

Dumond, D. E.    1975    The limitation of human population: A natural history. *Science 187:* 713–721.

Dunbar, R. I. M., and P. Dunbar    1974    On hybridization between *Theropithecus gelada* and *Papio anubis* in the wild. *Journal of Human Evolution 3:* 187–192.

Dunn, F. L.    1966    Patterns of parasitism in primates: Phylogenetic and ecological interpretations, with particular reference to the Hominoidea. *Folia Primatologica 4:* 329–345.

Durham, N. M.    1969    Sex differences in visual threat displays of West African vervets. *Primates 10:* 91–95.

Durham, N. M.    1971    Effects of altitude differences on group organization of wild black spider monkeys *(Ateles paniscus). Proceedings 3rd International Congress on Primates 3:* 32–40. Basel, Switzerland: Karger.

Eaton, J. W., and A. J. Mayer    1953    The social biology of very high fertility among the Hutterites: The demography of a unique population. *Human Biology 25:* 206–264.

Eisenberg, J. F., N. A. Muckenhirn, and R. Rudin    1972    The relation between ecology and social structure in primates. *Science 176:* 863–874.

Ellefson, J. O.    1968    Territorial behavior in the common white-handed gibbon, *Hylobates lar* Linn. In P. C. Jay (Ed.), *Primates: Studies in adaptation and variability.* New York: Holt.

Emiliani, C.    1971    Paleotemperature variations across the Plio-Pleistocene boundary. *Science 171:* 60–62.

Ericson, D. B., and G. Wollin    1968    Pleistocene climates and chronology in deep-sea sediments. *Science 162:* 1227–1234.

Erlenmeyer-Kimling, L., and L. F. Jarvik    1963    Genetics and intelligence: A review. *Science 142:* 1477–1479.

Eveleth, P. B., and J. A. de Souza Freitas    1969    Tooth eruption and menarche of Brazilian-born children of Japanese ancestry. *Human Biology 41:* 176–184.

Ferguson, C. W.    1968    Bristlecone pine: Science and esthetics. *Science 159:* 839–846.

Fishberg, M.    1905    Materials for the physical anthropology of the Eastern European Jew. *Annals of the New York Academy of Science 16:* 155–297.

Fisher, R. A.    1930    *The genetical theory of natural selection.* Oxford: Oxford University Press.

Fitch, W. M., and E. Margoliash    1967    Construction of phylogenetic trees. *Science 155:* 279–284.

Fossey, D.    1970    Making friends with mountain gorillas. *National Geographic 137:* 48–67.

Fox, S. W.    1960    How did life begin? *Science 132:* 200–208.

Frayer, D. W.    1973    *Gigantopithecus* and its relationship to *Australopithecus. American Journal of Physical Anthropology 39:* 413–426.

Friedmann, N., and S. L. Miller    1969    Phenylalanine and tyrosine synthesis under primitive earth conditions. *Science 166:* 766–767.

Frisancho, A. R.    1969    Human growth and pulmonary function of a high altitude Peruvian Quechua population. *Human Biology 41:* 365–379.

Frisancho, A. R. 1975 Functional adaptation to high altitude hypoxia. *Science 187:* 313–319.

Frisancho, A. R., and P. T. Baker 1970 Altitude and growth: A study of the pattern of physical growth of a high altitude Peruvian Quechua population. *American Journal of Physical Anthropology 32:* 279–292.

Frisch, R., and R. Revelle 1969 The height and weight of adolescent boys and girls at the time of peak velocity of growth in height and weight: Longitudinal data. *Human Biology 41:* 536–559.

Froehlich, J. W. 1970 Migration and plasticity of physique in the Japanese Americans of Hawaii. *American Journal of Physical Anthropology 32:* 429–442.

Gardner, R. A., and B. T. Gardner 1969 Teaching sign language to a chimpanzee. *Science 165:* 644–672.

Garn, S. M. 1963 Culture and the direction of human evolution. *Human Biology 35:* 221–236.

Garn, S. M. 1970 *Human races* (ed. 3). Springfield, Illinois: Charles C Thomas.

Garn, S. M., and C. S. Coon 1955 On the number of races of mankind. *American Anthropologist 57:* 996–1001.

Garn, S. M., and A. B. Lewis 1958 Tooth size, body-size and "giant" fossil man. *American Anthropologist 60:* 874–880.

Garn, S. M., A. B. Lewis, and R. S. Kerewsky 1968 The magnitude and implications of the relationship between tooth size and body size. *Archives of Oral Biology 13:* 129–131.

Garn, S. M., and Zvi Shamir 1958 *Methods for research in human growth.* Springfield, Illinois: Charles C Thomas.

Garn, S. M., F. N. Silverman, K. P. Hertzog, and C. G. Rohmann 1968 Lines and bands of increased density: Their implication to growth and development. *Medical Radiography and Photography 44:* 58–89.

Garrett, J. W., and K. W. Kennedy 1971 *A collation of Anthropometry.* Aerospace Medical Research Laboratory, Wright-Patterson Air Force Base, Ohio. 2 vols.

Garrod, A. E., 1902 The incidence of alkaptonuria: A study in chemical individuality. *Lancet 2:* 1616–1620.

Garrod, A. E. 1923 *Inborn errors of metabolism.* London: Henry Frowde and Hodder and Stoughton.

Gartlan, J. S., and C. K. Brain 1968 Ecology and social variability in *Cercopithecus aethiops* and *C. mitis.* In P. C. Jay (Ed.), *Primates.* New York: Holt, pp. 253–292.

Genovés, S. 1970 *Is peace inevitable?: Aggression, evolution and human destiny.* New York: Walker.

Gibaut, A., and G. Oliver 1965 *Anthropologie des Tibetains orientaux.* Paris: L'École Français d'Extreme-Orient.

Giblett, E. R. 1969 *Genetic markers in human blood.* Oxford: Blackwell.

Giles, E., R. J. Walsh, and M. A. Bradley 1966 Micro-evolution in New Guinea: The role of genetic drift. *Annals of the New York Academy of Science 134:* 655–665.

Giles, E., E. Ogan, and A. G. Steinberg 1965 Gamma globulin factors (Gm and Inv) in New Guinea: Anthropological significance. *Science 150:* 1158–1160.

Giles, E., S. Wyber, and R. J. Walsh 1970 Micro-evolution in New Guinea: Additional evidence for genetic drift. *Archaeology and Physical Anthropology in Oceania 5:* 60–72.

Glanville, E. V. 1969 Nasal shape, prognathism and adaptation in man. *American Journal of Physical Anthropology 30:* 29–37.

Glass, B., M. S. Sacks, E. F. Jahn, and C. Hess   1952   Genetic drift in a religious isolate: An analysis of the causes of variation in blood group and other gene frequencies in a small population. *The American Naturalist 86:* 145–159.

Goldstein, M. S.   1943   *Demographic and bodily changes in descendants of Mexican immigrants.* Austin: University of Texas, Institute of Latin American Studies.

Goldstein, Marcus S.   1956   Review of: *The Physical Anthropology of Ireland* by Earnest A. Hooton and C. Wesley Dupertuis. *American Journal of Physical Anthropology 14:* 328–333.

Goodall, J.   1963   Feeding behavior of wild chimpanzees. *Symposia of the Zoological Society,* London *10:* 39–47.

Goodall, J.   1965   Chimpanzees of the Gombe Stream Reserve. In I. DeVore (Ed.), *Primate behavior.* New York: Holt, pp. 425–473.

Goodall, J. van Lawick-   1968   A preliminary report on expressive movements and communication in the Gombe Stream chimpanzees. In P. C. Jay (Ed.), *Primates.* New York: Holt, pp. 313–374.

Goodman, M.   1963a   Man's place in the phylogeny of the primates as reflected in serum proteins. In S. L. Washburn (Ed.), *Classification and human evolution.* Chicago: Aldine, pp. 204–234.

Goodman, M.   1963b   Serological analysis of the systematics of recent hominoids. *Human Biology 35:* 377–436.

Goodman, M.   1966   Phyletic position of tree shrews. *Science 153:* 1550.

Goodman, M.   1968   Evolution of the catarrhine primates at the macromolecular level. *Primates in Medicine 1:* 10–26.

Goodman, M., J. Barnabas, G. Matsuda, and G. W. Moore   1971   Molecular evolution in the descent of man. *Nature 233:* 604–613.

Goodman, M., A. Koen, J. Barnabas, and G. W. Moore   1972   Evolving primate genes and proteins. In A. B. Chiarelli (Ed.), *Comparative genetics in monkeys, apes and man.* New York: Academic Press, pp. 153–212.

Goodman, M., A. Kulkarni, E. Poulik, and E. Reklys   1965   Species and geographic differences in the transferrin polymorphism of macaques. *Science 147:* 884–886.

Goodman, M., G. W. Moore, W. Farris, and E. Poulik   1970   The evidence from genetically informative macromolecules on the phylogenetic relationships of the chimpanzees. In G. H. Bourne (Ed.), *The chimpanzee.* Basel, Switzerland: Karger, pp. 318–360.

Goodman, M., G. W. Moore, and G. Matsuda   1975   Darwinian evolution in the genealogy of haemoglobin. *Nature 253:* 603–608.

Goodman, M., N. W. Sorenson, W. Farris, and E. Poulik   1969   Immunodiffusion systematics of *Tarsius syrichta. American Journal of Physical Anthropology 31:* 266.

Goodman, M., W. G. Wisecup, H. H. Reynolds, and C. H. Kratochvil   1967   Transferrin polymorphism and population differences in the genetic variability of chimpanzees. *Science 156:* 98–100.

Greulich, W. W.   1957   A comparison of the physical growth and development of American-born and native Japanese children. *American Journal of Physical Anthropology 15:* 489–515.

Greulich, W. W., and S. I. Pyle   1959   *Radiographic atlas of skeletal development of the hand and wrist* (ed. 2). Palo Alto, California: Stanford University Press.

Guyton, A. C.   1956   *Textbook of medical physiology.* Philadelphia: Saunders.

Haldane, J. B. S.   1932   *The causes of evolution.* London: Longmans.

Hall, K. R. L., and I. DeVore   1965   Baboon behavior. In I. DeVore (Ed.), *Primate behavior*. New York: Holt, pp. 53–110.

Hanna, J. M.   1970   The effects of coca chewing on exercise in the Quechua of Peru. *Human Biology 42:* 1–11.

Hanna, J. M.   1971   Further studies on the effects of coca chewing on exercise. *Human Biology 43:* 200–209.

Hanson, E. D.   1966   Evolution of the cell from primordial living systems. *Quarterly Review of Biology 41:* 1–12.

Hardin, G.   1959   *Nature and man's fate.* New York: Holt.

Hardy, Sir A.   1965   *The living stream: Evolution and man.* New York: Harper & Row.

Hardy, G. H.   1908   Mendelian proportions in a mixed population. *Science 28:* 49–50.

Harrison, G. A., J. S. Weiner, J. M. Tanner, and N. A. Barnicot   1964   *Human biology.* New York: Oxford University Press.

Harrison, T.   1957   The great cave of Niah. *Man 57:* 161–166.

Heim, J.-L.   1970   L'encéphale Néandertalien de l'homme de La Ferrassie. *L'Anthropologie 74:* 527–572.

Heintz, N.   1964   Aspects infantiles tardifs de la croissance du crâne humain. *Comptes Rendus de l'Académie des Sciences,* Paris 259: 2297–2299.

Heintz, N.   1966   Le crâne des anthropomorphes. *Musée Royal de L'Afrique Centrale, Tervuren, Belgique: Annales.* N. S. 4. No. 6.

Hershey, A. D., and M. C. Chase   1952   Independent functions of viral protein and nucleic acid in growth of bacteriophage. *Journal of General Physiology 36:* 39–56.

Hiernaux, J.   1968   *La diversité humaine en Afrique subsaharienne.* Institut de Sociologie de l'Université Libre de Bruxelles.

Hill, J. H.   1972   On the evolutionary foundations of language. *American Anthropologist 74:* 308–317.

Hoff, C.   1974   Altitudinal variations in physical growth and development of Peruvian Quechua. *Homo 24:* 87–99.

Hoffstetter, R.   1972   Relationships, origins and history of the Ceboid monkeys and the caviomorph rodents. In Th. Dobzhansky (Ed.), *Evolutionary Biology.* New York: Appleton-Century-Crofts, Vol. 6, pp. 323–347.

Holliday, R., and J. E. Pugh   1975   DNA modification mechanisms and gene activity during development. *Science 187:* 226–232.

Holloway, R. L.   1972   Australopithecine endocasts, brain evolution in the hominoidea, and a model of hominid evolution. In R. Tuttle (Ed.), *The functional and evolutionary biology of primates.* Chicago: Aldine, pp. 185–203.

Hooton, E. A., and C. W. Dupertuis   1955   The physical anthropology of Ireland. *Papers of the Peabody Museum of Archaeology and Ethnology,* Harvard University 30: Nos. 1–2.

Hopkins, D. M.   1959   Cenozoic history of the Bering land bridge. *Science 129:* 1519–1528.

Horowitz, N. H.   1945   On the evolution of biochemical syntheses. *Proceedings of the National Academy of Sciences 31:* 153–157.

Howell, F. C.   1951   The place of Neanderthal man in human evolution. *American Journal of Physical Anthropology 9:* 379–416.

Howell, F. C.   1967   Review of *Man Apes or Ape-Men?* by W. E. Le Gros Clark. *American Journal of Physical Anthropology 27:* 95–101.

Howell, F. C.   1969   Remains of Hominidae from Pliocene/Pleistocene formations in the Lower Omo Basin, Ethiopia. *Nature 223:* 1234–1239.

Howell, F. C., and B. A. Wood 1974 Early Hominid ulna from the Omo Basin, Ethiopia. *Nature 249:* 174–176.

Howells, W. W. 1970 Mount Carmel man: Morphological relationships. *Proceedings of the VIII International Congress of Anthropological and Ethnological Sciences, Tokyo and Kyoto, 1968.* Vol. 1. pp. 269–272.

Howells, W. W. 1974 Neanderthals: Names, hypotheses, and scientific method. *American Anthropologist 76:* 24–38.

Huang, S. S., and T. M. Bayless 1968 Milk and lactose intolerance in healthy Orientals. *Science 160:* 83–84.

Hulse, F. S. 1955 Technological advance and major racial stocks. *Human Biology 27:* 184–192.

Hulse, F. S. 1957a Exogamie et hétérosis. *Archives suisse d'Anthropologie général 22:* 103–127. Translated into English (1964) in *Physical Anthropology 1953–1961.* G. W. Lasker (Ed.), *Yearbook of Physical Anthropology 9:* 240–257.

Hulse, F. S. 1957b Some factors influencing the relative proportions of human racial stocks. *Cold Spring Harbor Symposia on Quantitative Biology 22:* 33–45.

Hulse, F. S. 1962 Race as an evolutionary episode. *American Anthropologist 64:* 929–945.

Hulse, F. S. 1967 Selection for skin color among the Japanese. *American Journal of Physical Anthropology 27:* 143–155.

Hulse, F. S. 1968 Migration and cultural selection in human genetics. *The Anthropologist.* Special volume, pp. 1–21.

Hunt, E. E., Jr. 1959 Anthropometry, genetics and racial history. *American Anthropologist 61:* 64–87.

Hurme, V. O. 1948 Standards of variation in the eruption of the first six permanent teeth. *Child Development 19:* 213–232.

Hürzeler, J. 1958 *Oreopithecus bambolii* Gervais: A preliminary report. *Verhandlungen Naturforschende Gesselschaft in Basel 69:* 1–48.

Huxley, J. 1943 *Evolution: The modern synthesis.* New York: Harper & Row.

Huxley, T. H. 1863 *Evidence as to man's place in nature.* London: Williams & Norgate.

Imanishi, Kinji 1960 Social organization of subhuman primates in their natural habitat. *Current Anthropology 1:* 393–407.

Ingram, V. M. 1958 Abnormal human haemoglobins. *Biochimica et Biophysica Acta 28:* 539–545.

Ito, P. K. 1942 Comparative biometrical study of physique of Japanese women born and reared under different environments. *Human Biology 14:* 279–351.

Jacob, T. 1966 A sixth skull cap of *Pithecanthropus erectus. American Journal of Physical Anthropology 25:* 243–259.

Jacob, T. 1973 Morphology and paleoecology of early man in Java. Chicago: IXth International Congress of Anthropological and Ethnological Sciences. Paper No. 0106.

Jay, P. 1965 The common langur of North India. In I. DeVore (Ed.), *Primate behavior.* New York: Holt, pp. 197–249.

Jay, P. C. (Ed.) 1968 *Primates: Studies in adaptation and variability.* New York: Holt.

Johnston, F. E., B. S. Blumberg, S. S. Agarwal, L. Melartin, and T. A. Burch 1969 Alloalbuminemia in Southwestern U.S. Indians. *Human Biology 41:* 263–270.

Johnston, F. E., and R. M. Malina 1966 Age changes in the composition of the upper arm of Philadelphia children. *Human Biology 38:* 1–21.

Jolly, A. 1966 *Lemur behavior.* Chicago: University of Chicago Press.

Jolly, A. 1972 *Evolution of primate behavior.* New York: Macmillan.

Jones, J. A. 1964 Rio Grande Pueblo albinism. *American Journal of Physical Anthropology 22:* 265–270.

Kabat, D. 1972 Gene selection in hemoglobin and in antibody synthesizing cells. *Science 175:* 134–140.

Kaplan, B. A. 1954 Environment and human plasticity. *American Anthropologist 56:* 780–800.

Kaplan, B., E. Richards, and G. W. Lasker 1946 A seminar in physical anthropology. *Yearbook of Physical Anthropology—1945,* pp. 5–11.

Kass, L. R. 1971 The new biology: What price reliving man's estate? *Science 174:* 779–788.

Keosian, J. 1964 *The origin of life.* New York: Reinhold.

King, J. L., and T. H. Jukes 1969 Non-Darwinian evolution. *Science 164:* 788–798.

King, M.-C., and A. C. Wilson 1975 Evolution at two levels in humans and chimpanzees. *Science 188:* 107–116.

Kirk, R. L. 1970 The haptoglobin groups in man. *Monographs in Human Genetics,* Vol. 4.

Klein, R. G. 1973 Geological antiquity of Rhodesian man. *Nature 244:* 311–312.

Klineberg, O. 1935 *Race differences.* New York: Harper & Row.

Knip, A. S. 1969 Measurement and regional distribution of functioning eccrine sweat glands in male and female Caucasians. *Human Biology 41:* 380–387.

Koenigswald, G. H. R. von 1973 Java: Early man, catalogue and problems. Chicago: *IXth International Congress of Anthropological and Ethnological Sciences.* Paper No. 1631.

Kohne, D. E. 1970 Evolution of higher organism DNA. *Quarterly Review of Biophysics 33:* 327–375.

Kraus, B. S. 1964 *The basis of human evolution.* New York: Harper & Row.

Kroeber, A. L. 1948 *Anthropology* (revised ed.). New York: Harcourt.

Krogman, W. M. 1972 *Child growth.* Ann Arbor: University of Michigan Press.

Küchemann, C. F., A. J. Boyce, and G. A. Harrison 1967 A demographic and genetic study of a group of Oxfordshire villages. *Human Biology 39:* 251–283.

Kummer, H. 1968 *Social organization of Hamadryas baboon.* Chicago: University of Chicago Press.

Kummer, H. 1971 *Primate societies.* Chicago: Aldine.

LaBarre, W. 1954 *The human animal.* Chicago: University of Chicago Press.

LaFarge, O. 1960 The enduring Indian. *Scientific American 202:* 37–45.

Lancaster, J. B., and R. B. Lee 1965 The annual reproductive cycle of monkeys and apes. In I. DeVore (Ed.), *Primate behavior.* New York: Holt.

Landsteiner, K. 1945 *The specificity of serological reactions.* Cambridge: Harvard University Press.

Landsteiner, K., and P. Levine 1927 A new agglutinable factor differentiating individual human bloods. *Proceedings of the Society for Experimental Biology, New York. 24:* 600–602.

Landsteiner, K., and A. S. Wiener 1940 An agglutinable factor in human blood recognized by immune sera for rhesus blood. *Proceedings of the Society for Experimental Biology, New York, 43:* 223.

Lasker, G. W. 1941 The process of physical growth of the Chinese. *The Anthropological Journal of The Institute of History and Philology, Academia Sinica 2:* 58–90.

Lasker. G. W.   1946   Migration and physical differentiation. *American Journal of Physical Anthropology 4:* 273–300.

Lasker, G. W.   1952   Environmental growth factors and selective migration. *Human Biology 24:* 262–289.

Lasker, G. W.   1954   The question of physical selection of Mexican migrants to the U.S.A. *Human Biology 26:* 52–58.

Lasker, G. W.   1961   *The evolution of man.* New York: Holt.

Lasker, G. W., and F. G. Evans   1961   Age, environment and migration: Further anthropometric findings on migrant and non-migrant Mexicans. *American Journal of Physical Anthropology 19:* 203–211.

Lasker, G. W., and H. Womack   1975   An anatomical view of demographic data: Biomass, fat mass and lean body mass of the United States and Mexican human populations. In F. E. Johnston, E. Watts, and G. W. Lasker (Eds.), *Biosocial interrelations in population adaptation.* The Hague: Mouton, pp. 43–53.

Laughlin, W. S.   1968   Adaptability and human genetics. *Proceedings of the National Academy of Sciences 60:* 12–21.

Leakey, L. S. B.   1961   A new Lower Pliocene fossil primate from Kenya. *Annals and Magazine of Natural History.* Ser. 13, *4:* 689–696 and Plate XVIII.

Leakey, L. S. B., P. V. Tobias, and J. R. Napier   1964   A new species of the genus *Homo* from Olduvai Gorge. *Nature 202:* 5–9.

Leakey, R. E. F.   1969   Early *Homo sapiens* remains from the Omo River region of southwest Ethiopia. *Nature 222:* 1132–1134.

Leakey, R. E. F.   1970   In search of man's past at Lake Rudolf. *National Geographic 137:* 712–733.

Leakey, R. E. F.   1973   Australopithecines and Hominines: A summary of the evidence from the early Pleistocene of Eastern Africa. In S. Zuckerman (Ed.), *The concepts of human evolution.* Symposia of the Zoological Society of London, No. 33. London: Academic, pp. 53–69.

Leakey, R. E. F., J. M. Mungai, and A. C. Walker   1971, 1972   New Australopithecines from East Rudolf, Kenya. *American Journal of Physical Anthropology 35:* 175–186; *36:* 235–251.

Leakey, R. E. F., and B. A. Wood   1973   New evidence of the genus *Homo* from East Rudolf, Kenya: II. *American Journal of Physical Anthropology 39:* 355–368.

Lee, M. M. C., and G. W. Lasker   1959   Sun-tanning potential of human skin. *Human Biology 31:* 252–260.

LeMay, M.   1975   The language capacity of Neanderthal man. *American Journal of Physical Anthropology 42:* 9–14.

Lerner, I. M.   1968   *Heredity, evolution, and society.* San Francisco: Freeman.

Leutenegger, W.   1974   Functional aspects of pelvic morphology in simian primates. *Journal of Human Evolution 3:* 207–222.

Levine, P.   1958   The influence of the ABO system on Rh hemolytic disease. *Human Biology 30:* 14–28.

Levine, P., and R. E. Stetson   1939   An unusual case of intragroup agglutination. *Journal of the American Medical Association 113:* 126–127.

Lewis, O. J.   1972   Osteological features characterizing the wrists of monkeys and apes, with a reconsideration of this region in *Dryopithecus (Proconsul) africanus. American Journal of Physical Anthropology 36:* 45–58.

Li, C. C.   1967   Castle's early work on selection and equilibrium. *American Journal of Human Genetics 19:* 70–74.

Lieberman, P., E. S. Crelin, and D. H. Klatt   1972   Phonetic ability and related anatomy of the newborn and adult human, Neanderthal Man, and the chimpanzee. *American Anthropologist 74:* 287–307.

Lindburg, D. G.   1969   Rhesus monkeys: Mating season mobility of adult males. *Science 166:* 1176–1178.

Linnaeus, C.   1758   *Systema naturae per regna tria naturae secundum classes, ordines, genera, species cum characteribus, differentiis, synonymis, locis.* Stockholm: Laurentii Salvii.

Lisowski, F. P., G. H. Albrecht, and C. E. Oxnard   1974   The form of the talus in some higher primates: A multivariate study. *American Journal of Physical Anthropology 41:* 191–216.

Little, M. A.   1970   Effects of alcohol and coca on foot temperature responses of highland Peruvians during a localized cold exposure. *American Journal of Physical Anthropology 32:* 233–242.

Little, M. A., R. B. Thomas, R. B. Mazess, and P. T. Baker   1971   Population differences and development changes in extermity temperature responses to cold among Andean Indians. *Human Biology 43:* 70–91, 581.

Livingstone, F. B.   1960   Natural selection, disease, and ongoing human evolution, as illustrated by the ABO blood groups. *Human Biology 32:* 17–27. Reprinted in G. W. Lasker (Ed.), *The processes of ongoing human evolution.* 1960. Detroit: Wayne State University Press.

Livingstone, F. B.   1967   *Abnormal hemoglobins in human populations.* Chicago: Aldine.

Livingstone, F. B.   1969a   Gene frequency clines of the beta hemoglobin locus in various human populations and their simulation by models involving differential selection. *Human Biology 41:* 223–236.

Livingstone, F. B.   1969b   Polygenic models for the evolution of human skin color differences. *Human Biology 41:* 480–493.

Loehlin, J. C., G. Lindzey, and J. N. Spuhler   1975   *Race differences in intelligence.* San Francisco: Freeman.

Loomis, W. F.   1967   Skin pigment regulation of vitamin-D biosynthesis in man. *Science 157:* 501–506.

Lovejoy, C. O., and K. G. Heiple   1970   A reconstruction of the femur of *Australopithecus africanus. American Journal of Physical Anthropology 32:* 33–40.

de Lumley, H. and M.-A.   1971   Découverte de restes humaines anténéandertaliens datés du début du Riss a la Caune de L'Arago (Tautavel, Pyrénées Orientales). *Comptes Rendus de l'Académie des Sciences,* Paris. Série D, 272: 1739–1742.

Luzatto, L., E. A. Usanga, and S. Reddy   1969   Glucose-6-phosphate dehydrogenase deficient red cells: Resistance to infection by malarial parasites. *Science 164:* 839–842.

Lynch, T. F., and K. A. R. Kennedy   1970   Early human cultural and skeletal remains from Guitarrero Cave, Northern Peru. *Science 169:* 1307–1309.

Macintosh, N. W. G.   1967   Recent discoveries of early Australian man. *Annals of the Australian College of Dental Surgeons 1:* 104–126.

MacMahon, B., and J. C. Folusiak   1958   Leukemia and ABO blood group. *American Journal of Human Genetics 10:* 287–293.

MacRoberts, M.   1970   The social organization of Barbary apes (*Macaca sylvana*) on Gibraltar. *American Journal of Physical Anthropology 33:* 83–99.

Mann, A.   1970   "Telanthropus" and the single species hypothesis: A further comment. *American Anthropologist 72:* 607–609.

Marshall, W. A.   1971   Anthropometric measurements of Tristan da Cunha islanders. *Human Biology 43:* 112–139.

Marston, A. T.   1937   The Swanscombe skull. *Journal of the Royal Anthropological Institute 67:* 339–406.

Martin, A. O.   1970   The founder effect in a human isolate: Evolutionary implications. *American Journal of Physical Anthropology 32:* 351–368.

Martin, R.   1928   *Lehrbuch der Anthropologie* (ed. 2). Jena: Gustav Fisher, 3 vols.

Martin, R., and K. Saller   1957   *Lehrbuch der Anthropologie* (ed. 3). Stuttgart: Gustav Fischer, 2 vols.

Mazess, R. B., E. Picon-Reategui, R. B. Thomas, and M. A. Little   1968   Effects of alcohol and altitude on man during rest and work. *Aerospace Medicine 39:* 403–406.

McCown, T. D., and A. Keith   1939   *The stone age of Mt. Carmel.* Vol. 2: *The fossil human remains from the Levalloiso-Mousterian.* Oxford: Clarendon Press.

McCracken, R. D.   1971   Lactase deficiency: An example of dietary evolution. *Current Anthropology 12:* 479–517.

McHenry, H.   1974   How large were the australopithecines? *American Journal of Physical Anthropology 40:* 329–340.

McHenry, H. M.   1975   A new pelvic fragment from Swartkrans and the relationship between the robust and gracile australopithecines. *American Journal of Physical Antrhopology 43:* 245–261.

Mednick, L. W., and S. L. Washburn   1956   The role of the sutures in the growth of the braincase of the infant pig. *American Journal of Physical Anthropology 14:* 175–191.

Mendel, G.   1866   Versuche über Pflanzen Hybriden. Translated in J. A. Peters (Ed.), *Classic papers in genetics.* Englewood Cliffs, New Jersey: Prentice-Hall, 1959.

Merbs, C. F.   1966   *Dating.* Chicago: Anthropology Curriculum Study Project.

Merbs, C.F.   1971   Anthropology. *Science Year 1972,* 256–258.

Meredith, H. V.   1939   Length of head and neck, trunk and lower extremities of Iowa City children aged seven to seventeen years. *Child Development 10:* 129–144.

Meredith, H. V.   1963   Changes in stature and body weight of North American boys. In L. P. Lipsitt and C. C. Spiker (Eds.), *Advances in child development and behavior,* Vol. 1. New York: Academic Press.

Meredith, H. V.   1970   Body weight at birth of viable human infants. *Human Biology 42:* 217–264.

Miller, O. L., and B. R. Beatty   1969   Visualization of nucleolar genes. *Science 164:* 955–957.

Miller, S. L.   1953   A production of amino acids under possible primitive earth conditions. *Science 117:* 528–529.

Moorrees, C. F. A.   1957   *The Aleut dentition.* Cambridge: Harvard University Press.

Morant, G. M.   1930–1931   Studies of Palaeolithic man: Part IV, A biometric study of the upper Palaeolithic skulls of Europe and of their relationships to earlier and later types. *Annals of Eugenics 4:* 109–214.

Morbeck, M. E.   1975   Problems in reconstruction of the *Dryopithecus (Proconsul) africanus* wrist complex. (Abstract.) *American Journal of Physical Anthropology 42:* 319.

Morgan, T. H.   1911   Random segregation versus gametic coupling in Mendelian inheritance. *Science 34:* 384.

Morris, D. H.   1970   On deflecting wrinkles and the *Dryopithecus* pattern in human mandibular molars. *American Journal of Physical Anthropology 32:* 97–104.

Moss, M. L., and R. W. Young   1960   A functional approach to craniology. *American Journal of Physical Anthropology 18:* 281–292.

Motulsky, A. R.   1960   Metabolic polymorphisms and the role of infectious diseases in human evolution. *Human Biology 32:* 28–62.

Mourant, A. E.   1954   *The distribution of the human blood groups.* Oxford: Blackwell.

Mourant, A. E., A. C. Kopec, and K. Domaniewska-Sobczak   1958   *The ABO blood groups.* Oxford: Blackwell.

Movius, H. L.   1949   Lower paleolithic archaeology in southern Asia and the Far East. In W. W. Howells (Ed.), *Early man in the Far East.* Studies in Physical Anthropology No. 1, American Association of Physical Anthropologists, pp. 17–82.

Muller, H. J.   1950   Our load of mutations. *American Journal of Human Genetics 2:* 111–176.

Napier, J.   1963   Brachiation and brachiators. *Symposia of the Zoological Society of London,* No. 10, 183–195.

Napier, J. R.   1964   The evolution of bipedal walking in the hominids. *Archives de Biologie 75* (Supplement): 673–708.

Napier, J. R., and P. H. Napier   1967   *A handbook of living primates.* New York: Academic Press.

Neel, J. V.   1951   The inheritance of the sickling phenomenon with particular reference to sickle cell disease. *Blood 6:* 389–412.

Neel, J. V.   1970   Lessons from a "primitive" people. *Science 170:* 815–822.

Newman, H. H., F. M. Freeman, and K. J. Holzinger   1937   *Twins: A study of heredity and environment.* Chicago: University of Chicago Press.

Newman, M. T.   1961   Biological adaptation of man to his environment: Heat, cold, altitude and nutrition. *Annals of the New York Academy of Science 91:* 617–633.

Newman, M. T., and C. Collazos   1957   Growth and skeletal maturation in malnourished Indian boys from the Peruvian Sierra. *American Journal of Physical Anthropology 15:* 431.

Newman, R. W.   1970   Why man is such a sweaty and thirsty naked animal: A speculative review. *Human Biology 42:* 12–27.

Newman, R. W., and E. Munro   1955   The relation of climate and body size in U.S. males. *American Journal of Physical Anthropology 13:* 1–17.

Nirenberg, M. W., O. W. Jones, P. Leder, B. F. C. Clark, W. S. Sly, and S. Pestka 1963   On the coding of genetic information. *Cold Spring Harbor Symposia on Quantitative Biology 28:* 549–557.

Oakley, K. P.   1950   *Man the toolmaker.* London: The British Museum (Natural History).

Oakley, K. P.   1961   Possible origin of the use of fire. *Man 61:* 207.

Oakley, K. P.   1966   *Frameworks for dating fossil man* (ed. 2). Chicago: Aldine.

Olshan, A. F.   1975   Hominid sympatry at East Rudolf. (Abstract.) *American Journal of Physical Anthropology 42:* 321.

Olson, E. C.   1964   The geology and mammalian faunas of the Tertiary and Pleistocene of South America. *American Journal of Physical Anthropology 22:* 217–225.

Oparin, A.   1957   *Origin of life on earth* (ed. 3). New York: Academic Press.

Orr, P. C.   1962   Arlington Springs man. *Science 135:* 219.

Oschinsky, O.   1964   *The most ancient Eskimos.* Ottawa, Canada: Canadian Research Centre for Anthropology.

Patterson, B., A. K. Behrensmeyer, and W. D. Sill   1970   Geology and fauna of the new Pliocene locality in North-western Kenya. *Nature 226:* 918–921.

Patterson, B., and W. W. Howells   1967   Hominid human fragment from Early Pleistocene of Northwest Kenya. *Science 156:* 64–66.

Pearson, K.   1896   Mathematical contributions to the theory of evolution: III. Regression, heredity and panmixia. *Philosophical Transactions, Royal Society of London,* series A *187:* 253–318.

Pei, W.   1957   Découverte en Chine d'une mandibule de singe géant. *l'Anthropologie 61:* 77–83.

Pilbeam, D.   1966   Notes on *Ramapithecus,* the earliest known hominid, and *Dryopithecus. American Journal of Physical Anthropology 25:* 1–5.

Pilbeam, D.   1968   The earliest hominids. *Nature 219:* 1335–1338.

Pilbeam, D.   1972   *The ascent of man.* New York: Macmillan.

Poirier, F. E.   1969   Behavioral flexibility and intergroup variation among Nilgiri langurs *(Presbytis johnii)* of South India. *Folia Primatologia 11:* 119–133.

Post, P. W., F. Daniels, Jr., and R. T. Binford   1975   Cold injury and the evolution of "white" skin. *Human Biology 47:* 65–80.

Post, R. H.   1962   Population differences in red and green color vision deficiency: A review, and a query on selection relaxation. *Eugenics Quarterly 9:* 131–146.

Premack, D.   1971   Language in chimpanzee? *Science 172:* 808–822.

Prost, J. H.   1965   The methodology of gait analysis and gaits of monkeys. *American Journal of Physical Anthropology 23:* 215–240.

Prost, J. H.   1967   Bipedalism of man and gibbon compared using estimates of joint motion. *American Journal of Physical Anthropology 26:* 135–148.

Race, R. R., and R. Sanger   1954   *Blood groups in man.* Springfield, Illinois: Charles C Thomas.

Randall, J. E.   1973   Size of the great white shark *(Carcharodon). Science 181:* 169–170.

Read, D. W.   1975   Hominid teeth and their relationship to hominid phylogeny. *American Journal of Physical Anthropology 42:* 105–125.

Reed, C. A.   1967   The generic allocation of the hominid species *habilis* as a problem in systematics. *South African Journal of Science 63:* 3–5.

Retzius, A. A.   1860   De brachycephaliska och dolichocephaliska folkslagens geografiska utbredning forklaring til attoljande karta. *K. Vet. Akad. Fork.,* No. 2: 99–101.

Reynolds, V., and F. Reynolds   1965   Chimpanzees of the Budango Forest. In I. DeVore (Ed.), *Primate behavior.* New York: Holt, pp. 368–424.

Richmond, R. C.   1970   Non-Darwinian evolution: A critique. *Nature 255:* 1025–1028.

Riesenfeld, A.   1955   The variability of temporal lines, its causes and effects. *American Journal of Physical Anthropology 13:* 599–620.

Ripley, S.   1967   Intertroop encounters among Ceylon Gray langurs *(Presbytis entellus).* In S. Altmann (Ed.), *Social communication among primates.* Chicago: University of Chicago Press, pp. 237–253.

Roberts, D. F.   1952   Basal metabolism, race and climate. *Journal of the Royal Anthropological Institute 82:* 169–183.

Roberts, D. F.   1953   Body weight, race and climate. *American Journal of Physical Anthropology 11:* 533–558.

Roberts, D. F.   1956   A demographic study of a Dinka Village. *Human Biology 28:* 323–349.

Roberts, D. F.   1968   Genetic fitness in a colonizing human population. *Human Biology 40:* 494–507.

Roberts, D. F., and D. R. Bainbridge   1963   Nilotic physique. *American Journal of Physical Anthropology 21:* 341–370.

Robertson, G. G.   1966   Developmental anatomy. In B. J. Anson (Ed.), *Morris' human anatomy.* New York: McGraw-Hill Book Company.

Robinson, J. T.   1953   Telanthropus and its phylogenetic significance. *American Journal of Physical Anthropology 11:* 445–501.

Robinson, J. T.   1964   Some critical phases in the evolution of man. *South African Archaeological Bulletin 19* (73): 3–12.

Robinson, J. T.   1972   *Early hominid posture and locomotion.* Chicago: University of Chicago Press.

Robinson, J. T., and E. F. Allin   1966   On the Y of the dryopithecus pattern of mandibular molar teeth. *American Journal of Physical Anthropology 25:* 323–324.

Roche, A. F., A. Wainer, and D. Thissen   1975   Predicting adult stature for individuals. *Monographs in Paediatrics, 3.* Basel, Switzerland. Karger.

Roche, F. J. da, R. S. Spielman, and J. V. Neel   1974   A comparison of gene frequency and anthropometric matrices in seven villages of four Indian tribes. *Human Biology 46:* 295–310.

Romer, A. S.   1969   Cynodont reptile with incipient mammalian jaw articulation. *Science 166:* 881–882.

Ruffié, J.   1971   Les données de l'immunogénétique et de la cytogénétique et la monophyletisme humain. *L'Anthropologie 75:* 57–84.

Sabharwal, K. P., S. Morales, and J. Méndez   1966   Body measurements and creatinine excretion among upper and lower socio-economic groups of girls in Guatemala. *Human Biology 38:* 131–140.

Sade, D. S.   1965   Some aspects of parent-offspring and sibling relations in a group of rhesus monkeys, with a discussion of grooming. *American Journal of Physical Anthropology 23:* 1–18.

Sagan, C., and B. N. Khare   1971   Long wave-length ultraviolet photoproduction of amino acids on the primitive earth. *Science 173:* 417–420.

Sager, Ruth, and Francis Ryan   1961   *Cell heredity.* New York: Wiley.

Sarich, V.   1969   The phyletic position of the Tupaiiformes. *American Journal of Physical Anthropology 31:* 266.

Sarich, V. M., and A. C. Wilson   1967   Immunological time scale for hominid evolution. *Science 158:* 1200–1203.

Sax, K.   1956   *The population explosion.* Foreign Policy Association Headline Series, No. 120.

Scammon, R. E.   1927   The first seriatim study of human growth. *American Journal of Physical Anthropology 10:* 329–336.

Schaller, G. B.   1963   *The mountain gorilla: Ecology and behavior.* Chicago: University of Chicago Press.

Schaumburg, H. H., R. Byck, R. Gersti, and J. H. Mashman   1969   Monosodium l-glutamate: Its pharmacology and role in the Chinese restaurant syndrome. *Science 163:* 826–828.

Schonlander, P. F., H. T. Hammel, J. S. Hart, D. H. LeMessuria, and J. Stem    1958    Cold adaptation in Australian aborigines. *Journal of Applied Physiology 13:* 211–218.

Schreider, E.    1951    Anatomical factors of body-heat regulation. *Nature 167:* 823–824.

Schreider, E.    1953    Regulation thermique et evolution humaines: Recherches statistiques et experimentales. *Bulletin et Memoires de la Société d' Anthropologie de Paris,* 10th Ser. *4:* 138–148.

Schull, W. J. (Ed.)    1962    *Mutations.* Ann Arbor: University of Michigan Press.

Schull, W. J., and J. V. Neel    1965    *The effects of inbreeding on Japanese children.* New York: Harper & Row.

Schultz, A. H.    1940    The size of the orbit and of the eye in primates. *American Journal of Physical Anthropology 26:* 389–408.

Schultz, A. H.    1947    Variability in man and other primates. *American Journal of Physical Anthropology 5:* 1–14.

Schultz, A. H.    1948    The relation in size between premaxilla, diastema, and canine. *American Journal of Physical Anthropology 6:* 163–179.

Schultz, A. H.    1949    Ontogenetic specializations of man. *Archiv Julius Klaus-Stiftung 24:* 197–216.

Schultz, A. H.    1969    Observations on the acetabulum of primates. *Folia Primatologica 11:* 181–199.

Sebeok, T. A.    1965    Animal communication. *Science 147:* 1006–1014.

Shapiro, H. L.    1931    The Chinese population in Hawaii: Preliminary paper prepared for the fourth general session of the Institute of Pacific Relations, New York, pp. 3–29.

Shapiro, H. L.    1939    *Migration and environment.* New York: Oxford University Press.

Sheldon, W. H., S. S. Stevens, and W. B. Tucker    1940    *The varieties of human physique.* New York: Harper & Row.

Simmons, K., and W. W. Greulich    1943    Menarcheal age and the height, weight and skeletal age of girls age 7 to 17 years. *Journal of Pediatrics 22:* 518–548.

Simmons, R. T., N. B. Tindale, and J. B. Birdsell    1962    A blood group genetical survey in Australian aborigines of Bentinck, Mornington and Forsyth Islands, Gulf of Carpentaria. *American Journal of Physical Anthropology 20:* 303–320.

Simonds, P. E.    1965    The bonnet macaque in South India. In I. DeVore (Ed.), *Primate behavior.* New York: Holt, pp. 175–196.

Simons, E. L.    1964a    The early relatives of man. *Scientific American 211* (1): 50–62.

Simons, E. L.    1964b    On the mandible of *Ramapithecus. Proceedings of the National Academy of Science 51:* 528–535.

Simons, E. L.    1967a    Review of the phyletic interrelationships of Oligocene and Miocene Old World Anthropoidea. *Problems Actuels de Paleontologie (Evolution des Vertebres),* Col. Int. Cent. Nat. Recherche Sci., No. 163, pp. 597–602.

Simons, E. L.    1967b    Fossil primates and the evolution of some primate locomotor systems. *American Journal of Physical Anthropology 26:* 241–253.

Simons, E. L.    1967c    The significance of primate paleontology for anthropological studies. *American Journal of Physical Anthropology 27:* 307–332.

Simons, E. L.    1968a    New fossil primates: A review. In S. L. Washburn and P. C. Jay (Eds.), *Perspectives on human evolution.* New York: Holt, pp. 41–60.

Simons, E. L.    1968b    Assessment of a fossil hominid. *Science 160:* 672–675.

Simons, E. L.    1969a    Recent advances of paleoanthropology. *Yearbook of Physical Anthropology—1967,* pp. 14–23.

Simons, E. L.    1969b    The origin and radiation of the primates. *Annals of the New York Academy of Science 167:* 319–331.

Simons, E. L.    1970    The deployment and history of Old World monkeys (Cercopithecidae, primates). In J. R. Napier and P. H. Napier (Eds.), *Old World monkeys.* New York: Academic Press.

Simons, E. L., and P. C. Ettel    1970    Gigantopithecus. *Scientific American 222:* 77–85.

Simons, E. L., and D. Pilbeam    1971    A gorilla-sized ape from the Miocene of India. *Science 173:* 23–27.

Simpson, G. G.    1945    The principles of classification and a classification of mammals. *Bulletin of the American Museum of Natural History,* New York, No. 85.

Simpson, G. G.    1963    The meaning of taxonomic statements. In S. L. Washburn (Ed.), *Classification and human evolution.* Chicago: Aldine, pp. 1–31.

Simpson, G. G.    1967    *The meaning of evolution.* New Haven: Yale University Press.

Siniscalco, M., L. Bernini, G. Fillipi, B. Latte, P. Meera Khan, S. Piomelli, and M. Rattazzi    1966    Population genetics of haemoglobin variants, thalassemia and glucose-6-phosphate dehydrogenase deficiency, with particular reference to the malaria hypothesis. *Bulletin of the World Health Organization 34:* 379–393.

Singer, R., and J. S. Weiner    1962    Biological aspects of some indigenous African populations. *Southwestern Journal of Anthropology 19:* 168–176.

Sofaer, J. A., C. S. Chung, J. D. Niswander, and D. W. Runck    1971    Developmental interaction, size and agenesis among permanent maxillary incisors. *Human Biology 43:* 36–45.

Solecki, R. S.    1963    Prehistory in Shanidar Valley, northern Iraq. *Science 139:* 179–193.

Southwick, C. H., M. A. Beg, and M. R. Siddiqi    1965    Rhesus monkeys in North India. In I. DeVore (Ed.), *Primate behavior.* New York: Holt, pp. 111–159.

Spuhler, J. N.    1959    Somatic paths to culture. *Human Biology 31:* 1–13.

Srb, A. M., R. D. Owen, and R. S. Edgar    1963    *General genetics* (ed. 2). San Francisco: Freeman.

Steegmann, A. T., Jr.    1967    Frostbite of the human face as a selective force. *Human Biology 39:* 131–144.

Steegmann, A. T., Jr.    1970    Cold adaptation and the human face. *American Journal of Physical Anthropology 32:* 243–250.

Stein, Z., M. Susser, G. Saenger, and F. Marolla    1975    *Famine and human development: The Dutch hunger winter of 1944/45.* New York: Oxford University Press.

Stephen-Sherwood, E., J. Oro, and A. P. Kimball    1971    Thymine: A possible prebiotic synthesis. *Science 173:* 446–447.

Stern, C.    1960    *Principles of human genetics.* San Francisco: Freeman.

Stewart, T. D.    1960    A physical anthropologist's view of the peopling of the New World. *Southwestern Journal of Anthropology 16:* 259–273.

Stewart, T. D., and M. Trotter (Eds.)    1954    *Basic readings on the identification of human skeletons: Estimation of age.* New York: Wenner-Gren Foundation for Anthropological Research.

Stoudt, H. W., A. Damon, and R. A. McFarland    1960    Heights and weights of white Americans. *Human Biology 32:* 331–341.

Straus, W. L., Jr.   1949   The riddle of man's ancestry. *The Quarterly Review of Biology 24:* 200–223. Reprinted in *Yearbook of Physical Anthropology—1949,* pp. 134–157.

Straus, W. L., Jr.   1963   The classification of *Oreopithecus.* In S. L. Washburn (Ed.), *Classification and human evolution.* Chicago: Aldine, pp. 146–177.

Straus, W. L., Jr., and A. J. E. Cave   1957   Pathology and posture of Neanderthal man. *Quarterly Review of Biology 32:* 348–363.

Strickberger, M. W.   1968   *Genetics.* New York: Macmillan.

Stringer, C. B.   1974   A multivariate study of the Petralona skull. *Journal of Human Evolution 3:* 397–404.

Struhsaker, T. T.   1967   Behavior of vervet monkeys and other cercopithecines. *Science 156:* 1197–1203.

Sturtevant, A. H., and G. W. Beadle   1962   *An introduction to genetics.* New York: Dover.

Suzuki, H., and F. Takai (Eds.)   1970   *The Amud man and his cave site.* Tokyo, Japan: University of Tokyo.

Swedlund, A. C.   1974   The use of ecological hypotheses in australopithecine taxonomy. *American Anthropologist 76:* 515–529.

Swedlund, A. C., and W. D. Wade   1972   *Laboratory methods in physical anthropology.* Prescott, Arizona: Prescott College Press.

Tanner, J. M.   1962   *Growth at adolescence* (ed. 2). Oxford: Blackwell.

Tanner, J. M.   1966   Growth and physique in different populations of mankind. In P. T. Baker and J. S. Weiner (Eds.), *The biology of human adaptability.* Oxford: Clarendon Press, pp. 45–66.

Tanner, J. M., and R. H. Whitehouse   1959   *Standards for skeletal maturity: Part I.* Paris: International Children's Centre.

Tanner, J. M., R. H. Whitehouse, and M. J. R. Healy   1962   *A new system for estimating the maturity of the hand and wrist with standards derived from 2,600 healthy British children. Part II: The scoring system.* Paris: International Children's Centre.

Tashian, R. E., R. J. Tanis, R. E. Ferrell, S. K. Stroup, and M. Goodman   1972   Differential rates of evolution in the carbonic anhydrase isozymes of catarrhine primates. *Journal of Human Evolution 1:* 545–552.

Taylor, J. H.   1958   Sister chromatid exchanges in tritium-labeled chromosomes. *Genetics 43:* 515–529.

Taylor, J. H., P. S. Woods, and W. T. Hughes   1957   Organization and duplication of chromosomes as revealed by autographic studies using tritium-labelled thymidine. *Proceedings of the National Academy of Sciences 43:* 122.

Teilhard de Chardin   1959   *The phenomenon of man.* New York: Harper.

Teleki, G.   1973   *The predatory behavior of wild chimpanzees.* Lewisburg, Pennsylvania: Bucknell University Press.

de Terra, H., J. Romero, and T. D. Stewart   1949   *Tepexpan man.* New York: Viking Fund Publications in Anthropology, Number 11.

Thieme, F. P.   1952   The population as a unit of study. *American Anthropologist 54:* 504–509.

Thieme, F. P.   1957   A comparison of Puerto Rican migrants and sedentes. *Papers of the Michigan Academy of Science, Arts and Letters 42:* 249–256.

Thomas, R. B.    1971    Growth retardation and limited energy flow in a high Andean population. *American Journal of Physical Anthropology 35: 297–298.*

Thomas, R. B.    In press    Energy flow at high altitude. In P. T. Baker and M. A. Little (Eds.), *Man in the Andes: A multidisciplinary study of high-altitude Quechua.* Stroudsberg, Pa.: Dowden, Hutchinson, and Ross.

Tobias, P. V.    1962    Early members of the genus Homo in Africa. In G. Kurth (Ed.), *Evolution and hominisation.* Stuttgart: Fischer, pp. 191–204.

Tobias, P. V.    1965    Early man in East Africa. *Science 149: 22–23.*

Tobias, P. V.    1967    The cranium and maxillary dentition of *Australopithecus* (Zinjanthropus) *boisei. Olduvai Gorge,* vol. 2. New York: Cambridge University Press.

Tobias, P. V.    1969    Commentary on new discoveries and interpretations of early African fossil hominids. *Yearbook of Physical Anthropology—1967,* pp.24–30.

Tobias, P. V.    1970    Brain size, grey matter and race—fact or fiction? *American Journal of Physical Anthropology 32: 3–25.*

Tobias, P. V.    1971a    Human skeletal remains from the Cave of the Hearths, Makapansgat, Northern Transvaal. *American Journal of Physical Anthropology 34: 335–367.*

Tobias, P. V.    1971b    *The brain in hominid evolution.* New York: Columbia University Press.

Tobias, P. V., and G. H. R. von Koenigswald    1964    A comparison between the Olduvai hominines and those of Java and some implications for hominid phylogeny. *Nature 204: 515–518.*

Todd, T. W.    1937    *Atlas of skeletal maturation: I. The hand.* St. Louis: Mosby.

Turner, C. G., II.    1969    Microevolutionary interpretations from the dentition. *American Journal of Physical Anthropology 30: 421–426.*

Tuttle, R. H.    1967    Knuckle-walking and the evolution of hominid hands. *American Journal of Physical Anthropology 26: 171–206.*

Urey, H. C.    1962    Lifelike forms in meteorites. *Science 137: 623–628.*

Vallois, H. V.    1949    The Fontechévade fossil men. *American Journal of Physical Anthropology 7: 339–362.*

Vallois, H. V.    1956    The Pre-Mousterian human mandible from Montmaurin. *American Journal of Physical Anthropology 14: 319–323.*

Vallois, H. V.    1961    The social life of early man: The evidence of skeletons. In S. L. Washburn (Ed.), *Social life of early man.* New York: Viking Fund Publications in Anthropology, Number 31, pp. 214–235.

Vallois, H. V.    1969    Le temporal Neanderthalien H 27 de la Quina: Étude anthropologique. *L'Anthropologie 73: 365–400; 525–544.*

Van Valen, L.    1969    A classification of the primates. *American Journal of Physical Anthropology 30: 295–296,*

Van Valen, L., and R. E. Sloan    1965    The earliest primates (mid-Paleocene *Purgatorius*). *Science 150: 743–745.*

Vandenberg, S. G.    1967    Hereditary factors in psychological variables in man, with special emphasis on cognition. In J. N. Spuhler (Ed.), *Genetic diversity and human behavior.* Chicago: Aldine, pp. 99–133.

Vander, A., J. H. Sherman, and D. Luciano    1970    *The mechanisms of body function.* New York: McGraw-Hill.

Vlastovsky, V. G.    1966    The secular trend in the growth and development of children and young persons in the Soviet Union. *Human Biology 38: 218–250.*

Vos, G. H., R. L. Kirk, and A. G. Steinberg  1963  The distribution of the gamma globulin types Gm(a), Gm(b), Gm(x) and Gm-like in South and Southeast Asia and Australia. *American Journal of Human Genetics 15:* 44–52.

Wagley, C.  1971  The formation of the American population. In F. M. Salzano (Ed.), *The ongoing evolution of Latin American populations.* Springfield, Illinois: Charles C Thomas, pp. 19–39.

Walcher, G.  1905  Ueber die Entstehung von Brachy- und Dolichocephalie durch willkürliche Beinflussung des kindlichen Schädels. *Zentralblat für Gynäkologie 29:* 193–196.

Washburn, S. L.  1947  The relation of the temporalis muscle to the form of the skull. *Anatomical Record 99:* 239–248.

Washburn, S. L.  1951  The new physical anthropology. *Transactions of the New York Academy of Sciences 13:* 298–304. Reprinted in *Yearbook of Physical Anthropology—1951,* pp. 124–130.

Washburn, S. L.  1959  Speculation on the interrelations of the history of tools and biological evolution. *Human Biology 31:* 21–31.

Washburn, S. L., and R. L. Ciochon  1974  Canine teeth: Notes on controversies in the study of human evolution. *American Anthropologist 76:* 765–784.

Washburn, S. L., and S. R. Detwiler  1943  An experiment bearing on the problems of physical anthropology. *American Journal of Physical Anthropology 1:* 171–190.

Washburn, S. L., and I. DeVore (Eds.)  1961  The social life of baboons. *Scientific American 204* (6): 62–71.

Washburn, S. L., and D. A. Hamburg  1965  The study of primate behavior: The implications of primate research. In I. DeVore (Ed.), *Primate behavior.* New York: Holt, pp. 1–13; and 607–622.

Washburn, S. L., P. C. Jay, and J. B. Lancaster  1965  Field studies of Old World monkeys and apes. *Science 150:* 1541–1547.

Watson, J. D., and F. H. C. Crick  1953a  Molecular structure of nucleic acid. *Nature 171:* 737–738.

Watson, J. D., and F. H. C. Crick  1953b  The structure of DNA. *Cold Spring Harbor Symposia on Quantitative Biology 18:* 123–131.

Weidenreich, F.  1927  Der Schadel von Weimar-Ehringsdorf. *Verhandl. der Gesellschaft für Phys. Anthrop. 2:* 34–41.

Weidenreich, F.  1936  The mandibles of *Sinanthropus pekinensis:* A comparative study. *Palaeontologia Sinica,* series D, 7: 1–162.

Weidenreich, F.  1937  The dentition of *Sinanthropus pekinensis:* A comparative odontography of the hominids. 2 vol., *Palaeontologia Sinica,* new series D, No., 1, whole series No. 101.

Weidenreich, F.  1939  On the earliest representatives of modern mankind recovered on the soil of East Asia. *Peking Natural History Bulletin 13:* 161–174.

Weidenreich, F.  1941  The extremity bones of *Sinanthropus pekinensis. Palaeontologia Sinica,* new series D, No. 5, whole series No. *115:* 1–150.

Weidenreich, F.  1943  The skull of *Sinanthropus pekinensis:* A comparative study on a primitive hominid skull. *Palaeontologia Sinica,* new series D, No. 10, whole series No. *127:* 1–484.

Weidenreich, F., and G. H. R. von Koenigswald  1951  Morphology of Solo man. *Anthropological Papers of the American Museum of Natural History 43:* 205–290.

Weiner, J. S. 1954 Nose shape and climate. *American Journal of Physical Anthropology 12:* 615–618.

Weiner, J. S. 1964 The biology of social man. *Journal of the Royal Anthropological Institute 94* (part 2): 230–240.

Weiner, J. S., and J. A. Lourie 1969 *Human biology: A guide to field methods.* IBP Handbook No. 9. Philadelphia: Davis.

Weiner, J. S., K. P. Oakley, and W. E. Le Gros Clark 1953 The solution of the Piltdown problem. *Bulletin of the British Museum (Natural History),* Geological series, 2, No. 3.

Wendorf, F., A. D. Krieger, and C. C. Albritton 1955 *The Midland discovery.* Austin: University of Texas Press.

Westmoreland, B. C., W. Szybalski, and H. Ris 1969 Mapping of deletions and substitutions in heteroduplex DNA molecules of bacteriophage lambda by electron microscopy. *Science* 163: 1343.

White, L. A. 1959 Summary review. In J. N. Spuhler (Ed.), *The evolution of man's capacity for culture.* Detroit: Wayne State University Press, pp. 74–79.

Whittaker, R. H. 1969 New concepts of kingdoms of organisms. *Science 163:* 150–160.

Wiener, A. S., and J. Moor-Jankowski 1972 Blood groups of non-human primates and their relationship to the blood groups of man. In A. B. Chiarelli (Ed.), *Comparative genetics in monkeys, apes and man.* New York: Academic, pp. 71–95.

Williams, R. C., and H. W. Fisher 1974 *An electron micrographic atlas of viruses.* Springfield, Illinois: Charles C Thomas.

Wilson, A. C., and V. M. Sarich 1969 A molecular time scale for human evolution. *Proceedings of the National Academy of Science 63:* 1088–1093.

Wilson, D. R. 1972 Tail reduction in *Macaca.* In R. Tuttle (Ed.), *The functional and evolutionary biology of primates.* Chicago: Aldine, pp. 241–261.

Winchester, A. M. 1969 *Biology and its relation to mankind* (ed. 4). New York: Van Nostrand.

Witkop, C. J. 1963 Advances in dental genetics. *Journal of Dental Research 42:* 1262–1275.

Wollin, G., and D. B. Ericson 1971 Amino acid synthesis from gases detected in interstellar space. *Nature 233:* 615–616.

Wolpoff, M. H. 1968a Climatic influence on the skeletal nasal aperture. *American Journal of Physical Anthropology 29:* 405–423.

Wolpoff, M. H. 1968b "Telanthropus" and the single species hypothesis. *American Anthropologist 70:* 477–493.

Wolpoff, M. H. 1970 The evidence for multiple hominid taxa at Swartkrans. *American Anthropologist 72:* 576–607.

Wolpoff, M. H. 1971 Vertesszöllös and the presapiens theory. *American Journal of Physical Anthropology 35:* 209–215.

Wolpoff, M. H. 1974 Sagittal cresting in the South African australopithecines. *American Journal of Physical Anthropology 40:* 397–408.

Woo, J. K. 1956 Human fossils found in China and their significance in human evolution. *Scientia Sinica 5:* 389–397.

Woo, J., and T. Chao 1959 New discovery of *Sinanthropus* mandible from Choukoutien. *Vertebrata Palasiatica 3:* 169–172.

Woo, J., and R. Peng 1959 Fossil human skull of early paleoanthropic stage found at Mapa, Shaoquan, Kwantung Province. *Vertebrata Palasiatica 3:* 176–182.

Wood, B. A.    1974    Olduvai Bed I post-cranial fossils: A reassessment. *Journal of Human Evolution 3:* 373–378.

Woolf, C. M., and F. C. Dukepoo 1964    Hopi Indians, interbreeding and albinism. *Science 164:* 30–37.

Workman, P. L., B. S. Blumberg, and A. J. Cooper    1963    Selection, gene migration and polymorphic stability in a U.S. white and Negro population. *American Journal of Human Genetics 15:* 429–437.

Wright, S.    1931    Evolution in Mendelian populations. *Genetics 16:* 97–159.

Wright, S.    1932    The roles of mutation, inbreeding, crossbreeding and selection in evolution. *Proceedings of the Sixth International Congress of Genetics 1:* 356–366.

Wright, S.    1938    Size of population and breeding structure in relation to evolution. *Science 87:* 430–431.

Yoshiba, K.    1968    Local and intergroup variability in ecology and social behavior of Common Indian Langurs. In P. C. Jay (Ed.), *Primates.* New York: Holt, pp. 217–242.

Yount, J. L.    1967    On teaching homology, homoplasy, and analogy. *Turtox News 45:* 138–139.

Yulish, S. M.    1970    Anterior tooth reduction in *Ramapithecus. Primates 11:* 255–263.

Zapfe, H.    1958    The skeleton of *Pliopithecus* (Epipliopithecus) *vindobonensis* Zapfe and Hurzeler. *American Journal of Physical Anthropology 16:* 441–455.

Zuckerman, S.    1932    *The social life of monkeys and apes.* London: Kegan Paul.

Zuckerman, S.    1933    *Functional affinities of man, monkeys and apes.* New York: Harcourt.

# NAME INDEX

# SUBJECT INDEX

# SITES OF FOSSILS SIGNIFICANT IN THE TRACING
OF HUMAN EVOLUTION (SEE END PAPERS)

| Country | Site | Location on map | |
|---------|------|------|------|
| South Africa | Taung | 1 | First *Australopithecus africanus* skull |
| | Sterkfontein | | Several specimens of *Australopithecus africanus* (all gracile) |
| | Swartkrans | 2 | *Australopithecus* (robust); "Telanthropus"; crude stone tools |
| | Kromdraai | | *Australopithecus* (robust) |
| | Saldanha | 3 | Neanderthaloid skull cap and mandible |
| | Florisbad, | 4 | *Homo sapiens;* Middle Stone Age tools |
| | Makapan | 5 | *Australopithecus* (gracile); Cave of the Hearths mandible with Acheulian stone tools |
| Zambia | Broken Hill | 6 | Neanderthaloid |
| Tanzania | Peninj | 7 | *Australopithecus* mandible (robust) |
| | Olduvai Gorge | 8 | *Australopithecus* ("Zinjanthropus"); "Homo habilis"; *Homo erectus;* stone tools of Olduwan and Chellean types |
| Kenya | Lothagam Hill | 9 | Oldest *Australopithecus* specimen known |
| | East Rudolf | 10 | *Australopithecus* (robust) skulls and other bones; a still-undescribed "third" hominid |
| | Fort Ternan | 11 | *Ramapithecus* |
| Ethiopia | Omo River Basin | 12 | Many specimens of *Australopithecus:* three early *Homo* skulls |
| Morocco | Jebel Irhoud | 13 | Neanderthal or Neanderthaloid skull; stone flake tools |
| Algeria | Afalou | 14 | 50 skeletons of *Homo sapiens sapiens* |
| | Ternifine | 15 | *Homo erectus:* Chelles-Acheul stone tools |
| Libya | Haua Fteah | 16 | 2 Neanderthaloid mandibles; Levalloiso-Mousterian tools |
| Egypt | Fayum | 17 | *Apidium; Parapithecus; Aelopithecus; Propliopthecus; Aegyptopithecus* |
| Greece | Petralona | 18 | Neanderthaloid |
| Hungary | Vertesszöllös | 19 | *Homo erectus?* |
| Czechoslovakia | Brno; Pavlo; Mladeč; Predmost | 20 | Early *Homo sapiens sapiens* |
| Italy | Tuscany | 21 | *Oreopithecus* |
| | Monte Circeo and Saccopastore | 22 | *Homo sapiens neanderthalensis* |

## SITES OF FOSSILS SIGNIFICANT IN THE TRACING
## OF HUMAN EVOLUTION *(Continued)*

| Country | Site | Location on map | |
|---------|------|:---:|---|
| Germany | Ehringsdorf | 23 | Fossil (Neanderthaloid) skull with pre-Mousterian tools |
| | Steinheim | 24 | Early fossil skull (Neanderthaloid?) |
| | Rhunda | 25 | Skull transitional from Neanderthaloid to *Homo sapiens sapiens* |
| | Mauer | 26 | Heidelberg jaw |
| | Neanderthal | 27 | Original specimen of *Homo sapiens neanderthalensis* |
| England | Swanscombe | 28 | Skull of uncertain affinities, with Acheulian tools |
| France | Chancelade | | *Homo sapiens sapiens;* Magdalenian cultural remains |
| | Montmaurin | | Preneanderthal mandible |
| | La Chapelle-aux-Saints | | *Homo sapiens neanderthalensis* |
| | La Ferrassie | 29 | *Homo sapiens neanderthalensis* |
| | Cro-Magnon | | *Homo sapiens sapiens* |
| | Combe-Capelle | | Earliest dated *Homo spaiens sapiens* |
| | Fontéchevade | | Two fragments of skull vault; Tayacian pre-Mousterian tool types |
| | La Quina | | *Homo sapiens neanderthalensis* |
| | Arago | 30 | Preneanderthal |
| Monaco | Grimaldi Cave | 31 | *Homo sapiens sapiens;* Aurignacian cultural remains |
| Spain | Gibralta | 32 | *Homo sapiens neanderthalensis* |
| | Cariquela a Piñar | | *Homo sapiens neanderthalensis* |
| Israel | Amud | 33 | Transitional Neanderthal |
| | Tabūn | | Neanderthal; Levalloiso-Mousterian industry |
| | Skhūl | | Neanderthal (transitional); Levalloiso-Mousterian industry |
| Iraq | Shanidar | 34 | Many Neanderthal fossils; Eastern Mousterian industry |
| Iran | Hotu | 35 | Three Upper Paleolithic *Homo sapiens sapiens* |
| USSR | Teshik-Tash, Uzbekistan | 36 | Neanderthal child |
| India | Siwalik Hills | 37 | *Dryopithecus; Ramapithecus; Gigantopithecus* |
| China | Mapa, Kwangtung | 38 | Neanderthaloid |
| | Leng-Chai-Shan, | 39 | *Gigantopithecus* mandibles |
| | Lantian, Shensi | 40 | *Homo erectus* |

## SITES OF FOSSILS SIGNIFICANT IN THE TRACING OF HUMAN EVOLUTION *(Continued)*

| Country | Site | Location on map | |
|---------|------|-----------------|---|
| | Choukoutien | 41 | Many specimens of *Homo erectus* (Peking man); hearths; 3 Upper Cave *Homo sapiens sapiens*; cultural remains |
| Indonesia | Neah Cave Borneo | 42 | *Homo sapiens sapiens* with Paleolithic artifacts |
| | Trinil, Java | 43 | First specimen of *Homo erectus* (Java man) |
| | Modjokerto, Java | | *Homo erectus* |
| | Solo River Valley | | *Homo erectus*; "Meganthropus"; Solo man |
| Australia | Lake Mungo | 44 | Early cremated skeleton |
| USA | Los Angeles, California | 45 | Early *Homo sapiens* |
| | Arlington Springs, California | | Early *Homo sapiens sapiens* |
| | Midland, Texas | 46 | Early *Homo sapiens sapiens*; Folsom type tool |
| Mexico | Tepexpan | 47 | Early *Homo sapiens sapiens* |
| Peru | Guitarrero Cave | 48 | Early human remains; domesticated common beans and lima beans |

## SITES OF FOSSILS SIGNIFICANT IN THE
## TRACING OF HUMAN EVOLUTION

| Location | Site |
|---|---|
| 1 | Taung |
| 2 | Sterkfontein; Swartkrans; Kromdraai |
| 3 | Saldanha |
| 4 | Florisbad |
| 5 | Makapan |
| 6 | Broken Hill |
| 7 | Peninj |
| 8 | Olduvai Gorge |
| 9 | Lothagam Hill |
| 10 | East Rudolf |
| 11 | Fort Ternan |
| 12 | Omo River Basin |
| 13 | Jebel Irhoud |
| 14 | Afalou |
| 15 | Ternifine |
| 16 | Haua Fteah |
| 17 | Fayum |
| 18 | Petralona |
| 19 | Vertesszöllös |
| 20 | Brno; Pavlo;Mladeč; Predmost |
| 21 | Tuscany |
| 22 | Monte Circeo and Saccopastore |
| 23 | Ehringsdorf |
| 24 | Steinheim |
| 25 | Rhunda |
| 26 | Mauer |
| 27 | Neanderthal |
| 28 | Swanscombe |
| 29 | Chancelade; Montmaurin; La Chapelle-aux-Saints; La Ferrassie; Cro-magnon; Combe-Capelle; Fontéchevade; La Quina |
| 30 | Arago |
| 31 | Grimaldi Cave |
| 32 | Gibralta; Cariquela a Piñar |
| 33 | Amud; Tabūn; Skhūl |
| 34 | Shanidar |
| 35 | Hotu |
| 36 | Teshik-Tash, Uzbekistan |
| 37 | Siwalik Hills |
| 38 | Mapa, Kwangtung |
| 39 | Leng-Chai-Shan, Kwangsi |
| 40 | Lantian, Shensi |
| 41 | Choukoutien |
| 42 | Néah Cave, Borneo |
| 43 | Trinil, Java; Modjokerto, Java; Solo River Valley |
| 44 | Lake Mungo |
| 45 | Los Angeles, California; Arlington Springs,California |
| 46 | Midland, Texas |
| 47 | Tepexpan |
| 48 | Guitarrero Cave |

45

46

47

48